Employee Relations

THIRD EDITION

John Gennard is the CIPD professor of Human Resource Management at the University of Strathclyde and has written extensively on employee relations and industrial relations institutions. His most recent research looks at the role of personnel directors in devising and developing corporate strategy, and the career routes whereby people become personnel directors. He is chief examiner (Employee Relations) for the CIPD and a fellow of the CIPD.

Graham Judge is group human resources executive for Yattendon Investment Trust plc which has interests in regional newspapers, television and the marine leisure industry. He has held a number of personnel and training posts within the publishing, printing and packaging industries, and has lectured extensively on a range of management issues. He is an associate examiner (Employee Relations) for the CIPD and a fellow of the CIPD.

• Other titles in the series

The Chartered Institute of Personnel and Development is the leading publisher of books and reports for personnel and training professionals, students, and all those concerned with the effective management and development of people at work.
For details of all our titles, please contact the Publishing Department:
tel 020 8263 3387
fax 020 8263 3850
e-mail publish@cipd.co.uk
The catalogue of all CIPD titles can be viewed on the CIPD website:
www.cipd.co.uk/bookstore

Employee Relations

THIRD EDITION

John Gennard

and

Graham Judge

Chartered Institute of Personnel and Development

© John Gennard and Graham Judge 1997, 1999, 2002

First published in 1997
Reprinted 1998
Second edition published 1999
Reprinted 2000
This edition published 2002
Reprinted 2002

Design by Curve

Typeset by Fakenham Photosetting Ltd, Fakenham, Norfolk

Printed in Great Britain by
the Cromwell Press, Trowbridge, Wiltshire

British Library Cataloguing in Publication Data
A catalogue record of this book is available from
the British Library

ISBN 0 85292 940 4

The views expressed in this book are the authors' own and may not
necessarily reflect those of the CIPD.

CIPD Enterprises Ltd has made every effort to trace and acknowledge
copyright holders. If any source has been overlooked, CIPD Enterprises
would be happy to redress this for future versions.

Chartered Institute of Personnel and Development, CIPD House,
Camp Road, London SW19 4UX
Tel: 020 8971 9000   Fax: 020 8263 3333
E-mail: cipd@cipd.co.uk Website: www.cipd.co.uk
Incorporated by Royal Charter. Registered Charity No. 1079797.

• Contents

Editor's foreword

HRM is now more important than ever. Organisations increasingly compete with each other on the basis of effective people management and development by tapping into the ideas of workers and organising their work in more efficient ways. Much of this relies on line managers in their day-to-day interactions with the people who work for them. However, line managers are busy individuals who need the support of HR specialists – internal or external to the organisation – to help them make sense of what is happening in the field. Contemporary initiatives in learning and development, recruitment and selection, employee relations, reward management, appraisal and performance review need to be interpreted for different organisational contexts. HR specialists not only need to display a sound understanding of the main HR issues, but also show awareness of business issues and have an acute sensitivity to how change can be managed effectively. In addition, HR specialists need to demonstrate a commitment to professional and ethical standards, and be able to provide sound advice based on an extensive knowledge of high-quality research and contemporary organisational practice.

With this in mind, the CIPD is publishing a series of books designed to address key issues in people management and development. This book is one of the series focusing on the CIPD Standards in People Management and Development, Learning and Development, Employee Relations, People Resourcing, and Employee Reward. The series provides essential guidance and points of reference for all those interested in learning more about the management of people in organisations. It covers the main sets of CIPD Standards in a systematic and comprehensive manner, and as such is essential reading for all those preparing for CIPD examinations. In addition, however, the books are also excellent core texts for those studying for courses in human resource management at postgraduate and advanced undergraduate levels. Moreover, practitioners should also find the books invaluable for information and reference to sources of specialist advice. Underpinning the series is the CIPD notion of 'the thinking performer' that is central to the Professional Development Scheme.

People Management and Development: HRM at Work, written by Mick Marchington and Adrian Wilkinson, analyses the essential knowledge and understanding required of all personnel and development professionals. The book comprises a number of sections, commencing with an examination of the factors shaping HRM at work – including the legal and institutional forces as well as the changing nature of work and employment. A recurring theme throughout the book is the integration of HRM with business objectives and the degree to which it is able to add value. Later chapters in the book consider each of the main components of HRM at work, seeking to show how these interrelate with each other in a wide range of differing organisational contexts. The authors are both well-known researchers and professors of HRM at two of the UK's premier management schools – UMIST and the University of Loughborough, respectively. Professor Marchington is also Chief Moderator, Standards for the CIPD.

Learning and Development is written by the CIPD's Chief Examiner for the subject, Rosemary Harrison. Building on her extremely popular previous book on training and development, this also provides an extended analysis of learning and development that is based on the CIPD Standards. The book focuses on the main areas of the field – national policy frameworks, professional and ethical considerations, the delivery of learning and development, and career and management development. Given the comprehensive treatment of learning and development in this book, it is also eminently suitable for students on all courses – including CIPD – as well as for practitioners.

Employee Reward has also been fully revised and restructured to address the CIPD Professional Development Scheme Standards in the area. The author, Michael Armstrong, is a well-known and experienced writer and consultant in employee reward, and he was one of the CIPD's chief examiners until 2001. The book is divided into nine sections, each of which analyses a key component of reward management. This includes chapters on reward processes, job evaluation and competency frameworks, pay structures and systems, performance management and employee benefits. The book provides a highly practical and systematic coverage of employee reward that is likely to offer students an invaluable resource as well as give practitioners vital sources of information and ideas.

Employee Relations, like all the other books in the series, has been thoroughly updated in order to cover the CIPD Standards in the subject. The authors, John Gennard and Graham Judge, have an immense amount of academic and practical experience in employee relations, and they have combined forces again to offer students on CIPD courses an unparalleled text. The book deals systematically with all of the key components of employee relations. It provides an overview of the economic, corporate and legal environment and it focuses on the increasing influence of the European Union on employee relations. Subsequent parts of the book examine the processes and policies used by organisations, and the practice and skills required of HR professionals. John Gennard is Professor of HRM at the University of Strathclyde and Graham Judge is a practising personnel professional.

People Resourcing is written by Stephen Taylor, who is a senior lecturer at Manchester Metropolitan University, one of the CIPD's centres of excellence. This is an updated version of his earlier book on employee resourcing, and it provides a highly practical and accessible text for students taking CIPD examinations. All the main elements of people resourcing are examined in detail in the book. There is a particular focus on human resource planning, recruitment and selection, performance management, dismissal and redundancy. A wide range of examples drawn from different sectors and occupational groups illustrates the core concepts. The author is one of the CIPD's national examiners for Core Management and has a wide range of experience marking scripts in the people management and development area.

Essentials of Employment Law, now in its seventh edition, is firmly established as the most authoritative textbook on employment law for all students of human resource management. The authors are both from Middlesex University – David Lewis is professor of employment law and Malcolm Sargeant is reader in employment law. The text covers the CIPD employment law specialist elective and is an invaluable source of reference to students studying any area of HRM. It covers the key areas of employment law from the formation of contracts of employment to human rights and discrimination issues.

In drawing upon a team of such distinguished and experienced writers, this series provides a range of up-to-date, practical and research-led texts essential for those studying for the CIPD qualifications. Each of the books provides a systematic and comprehensive analysis of its subject area and as such can be used as core texts for all students on postgraduate and advanced undergraduate courses.

Mick Marchington
CIPD Chief Moderator, Standards

• Acknowledgements

We would like to thank the following individuals for their help and assistance with this book: Robert Foss for his tolerance over deadlines; Debbie Campbell, John's secretary, who did a great deal of work on co-ordinating this project, and Graham's present and former secretaries Jennie Allan and Geraldine Ford. Thanks also to Dr Adrian Murton and Dr Peter Fenwick for their invaluable comments and feedback. John would like to thank Anne for her support, while Graham would like to thank Kim for her patience and understanding when things got a little stressful.

John Gennard
Graham Judge
April 2002

PART 1 INTRODUCTION

1

Introduction

Key themes

The CIPD Graduate Professional Qualification is not an academic qualification. It indicates to employers that its holders can be reasonably expected to be aware of, to be informed about and to understand prevailing trends, topics and management techniques deployed in employee relations, and to be able to display an acceptable level of proficiency in operational skills. A CIPD qualification indicates the competence of personnel managers to solve people management problems by the application of their acquired knowledge and understanding using appropriate management skills. Knowledge and understanding are essential but limited if managers lack the practical skills to apply them. Holders of a CIPD professional qualification should be capable of entering a personnel department and operating without causing mayhem when asked to undertake tasks with little or no supervision.

University degree/diploma qualifications have a balance in curriculum between theoretical and vocational needs of students that is different from the CIPD's graduate professional qualification. University degrees require students to be aware of the plurality of perspectives on issues and themes. CIPD professional qualifications are management qualifications, and students who seek CIPD qualifications should be taught from a management perspective. CIPD graduates must be capable of demonstrating an ability to identify, define and explain the significance of employee relations managers' possessing (or not possessing) specific skills to solve people management problems. This book is written solely from a professional management perspective and draws on the experience of practising personnel professionals operating in both unionised and non-unionised environments. It explains why personnel managers require specific skills. It is a 'how to do it' book in which the importance of proceeding on the basis of good practice is to the fore.

But – and this is important – it should not be the only book that you should read. You must use a range of materials, from the more academic texts such as Salamon, and other writers, through to journals such as *People Management*. It is important to be aware of current trends, ideas and research in the field of personnel management, and we would also recommend that you use the extensive number of HR-specific websites that are now available.

It is an acute misunderstanding to believe that employee relations is only a relevant management activity if the organisation deals with trade unions. In non-unionised environments, as in unionised ones, collective relationships exist. In non-unionised firms there are employee representative bodies (for example, employee councils, works councils, joint consultative committees), and just as in unionised environments employee grievances have to be resolved, disciplinary matters processed, and procedures devised, implemented, operated and monitored. In addition, in non-unionised situations as well as in unionised ones, support and loyalty from one's management colleagues, at all levels of seniority, has to be gained by using *inter alia* negotiating, interviewing and communication skills. Employee relations knowledge, understanding and skills acquisition are just as relevant to non-union environments as to unionised environments.

As we shall explain, an important employee relations concept is the relative balance of bargaining power between the buyers and sellers of labour services, and that important determinants of this relationship are external to the organisation – for example, government economic and legislative policies. One result of this is that the key employee relations policies and practices can be rendered irrelevant, illegal or more expensive to operate because of legislative intervention. Instances include the changes in representational rights in grievance and disciplinary procedures and the statutory recognition procedures contained in the Employment Relations Act (1999), or the changes in maternity leave, disciplinary procedures, etc, introduced by the Employment Act 2002. The professional personnel manager has to be capable of offering advice on how the organisation might deal with such situations that stem from decision-making sources over which companies have no direct control. This book is designed to help in this regard.

Changes in the corporate environment that have influenced the balance of bargaining power help to explain changes over time (for example, the present decade relative to the 1970s) in the employee relations behaviour of employees and employers in terms of the processes used, the rules, regulations and agreements, and their authorship. In the 1970s when the corporate environment was very different from today, trade unions grew steadily, strike action was more frequent and higher wage increases were gained by employees from their employers. In today's corporate environment trade union membership has fallen, strike action has fallen, employers are able to decide unilaterally on the rules and regulations governing employment and, courtesy of low inflation, wage increases are much smaller. Personnel managers/professionals require an understanding of the impact of changes in the corporate environment on management–employee relations strategy, policies and agreements in order to predict the impact of possible external changes on the organisation's employee relations and determine how they might seek to mitigate them.

In conducting their employee relations activities, professional managers should behave in a fair and reasonable manner; and seek to persuade their management colleagues to behave in a like way. This means acting with just cause (for example, having a genuine reason to dismiss a worker or for selecting an employee for redundancy) and behaving in procedural terms via a series of stages in which behaviour is compatible with the standards of natural justice – for instance, a statement is made of the complaint against an individual, a proper investigation is undertaken, the accused is given the opportunity to cross-examine witnesses, there is sufficient time made available for the accused to prepare a defence, an appeals procedure exists, and different individuals are involved at the different stages in the operation of the procedure.

It is important for personnel managers to appreciate that the underlying principle of employee relations procedures is that they establish standards of behaviour that will pass the test of reasonableness. However, personnel managers must not only appreciate what constitutes fair and reasonable behaviour but why such good practice is essential to protecting and advancing management's interests – namely, the avoidance of adverse financial consequences through the payment of compensation to individuals wronged by such action, and the simultaneous avoidance of damaging the organisation's labour market image in the eyes of the sellers of labour services. As we have already indicated, managers by behaving in a fair and reasonable manner (good practice) help to add value to the business. This is a key theme of the book.

Change and innovation in employee relations policies and practices to gain a competitive advantage or to deliver a service at a higher quality is essential in a modern competitive-based economy. New and developing management practices (for example, performance-related pay, single-union/no-strike agreements) of the 1980s have been successfully introduced into organisations. However, personnel managers cannot assume that such practices can automatically be transferred successfully to their own organisation which may be operating in a very different environment. They must be able to evaluate whether practices successfully introduced in one organisation can be successfully transplanted into their own. Organisations cannot change policies and practices constantly without any reference to organisational needs or existing practices. A further assumption in this book is that 'new initiatives' in management practice have to be evaluated in a rational manner over whether they can be introduced with equal success into another organisation.

A further theme of this book is the importance of personnel managers' understanding why negotiating skills are necessary for the effective solution of people management problems. They have to be able to identify the different negotiating situations (grievance-handling, bargaining, group problem-solving) in which managers may find themselves, appreciate the different stages through which negotiation may proceed, and the skills required in different negotiation situations.

The influential manager

If personnel-HRM managers, at any level of seniority, are to be proactive and to have influence in an organisation, they must demonstrate certain abilities (see Figure 1). First, they require a successful record of professional competence in the personnel-HRM field that is recognised by managerial colleagues both within and outside the personnel function. Second, they must demonstrate an understanding of the personnel-HRM function as a whole and of how its separate components integrate. Third, they must understand the interests of the business/organisation as a whole, and that these take preference over those of any management function as a unit or as that unit's component parts. Fourth, they must develop a network of contacts with managers, both within and outside the personnel-HRM function, in their own organisation and with managers in other organisations, including employers' associations and professional bodies such as the Chartered Institute of Personnel and Development (CIPD) and the British Institute of Management (BIM). Finally, they also require to build fruitful relationships with their superiors and to possess excellent interpersonal skills, particularly with respect to communications and teambuilding. Each of these five abilities is a necessary condition for an effective and influential personnel-HRM manager, but each is an insufficient ability on its own.

All people managers regardless of their seniority (personnel assistant, officer, manager, executive, etc) must understand the nature of the

Figure 1 Necessary conditions for an effective and influential personnel manager

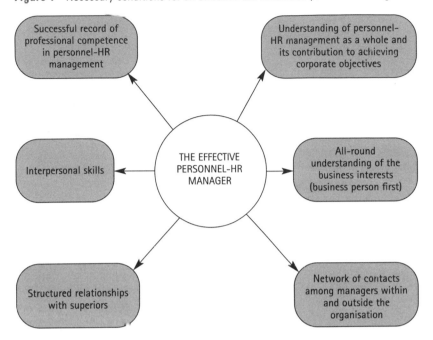

business of the organisation in which they manage, in terms of the organisation's mission, objectives, strategies and policies. In the private sector the effective and influential personnel-HRM manager will understand the 'bottom line' for the business and be able to contribute constructively, at the appropriate level of decision-making (department, section, management team, working-party, etc) to discussions on how the business might be developed and expanded. In the public sector the effective and influential personnel manager will understand the objectives of efficiency, effectiveness, economy, 'value for money' and the quality of service delivery to the customer or client.

The effective personnel-HRM manager understands how the people management function contributes to the achievement of the organisation's commercial and/or social objectives. He or she is able to explain to other managers, particularly outside personnel-HRM, how the function's strategies and policies help the business to develop and grow, add value to the business as a whole, and help provide a higher quality of service to the customer or client. In a nutshell, the personnel-HRM manager can explain to the other managers how the activities of the personnel-HRM function match with the overall objectives of the organisation. This is vertical integration of a management function with the overall business objectives.

In addition, the effective personnel-HRM manager can explain how the various components of people management – resourcing, development, reward and relations – contribute to the achievement of the objectives of the personnel-HRM function. This means that he or she must fully understand how the strategies and policies of the components of the personnel function link together to achieve the goals of the function. This horizontal integration of the personnel-HRM function will not be new to you because it has been a central theme in your core personnel and development studies. It is important during your employee relations studies that you understand vertical and horizontal integration.

The effective personnel-HRM manager in a management team has a proven competence recognised by management colleagues in employee relations as well as in employee resourcing, training and development, and pay and reward. It is essential, therefore, if personnel managers are to be effective, that they have an adequate knowledge and understanding of employee relations and have acquired the appropriate skills to apply that knowledge and understanding to solve employee relations problems to enable the organisation achieve its commercial and/or societal objectives. An implication of this statement is that it is not only existing, and prospective, personnel managers who need to acquire employee relations knowledge, understanding and skills, but *all* managers, regardless of their seniority or specialism.

The personnel-HRM manager who lacks professional competence in employee relations will be a less effective manager. The trend in many organisations to devolve their personnel-HRM function across management teams reinforces this view. Devolution often means that the services of a personnel manager with a specialism are not always required. However, the activities of the employee relations function (for example, being responsible for communications policy, handling employee grievances, dealing with disciplinary matters, and monitoring the size of the workforce) nevertheless must be delivered to the management team. Generalist personnel managers with employee relations skills are essential to any management team. Specialist personnel managers are less attractive to a management team.

This book therefore aims to provide the generalist personnel-HRM manager – and any other individuals who have to manage people – with the appropriate employee relations knowledge. And it aims to provide them with the awareness and skills they require to apply that knowledge and understanding to solving people management problems. This in turn will contribute to the organisation's achieving its commercial and/or social objectives. It will have the additional advantage of enhancing the creditability of the personnel-HRM manager in the eyes of his or her managerial colleagues both within and outside the personnel-HRM function.

A central theme of the book is that 'good practice' in the delivery of the personnel-HRM strategy and policies adds value to the business and thereby contributes to the achievement of the corporate-organisational economic and social objectives. The text explains not only what constitutes good practice (that this is acting with just cause and behaving fairly and reasonably) but why operating to good practice standards is sound business sense – for example, falling foul of industrial tribunal decisions may result in the exposure of 'bad' practices that are embarrassing to the organisation. The book also aims to help personnel managers/professionals develop and acquire skills, not only to solve people management problems but also to improve their own interpersonal skills and thereby enhance the quality of their relationships with superiors.

If personnel manages are to be effective and influential, they require to be both 'generalist' and 'specialist' as personnel managers. Generalist personnel managers have at least an adequate knowledge and understanding of the skills to be applied in employee relations. If they neglect this and concentrate exclusively on development, resourcing and reward, they will be less effective managers.

Employee relations activities

The purpose of employee relations activity is to reconcile the different interests of the buyers of labour services (employers) and the sellers of labour services (employees), and in so doing assist the organisation to achieve its business and/or social objectives. This difference of interests revolves around the 'price' (including the quality and quantity) at which labour services will be bought and sold. Although there is this difference of interests, both management and employees have a common need to reconcile the difference. The alternative is mutual destruction of the organisation. The closure of the enterprise is of no benefit to employers or employees. There is mutual advantage to both employers and employees in resolving their differences as buyers and sellers of labour market services. They accommodate their respective interests by making agreements, rules and regulations through the use of various employee relations processes – employee involvement, collective bargaining, unilateral imposition by management, joint consultation, arbitration, mediation and conciliation, and Parliamentary legislation.

The agreements, rules and regulations express the price at which labour services are to be bought and sold, and are made at different levels (workplace, company, industry) and have different degrees of authorship. Some are written solely (imposed) by the employer with little or no influence from the employees, whereas others, usually as a result of collective bargaining, are jointly authored by the employer and representatives of their employees. Agreements, rules and regulations cover two broad range of issues. One is substantive issues (pay, holidays, hours of work, incentive schemes, pensions, sick pay, maternity leave, family-friendly policies, etc) and the other comprises procedural issues. Employee relations procedures provide fair and reasonable standards of behaviour to resolve in a peaceful way issues over which employers and employees have differences. Such procedures normally apply to the resolving of issues such as employee complaints against the behaviour of employers (known as grievances), employer complaints about the behaviour of employees (referred to as disciplinary matters), the need to reduce the size of the workforce (redundancy), employee claims that the responsibilities of their jobs have increased (job grading) and employee requests for union representation (union recognition procedures).

The content of agreements, rules and regulations and the employee relations processes used to secure them reflect the relative balance of bargaining power between employers and employees. This balance is heavily influenced by changes in the corporate environment in which an organisation undertakes its employee relations activity. The major factors that shape the external corporate environment are the economic and legal policies of national governments and European Union political decision-making institutions. In an attempt to enhance their economic interests, both employers and employees, via representative organisations, spend relatively large sums of money on the political lobbying process to persuade the government to introduce appropriate economic and legal policies. A further factor in the external corporate environment that influences employee relations is the implementation by employers of technological change.

The balance of bargaining power is a central concept that must be understood by employee relations managers. It helps to explain the constraints within which managements can exercise their power. Abusing one's power to obtain one's aims is not professional behaviour. It will inevitably lead to pressure for legal restraints to be imposed to curb the abuse. Unprofessional behaviour that relies on a sense of 'might is right' will cause employees to behave in a reciprocal way when the balance of bargaining power shifts away from management towards the employees. Professionalism means tackling matters in a systematic and careful manner. The fact that the state of balance of bargaining power currently means that management can 'succeed' without trying to continually dominate is no excuse for managers not to behave in a professional way. Good practice dictates that they behave in a professional manner, gaining consent by discussion, consultation, negotiation and involvement, not through the crude exercise of power.

However, personnel managers/professionals require more than just knowledge and understanding of employee relations parties, processes, agreements, rules and regulations and the external environment in which these activities take place if they are to solve people management problems effectively. Employee relations problem-solving also requires the development and application of certain skills, of which the most significant are communication (oral and written), interviewing, listening, negotiating, evaluating and analysing.

This book thus endeavours to widen and develop the employee relations knowledge and understanding you acquired in your core personnel and development studies. It provides sufficient knowledge, understanding and skills for personnel managers and those who manage people in other functions, to operate as professional people managers in a number of different situations, including both union and non-union environments. The book also aims to introduce you to how essential it is for personnel managers/professionals to become effective and influential in the organisation by understanding the concepts of good practice and the balance of bargaining power, and by acquiring and developing the general management skills referred to above.

The book and the CIPD syllabus

The CIPD Professional Development Scheme's standards on employee relations is arranged under five headings:

- Employee relations management in context

- The parties in employee relations

- Employee relations processes

- Employee relations outcomes

- Employee relations skills.

In this book, the sections that fall within *employee relations management in context* describe the corporate environment in which organisations undertake their internal employee relations activities. A growing and important part of this external environment is the evolution of the 'social' dimension (Social Chapter, Social Charter) of the European Union. This section of the standards also covers the role of the national government as an economic manager and as a law-maker, as well as 'state agencies' such as the Advisory, Conciliation and Arbitration Service (ACAS) and the employment tribunal system. The *employee relations management in context* part of the standards is covered by Chapter 1 (Employee relations: an overview), Chapter 2 (The economic and corporate environment), Chapter 3 (The legislative framework) and Chapter 4 (The European Union).

The sections on *the parties in employee relations* deal with management objectives and styles, employee relations strategies, gaining employee commitment and participation, and managing with or without unions. It also covers the changing role and functions of employers' associations – such as the Confederation of British Industry (CBI) and the Engineering Employers' Federation – and management associations organised at the level of the European Union. The section of the standards that covers employee organisations (trade unions, professional associations, staff/employee associations, etc) is dealt with in Chapter 5 (Employee relations institutions). Chapter 6 looks at management strategy and policies together with issues such as management style and the management of change.

There is a wide range of *employee relations processes* which impact on employment relationships in organisations – joint consultation, employee involvement schemes, third-party intervention (arbitration and conciliation), collective bargaining, industrial sanctions (lock-outs, suspension, collective dismissals) and parliamentary legislation. This part of the standards is covered by Chapters 5, 6, 7 and 8.

The *employee relations outcomes* component of the standards concerns the various dimensions of agreements (both collective and individual), their types (substantive and procedural), their authorship (joint or by employer alone), the levels at which they are concluded, and their scope (the subjects covered by the agreements, rules and regulations). This section of the standards is dealt within Chapter 5.

The *employer relations skills* section of the standards covers the definition of negotiations, the different types of negotiating situations and the various stages involved in the negotiating process. It also covers the skills required by managers in preparing for and conducting bargaining, in presenting claims/offers and counter-offers, in searching for common ground, in concluding the negotiations, and in writing up the agreement.

The standards also cover the skills required by a manager (or management team) in handling employee complaints against management behaviour (commonly referred to as grievances), in handling disciplinary proceedings, in managing a redundancy situation and in managing health and safety. It also deals with management skills and the knowledge and understanding required to devise, review and monitor procedural arrangements.

Chapter 9 deals with negotiation in general terms (that is, its definition, its different types and its component stages) and with bargaining collectively with the workforce. The chapter places great stress on the skills required of management in the preparation stages, in grievance-handling and bargaining, and in particular in identifying any common ground with the other party via the use of such techniques as 'if and then' and the 'aspiration grid'.

Chapter 10 deals with handling employee behaviour and performance issues (including disciplinary proceedings), and stresses the importance of management's behaving in a fair and reasonable manner (good practice). Chapter 11 covers grievance-handling. Chapter 12 centres on managing redundancy situations and the devising, reviewing and monitoring of redundancy procedures. Chapter 13 concentrates on the management of health and safety, and emphasises the need for health and safety aspects to be taken seriously and integrated with other people management policies.

Chapter 14, the concluding chapter, offers help and advice to students when preparing for the Professional Development Scheme employee relations examination. Some specimen case studies and questions are discussed.

We hope you enjoy reading this book. If you can acquire and develop a deep understanding and appreciation of its contents, you have an excellent chance of gaining a CIPD professional qualification.

John Gennard
Graham Judge

PART 2

EMPLOYMENT RELATIONS MANAGEMENT IN CONTEXT

• Employee Relations: An Overview

CHAPTER OBJECTIVES

This chapter introduces you to the components of any employee relations system at an international, national, company or enterprise level:

● the different, and the common, interests of the 'buyers' (the employers) and the 'sellers' of labour services (employees) in the management of employees

● the mechanisms (processes) available to employers and employees whereby they agree rules and regulations to govern the employment relationship and at the same time accommodate their differing interests

● the rules, regulations and agreements made (and by whom) to regulate the employment relationship – this affects the 'price' at which labour services are exchanged in the labour market

● the relative balance of bargaining power between employers and employees, and how this influences the mechanisms used to establish employment rules, etc, and the content of those rules, regulations and agreements.

Introduction

Some people view employee relations as being about trade union behaviour, collective bargaining, industrial disputes and UK Government– trade union relationships. Trade unions are regarded as workplace adversaries negotiating with employers and also as social partners expressing an 'employee view' on economic and social matters, particularly through the Trades Union Congress, to governments. Although the extent to which this employers-propose/unions-oppose approach squares (or squared) with reality can be questioned, there is no doubt that the perspective is of lesser relevance to today's employment relationship. The institutions of trade unions, collective bargaining procedures and arrangements, strikes and tripartism have declined steadily over the last two decades. Indeed, the 1998 Workplace Employee Relations Survey reported that 47 per cent of workplaces have no union members at all.

Attitudes to work and relationships at work have certainly changed since the late 1970s. The driving forces for this have been increased competition, reductions in international trade barriers, public sector financial constraints, pressures for higher value-for-money, rapidly changing and easily transferable technologies, and customer demands for products and services increasingly customised to their needs. In this changed environment of the last 20 years, many employers now view employee relations as having a relatively greater focus on the individual employee than on the employees as a collective body, and on partnership between employees and employers in which both parties are motivated to add value to the organisation. Such changed relationships are thought to be based on:

- the success of the enterprise

- building employee trust, feelings of fairness and greater commitment

- enhancing the satisfaction employees get from their work

- providing all employees with the opportunity to influence and be involved in decisions that are likely to affect their interests ('employee voice')

- helping the organisation to improve productivity, profitability and efficiency.

These changing attitudes are reflected in the management-led changes in communication methods (for example, team briefing), in work organisation (quality circles, teamworking and single status), in changes in payment systems (for example, performance-related pay), in changes in employees' representative systems (business-focused consultation arrangements), in the recognition of the employees' need for employment security (training and development of employees), in attitudes towards trade union recognition, in patterns of working (part-time, shift work, annualised hours) and in employment status (temporary/agency workers, fixed-term contract). Employee relations is a study of the rules, regulations and agreements by which employees are managed both as individuals and as a collective group, the priority given to the individual as opposed to the collective relationship varying between companies depending on the values of management. As such it is concerned with how to gain people's commitment to the achievement of an organisation's business goals and objectives in a number of different situations. Employee relations management is also about ensuring that organisational change is accepted and then implemented.

An IPD Position Paper (1997) advocated an employee relations system built on higher skills, better skill utilisation, greater co-operation within the workplace and the use of initiatives to develop higher added value through differentiated goods and services. In this model of employee relations, organisations succeed by:

- raising the skills of their employees

- providing high-quality services and products

- giving excellent customer service.

These in turn generate high profits, high earnings and a relatively more secure future for employees. In practical terms, the model embraces effective performance, good people management practices based on trust, fairness and delivery of the deal, a knowledge and understanding of employees' aspirations, and attention to the 'employee voice' obtained through a variety of channels (for example, employee involvement and participation, and trade union representatives).

The components of employee relations systems

Employee relations systems in any organisation have a number of components. These are shown in Figure 2 overleaf. First, there are the 'players' in employee relations activities. The principal 'players' are:

- individual employers

- individual employees

- employee representative bodies (staff associations, trade unions, works councils, etc)

- employers' associations

- private companies

- public bodies

- voluntary organisations (for example, Save the Children Fund).

These 'players' operate in a labour market in which they attempt to protect and advance their respective economic interests relative to each other. Although sellers (employees) in the labour market have interests that are different from the buyers' (employers), both have a common interest in finding their opposite number. Both employees and employers have a common interest in the survival of the employing enterprise, even though they may disagree on how any surplus generated by the sales of its products or services should be divided among themselves. They have a mutual interest in resolving this problem because not to do so will result in mutual destruction. An analysis of the interests of the 'players' in an employee relations system is thus a central concern of employee relations.

The employee relations 'players' also have expectations of how each will behave towards the other. This is referred to as the 'psychological contract', which has been described by Schein (1978) as 'a set of unwritten, reciprocal expectations between an individual employee and the organisation'. It is based on the notion that in addition to the formal employment contract, employees develop a set of informal unwritten assumptions about and expectations from their employing organisation. These are said to depend on employee trust, perceptions of fairness and reliable delivery of the deal over a range of issues such as job satisfaction, career progression, reward, relationships with managers, wellbeing (employment security, involvement via voice to the employer

Figure 2   Employee relations: reconciliation of interests

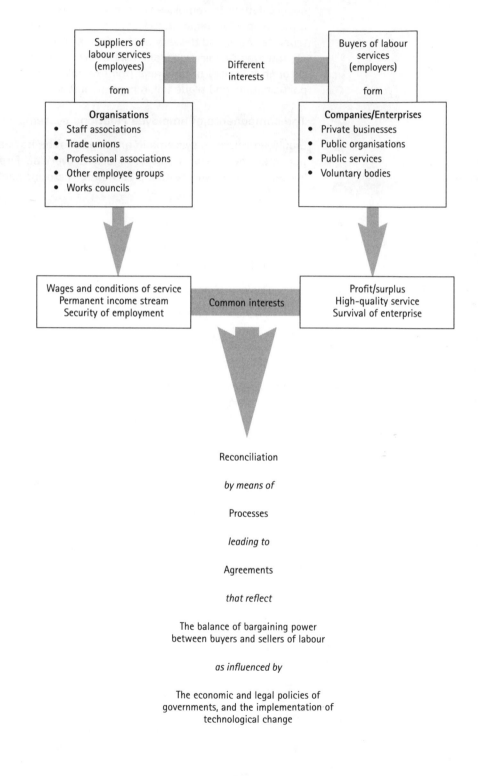

and skill development) and technology upgrading. It is a concept that enables conclusions to be drawn about the quality of the employment relationship in the UK (IPD, 1998).

Second, there are mechanisms available to the buyers and sellers of labour services by which they agree rules and regulation to govern the employment relationship and at the same time accommodate their different economic interests. These mechanisms include:

- consultation
- employee involvement and participation
- communication processes
- collective bargaining
- legal regulation by the UK Government and the European Union.

The third component is the agreements and regulations (ie the rules) that govern the employment relationship for an individual and/or group of employees and that result from the use of these mechanisms. These rules also constitute a statement of the rights, responsibilities and obligations employers and employees have towards each other.

The external environment

The selling and buying of labour services also takes place in the context of an external environment. The UK Government, through its economic and legislative policies, and directed increasingly by the European Union through its legal instruments, sets minimum standards of behaviour for the buyer and sellers of labour services. Employment legislation stipulates the redress one party can seek from the other if it steps outside these standards of behaviour. The UK Government's economic and legal policies influence, at the macro level, the relative bargaining power between the buyers and sellers of labour services, which then affects the choice of employee relations processes used as well as the outcomes from their use. If UK Government economic and legal policies are more favourable to the interests of employees (for example, by pursuit of full employment policies), it will be reflected in the content of the 'rules' regulating the employment relationship.

The mechanism used and the output of an employee relations system in any organisation are also influenced by the balance of bargaining power at the sector and enterprise level. This requires the employee relations professional to analyse variables such as the strategic position workers hold in the production or service provision process and the availability of an alternative workforce to the one currently employed. If a group of workers who have the power to stop an organisation's activities are willing to exercise that power, and have exercised it successfully in the past, they will have a relatively greater bargaining power than their employer and will be able to obtain a 'price' for their labour services that is closer to their ideal economic objectives than it is to the economic objectives of the employer. This concept of the relative bargaining power between the buyers and sellers of labour services is the fourth component of any employee relations system in any organisation.

> What are the four main components of an employee relations system in any organisation?

Employers' interests in the labour market

Employee relations is a management problem-solving activity designed to establish the rules, regulations and agreement by which – that is, the 'price' at which – labour services are to be exchanged in the labour market. The word 'price' is in quotation marks because employers seek to secure labour services on the most advantageous terms they can through offering a package of employment conditions that contains monetary (pay, paid holidays, etc) and non-monetary (opportunities for career development, good work colleagues) advantages and disadvantages.

The employer's employment package

Monetary considerations taken into account by an employer in purchasing labour services include:

- pay
- hours of work
- paid holidays
- sick-pay schemes
- incentive schemes
- pension arrangements
- the provision of family-friendly measures such as childcare facilities.

In return for providing these items, employers expect their employees to provide, depending on the skill and status of the job:

- flexibility between tasks (functional flexibility)
- minimum standards of competency in the task for which they are being hired, as expressed in qualifications, training received and the employee's experience
- a willingness to change (aptitude and adaptability)
- an ability to work as a member of a team

- a capability to show initiative
- a talent to give discretionary effort
- a demonstrable commitment to the organisation's objectives.

In recruiting labour services, the employer trades off items in a package of conditions. A management that would, for example, like to be able to hire and fire labour services at will (numerical flexibility) may be willing to offer potential employees – depending on the state of the labour market – a higher financial reward to compensate for the reduced job security. However, if jobs are scarce, an employer may not have to make such a trade-off. Employers who prefer to deploy any labour services they purchase, thereby requiring flexibility between various tasks, are likely to offer a package of higher financial rewards in order to attract employees who can adapt relatively easily to change.

If employers wish to purchase high-quality labour services, in terms of skills, attitude, etc, they may offer a package of financial rewards that is more advantageous than those offered by employers who are happy to purchase lower-quality labour services. In every sector of the economy there are those employers who are more prepared than their competitors to invest in better employment conditions. The argument is that the higher financial rewards afforded to the employees are more than offset by the increased productivity, lower labour turnover, greater motivation, etc, that results from purchasing higher-quality labour services.

In purchasing labour services, employers cannot ignore the longer-term interests of their organisations. Although employers may like to hire and fire employees at will, they nevertheless require a core of permanent employees to provide continuity and some stability if they are to survive in the marketplace. The size of this core workforce, in relation to those who actually are hired and fired at will, is a matter for commercial judgement by each organisation.

The package offered to, and accepted by, the suppliers of labour services may be minimal, consisting of low wages, long hours, few opportunities to acquire and develop skills and little employment security. The suppliers of labour services may be prepared to accept such a package because the alternative is unemployment. However, suppliers of labour services who work under such an employment package are likely to have low morale, perform at standards below their capability and feel no commitment or loyalty to the purchaser of their labour services. Low morale and low commitment have adverse consequences for an organisation's economic performance and/or the quality of service offered to customers. In the long run, the employment of poor-quality labour services increases an organisation's costs, reduces its competitiveness in the product market and puts at risk its very survival.

In purchasing labour services, the package of conditions the buyers will have to offer is influenced by the relative balance of bargaining power between buyers and sellers. If the relative bargaining power favours the buyers, the buyers will purchase labour services for a lesser package of conditions than if the power relationship were reversed. But if the buyers of labour services abuse this market power by offering unacceptably low wages and conditions, then pressures will develop for the state to restrain – by legal regulation – the misuse of such power. It was such behaviour – admittedly, on behalf of a small number of employers – that led to the imposition by the UK Government, from 1 April 1999, of a national minimum wage to be paid to all those in paid employment aged over 18. So in offering a package of conditions to employees, employers should have regard to longer-term considerations and not merely to what can be 'got away with' in the short run.

> Consider a group of employees in your organisation. What package of monetary and non-monetary employment conditions does your organisation offer to attract that group to come to work for it, and to continue to work for it? Why that package?

Employees' interests in the labour market

In the labour market, the sellers of labour services seek from employers (the buyers) the best possible package of monetary and non-monetary employment conditions available. The monetary aspects include wage/salary rates, hours of work, paid holidays, pension schemes, sick-pay arrangements, incentive schemes and childcare facilities. The non-monetary elements involve such items as:

- employment security

- the opportunity to work with good colleagues in a sociable atmosphere

- the potential for advancement and promotion

- access to training and development opportunities to upgrade skills, acquire new skills, etc

- being treated as a human being, not merely a commodity

- job satisfaction in relation to job design, degree of control over the job (empowerment)

- family-friendly employment measures (eg childcare facilities) which enable a balance to be achieved between the need to be a family person and the need to take paid employment to provide for that family

- fair and consistent treatment by managers relative to other employees

- influence over the day-to-day operations at the workplace and at policy level (a voice in relation to management).

Like the buyers of labour services, the sellers also give different weight to the items in the package of employment conditions on offer. They may, for example, be prepared to work for 'lower' wages if that is compensated for by greater employment security. Some employees may, for example, stay with an organisation even though it pays below the market rate because it practises employee involvement and empowerment by vesting decision-making with the team leaders or promotes self-managing teams.

It is impossible to tell what a 'standard mix' of benefits sought from employment by employees would include. Motivation theory postulates that each individual is stimulated by his or her own package, and that as economic and social conditions change, the pressures on employees alter with them. The balance between the various items in the package depends on many factors, including age, family circumstances, local and industry-specific employment conditions and the national scene. Nevertheless, employers – like any seller in a marketplace – seek the best possible package of monetary and non-monetary employment conditions.

> What is your monetary and non-monetary package of employment conditions? Which are the most important to you? Why?

The employment relationship

The employment relationship has some similarities with all transactions. A golden rule of buying is to purchase goods or services of acceptable quality at the lowest price obtainable. The seller meanwhile wishes to sell at the highest possible price. To reach agreement buyer and seller must accommodate each other's interests and establish an appropriate price.

However, the employment relationship is more stable and longer-term than that between the buyer and seller of a commodity such as a house or piece of equipment, furniture, etc. In that kind of activity, the buyers and sellers engage in a one-off and immediate exchange relationship. The parties involved in the labour market, on the other hand, are entering what is expected to be a long-standing relationship involving terms that will be reviewed periodically and amended if necessary. In short, a particular feature of the employment relationship is that it has a future.

Different interests within management

There are differences of interest within management at all levels of an organisation, including the workplace. Although working to a common end, management is not a united whole. Managers have differences, which, like those between the buyers and sellers of labour services, have to be reconciled if corporate objectives are to be achieved.

In larger organisations, management activities are divided into different functions – for example, marketing, production-operations, personnel, and finance. These management interest groups have a common interest in the survival and growth of the business but often have different and competing interests at the same time. While the aim of all is to ensure that the products or services reach their destination at the right time and are of the right quality, internal power struggles (management politics) and competition for shares of a finite budget often play off one management interest against another.

The main objective of production-operations management is usually the achievement of production targets, and to this end they may consider the organisation's best interests are served by employment policies that freely permit the hiring and firing of labour and the granting of employee demands to prevent production-service disruptions. This approach conflicts with that of people managers, who believe the organisation's interests are best served by recruiting, selecting and/or dismissing employees in accordance with good personnel practices, and rewarding them on objective criteria rather than in order solely to meet market demand at all costs.

Differences between interest groups within management are resolved by negotiation between themselves or through arbitration by a more senior manager. Using persuasion and perhaps making constructive compromises, managers seek to gain the commitment of their managerial colleagues to their proposed course of action. Should managers at the same level of seniority be unable to settle their differences by negotiation, then a senior manager will arbitrate and decide the appropriate course of action to be adopted.

Employee relations professionals cannot take it for granted that what they propose will be accepted at once and without question by other managers. However, differences between managers have to be reconciled in a constructive, and not a destructive, manner. Most management differences can be resolved quickly. As an employee relations professional, you will find yourself frequently negotiating with your management colleagues (at the same, at a lower or at a higher level of seniority) to resolve differences over what constitutes the 'best' employee relations policies and practices to be implemented if the organisation is to achieve its objectives.

> When did you last have a difference with a colleague over how a problem should be resolved? What was the problem about? What were the differences between you? What was the resolution of the difference? Why was there a difference in the first place?

Different interests among employees

Just as there are a plurality of interests within and between groups of managers, so there are within and between groups of employees. In a workplace, different types of employees (technical, clerical, administrative, craft manual, semi-skilled and unskilled, etc) are employed and have different interests from each other. Non-manual employees usually expect a positive employment conditions differential over manual workers. Craft manual workers see their interests, relative to those of lesser skilled workers, best served by pay differentials expressed in percentage terms. If this percentage figure is reduced, craft workers usually demand improvements in pay and conditions to re-establish accepted percentage differentials.

Lesser skilled manual workers (who also tend to be low-paid) view their interests, relative to those of craft manual workers, best served by pay differentials expressed in monetary terms. They oppose percentage increases in pay on the grounds that such increases widen monetary differentials.

Such differences between the various groups of employees continue. They are particularly acute in the public sector. In 1999 schoolteachers expressed fierce opposition to the Government's proposal to make teaching a more attractive profession by the creation of a more highly paid super-teacher. Differences of interests between different groups of employees often makes it difficult for them to support each other in differences with employers.

The recognition of different interests

Employee relations aims to resolve differences between the various interest groups regardless of whether these groups comprise different categories of managers or of employees. The bottom line is that the activity of the organisation must continue even if the behaviour to make it happen must alter, depending on the current situation and the underlying climate of employee relations. In organisations, whether non-union or unionised, where the emphasis is on problem-solving, consultation and communications procedures, these differences of interests, between employers and employees, are formally recognised in written statements of policy and procedures and/or in collective agreements with trade unions. For example, Clauses 2.3 and 2.4 (General principles) of a 'recognition procedural agreement' between Kingsmead Carpets Ltd, Cumnock, and the Scottish Carpet Workers Union signed in 1997 state that:

2.3   The union recognises management's responsibility to plan, organise and manage the company's operation.

2.4   The company recognises the union's responsibility to represent the interests of its members and to maintain or improve their terms and conditions of employment and work within the constraints imposed on the plant by corporate policy and finance.

Another example can be drawn from a recognition and procedural agreement between a food manufacturer and the Amalgamated Engineering and Electrical Union signed in 1995, which states in its preamble:

> The company recognises the union as the sole collective bargaining agent in respect of the categories of employees coming within the scope of this agreement.
>
> The union recognises management's responsibility to manage its establishments and accepts that the company must continue with new and improved methods of work and that the company must be able to make free and intelligent use of its labour force to achieve the highest quality of service and obtain maximum efficiency . . .

Yet another example of the recognition of the difference of interests between employers and employees is seen in the recognition agreement between Volex Powercords and the Transport and General Workers Union, which contains the following:

3 General principles
a) The company has the right to manage the business and direct its affairs and workforce in the efficient pursuit of the organisation's business.
b) The company recognises the union's responsibility to manage its affairs and to represent the interests of its members.
c) Both parties agree the need to maintain open and direct communications with all employees on matters of mutual interest and concern.

The aim of employee relations is to resolve areas of conflicting interests and to identify and pursue areas of common interest so as to maintain the business organisation. We now turn to these common interests.

Employer–employee common interests

Unless the organisation keeps running, there is nothing to manage, no profit to be made, no service to provide and no pay for work done. Although, as buyers and sellers of labour services, employers and employees have different interests, they have a common interest in ensuring that their different interests are reconciled. There are strong economic pressures on employers and employees to accommodate each other's interests rather than to perpetuate their differences.

Costs to employers

If employers fail to reconcile their different interests with their employees, a number of costs arise:

- The employer has no goods/services to sell in the marketplace.

- The employer cannot earn profit or provide services at value-for-money.

- Goods and services cannot be supplied to the marketplace at the right price or of the right quality.

- Customer needs cannot be satisfied.

- Factories, offices and shops, etc, lie idle or close down.

- Customers take their business to competitor firms.

Costs to employees

The consequences for employees who fail to resolve their different interests from employers are equally obvious:

- They do not remain in employment.

- They do not receive a steady income.

- They have no power as consumers.

- They cannot enter into long-term financial commitments (eg mortgages, bank loans, hire purchase contracts).

- They accumulate no employment benefits based on continuity of employment (eg paid holidays and sick pay).

- There is no certainty as to the future level of income.

If employees receive no income from employment, they become dependent on the state for a minimum level of income to satisfy their basic needs of housing, heating, lighting, food, etc.

The recognition of common interests

Both employers and employees have an enlightened self-interest in ensuring that their differing interests are reconciled. Enlightened self-interest also helps produce a bottom line, beyond which it is not worth pushing for one's own interest against the interest of the other party. Interest reconciliation brings mutual gain. Employers secure the survival of their enterprises, gain profit or provide services at value-for-money, and satisfy the needs of their customers. Employees obtain job security, and benefit from more income security, consumer power and status by being employed. Both employers and employees have a common interest in ensuring that companies/enterprises are successful. However, there are occasions when this common interest might not seem particularly common to employees, especially if they are told by management that they are to be made redundant because cost cuts are required to re-establish the viability of the enterprise.

The recognition of this common interest is so important that it is normally formally stated in agreements between employers and employees. For example, the 2002 national agreement between the Scottish Print

Employers Federation and the Graphical, Paper and Media Union declares:

2 Unit cost and competitiveness

The parties recognise that the whole basis of the market for printed products is changing rapidly, posing new challenges for everyone engaged in the industry. It is of fundamental importance that those challenges are met with a positive response from employers and employees in order to secure the future of Scottish printing in the face of intensifying domestic and international competition. The parties willingly accept the need for companies to attain the highest standards in meeting customers' requirements, in particular the need for continuous improvement in increasing efficiency at reducing unit costs.

It is therefore agreed that at individual company level, management and chapel [branch] representatives will co-operate fully in identifying, discussing and implementing any changes necessary to achieve increased output and lower unit costs through the most effective use of people, materials and machines.

It is further agreed that where practical, managements and chapels will agree and implement efficiency and productivity measures sufficient to offset in full additional costs arising from the national wages and conditions settlement. Such measures can be wide-ranging in scope.

No person will be made redundant as a direct result of implementing this clause . . .

Similarly, the Constitution and Memorandum of Agreement between the Transport and General Workers Union and the Road Haulage Association Ltd for the road haulage industry (hire and reward) contains the following paragraph:

Objects and functions:

3 The objects of the Council should be to promote joint action for their mutual benefit by organisations of employers and working people.

Clauses 6.2 and 6.3 of Section 6 entitled 'Competitive advantage' of the pay and conditions agreement between Scottish Power, Power Systems, Scotland and the Amalgamated Engineering and Electrical Union, GMB, the Transport and General Workers and UNISON states:

6.2 A key part of the competitive advantage strategy will be continuous improvement in all Power Systems activities to ensure that changing business demands can be rapidly met and best working practices, identified through benchmarking and other means, are safely implemented within the normal joint processes so that competitive advantage can be developed and maintained.

6.3 The Division and the Trade Unions agree that to achieve and maintain competitive advantage, continuous improvement and the changes which will result will be implemented on an ongoing basis, subject to the normal joint processes.

An agreement in the further education sector also recognises the common interests between the buyers and sellers of labour services with a clause that states:

It is in the mutual interest of the Board of Management and its employees that the college should function effectively thus providing a quality service to all students and the community.

The common requirement between employers and employees to reconcile their different interests to mutual advantage was stressed in the Trades Union Congress document, *Partners for Progress: Next steps for the New Unionism*, in the following paragraph:

3 The theme of this statement is partnership, a recognition that trade unions must not be seen as part of Britain's problems but as part of the solution to the country's problems. At the workplace, social partnership means employers and trade unions working together to achieve common goals such as fairness and competitiveness; it is a recognition that, although they have different constituencies, and at times different interests, they can serve these best by making common cause wherever possible. At the national level, partnership means government discussing issues with employers and trade unions on a fair and open basis where a common approach can reap dividends – for example, attracting inward investment and promoting training and equal opportunities.

One of the methods by which the different labour market interests of employers and employees are accommodated is by negotiation, which involves the two parties (employers and employees) coming together to make an accommodation (agreement) by purposeful persuasion (the use of rational argument) and by making constructive compromises (identifying the common ground for a basis for agreement) towards each other's position. There are different types of negotiating situations (see Chapter 9) but the most usual of those that involve employers and employees are:

- grievance-handling to resolve a complaint by an employee that management behaviour has infringed his or her employment 'rights'

- bargaining, during which employers and employees 'trade' items within a list of demands they have made of each other

- group problem-solving, in which the employer settles the details upon which the employees will co-operate with a request from management to assist in obtaining information to help solve a problem of mutual concern.

Why do you think it is essential for employees and employers to reconcile their differences?

Alternative interest-resolution mechanisms

There are, however, other ways in which the conflict of interests may be accommodated. In some cases, individuals who find that their aspirations (for example, for promotion or for higher pay) cannot be met with their present employer, resign their employment and go and work for another somewhere where their interests can be, or are more likely to be, better accommodated. Although labour turnover represents a peaceful method of resolving the differences of interests between employers and employees, management has to keep voluntary disengagements in such cases to manageable proportions, for labour turnover is not without cost to the employer.

In other circumstances accommodation is achieved by the employer's dismissing the employee. Here, the employer says it is not in the interest of the company to continue to employ the individual concerned. The employee, however, is virtually bound to hold the opposite view and see his or her interest best advanced by continuing in employment with that employer. Such opposing positions cannot be reconciled, so the employer forces the issue by dismissing the employee – who may or may not respond by complaining to an employment tribunal that he or she has been dismissed unfairly. The tribunal must then come to a decision in favour either of the employer or of the employee – a decision that may stipulate reinstatement, re-engagement or financial compensation. Ultimately, the tribunal resolves differences of interest between the employer and the employee.

Where are labour services employed?

Workplace size

The 1998 Workplace Employment Relations Survey found that workplaces employing between 25 and 49 employees accounted for 52 per cent of all workplaces but only 17 per cent of all workplace employees. On the other hand, workplaces employing 500 or more accounted for only 3 per cent of all workplaces but almost 30 per cent of all workers, the remaining 70 per cent fairly evenly distributed across other size bands (see Table 1).

Sector distribution

Table 2 shows the extent to which labour services are purchased by sectors of the economy. Some 18 per cent of workplaces were in the

Table 1 Distribution of workplaces and employment by workplace size

Workplace size	Percentage of all workplaces	Percentage of all employees
25–49 employees	52	17
50–99 employees	25	16
100–199 employees	12	16
200–499 employees	8	22
500 or more employees	3	30

Source: 1998 Workplace Employment Relations Survey

manufacturing sector, which was predominately privately owned. This same pattern existed for wholesale and retail distribution. Marked differences were apparent in the workforce composition across the groups (see Table 2).

Workplaces making or doing different things had differing skill requirements, and there were substantial differences in occupational composition by industry. For example, 70 per cent of education workplaces employed professional people. Plant and machine operatives worked mostly in manufacturing and transport and communications. Craft and related occupations were mainly in public utilities and construction. The

Table 2 Distribution of workplace by industry and sector

Industry	Percentage of workplaces in private sector	Percentage of workplaces in public sector	All workplaces
Manufacturing	99	1	18
Electricity, gas and water	85	15	–
Construction	88	12	4
Wholesale and retail	99	1	18
Hotels and restaurants	96	4	6
Transport and communications	78	22	5
Financial services	100	0	3
Other business services	87	13	9
Public administration	–	100	6
Education	13	87	14
Health	57	43	13
Other community services	71	29	4
All workplaces	72	28	100

Source: 1998 Workplace Employment Relations Survey

1998 Workplace Employment Relations Survey also reported that some 29 per cent of workplaces employed mainly women to the extent that at least three quarters of their employees were female; 27 per cent of workplaces employed mainly male labour services; and 44 per cent employed both male and female employees. Under a quarter of private sector workplaces had a largely female workforce compared to nearly a half in the public sector. Women employees dominated workplace employment in health (84 per cent) and education (63 per cent), whereas males dominated in construction (85 per cent), transport and communications (71 per cent), and electricity, gas and water (70 per cent).

Part-time workers – defined as those who worked fewer than 30 hours per week – accounted for a quarter of all jobs in workplaces with 25 or more employees. Sixteen per cent of workplaces employed no part-time workers, whereas in 26 per cent of workplaces part-timers formed the majority of the workforce. Substantial proportions of workplaces in manufacturing, the public utilities and construction used no part-timers at all, while similarly high proportions of workplaces in wholesale and retail, hotels and restaurants, education and health employed a majority part-time workforce.

The number of employees in January 2002 (*Labour Market Trends*, 2002) was 24.8 million, of which 4 million (16 per cent) were employed in the manufacturing sector. In 1971, manufacturing employed 8.1 million (36.3 per cent) of the workforce. In 2002, the service sector employed 20.5 million, which was 7.5 per cent of the total workforce. In 1971, the share of service sector employment was almost 53 per cent. In 2002, 6.3 million (more than in the whole of manufacturing) were employed in public administration, education and health, 5 million in banking, finance and insurance, and 5 million in retail and wholesale distribution, hotels and restaurants.

Interest-enhancing institutions

Employers

The buyers of labour services seek to maintain and enhance their interests by organising themselves into companies or enterprises, of which there are four main types :

- private businesses in which a distinction can be made between:

    - the private company owned by either an individual or a family and which has no shareholders. Such companies retain control of the decision whether to sell themselves to another company.

    and

    - the private company owned by shareholders but controlled by managers. Such companies can be acquired by other companies with the agreement of the shareholders irrespective of the views of the managers

- public corporations
- central and local government
- voluntary bodies.

Private businesses employ some 18 million people. Although there are large numbers of small incorporated businesses, the most common form of organisation is the registered company. A major feature of the corporate sector is the concentration of output into a small number of very large private limited companies (many of which have production or service capacity in more than one country) alongside a substantial but growing number of much smaller private firms serving local 'niche' markets. This concentration of output into fewer enterprises is the result of corporate mergers within countries and across national boundaries.

There is, in large, private sector businesses, a divorce of ownership by individual and institutional shareholders (such as banks and pension fund managers) and management control which lies with a team of professional managers who are accountable to the owners for the performance of the company. Corporate strategy and its associated policies are normally decided by an executive group selected by the chief executive officer/managing director. This strategy is then taken to the plc board of directors for approval, modification or rejection. Senior, middle and junior managers are appointed to implement the policies in order to achieve the corporate strategy. In private corporations, the authority chain is from the top downwards through management structures.

Public sector organisation can be divided into public corporations, central government and local authorities. Public corporations, which include organisations such as the Royal Mail and NHS Trusts, in 2002 employed some 1 million people. In the same year the central government employed just under three quarters of a million people, of whom half worked for the Civil Service. The numbers employed in local authorities in 2002 was some 2.0 million. By 2001, employment in the public sector had fallen to its lowest level in the post-World War II period.

Voluntary bodies are usually small, not-for-profit organisations with social rather than economic objectives. They include organisations such as Oxfam, Save the Children Fund, The British Heart Foundation and local housing associations. The voluntary sector also contains worker or producer co-operatives in which the enterprise is owned and controlled by its members. In 2002 it was estimated that some 0.5 million were employed in voluntary organisations.

Employers' associations are also used by employers to protect and advance their interests. The annual report of the Certification Officer in

2000/2001 states that in 2000 there were 98 such associations. Some of these were national bodies covering a whole industry (for example, the Engineering Employers' Federation), others were specialised bodies representing a segment of an industry (for example, the Newspaper Society, which represents the interests of provincial newspaper employers in England, Wales and Northern Ireland), and yet others were local associations representing regional industrial interests (for example, the Lancashire Textile Manufacturers' Association). Employers' associations' major activities fall into the following areas:

- assistance to member firms in the resolution of disputes with their employees

- general help and advice on good practice in employee relations matters

- representation of members' interests to political decision-makers at all levels

- representation of members' interests at employment tribunals

- in some cases, negotiation of collective agreements with trade unions.

The ways in which employers' associations can assist the employee relations specialist in his/her everyday job is examined in Chapter 5.

Employees

Some employees attempt to strengthen and enhance their interests in the labour market by presenting a collective face to the employer, notably in relation to minimum conditions on which they are content to supply their labour services to the employer. The most numerous employee labour market organisations are:

- professional associations

- staff associations

- trade unions.

In enterprises where such organisations do not exist, employers often create a collective employee organisation (sometimes called an employee council, a works council, a representative committee, a business involvement group, etc) so that they can obtain a collective and representative voice from their employees. It is only in very small firms that a truly individual and personal relationship can exist between an employer and employee. Once an organisation grows, in employment terms, beyond a critical size, the views of the employees are best collected (in time and efficiency terms) through some representative organisation. It becomes too time-consuming to talk to each separate employee. Employers' interests may therefore be enhanced by their employees' having a representative body. However, employers' attitudes vary over what form of collective employee organisation best serves the company's interests.

Professional associations

Professional associations are not central employee relations agencies. They usually control the education and training of new members to the profession by acting as 'qualifying associations'. They also establish, maintain and review professional and ethical standards for their members. In addition, they advance the standing and status of the profession in the wider community. However, some professional associations – especially those whose members are mainly employed in the public sector – also protect and improve their members' employment interests in pay bargaining. In the health service, for example, there are groups of professional employees, such as nurses and midwives, who use their professional associations in the dual capacity of a professional and bargaining body.

Staff associations

Staff associations are in some cases the creation of employers who wish to keep their business non-unionised. The majority, however, are independent of the employer. Despite low membership subscriptions and lack of militancy, staff associations can, and do, provide an acceptable alternative to trade unions. This is particularly true of certain white-collar groups. Nevertheless, most staff associations are characterised by weak finances and a narrow membership-base confined to a single employer.

Larger staff associations tend to acquire their own staff and premises and rely less on the employer for services and facilities. In 2001 the Certification Officer's list of employee organisations contained some 50 staff associations, concentrated mainly in the financial sector, of which 25 were recognised to be independent of employer influence and domination. These staff associations are characterised by high membership density, often exceeding 75 per cent.

Trade unions

Trade unions are the best-known form of employee representative organisation. They were formed to protect and advance the interests of their members against employers and members of other trade unions. In the UK, trade unions have different recruitment strategies. Craft and occupational unions (for example, the AEEU, the GPMU) focus on recruiting employees who perform certain jobs. Some unions confine their recruitment to all grades of employees employed in a particular industry. These are referred to as industrial unions. General unions, such as the T&GWU and the GMB, organise workers across the boundaries within and between industries. They take into membership any worker regardless of the job he or she does and the industry in which he or she does it.

In the UK, trade union organisation is characterised by the co-existence of a large number of small unions together with a very small number of large trade unions. In 2000, 83 per cent (171) of the total number of trade unions registered with the Certification Officer had memberships of less than 5,000. On the other hand, 7 per cent (16) of the unions had memberships in excess of 100,000.

Unions represent different interests in terms of jobs, types of workers, industries, services and the public and private sectors of the economy. They also have different interests within them (skilled, unskilled, non-manual workers, etc) but these are accommodated through their decision-making procedures which are based on the principle of repre-sentative democracy. Trade unions in the UK are:

- job-, not class-centred
- concerned more to achieve their objectives by industrial methods (for example, through collective bargaining) than by political means (for example, by taking industrial action against govern-ment measures they dislike)
- motivated by pragmatism rather than by principle.

Trade unions are discussed in more detail in Chapter 5.

Employee relations processes

The accommodation of the interests of employers and employees by the establishment of rules, regulations and agreements to govern their exchange of labour services (and so regulate employment) is achieved by the use of employee relations processes (mechanisms) of which the most important are :

- unilateral action
- employee involvement and participation schemes
- collective bargaining
- third-party intervention
- industrial sanctions.

In addition to these processes, the state can intervene in the buying and selling of labour services by establishing minimum terms that the buyers must offer the sellers. It does this by way of legal regulation. Unlike the other processes listed above, management has no direct con-trol over what legal regulation the government or the European Union introduces. However, management does try to influence such regulation via its political lobbying activities. For example, in 1998 the employers succeeded in persuading the Labour Government to alter its original proposal, contained in its White Paper *Fairness at Work*, that there should be no limit on the amount of compensation that could be awarded to an individual who is unfairly dismissed by his or her employer. As a result of employer pressure, the Government decided to raise the limit on such compensation from £12,000 to £50,000.

Unilateral action

Unilateral action is where the employer is the sole author of the rules, agreements and regulations that govern the conditions under which employees work. In deciding employment conditions in this way, the employer may or may not give attention to the views ('voice') of the employees. It is a methodology that was formerly mostly associated with non-union companies, but in the last 20 years there has been an increase in the number of employers stressing the need for business efficiency, claiming management's right to manage and to impose decisions on employees. However, even in highly unionised organisations (for example, commercial television companies and the NHS Trusts) there have been examples of unilateral changes by management on issues such as overtime opportunities, and changes in job descriptions. At the extreme, managers who impose unilateral changes to their employees' employment conditions are effectively saying 'Accept these new terms, or consider yourself dismissed' – take it or leave it.

Another area in which employers exercise unilateral action is the devising of company rules, which are applicable to all employees and set out in the company handbook/rule-book. If employees breach these rules, serious consequences – including dismissal – can arise. Such rules usually include the steps to be followed in the event of an accident, directions on maintaining security, safety and hygiene, the dress code, and an obligation on employees to report to the employer a change of address.

It is difficult to find out exactly how many management-imposed changes are made to the employment conditions of employees since there is no regular source of such information. The Workplace Industrial Relations Survey series, however, provides some information in respect of pay determination. The 1998 Employee Relations Survey revealed, over the economy as a whole, that more than 70 per cent of employees had their pay determined by non-collective bargaining mechanisms, and that 30 per cent of employees (compared with 21 per cent in 1984) had their pay determined by workplace management. For a further 25 per cent (11 per cent in 1984) pay was determined by a higher level (than workplace) of management in the organisation. In 1998, in the private manufacturing and extraction sector, 48 per cent of employees (as opposed to 33 per cent in 1984) had their pay determined by workplace management, and a further 24 per cent (11 per cent in 1984) by a higher level of management in the organisation. In private services in 1998, 39 per cent of employees had their pay settled by workplace management, and 36 per cent by a higher level of management in the organisation. In the public sector, on the other hand, in 1998 only 2 per cent of employees had their pay determined by management at the workplace and 6 per cent by a higher level of management in the organisation. The 1998 Employee Relations Workplace Survey concluded that in 32 per cent of the workplaces it surveyed, there was an absence of any formal structure for employees to relay their voice to their employer.

Employee involvement

Employee involvement is a broad term which covers a range of processes designed to enable employees to voice their views to the employer and so have an involvement in management decision-making and the feeling of participation in the development of the business. There is, however, no commitment on the part of management to act on the employees' views. These processes include indirect forms of participation, such as consultative committees or works councils, as well as direct communications forms such as regular workforce meetings between senior management and the workforce, problem-solving groups that discuss aspects of performance (for example, quality), and briefing groups which usually involve regular meetings between junior managers and all the workers for whom they are responsible.

Consultation is different from communication because it invites the participation of staff by seeking views, bringing individuals in to the decision-making process and delegating a measure of autonomy through empowerment. Consultation can take place either directly with staff or through a representative forum (such as a works council) or some other form of joint consultation machinery.

Each of the elements of the employee involvement mix is linked. It is not always clear where communication ends and consultation begins. Organisations which pursue employee involvement typically use a wide range of differing activities to develop the mix needed to achieve success in the marketplace. Employee involvement is analysed in greater detail in Chapter 7.

In joint consultation, management seeks views, feelings and ideas from employees and/or their representatives prior to making a decision. Although joint consultation may involve a discussion of mutual problems, it leaves management to make the final decision. There is no commitment to action on the employees' views. Issues dealt with by joint consultation vary from social matters, such as the provision of canteen or sports facilities, to issues such as the scheduling of production.

The Workplace Employee Relations Survey (1998) provides information on the extent of joint consultative arrangements in establishments employing 25 or more employees. It revealed that 23 per cent of workplaces had a functioning joint consultative committee (JCC) at the workplace. These committees were responsible for discussing a range of topics rather than a single issue such as health and safety. In the private sector, only 20 per cent of workplaces had a JCC, compared with 32 per cent in the public sector. Workplace committees are much more frequent amongst large workplaces, and higher-level committees – through which management prefers to consult with employees on a multi-site basis rather than have a consultative committee for each establishment – are more frequent in larger organisations. All in all, some 67 per cent of employees work in places with joint consultative arrangements at either the workplace or a higher level in the organisation.

Collective bargaining

Collective bargaining is a method of determining the 'price' at which employee services are bought and sold – a system of industrial governance whereby unions and employers jointly reach decisions concerning the employment relationship. It involves employees' – via their elected representatives and unions – participating in the management of the enterprise. Collective bargaining is a problem-solving mechanism but can only take place if employees are organised and if the employer is prepared to recognise the trade union(s) for collective bargaining purposes.

In practice, the outcome of collective bargaining is not confined to union members. Unionised companies apply collectively bargained terms and conditions of employment to their non-union employees as well as to their unionised ones. Companies that do not recognise unions have regard to collectively bargained rates in their industry or in comparator firms when deciding on their own employees' employment conditions if they are to remain competitive in the labour market. Many non-unionised companies (for example, Marks & Spencer, IBM, Mars) seek to retain union-free workplaces by rewarding above the union-negotiated pay and other employment conditions. This means that such companies must have an interest in the outcome of collective bargaining although they are not direct parties to it.

Over the period 1984–1998 inclusive, the proportion of workers covered directly by collective bargaining has declined. The 1990 WIRS revealed that the overall proportion of employees covered by collective bargaining was 70 per cent in 1984, 54 per cent in 1990, and 41 per cent in 1998. In the public sector, the coverage of collective bargaining in 1998 was 63 per cent, compared with 80 per cent in 1990. In private manufacturing, the corresponding figures were 51 per cent and 46 per cent respectively. The largest proportionate fall in collective bargaining coverage has been in private services, involving a fall from 33 per cent in 1990 to 22 per cent in 1998.

What are the main processes used to regulate employment conditions in your organisation? Why are these the main processes, rather than others?

Third-party intervention

In situations where the employer and employees are unable to resolve their collective differences, they may agree voluntarily to seek the assistance of an independent third party. Third-party intervention can take one of three forms:

- conciliation
- mediation
- arbitration.

In the case of disputes between an employer and an individual employee over unfair dismissal, non-payment of a termination of employment payment or commission, or sex, race, equal pay or disability discrimination, the law requires the Advisory, Conciliation and Arbitration Service (ACAS) to attempt a conciliated settlement before the claim can proceed to an employment tribunal.

In conciliation, the role of the third party is to keep the two sides talking and assist them to reach their own agreement. The conciliator acts as a link between the disputing parties by passing on information, which the parties will not pass directly to each other, from one side to the other until either a basis for agreement is identified or both parties conclude that there is no basis for an agreed voluntary settlement to their problem. Conciliation permits each side to reassess its situation continually. The conciliator plays a passive role and does not impose any action or decision on the parties.

A mediator listens to the arguments of the two sides and makes recommendations on how their difference(s) might be resolved. The parties are free to accept or reject these recommendations. Arbitration removes from employers and employees control over the settlement of their differences. The arbitrator hears both sides' case and decides the solution to the parties' differences by making an award. Both parties, having voluntarily agreed to arbitration, are morally obliged, but not legally bound, to accept the arbitrator's award. Pendulum arbitration is a specific form of arbitration which limits the third party to making an award which accepts fully either the final claim of the union or the final offer of the employer. It reduces arbitration to an all-or-nothing win-or-lose outcome for the disputants. By creating an all-or-nothing expectation, pendulum arbitration is said to provide the incentive for bargainers to moderate their final positions and reach a voluntary agreement.

Third-party intervention is facilitated by ACAS, established by Royal Commission in 1974 and put on a statutory basis by the Employment Protection Act (1975). Mediation and arbitration is undertaken by an independent person (or occasionally persons) selected jointly by the parties to the dispute, from a list held by ACAS of competent arbitrators made up of academics, trade union officers, and employers. The listed members of this panel are all experienced and knowledgeable in employee relations. There is also the Central Arbitration Committee (CAC) which is a standing independent arbitration body. Originally established as the Industrial Court in 1919, it can deal with issues relating to industrial disputes, to a single employer or to a particular employee group. As well as providing voluntary arbitration in trade disputes, it arbitrates on claims by trade unions over alleged failure of employers to disclose information for collective bargaining purposes, in disputes over the establishment of European Works Councils, and in disputes that arise from the operation of the statutory trade union recognition procedure contained in the Employment Relations Act (1999). The roles of ACAS and the CAC are discussed more fully in Chapter 5.

Third-party intervention is a little-used employee relations process. The number of completed collective conciliation cases handled by ACAS fell from 2,284 in 1979 to 1,226 in 2000/2001. Mediation is rarely used. In the whole of 2000/2001, there were only five mediation hearings arranged by ACAS, whereas in 1998 there were none. Throughout the 1990s, the number of arbitration hearings arranged by ACAS fell. In 1990 there were 190 such hearings, but in 2000/2001 there were only 55. The process of third-party intervention in employee relations is discussed and analysed in detail in Chapter 5.

Industrial sanctions

The use of industrial sanctions is generally a last resort because it is costly to both sides to impose them on each other. The main sanctions available to the employer are:

- locking out some, or all, of the workforce
- closing the factory
- relocating operations to another site
- dismissing employees who participate in industrial action.

The main industrial sanctions that employees can impose on employers are:

- a ban on overtime
- working-to-rule
- imposing a selective strike
- calling an all-out strike.

The threat of the imposition of industrial sanctions can be important in bringing about a reconciliation of the different interests of employers and employees. The threat that one side might impose industrial sanctions, with their ensuing costs, on the other may actually be as important as if sanctions were imposed. It is the threat that can oblige the parties to adjust their position and negotiate a peaceful settlement. Both parties will be reluctant to go ahead and impose industrial sanctions because of their associated costs. However, the possibility means that the parties have to have regard to them and adjust their behaviour accordingly.

Employers and employees have to think carefully before imposing or threatening to impose industrial sanctions. There is little to be gained in imposing industrial action if it is unlikely to be successful, especially if economic pressures may quickly mount as the organisation's product market competitors take advantage of its industrial problems to poach its customers. It is pointless to relocate operations to another site unless an alternative and fully competent workforce is available (or can

Table 3 Industrial stoppages in the UK, 1979–2001

Year	Number of stoppages in progress	Number of workers involved (000s)	Number of working days lost (000s)
1979	2,125	4,608	29,474[1]
1980	1,348	834	11,964[2]
1981	1,344	1,513	4,266
1982	1,538	2,103	5,313
1983	1,364	574	3,754
1984	1,221	1,464	27,135[3]
1985	903	791	6,402[4]
1986	1,074	720	1,920
1987	1,016	887	3,546
1988	781	790	3,702
1989	701	727	4,128[5]
1990	630	298	1,903
1991	369	176	761
1992	253	148	528
1993	211	385	649
1994	205	107	278
1995	234	173	415
1996	244	364	1,303
1997	216	130	235
1998	166	93	282
1999	205	140	242
2000	212	182	499
2001	194	167	525

[1] 54 per cent of total accounted for by a strike of engineering workers
[2] 74 per cent of total accounted for by national steel dispute
[3] 83 per cent of total accounted for by coal-mining strike
[4] 63 per cent of total accounted for by continuing miners' strike
[5] 49 per cent of total accounted for by strike of council workers
Source: Annual Report on Labour Disputes in Department of Employment *Gazette* and *Labour Market Trends*

be recruited) at the new site. To impose sanctions that fail to bring further concessions from the other party undermines, at a future date, the credibility of the threat to use them.

The extent of industrial action

In the UK, official statistics on the use of industrial sanctions relate only to strikes. They measure three dimensions of strike activity – their numbers (how frequent they are), their size (the number of workers involved) and their duration (the number of working days lost). This last measure is often distorted by a few big strikes. For example, in 1979 an engineering industry-wide strike accounted for 55 per cent of the 29.5 million working days lost in that year. In 2000 the number of working days lost in the UK was 499,00 (see Table 3).

However, disputes still happen – for example, the series of one-day stoppages in 2002 on the railways over the widening of pay differentials between drivers, who were in short supply, and other railway employees. The dearth of drivers meant that the railway employers wanted to give them higher pay rises than other staff. The latter then went on strike because of the smaller increases offered to them. The year 2002 also saw strikes in teaching in London, and threatened strikes in local government, the fire service and the Royal Mail.

Although dispute levels have declined through the 1990s and early 2000s, there are signs that some managers have been performing inadequately in managing their employee relations, in that there has been a dramatic growth in the number of complaints to employment tribunals by employees against employers' behaviour. In the 1980s the number of complaints reported to ACAS averaged about 45,000 per annum, but the number increased every year throughout the 1990s. In 2000 the number of such complaints exceeded 167,000. This would suggest a rising sense of individual grievances among people at work.

Legal intervention

The processes described above are private means by which the interests of employers and employees may be reconciled. Employers have some choice over which of these processes they will use. However, on occasions, the state intervenes in these private relationships and sets minimum employment conditions that employers must provide for their employees. Although employers have no control over parliamentary legislation, they can, by political lobbying, attempt to influence the details of proposed legislation to maximise its positive effects on their economic interests or to minimise its negative impact on their interests.

UK Parliament regulation

In the UK today, legal intervention comes from two sources – the UK Government and the European Union. The Labour Government elected in

1997 has introduced new minimum standards of protection for employees at the workplace. In April 1999 a national minimum wage of £3.60 for those aged over 21 and of £3 (which rose to £3.20 in 2001) for those aged 18 to 21 inclusive, was introduced. In October 2002 the rate was £4.20 for those over 21. The Employment Relations Act (1999) enabled employees to insist that a trade union be recognised by their employer where the majority of the relevant workforce wished it, created the right for employees to be accompanied by a fellow employee or trade union representative during grievance and disciplinary procedures over serious matters, and gave employees rights to extended maternity absence.

The European Union

The European Union is committed to establishing a 'level playing-field' of minimum social and employment standards in its Single European Market in which goods, capital, people and services can move freely. In 1997 the UK Government accepted that more social and employment measures should be harmonised between member states, through the use of the EU's qualified-majority-voting procedure. One implication of this is that an employee relations professional in the UK can expect to experience increasing legal regulation from the European Union (see Chapter 4). Chapter 4 shows how the EU has impinged on the work of the employee relations profession in the areas of equal opportunities, employment protection and working conditions, information and consultation rights, and health and safety.

Agreements, rules and regulations

The outcome of the use of employee relations processes is an 'agreement' which establishes the rules and regulations upon which labour services will be bought and sold. These rules and regulations may relate to a group of employees or may be the result of bargaining between an employer and an individual employee resulting in a personal contract. The distinguishing characteristic of such contracts is that none of its terms has been bargained collectively. The employee has negotiated as an individual – although in doing so he or she may have received assistance from a third party.

However, in practice, few personal contracts are genuinely individualised. At British Telecom, for example, all terms and conditions for senior managerial staff were standard across all personal contracts. The only difference was that pay was determined 'individually' so that there were no published rates (and thus there was no transparency in the criteria) by which pay increases were given to individuals.

Types of agreements

It is traditional to divide agreements into two broad types. First, there are substantive agreements which cover the money aspects of employment conditions (pay, hours of work, paid holidays, shift premiums, etc). An example of a substantive agreement is shown below.

Agreement between:
UNION OF SHOP, DISTRIBUTIVE AND ALLIED WORKERS (USDAW)
and
ABC LIMITED

The following has been agreed between USDAW and ABC Limited, regarding the 2002/03 Pay and Conditions claim.

The following are the rates of pay which now apply for a 39-hour week and are effective from Monday 5 June 2002.

Rates of pay

Boners	£170.82
Butchers	£156.47
M/c Op/Prep	£151.23
Gen Worker 'A'	£146.66
Gen Worker 'B'	£146.66
Drivers	£152.57

Nighshift premiums
Will be increased from their present levels to 18.5% of basic hourly rate.

Working hours
With immediate effect to become:

Dayshift	Monday to Friday	6.00 am until 2.30 pm
	or	8.00 am until 4.30 pm
Nightshift	Sunday to Thursday	9.00 pm until 5.18 am

Breaks
During each shift the following breaks will apply:

1 × 30-minute lunch break
1 × 15-minute tea break
2 × 10-minute tea breaks

Service day holidays
Qualification periods for five days' holiday to be reduced to 13 years.

Death in service
Sum assured benefit increased to £10,000.

Holidays
Five days of public holiday to become annual holiday, commencing 1 April 2003.

Second, there are procedural agreements which set standards of conduct to be met by employers and employees in resolving specific differences. In this sense, they provide the 'law and order' for the workplace. They constitute criteria by which reasonable, fair and consistent behaviour by employers can be judged by employees and by outside institutions such as employment tribunals. They provide quick and informal methods for resolving disputes. Procedures also send a message to all employees about how they will be treated should the specific issue arise.

In practice, employers have a wide range of procedural arrangements and agreements that cover such specific issues as:

- disputes
- employee grievances
- discipline
- redundancy
- union recognition
- grading
- health and safety
- promotion
- staff development and career review.

An example of a procedural agreement ('Appeals against grading') is shown below. The 1998 Employee Relations Workplace Survey reported that in 92 per cent of establishments surveyed there was an individual grievance procedure, and that a similar proportion of workplaces operated formal disciplinary procedures.

Clerical Staff Procedure Agreement

SECTION FIVE: APPEALS AGAINST GRADING

1 INDIVIDUAL RIGHT TO APPEAL
Where an employee is dissatisfied with the decision of the University at the annual review concerning an application for regrading on the grounds of increased duties and responsibilities, then he/she may apply in writing within three weeks to the Director of Personnel to have his/her case considered by an Appeals Panel constituted as below

2 APPEALS PANEL – MEMBERSHIP
The Appeals Panel shall consist of five members, as follows:
    (a) Two members nominated by the University
    (b) Two members nominated by the Association
    (c) One member, who shall act as Convenor, acceptable to the University and the Association.

PROCEDURE FOR APPEALS

(i) Persons involved in the hearing

    (a) The appellant

    (b) A colleague or Trade Union representative of the appellant, if he/she wishes

    (c) A Personnel Officer

    (d) The Head of Department or his/her nominee.

(ii) Prior to the hearing

    (a) The Panel shall have available to it all the original documentation

    (b) Each party shall make available a written statement of case to the Panel

    (c) Written statements and supporting documents, if any, should be in the hands of the Personnel Officer eight working days prior to the hearing. These together with copies of all the original documents will be circulated to the members of the Panel four working days prior to the hearing.

(iii) The hearing of the Appeal

    (a) The appellant or his/her representative may, if they wish, present a short summary of the case to the Panel

    (b) The members of the panel may then ask questions of any of those present

    (c) The appellant will withdraw from the hearing

    (d) The Personnel Officer will be asked to present the University's case

    (e) The Head of Department or his/her nominee will be asked to present the departmental view of the merits of the case, and the members of the Panel may ask questions.

(iv) Consideration of the Appeal

    (a) The Panel will then consider its decision after all parties have withdrawn

    (b) The decision will be by a simple vote of the Panel. The decision of the Panel is binding on all parties.

Select three procedures which operate in your organisation. Explain how they demonstrate that management behaves fairly and reasonably in operating these procedures.

The legal status of collective agreements

Collective agreements have a unique status in the UK in that they are not legally binding on the parties who have signed them. If either the union or management act contrary to the agreement, the other party cannot enforce its rights outlined in the agreement via the courts. Collective agreements are binding in honour only. In almost every democratic society, collective agreements between unions and employers are legally binding and enforceable through the Courts.

A consequence of having collective agreements that are not legally binding is that they are not comprehensive and their wording can be relatively imprecise. This reinforces the requirement for employers to have a disputes procedure to resolve differences with their employees over whether the agreement is being applied properly. The style of UK collective agreements also reflects that they are normally subject to review and renegotiation on an annual basis.

The dimensions of agreements

Agreements can be analysed by their dimensions. The main dimensions are:

- scope (ie the subjects covered)
- formality (ie whether they are written or unwritten)
- the level
- bargaining units (ie the employees covered).

The scope (ie the subjects covered) of both collective agreements and personal contracts varies widely, but normally includes some, or all, of the following:

- pay levels and structure
- overtime and shift payments
- incentive (bonus/performance-related pay) payments
- hours of work and paid holidays
- working arrangements and productivity
- training and retraining opportunities
- the means of resolving disputes, individual grievances, etc.

It is traditional for pay rates and working arrangements to be reviewed and amended annually by the signatories to the agreement. Hours of work and paid annual holidays are normally reviewed and changed at less frequent intervals. Procedural arrangements can remain unchanged for many years.

Agreements, rules and regulations governing employment conditions can also be analysed in terms of their formality. The vast majority of collective agreements are written out in full, but there are some that do not exist in written form. Such agreements are held to remain in force through 'custom and practice'. The employees have operated the working practice for many years. The employers have gone along with this behaviour although they have never formally agreed it with their employees. The practice has become accepted, and if management or the employees were to try to change it, the employees or the management will probably expect something in return.

Agreements, rules and regulations can be concluded at different levels. Some apply only to the place where those covered by it work; others apply to all workers in the company (referred to as company regulations), as is seen in the Ford Motor Company and ICI. Some cover a group of workers in an enterprise, whereas others relate to all (or certain grades of) workers in an industry, and this latter kind are commonly referred to as a national or industry-wide agreement or national or industry-wide rules and regulations. Over the past 15 years or so, many employers have withdrawn from operating under national agreements, often supplemented by local bargaining, preferring to bargain collectively (especially over pay) with their employees at a more decentralised level, considering this necessary to recruit, motivate, retain and reward the right calibre of employees if the success of the business is to be secured.

Agreements, rules and regulations can also be analysed in terms of the number of workers they cover. In the case of collectively bargained agreements, that number is referred to as 'the size' of the bargaining unit. In some unionised organisations, management operates by concluding separate agreements with separate trade unions that represent different groups of employees and that thus have a multiplicity of bargaining units and collective agreements. This is the classic multi-union situation.

However, other companies prefer to have a single set of rules and regulations to cover all relevant groups. They thus have one unit to cover significant numbers of employees and possibly a different number of trade unions or employee representative groups. In unionised situations this is referred to as 'single-table bargaining', in which all recognised trade unions sit at the same table with the employer. Yet other managements may believe the business objectives to be more achievable if they have one employing 'unit' in which all employees are represented by a single representative body – a situation that is known in unionised companies as having 'a single-union agreement'.

Non-unionised companies, like unionised ones, have substantive and procedural agreements, but they will have been written by the employer, and only the most professional of employers will have consulted with the workforce in doing so. In non-unionised companies, agreements, rules and regulations can also be analysed in terms of their scope (ie issues covered by information and consultation arrangements) and the number of workers to which they apply. Some information and communication systems apply to all workers in the enterprise, whereas others apply only to some groups. Quality circles, on the other hand, are usually confined to small groups from the same work area or who carry out similar job tasks and activities. Performance-related pay schemes often apply to certain occupational groups (eg managers in strategic positions) within an enterprise or workplace. Financial participation schemes again vary as to the workers covered. Some embrace all employees (eg profit-sharing and profit-related pay), whereas others are confined to certain occupational groups (eg share option schemes). Although the practices used in non-union companies may not be directly based on trade union organisation, they often parallel practices in unionised companies.

Workforce agreements

The Working Time Regulations (1998) have given rise to a new form of agreement known as a 'workforce agreement'. The Regulations allow for some of the measures to be adopted through agreements between workers and employers so as to allow flexibility in order to take account of the specific needs of local working arrangements. Employers and workers are expected to come to a consensus on which of three types of agreement – collective agreement, workforce agreement or relevant agreement – is the most appropriate to their circumstances.

Workforce agreements permit an employer to fix working-time arrangements with workers who do not have any terms or conditions set by a collective agreement. Workforce agreements allow employers to decide how to use the flexibilities permitted in the implementation of the Regulations. A workforce agreement may apply to the whole of the workforce or to a group within it. Where it is to apply to a group of workers, the group must share a workplace function or organisational unit within a business.

The balance of bargaining power

Whether the contents of agreements, rules or regulations on occupations are closer to satisfying the interests of the employers or of the employees is influenced heavily by the relative balance of bargaining power between them. Issues concerned with the relative balance of bargaining power are relevant to employers who bargain individually with their employees as well to those who bargain collectively with their workforce. The balance of bargaining power is a key employee relations concept which influences, *inter alia*, an employer's preferred employee relations process, the subject matter of agreements, rules and regulations, whether job regulations are jointly authored by employers and employees or solely written by one of the parties, and the actual content of the agreements, rules and regulations.

The macro level

The external environmental factors that influence the relative balance of bargaining power between employers and employees are:

- economic

- legal

- technological.

The Government's economic and legal policies have major implications for the outcome of employee relations activities. If economic policies are directed towards the creation of full employment and the maximising of economic growth, this weakens the bargaining power of the employer relative to that of the employees. In an expanding economy the demand for labour services increases, causing the price of those labour services to rise. On the other hand, if macro-economic policies are directed at restraining economic growth, the demand for labour services falls, resulting perhaps in redundancies and rising unemployment. In such circumstances the balance of bargaining power of the employer is strengthened relative to that of employees.

If the Government introduces legislation favourable to employers' interests – for example, by restricting the circumstances in which trade unions may instruct their members to undertake industrial action without employers' being able to seek redress through the Courts (to seek, for instance, compensation for a downturn in revenue through lost sales, etc) – the bargaining power of employers relative to employees is strengthened. The Conservative Governments of 1979 to 1997 inclusive enhanced employer bargaining power by passing nine pieces of parliamentary legislation which regulated the labour market activities of trade unions progressively more tightly.

If a government introduces legislation favourable to the interests of individual employees and trade unions, the bargaining power of employees relative to employers is increased. The present Labour Government via its Employment Relations Act (1999) – which, *inter alia*, introduced statutory trade union recognition, the minimum wages legislation and the implementation of legislation favourable to employees from the European Union – has enhanced employee/trade union bargaining power relative to the employer.

The implementation of new technology also impacts on the relative bargaining power of employees and employers. Technological developments based on computers, lasers and telecommunications have in some sectors of the economy destroyed jobs – for example, those of compositors (typesetters) in the printing industry – de-skilled jobs, blurred demarcation lines between existing jobs and industries, and created for employers an alternative and lower-paid workforce. These impacts have increased the bargaining power of the employer relative to the employee.

However, in other sectors of the economy, by creating new jobs, new skills and making some industries more capital-intensive, the implementation of technological change has strengthened the bargaining power of employees relative to the employer. For example, the growth of telephone banking services has created a new business, which in part replaces the jobs lost in traditional banks.

The economic and legal environment surrounding an employee relations system influences the relative bargaining power between employers and employees at the macro level. This is why employer and employee organisations spend large sums of money in lobbying political decision-makers.

> What factors determine at the national level the relative bargaining power between employers and employees? Explain, with appropriate examples, how the balance of bargaining power influences employer or employee behaviour in employee relations.

The micro level

An analysis of the relative bargaining power at the macro level cannot explain why some groups of employees retain their bargaining power vis-à-vis the employer despite recession and high unemployment, or why some employers are in a relatively weak bargaining position despite depressed economic activity. This is the relative bargaining power at the micro level.

At this level the balance of bargaining power is influenced by some of the following factors:

- whether employees can inflict costs on the organisation
- whether there is an alternative workforce available to the employer
- whether the group of employees is aware of its potential power
- whether the group of employees has previously exercised its power
- whether, if the group has exercised its power, the outcome was favourable to it.

For example, in assessing the relative bargaining power of a group of its employees, management has to consider how crucial the group is to the production/service supply process. The more central the group is to the workflow, the greater is its potential power within the organisation. In many organisations IT staff, for example, are now in strategic positions to disrupt workflow.

The bargaining power of a group of employees relative to management is strengthened if there is a lack of an appropriate alternative workforce available to undertake the group's work on an individual or a departmental basis. In short, a group of workers that is difficult to substitute has greater bargaining power relative to the employer than a group whose services are easily replaceable.

CONCLUSION

- This chapter identified the four main components of an employee relations system at an organisation, sector or national level – the different and the common interests of employers and employees; the processes by which employment conditions are regulated; the rules, regulations and agreements governing the employment relationship; and the balance of bargaining power.

- The processes by which the rules, regulations and agreements that govern the employment conditions are made are: unilateral action by management, employee involvement and participation schemes, communication processes (including employee voice), collective bargaining, third-party intervention, industrial sanctions, and legal regulation from the UK Government and the European Union.

- The rules, regulations and agreements that govern the employment relationship can be grouped into two broad categories – substantive issues (pay, holidays, hours of work, pensions, family-friendly benefits, etc) and procedural issues, which set out standards of behaviour to be met by employers and employees in resolving specific differences.

- The balance of bargaining power is a key employee relations concept which influences, *inter alia*, an employer's preferred employee relations processes, the subject matter of the rules, agreements and regulations, whether the job regulations are authored jointly by employers and employees or solely written by one party with or without consultation with the other, and the actual content of those rules, regulations and agreements.

Further reading

ADVISORY, CONCILIATION and ARBITRATION SERVICE *Annual Reports*.

BEARDWELL I. (ed.) (1996) *Contemporary Industrial Relations: A critical analysis*. Oxford University Press. Chapters 1, 3 and 7.

CENTRAL ARBITRATION COMMITTEE *Annual Reports*.

CERTIFICATION OFFICE FOR TRADE UNIONS and EMPLOYERS' ASSOCIATIONS *Annual Reports of the Certification Officer*.

CULLY, M., WOODLANDS S., O'REILLY A. and DIX G. (1999) *Britain at Work as Depicted by the 1998 Employee Relations Survey*. Routledge.

DEPARTMENT OF TRADE AND INDUSTRY (1998a) *Fairness at Work*, Cm 3968, May.

DEPARTMENT OF TRADE AND INDUSTRY (1998b) *National Minimum Wage Regulations*, September.

FARNHAM D. (2000) *Employee Relations in Context*. London, Institute of Personnel and Development. Chapters 1, 2, 3, 6, 8 and 10.

INSTITUTE OF PERSONNEL AND DEVELOPMENT (1995) *People Make the Difference: An IPD Position Paper*, January.

INSTITUTE OF PERSONNEL AND DEVELOPMENT (1997) *Employment Relations into the 21st Century: An IPD Position Paper*, December.

INSTITUTE OF PERSONNEL AND DEVELOPMENT (1998) *Fairness at Work and the Psychological Contract*.

INVOLVEMENT AND PARTICIPATION ASSOCIATION (1997) *Towards Industrial Partnership: New ways of working in British companies*, February.

MARTIN R. (1992) *Bargaining Power*. Oxford University Press. Chapter 3.

MILLWARD N., BRYSON A. and FORTH J. (2000) *All Change at Work? British Employment Relations, 1980-1984 as Portrayed by the Workplace Industrial Relations Survey Series*. Routledge.

TAYLOR R. (2000) *The Future of Employment Relations*. Economic and Social Research Council.

TRADES UNION CONGRESS (1997) *Partners for Progress: Next steps for the New Unionism*.

2 • The Economic and Corporate Environment

CHAPTER OBJECTIVES

When you have completed this chapter you should be able to:

- describe how the UK Government in its role as economic manager influences employee relations

- understand the principal economic theories that have been applied to the management of the economy since World War II

- explain how changes in the labour market have impacted on employee relations

- explain how the corporate environment affects the relative balance of bargaining power

- explain the impact of new technology on the working environment.

Introduction

In a 1997 statement on employee relations the CIPD drew attention to the need for every organisation to continually improve its performance because of the challenges that were constantly being imposed on them by the corporate environment. Whether those challenges were the intensifying product market competition, changes in the world economy, or the tight spending controls that continue to characterise the public sector, the pressure is much the same for all organisations. That statement is as true today as it was in 1997, and the pressures to which it refers are unlikely, in the short term, to diminish.

Those pressures are external to the organisation, and the purpose of this chapter is to examine the factors which, when taken together, are referred to as the external corporate environment in which all organisations have to operate. It matters not whether the organisation is a large multi-national, a National Health Service Trust or a medium-sized service company, its employee relations are influenced, and shaped, by the way in which the external corporate environment impacts on the workplace.

The context

In Chapter 1 we noted that the corporate environment had to be examined in the context of economic management, political/legal influences and technological changes. The legislative influences are more fully considered in Chapter 3, so this chapter concentrates more on the economic, political and technological factors. These three issues are important to understanding employee relations and why organisations choose to adopt particular policies, and how such policies have changed, or might change, over time.

The business environment in which employee relations professionals operate is constantly changing, and it is important for them not only to be aware of specific shifts in employee relations policies resulting from such changes, but to monitor the external environment to anticipate possible changes and developments and draw up a contingency plan to deal with the changes if and when they arise. Employee relations policies devised and implemented in this context have both a reactive and pro-active role – a strategic role that is central to the organisation's growth and survival.

Although each of the elements is crucial in determining the employee relations practices of employers, the response of individual employers to the impact on their own business or organisation is likely to be different. For example, a traditional non-union company such as Marks & Spencer is unlikely to have responded in the same way to the legislative changes introduced during the 1980s as a company will have done that was traditionally heavily unionised. Equally, non-union organisations may react in a completely different way to changes introduced by the Employment Relations Act (1999). The statutory rights on union recognition contained within the Act have caused many organisations to undergo a fundamental rethink in attitudes towards collectivism and the role the workforce may play in the process of change. The 1980s changes to the laws on strikes, picketing and closed shops opened the door to employers who wanted to force through change, and had a major impact on trade union membership and influence. An example of this was the radical transformation that occurred in the newspaper industry.

Now, however, as Cathy Cooper reported (*People Management*, 12 July 2001), 'The UK's unions seem to have at last broken out of their decline – with union membership rising and the number of recognition deals exceeding TUC expectations.' What is interesting about this change has been employers' willingness to enter into voluntary recognition arrangements rather than be forced to recognise unions under the new statutory framework. According to research from Incomes Data Services (IDS), nearly 500 voluntary recognition deals were signed in the two years to June 2001. This is partly explained by the concern that many employers have about whether the Central Arbitration Committee (CAC) adopts an even-handed approach to union recognition claims. Their approach in some disputed cases has been criticised because it is felt that they give trade unions preferential treatment, even though the legislation is not drafted in this way. Since the legislation came into force in June 2000, the ratio of voluntary to statutory recognition has been 4:1 in favour of voluntary. Fraser Younson (*People Management*, 7 March 2002: page 19) suggests that 'A voluntary agreement is more likely to be in a form an employer can live with.' IDS also reported some significant gains in trade union membership – up by 50,589 in 1997–98, and by 105,000 in 1998–99. TUC figures for 2000 showed a further increase of 60,000.

Notwithstanding this apparent acceptance by employers of trade unions and the IDS view that the large number of recognition agreements denotes 'a sea-change in British industrial relations', many employers now have real fears that the gains made in the last 20 years in eliminating outdated working practices are beginning to be eroded. There is concern that the resurgence in trade union membership will result in a return to militant behaviour by some sections of the workforce, and lead to an increase in industrial action. One of the more damaging aspects of British industrial relations in the 1960s and 1970s was the disputes involving differentials between groups of workers in the same organisation. Industrial action in the rail industry in 2002 heralded a return to this type of dispute as less-well-paid guards and other ancillary staff sought parity with drivers through a series of strikes.

How, and why, did your organisation – or one with which you are familiar – react to the statutory trade union recognition procedures introduced by the Employment Relations Act (1999)?

Change in organisations

All employers have their own objectives, their own styles of employee relations and their own structures of organisations and associations. These structures have changed in recent times, and it is important that the employee relations professional keeps up to date with new trends and developments. For example, the role of employers' organisations (see Chapter 4) has declined in recent years in response to moves to decentralise the levels at which collective bargaining takes place. In the private sector there is now little national bargaining, while in the public sector some local authorities have decentralised traditional systems of bargaining in favour of local wage determination.

Organisational structure has changed in both the public and private sector. The structure of the National Health Service today is radically different from what it was 20 years ago. This has meant changes in the way that it manages its employee relations. Changes have also occurred in respect of employees and their organisations. The UK Government economic policy and changes in legislation have altered the relative balance of bargaining power between employers and employees. This might explain *inter alia* changes in the level of membership of unions, causing individual unions to adapt their strategies to protect and advance their members' interests – for example, by merging with other unions to create a number of 'super-unions'. These issues are discussed in greater detail in Chapter 5.

The role of the state in influencing employee relations has also changed. The state has always been a major employer in its own right, and the post-war expectation was that it would be a 'model employer', proving its excellence by:

- encouraging collective bargaining

- ensuring that the pay of its employees was in line with that of the private sector

- resolving differences with its employees by arbitration and not through the use of industrial sanctions.

This concept has now changed as the whole nature of public sector employment has altered, so that what used to be civil servants now work for quasi-private sector employers. The growth of executive agencies such as the Prison Service and the Benefits Agency, the outsourcing of local authority services and the extension of privatisation has further undermined the concept of the 'public servant'. This dilution is set to spread as the concept of the public–private sector partnership is widened and expanded.

Most of this change resulted from the objective of successive Conservative administrations during the 1980s and 1990s to reduce the influence of government on people's lives. They saw the role of the UK Government as staying outside the employee relations arena, and although the state remains a large employer, it no longer views collective bargaining, pay comparability and arbitration as central to its employee relations policies. There continues to be strong encouragement to relate pay increases of government employees to improvements in individual performance. Although the present Labour Government is not as outwardly anti-union as its Conservative predecessors were perceived to be, there is significant evidence that the Labour Party's traditional links with the union movement are perceived as less important to Ministers than once they were. There is certainly no suggestion that the Government will actively promote an increase in collective bargaining in its employee relations policy towards those employees whose terms and conditions of employment it directly or indirectly finances.

All this change has impacted on the nature and style of employee relations processes. As the impact of collective bargaining – and thus collective agreements – has declined, there has been a growth in the use of other employee relations processes. Joint consultation – which although not a new concept has undergone a resurgence – and employee involvement schemes (for example, two-way communication, encouraging employees to contribute their knowledge and experience to operational decisions) have become much more important. This process is likely to be further strengthened when the EU Directive on information and consultation (which we examine in more detail in Chapter 3) is transposed into UK law.

The concept of the balance of bargaining power and how important it is to the selection, by the employer, of appropriate employee relations processes was introduced in Chapter 1. This balance is conditioned by changes in the economic, political and technological elements which taken together make up the corporate environment. In this chapter the concept is examined in greater detail and linked directly to the economic, legal and technical environment in which organisations exist and compete. The concept of the balance of power is also significant in helping to explain changes in the employee relations system over time – for example, why employee relations behaviour now is different from what it was in the 1970s.

List the economic, legal/political and technological factors that have impacted on your organisation in the last five to 10 years.

Economic management

The economic environment is influenced by the macro-economic policies a particular government chooses to implement. In the context of the UK, government policies in respect of the levels of

- employment
- inflation
- taxation
- interest rates
- exchange rates

have a direct effect on employee relations. This is because they have an impact on the relative balance of bargaining power between the buyers and sellers of labour services and thereby on the rules and regulations that govern employment conditions. For example, if we are in a period of high inflation, high levels of taxation and high interest rates, the stability of business is threatened. This can in turn lead to higher levels of unemployment and a consequent reduction in employment conditions or redundancies and lay-offs. Even when individuals are in work, a less favourable economic climate will alter their perception of continuing job security and will also have an impact on the relative balance of bargaining power.

However, it would be a mistake to assume that the UK Government has a completely free hand in deciding what economic policies to implement.

Like businesses, governments and their policies are affected by external events. Even before the catastrophic events of 11 September 2001 there was concern that a downturn in the global economy would have an adverse effect on Britain. Large parts of the US economy had ground to a halt, and Japan and other Far East economies were in difficulties. This situation clearly worsened after 11 September as in the aftermath of the terrorist attacks the financial markets went into what some described as panic mode. The Dow Jones and FTSE plunged as investors took fright, moving their cash out of shares and into safe havens like government bonds, and oil prices soared as the world feared a long-drawn-out war. Fortunately, within six months some of the panic sub-sided and share prices began to recover – but not before thousands of jobs were lost worldwide, primarily in airlines and other associated businesses. There is no doubt, however, that the effects of 11 September will linger on and will influence economic thinking, not just in the UK but also worldwide, for some considerable time.

In addition to the influences that worldwide events have, UK macro-economic policy will also be affected by any decisions the UK Government makes regarding European monetary union. Now that the euro is a reality and irrespective of whether the UK joins or stays out, the economy will not be immune to its impact. Many organisations have made arrangements to deal in euros and have set up systems that would allow their employees to be paid in the new currency. Some banks are establishing euro accounts for customers who want them, and many retail businesses have made it clear that they will accept the new currency. All of this could feed down into employee relations practices and policies at the workplace, particularly if the pro-euro campaigners are proved right and the eurozone economies grow at a faster rate than a non-euro UK, thereby putting pressure on jobs and wage rates.

If the UK were to join the euro, what do you think its impact would be on the employment relations policies of your organisation? Why?

However, whatever the degree of outside influence, the UK Government has the role of an economic manager. Although different political parties may have different ideologies and policies, the objectives of economic management, whichever party is in power, have been broadly similar. These have been:

- price stability
- full employment
- economic growth
- a balance-of-payments surplus.

On the other hand, the priorities allocated to these four objectives have differed between governments. The Conservative Governments (1979–1997) gave the greatest priority to price stability whereas previous Labour Governments (1974–1979) put the greatest emphasis on the full employment objective. The objective of the Labour Government from 1997 onwards has been slightly different. Although it has adopted many of the economic disciplines of the predecessor Conservative Governments, its principal aim has been to establish a stable economy. One of the difficulties that Britain has endured since World War II is a propensity to 'boom and bust' in the context of the economic cycle. In order to achieve better stability, the Labour Government has taken a number of steps, some of them reasonably straightforward – like controlling public spending – and some of them very radical – such as surrendering control of interest rates to the Bank of England. Monetary policy was subcontracted to the Bank of England immediately after the 1997 General Election, a decision that has, since then, broadly been seen as a success by all the main political parties. The Bank's monetary policy committee now makes decisions on interest rates, and this has helped to provide a degree of stability in Britain's financial markets. Of course, not everybody can always be satisfied, whoever sets policy, and indeed it would be possible to make a good argument for cutting rates, for increasing them, *and* for keeping them the same. Some commentators would argue that our present system is good news for Britain because, unlike the members of the eurozone, at least we still have control over monetary policy. Their interest rates are dictated by the European Central Bank (ECB), which has to have a policy that suits the whole of the zone. This may not necessarily be in the interests of individual countries whose economies may be growing at a faster rate than some of their euro partners. It is a difficulty that is used by the anti-euro camp to support their stance over non-membership.

Even though the two main political parties may have similar economic objectives when in government, the policies they implement to achieve them are likely to be different. The employee relations professional must therefore understand that the economic policies of a Conservative Government are likely to differ from those of a Labour Government, and that these distinctions in policy can have differing impacts on the relative balance of bargaining power. There are some politicians who believe that Britain should follow a policy of full employment, and that the achievement of this goal justifies a degree of direct UK Government intervention into the affairs of public and private enterprises. When this approach has been adopted, the outcome has been to give organised labour a relative advantage in the balance of relative bargaining power.

An important issue of economic policy is the level of public expenditure. The International Monetary Fund (IMF) has repeatedly warned that financial market confidence and long-term interest rates are adversely affected if governments pay insufficient attention to the need to reduce the public sector borrowing requirement. Despite such warnings, the present Labour Government has signalled its intention to increase the level of public spending in order to deliver on its promise to improve public services. This could mean that spending rises faster than output for the first time since Labour came into power, which for supporters of Keynesian economic theories is good news. Keynes taught that fiscal policy should be counter-cyclical – but there are dangers in this approach. External influences can impact on government economic policy, and if there were to be a series of events that impacted adversely upon the UK economy, the Government's spending plans may be unsustainable and cause a consequent rise in interest rates and unemployment.

The really important policies that might help to insulate the UK are structural ones. The UK needs to keep itself more attractive than its rivals as a place to work and invest. The Government recognises this, and has made it clear that it will develop policies that stimulate entrepreneurship. But many such policies are slow-burn. Starting a business that will be successful and create jobs does not happen overnight. It takes time. There are, however, some things that can be done. The key one is not to stifle growth where it wants to take place – for example, easing planning restrictions and giving fast-track clearance to companies trying to bring in skilled workers from overseas.

Despite signalling an intention to invest in public services, this Government is sticking to its principles – to keep public borrowing under some control because of the impact on inflation of not doing so. Translated into employee relations terms, this usually means keeping a tight control over increases in public sector pay. Among private sector employers there is always concern over the possibility of any government's taking a soft line on public sector pay. For example, the desire to improve rewards for groups such as nurses, the police or teachers in response to public opinion can create a knock-on effect across the board. If the government is unwilling, or unable, to keep a tight control over public sector pay settlements, then any appeals to the private sector to show restraint will fall on deaf ears. That is why one of the most important skills for the employee relations professional is the art of scanning the political and environmental landscape to establish the extent to which policy shifts may have an impact on employee relations in the future.

The present Government has repeatedly stated that it wants the UK to be a 'knowledge-based economy' – that it is human capital in the form of employees who help to create wealth, and that it is therefore of fundamental economic importance to create significant numbers of new jobs. If, through initiatives like the New Deal, the Government is successful in reducing the numbers of unemployed and creating a significant number of new skilled jobs, there could be a swing in the balance of power towards employees and away from employers. Evidence from the Audit Commission suggests that the New Deal has not been particularly successful to date, and that most new jobs would have been created without such an intervention. However, if unemployment decreases and if skills shortages increase, organisations could find themselves under pressure to increase wages in order to counteract this.

> Consider what occupational types, either within your own organisation or externally, might be in short supply in such circumstances. It is important that your organisation plans sufficiently far ahead in respect of its personnel requirements.

There is evidence that many organisations have, over time, failed to invest sufficiently in training. Once the pool of available labour is reduced, its 'price' goes up. These and other effects are not necessarily the immediate results of a change of UK government, but over time the needs of economic management changes and shifts. The strategic employee relations professional monitors and anticipates such changes in order to support and inform the organisation's future plans and objectives.

Globalisation

In economic terms, a further impact on employee relations comes from the growth in multi-national companies and the expansion of the global marketplace. 'Globalisation' is a word that is much in evidence today, but it is difficult to define. A possible all-embracing definition of it is as the process of developing markets in new parts of the world for products and services developed in another part of the world, with the intention of increasing profit and spreading opportunity for return on 'investment'. Using the benefits of technology it is possible to migrate employment around the world to the place where conditions are most ideal for the producer – for example, development in the 'First World', software in India, production in the Third World, and a global sales team based in Brussels. Globalisation is said to be breaking down old world divisions and creating new.

The globalisation of markets, products and businesses has been a driver of major change over the past 50 years. Supporters of globalisation would argue that for both consumer and employee it has built bridges, created a greater sense of global community, provided employment and opportunity for millions, and that this stimulus for change has generated actions and events that have, on the whole, had a major positive benefit for humankind. Opponents of globalisation would refute this. Their argument is that, on the whole, companies have invested in the Third World in order to take advantage of cheap labour and increase profits that have benefited Western societies. It is not our intention to agree or disagree with either of these views: our concern is with the impact globalisation has on employee relations.

Competition (which usually underpins the urge to globalise) breeds insecurity. Employees have a tendency to feel unsafe when they know that their employer is competing in the global marketplace. At any time, a new process, product or service can undermine the very basis of their jobs – and to know this can breed insecurity. It is certainly true that we live in a world of multi-nationals and that the intricacies of international finance have effects on employee relations at the local level. Indeed, they can influence the location of new employment opportunities and, in some cases, the underlying culture of employee relations practices.

Multi-nationals see wage rates, expansion and investment in the context of the global market, in much the same way that a national company makes decisions after taking into account subsidies from enterprise areas, development corporations, and so on. International competition affects employee relations in other ways. Firms from the USA and Japan who set up in the UK look for qualities such as flexibility and adaptability. This has caused some of the traditional demarcation lines in industry to become blurred or be altogether removed, to a great extent. The negotiation of such methods of working makes them important in the area of employee relations.

To understand how the UK Government's role as an economic manager can affect employee relations and the relative balance of bargaining power between employers and employees, it is important to review and understand the two principal economic theories that have been applied to the management of the UK economy since the end of World War II – not least because a reversal of the economic policies currently being applied could result in a high-wage, high-inflation economy.

The full employment/economic growth era

For nearly 30 years after World War II successive UK governments regardless of their political complexion were committed to a policy of full employment. During this period economic management was heavily influenced by the views of the economist John Maynard Keynes, whose basic ideas included:

- The general level of employment in an economy is determined by the level of spending power in the economy.

- The overall spending power in the economy depends upon the amount of consumption and investment undertaken by individual households and employing organisations, as well as UK Government expenditure on health, education, social security, defence, industrial assistance, etc.

- Full employment is achieved by government regulation of overall spending power in the economy by its fiscal (tax), monetary (interest rates), exchange rates (value of the pound relative to other currencies) and public expenditure policies.

- If unemployment rises owing to a lack of overall spending power in the economy, the government should inject spending power by reducing taxes on private and corporate incomes, property, expenditure (VAT, excise duties), by lowering interest rates, and/or by increasing its own expenditure.

Application of the Keynesian model of economic management led to economic growth, increased public provision (in such areas as housing, education and the National Health Service) and personal prosperity for the majority of households. From the perspective of trade unions, full employment provided them with increased bargaining power which, in many instances, led employers to concede inflationary wage settlements. Many of the craft unions – for example, printers, and engineers – operated policies aimed at restricting the number of new entrants to their particular craft, a policy that was said to delay the introduction of new working methods or technology. This behaviour created labour shortages in certain occupations and in others led to over-staffing. Attempts to resolve this problem caused considerable organisational conflict and evoked a perception that management was unable to implement effective policies to counteract many of these restrictions. This resulted, inevitably, in a worsening of management–union relationships.

However, notwithstanding the increase in the overall standard of living, the general level of performance of the British economy was one of slower economic growth compared to its major competitors'. This relative economic underperformance had many downside effects, one of which was less-than-constructive employee relations. By the latter part of the 1960s the effect of high wage settlements, together with unions' defensive attitudes and poor management, caused many commentators to take the view that this deterioration in competitiveness was a direct consequence of poor workplace industrial relations (Nolan and Walsh, 1995). It was a view supported by the report in 1968 of the Royal Commission on Trade Unions and Employers' Associations which had been established in 1965 under the chairmanship of Lord Donovan. The reform of workplace industrial relations thus became a major public policy priority. However, opinions on the type of reform, and how best to implement it, differed – particularly on the role of the law as a catalyst for bringing about change. Nonetheless, the need for reform was not questioned.

So by the mid-1960s concerns about the prevailing system of employee relations and its adverse impact on economic competitiveness via relatively higher UK prices and lower labour productivity levels than those of economic competitors became central to the political agenda. The Labour Government under Harold Wilson, which was elected in 1964, decided to try to re-establish UK economic competitiveness by direct intervention in the outcome of employee relations through a productivity, prices and incomes policy designed to control inflation by ensuring that income increases were linked to increases in productivity and not to changes in the rate of inflation or what other workers were receiving.

For followers of Keynesian economics, if creating full employment gave rise to inflation, then the implementation of productivity, prices and incomes policy was necessary. Because wage costs account for such a significant proportion of employers' total costs, excessive rises in wage levels affect the inflation spiral. As inflation rises, economic policy-makers are tempted to regulate economic activity by stifling demand, which, in turn, can lead to rises in unemployment. Keynes argued that increasing unemployment to control inflation could be avoided, and full employment could be maintained by the introduction of a productivity, prices and incomes policy.

The history of incomes policies over the period 1948–1979 shows that in the short run they were successful, but that after two or three years they broke down, usually in the face of a strike in support of a pay increase in excess of the policy. By the 1970s such policies were proving politically explosive. Attempts to limit wage settlements were seen by some as a deliberate endeavour to shift the balance of bargaining power towards the interests of employers, and were resisted by the unions to the point of industrial disputes – the most famous of which were the miners' strikes of 1972 and 1973–74, and the 'winter of discontent' in 1978–79.

Programme for Prosperity and Fairness

Although not an incomes policy in the accepted sense of the term, the Irish Government's Programme for Prosperity and Fairness (PPF) is, nevertheless, an attempt by the state to influence the scale of wage increases (*People Management*, 11 January 2001). The PPF, which was signed in January 2000, was a 33-month national pay agreement that allowed for a first-phase increase of 5.5 per cent, a further rise of 5.5 per cent for the second 12 months, and a final increase of 4 per cent for the remaining nine months. It was the successor to a series of tri-partite agreements that had started with the Programme for National Recovery in 1987, a rescue package for a nation then facing mass unemployment, declining living standards and unchecked public spend-ing. As with so many incomes policies and similar initiatives, it came under severe strain less than six months after it was signed, when the rate of inflation rose above the predicted level of 3 per cent. This resulted in the unions' calling for an early review of the agreement. The Government initially stalled on their demands, but eventually – following six months of industrial unrest – it entered negotiations with the Irish Congress of Trades Unions and employers represented by the Irish Business and Employers' Confederation. These talks engendered a 3 per cent top-up on the original deal. The top-up allowed for a further 2 per cent rise on the first phase and a 1 per cent lump-sum payment in April 2002, in effect making an increase of almost 18 per cent. The Irish Business and Employers' Confederation agreed to the revisions in return for renewed union commitments on industrial peace.

As part of the revised agreement the Government agreed to set up a new benchmarking body to consider a collection of special 'relativity' claims from key public sector groups. This benchmarking body was not due to report until the middle of 2002, and its recommendations were not expected to be implemented until 2003. But under the revised terms for the PPF, the Irish Government has guaranteed to backdate 25 per cent of any award to December 2001.The benchmarking body, which is meant to compare pay rates and duties between the private and public sectors, has a massive amount of work to do. Its initial programme alone involves studying at least 40 employee grades.

It is possible that Irish employers will find the PPF advantageous, but in the UK management was not always impressed by the arbitrary imposition of Government pay norms, and employers were often happy to work with their employees to find ways round them. Private sector employers were more interested in the continuation of production, and some were prepared to pay higher wages to avoid industrial action. Whereas we now live in a highly competitive world economy, in which maintaining some form of competitive advantage is essential for most businesses, this was not always the case in the three decades after World War II. During that period a much greater proportion of an organisation's customer-base was static, relative to today, and organisations therefore had a much greater ability to pass on increased wage costs in the form of increased prices. In the case of the public sector there was no serious long-term attempt to limit the growth in public expenditure, and companies and enterprises therefore learned to live with high inflation and its consequent impact on wages and prices.

Explain the main tenets of the Keynesian approach to macro-economic management. What are, with appropriate examples, its implications for employee relations at the workplace level?

'Irresponsible union' behaviour

Circumventing pay norms was but one example of a wider malaise. By the beginning of the 1960s the balance of power was firmly with the trade unions – and particularly in the car industry, where shop stewards at plant level were increasingly exercising this power. They were reluctant to abide by disputes procedures and to subject themselves to control by full-time officials, particularly those national trade union leaders who were prepared to co-operate with some form of pay restraint. Some industries – like shipbuilding, car manufacture and the ports – had their own agendas that tended to be parochial and, in the opinion of many employers, motivated by political and not industrial objectives. Many employers also questioned whether shop stewards in calling unofficial strikes (strike action not supported by the union) and unconstitutional strikes (strike action following less than all the stages of the agreed procedure) truly represented the wishes of the totality of their members. Such views about the internal democracy of trade unions was given credence in that many decisions to take industrial action were based on voting by a show of hands at mass meetings rather than by a secret ballot of those involved.

One common theme of the 1960s and 1970s was the perception – partly based on strike statistics, and on the trade unions' links with the Labour Party and therefore Labour Governments – that trade union leaders were more powerful than UK Government Ministers. Because poor workplace industrial relations were judged to have had a negative impact on economic performance, unions and their allegedly 'irresponsible' use of power were seen as major contributors to the UK's relative lack of economic competitiveness. If businesses were not investing sufficiently, it must be – so some claimed – the fault of the unions. If new technology was not embraced sufficiently quickly, again the unions were perceived to be at the root of the problem. If inflation was out of control, it was once more the fault of the unions. Although any objective examination of employee relations during this period would show that the unions ought indeed to accept a large part of the blame, weak management performance during the period was also a contributory factor. There was insufficient investment in training and development, and then as now, insufficient investment in innovation and research. The debate about skill levels within UK organisations relative to international competitors is still ongoing. Despite the investment in Training and Enterprise Councils, National Vocational Qualifications, and the National Curriculum that took place in the 1990s, there has been a continuing concern that some employers do not see any value in investing in people. A recurrent redesigning of the training infrastructure does not help, now that Training and Enterprise Councils are being replaced by Learning and Skills Councils. These Councils were the result of two government consultation exercises in 1998 and 1999 that then produced a Green Paper *The Learning Age*. Although it is always laudable that governments should try to underpin training and development with some form of statutory intervention, persistent tinkering with the infrastructure is confusing for employers and is likely to result in less, not more, training.

The rise of monetarism

The 1978–79 so-called 'winter of discontent', when low-paid public sector employees took strike action to gain pay increases in excess of the then Labour Government pay-increase norm, coincided with the end of the five-year electoral cycle. The incumbent Labour Government knew it had to call a General Election during 1979, and although they sought to postpone it for as long as possible, an election was duly held in May 1979. The Conservative Party campaigned promising better management of the economy, lower income taxes, less government expenditure and the curtailment of union power – all of which they claimed would help the UK economy to regain competitiveness. They committed themselves to introducing legislation designed to ensure that trade unions acted 'responsibly'.

During their period in opposition (1974–1979), a growing faction within the Conservative Party began to question the ability of Keynesian economic policies to provide price stability (commonly referred to as 'sound money'). Instead, what Keegan (1984) refers to as the 'economic evangelicalists' began to embrace the concept of monetarism as the means to control inflation and improve economic competitiveness. Monetarism can mean different things to different people, but its basic propositions are:

- If the general level of purchasing power in the economy as a whole grows quicker than the increase in the general level of goods and services produced in the economy as a whole, firms and households will have more money to purchase goods and services than are available in the economy as a whole.

- This could lead to a situation where there is 'too much money chasing too few goods and services', where demand is greater than supply. Shortages arise and market prices start to increase as consumers compete with each other for this reduced supply.

- Increasing inflation engenders expectations that future inflation rates will be even higher, resulting in (a) higher wage demands and settlements, and (b) a wages–prices inflationary spiral causing an increase in the general level of unemployment as the competitiveness of firms declines and workers 'price themselves out of jobs'.

- To prevent inflation, the increase in the overall level of purchasing power in the economy as a whole must match the rate of increase in the general output of goods and services in the economy as a whole.

- If the increase in the economy-wide level of purchasing power exceeds the increase in the general level of the supply of goods and services in the economy as a whole, spending power (demand) must be decreased by raising interest rates and reducing the level of UK Government (public) expenditure.

For monetarists, unemployment will only fall, in the longer term, if the productive capacity of the economy is increased. Measures to achieve such an increase are usually referred to as 'supply-side' economics. The key to reducing unemployment and controlling inflation is enhancing the ability of the economy to increase the supply of goods and services to the market more efficiently by:

- creating an environment conducive to private enterprise

- creating incentives for individuals to work

- creating incentives for firms to invest, produce goods and services and employ workers

- liberalising product markets

- privatising publicly owned enterprises

- reducing taxation

- deregulating labour markets.

The Conservatives won the 1979 election and began the process of applying monetarist policies to the management of the UK economy. Such policies have now been applied in one way or another since that time, and are being continued by the present Labour Government. However, 'New Labour' believes that competitive advantage comes from quality and added value and the provision of minimum standards of protection for employees – for example, the minimum wage. It may be that the application of economic policy is now less doctrinaire than in the past. There is a view that New Labour endorses and understands the concept of human capital much better than the Conservatives. By spreading opportunities through education and injecting more social justice into the equation, the present Government hopes the UK can become a 'knowledge-based economy' capable of competing with the best.

Labour market changes

The make-up of the UK economy changed radically in the last quarter of the twentieth century. One of the visible results of this, for the employee relations professional, has been a much more deregulated labour market. The reforms to the labour market have seen a move from employment in manufacturing to employment in the service industries, which has accounted for an increase in non-manual jobs at the expense of manual ones. Part-time employment has increased while full-time employment has decreased. The rise in part-time employment, when converted to full-time equivalents, does not compensate for this downturn in full-time work. Although it would be an over-simplification to blame all the changes in the labour market on monetarist policies, those policies were the engine by which the reforms were driven. The consequence of higher unemployment relative to the 1960s and 1970s has been a major impact on employee relations. Trade union influence may be lower and industrial disputes may have declined, but there has been a growth in employee insecurity and, if the number of cases being dealt with by ACAS and employment tribunals is any guide, a rise in the number of workplace grievances. In 2000–2001 ACAS reported that 167,000 cases were registered, and although 105,000 of these were either settled or withdrawn before reaching a tribunal, that total represents very high level of employee dissatisfaction. It also means that over 60,000 individuals felt so strongly about their treatment that they demanded a full tribunal hearing. Such high levels of employee insecurity are not helpful if organisations intend to continually improve their performance. The feelings of insecurity expressed by many employees are a major concern to employers and thus employee relations professionals.

> Do you monitor the indicators of employee insecurity, such as rises in grievances (individual or collective), rises in labour turnover, or increases in sickness absence?

The labour market

Some commentators have argued that the relative growth in jobs in this service sector relative to manufacturing sector has led to an increase in 'McJobs' – part-time, badly paid and with low status – which has contributed to the decline in trade union membership and influence. It is argued that the lack of security offered by this type of employment has made people less inclined to join trade unions because they are afraid to challenge their employer. The decline in traditional union strongholds such as mining and shipbuilding has had an effect, but as with most things in employee relations, the reality tends to be more complex.

If we are to understand the significance that the labour market has on employee relations we have to know more about the composition of the UK workforce. The 1998 Workplace Employee Relations Survey (WERS) provides useful data. As its authors point out:

commentators looking at the British labour market, often highlight the issue of flexibility [and they therefore consider it valid to look at the] extent to which workplaces contract out different services [because] if the extent of contracting out has been on the increase, it may have led to a reduction in direct employment in workplaces.

The Survey asked whether workplaces had contracted out services that would previously have been undertaken by people directly employed in the organisation, and found that a third of respondents said that that was the case. Furthermore, one third were using former employees of the workplace as the contractors. They found that 11 per cent of employers had transferred some employees to a different employer in the five years preceding the publication of their report, and that this proportion was far higher (22 per cent) in the public sector than in the private sector (6 per cent).

Another area which has had a major impact on the labour market is non-standard employment. This is generally defined as anything that is not permanent full-time work and embraces part-time working, the use of freelancers, outworkers and temporary and fixed-term contract employees.

Critics of labour market reforms have argued that there has been a growth in the use of part-time labour to the detriment of full-time jobs. The WERS provides information on the extent of part-time employment, which is defined as paid work for fewer than 30 hours per week. The

Table 4 The use of temporary agency workers and fixed-term contracts, by occupation

Occupation	Percentage of workplaces employing	
	Temporary agency workers	Fixed-term contracts
Managers and administrators	1	6
Professional	5	15
Associate professional and technical	5	6
Clerical and secretarial	17	13
Craft and related	2	3
Personal and protective services	2	5
Sales	0	4
Plant and machine operatives	4	2
Other occupations	5	6
None of these workers used	72	56

Base: workplaces with 25 or more employees
Figures are weighted and based on responses from 1,921 managers
Source: WERS (1998), page 8

Survey found that part-time workers accounted for a quarter of all jobs in workplaces with 25 or more employees, but that their distribution varied enormously across workplaces of different kinds.

The WERS revealed that the use of freelancers (13 per cent) and out-workers (6 per cent) is reasonably significant, but provided some reveal-ing data about temps and fixed-term contract employees. There has been a widely held perception that employers have placed a greater reliance on the use of temporary and fixed-term contract employees. Table 4 shows that this is not the case, and that the majority of work-places do not use temps or employ people on fixed-term contracts.

Whatever the statistics, there is no doubt that 'the ability of managers to adjust the size of their workforces in line with requirements and demand – usually referred to as "numerical flexibility" – appears to be widespread'. Table 5 shows that during the 1990s there was an increase in the use of non-standard employment.

Whatever type of organisation you work in, the impact of the labour market changes will have affected the way you do your job. In organis-ations that still rely on a greater proportion of traditional permanent full-time employees there is likely to be pressure for change. Employment costs are still, for most businesses, the most significant item in the management accounts and provide one of the better oppor-tunities to make savings. In the near future, as competition heightens, some form of the 'flexible firm' will have to become a reality for all

Table 5   Change in the use of different forms of labour, 1993–1998

Number	Percentage use in organisation of			
	Fixed-term contracts	Temporary agency workers	Contractors	Part-time employees
Gone up	20	17	26	40
Stayed about the same	43	40	60	48
Gone down	6	8	3	7
Never used	31	35	11	5

Base: all workplaces five or more years old (in 1998) with 25 or more employees

Figures are weighted and based on responses from 1,706 managers

Source: Adapted from WERS (1998), page 9

organisations – but this is not necessarily bad news, although the pessimistic view of the reformed labour market is the 'McJobs' thesis.

A report by the Institute for Employment Research (IER) at Warwick University in 1999 suggested that the reality is more encouraging. It predicted that over the period 1997–2006 1.4 million new jobs would be created, and that because this figure was higher than the expected increase in the population of working age, unemployment would stay low. The report also acknowledged that whereas many of the new jobs would be part-time and for women, some of the biggest increases in demand would be for professional and technical staff.

Job creation

Although it is expected that part-time jobs will account for most of the net job creation and that the proportion of women in the workforce will continue to rise, it would be wrong to interpret this as the creation of a second-class labour market. A closer look at the forecasts contained in the Warwick report shows job creation taking place in two broad categories. One is the 'personal and protective services', which includes security guards and carers. Although this could be made to fit the pessimistic thesis, the impact of the minimum wage, the Working Time Regulations, and the EU part-time work and temporary workers and fixed-term contract work Directives should help to mitigate some of the abuses involving long hours and low pay.

The second category is in managerial, professional and technical jobs that demand high levels of education and skill. The report predicted that on average by 2006 there will be 171,000 more jobs a year in these categories, compared to 77,000 a year in the personal and protective services category. The IER predicted big increases in retailing and tourism which, while they would require plenty of part-time labour, were also in the process of upskilling available jobs.

This forecast will have to be revised for a number of reasons. Both the 2001 foot-and-mouth epidemic and the 11 September terrorist attacks have had a major impact on jobs in the tourism and leisure sector. In the month after the 'twin towers' atrocity business travel fell by 40 per cent, and it is predicted that it will take some considerable time to recover. In addition, there have been significant job losses – British Airways alone shed 5,000 jobs and is planning further cuts. Paradoxically, security firms have enjoyed an unexpected boom as nervous companies ask them to vet new staff or test their safety procedures. These two seismic events demonstrate all too clearly how economic planning and economic forecasts can be blown off course by external events.

Furthermore, evidence from the Labour Force Survey would suggest that the number of newly created managerial, professional and technical jobs predicted in the Warwick report are masking a greater proliferation of lower-skilled, lower-paid jobs. In examining the role that the 'new economy' will play in both job creation and the changing nature of work, Peter Nolan (*People Management*, 27 December 2001) has made some very valid points. He says:

The new economy may yet succeed in transforming the future world of work, but all the signs today are pointing to the emergence of an hour-glass economy. The selective proliferation of highly-paid jobs, whose incumbents enjoy substantial discretion over the hours, places and patterns of their work, has helped to spur the growth of low-paid, routine and unglamorous jobs in the very same sectors commonly associated with the thriving new economy. For every entrepreneur, software engineer and professional networker there are thousands of support staff stuffing envelopes, stacking shelves and distributing products to people's homes.

Greater flexibility

But what does all this structural change in the labour market mean at the level of the individual firm? What is its impact on employee relations? Many of the changes that have taken place over the last two decades have been driven by the expansion of the global marketplace and by the need to develop organisations that can respond flexibly to the rapidly changing demands of that market. This has given rise to the concept known as the 'flexible firm', but the data from WERS indicates that the movement towards changing work patterns is at best mixed. Stredwick and Ellis (1998) identified a number of surveys that 'throw light on the reality of the movement towards flexible working'. They conclude that 'The evidence is strong all round that the move to greater flexibility is gathering pace, and that organisations see it as a means of achieving competitive advantage.'

Evidence concerning the employees' attitude to flexible working arrangements is thin, but Emmott and Hutchinson (1998) note that 'generally
they are perceived as a "good thing" [but] that there are negative implications'. This ties in with Stredwick and Ellis's conclusion that 'employees
are not always fully co-operative in these ventures', and it is this lack of
co-operation that is likely to present the greatest challenge to the
employee relations professional. If, as Stredwick and Ellis state,
employees are given little choice about embracing flexibility, this will
have a major impact on their sense of security and wellbeing.
Furthermore, if Stredwick and Ellis are right that few organisations are
embracing flexibility for strategic reasons, it might well mean that
organisations are inadvertently enhancing the ability of trade unions to
recruit workers as a means of resisting change.

The debate over the future of work will continue, and the major project
The Future of Work, launched by the Economic and Social Research
Council in October 1998, will help to fill the gaps in our knowledge. Its
aim is to provide evidence to enhance public understanding of the critical developments most likely to impact on people's working lives. A key
objective of the programme is to give breadth to accounts of the future
of work by producing a systematic mapping of past and present shifts
and continuities. As Moynagh and Worsley ask (*People Management*, 27
December 2001), is the workplace revolution over? Are the biggest
changes – the shift from manufacturing to services, more women in
work, and more part-timers – behind us?

As part of The Future of Work project, the Tomorrow Project has completed a programme of study and consultation and has concluded that
there are even bigger changes ahead that will raise major strategic
issues for employers, one of which will be a phase of radical outsourcing. We noted above that the WERS survey had identified that a growing number of organisations acknowledged outsourcing some
activities, and Moynagh and Worsley believe that outsourcing will be
taken further.

They acknowledge that there has always been a fierce 'debate about the
limitations of outsourcing, particularly on whether it means a loss of
control, quality and culture', and that:

*organisations will remain under intense pressure to increase
efficiency, but 'slash and burn' will not be enough, because they
can't go on cutting jobs indefinitely. They will find instead that
their survival hinges on reinventing products and processes –
doing new things better – which will require them to become
more focused.*

One organisation that has certainly taken a very close look at outsourcing is Abbey National. As Jane Pickard reports (*People Management*, 27
December 2001): 'The future is already here, as far as Abbey National

CASE STUDY: Abbey National

At the end of 2001 Abbey turned four of its branches into pilot franchises, selling local managers a 49 per cent stake. It has also been experimenting with 'café banks' run jointly with Costa Coffee.

Back-office operations are not immune either. MBNA now manages both the credit card operation (employing Abbey's former staff in that function) and customer relations – but not in a traditional outsourced capacity. The bank is also engaging in joint ventures.

Colin Brown, HR development manager at Abbey National, sees all this as the start of an entirely new type of organisation, held together by its brand, with far-reaching implications for the employment relationship.

'Employees could become the key parts of a networked organisation, with the company dependent on these individuals,' he says. 'So you can imagine lots of little bubbles with people in them. The company has a brand for customers, but actually they are separate little businesses.'

Brown believes the emphasis at present is on the employer adapting to the employee, partly because of the relatively stable economy. 'I think that will continue and we will have a situation where organisations cease to exist and it's the connections between people that will matter.' He predicts two different types of job function: knowledge workers and service workers [the latter of whom] provide hairdressing, healthcare and so on for the former.

In this environment, Brown says, HR becomes more about culture. 'You can no longer manage employees through a contract. Instead, you have more of a psychological contract. But how do you imbue your contractors, or other people not working directly for you, with enough of your values to get them to behave the way you want them to?

'You may want to find the right mix of culture between trust and training and, for instance, strong ideas and innovation. You need to give enough space for the company to grow while also retaining what the customer values,' Brown says. 'One of the errors in outsourcing used to be finding the cheapest supplier, which often meant that the service would deteriorate. So maybe it's a matter of paying for the culture of an organisation.'

Key lessons from Abbey National's experience include picking the right partners, having a very open style of communication, ensuring proper training and resources for managers, recruiting managers who can establish and maintain relationships with new groups of people, and learning how to get the right balance between close working relationships and looser ties.

'We are learning that this varies – and that we haven't quite sussed it out,' Brown admits. 'Sometimes you want a close relationship, and sometimes a more distant one. It's hard to know up front how to get that balance right.'

There are two kinds of franchised branches. In the first model – known as internal franchising – launched last year in one third of the bank's local markets, managers remain in post but risk a percentage of their salary on the business. In the latest pilots, in Belfast, Cardiff, London and Newcastle, managers have resigned and set up their own company, employing the rest of the staff but holding only 49 per cent of the business. They are risking a larger part of their salary, but come away with the national minimum wage if they fail to hit targets.

is concerned. Outsourcing has become almost passé as the company gets to grips with new forms of partnership (see case study).'

Many of the respondents to the Moynagh and Worsley research thought that

> *despite trade union opposition, the public sector would follow suit [in outsourcing]. Already the NHS is seeking to give hospitals greater independence, increase private-sector provision and let some surgeons own and run specialist surgeries. Perhaps the health service will in time become a 'brand management body', commissioning services, rating them and managing the NHS brand.*

The various pieces of research in The Future of Work programme are very important to the foreseeable work of personnel professionals, examining as they do issues with which those professionals will have to deal in managing the employment relationship into the future. For more information on the detail of the various projects you should visit www.leeds.ac.uk/erscfutureofwork.

The state as an employer pre-1979

During the post-war period, the state always sought to give a lead to the private sector as a model and good employer, as expressed in the implementation of particular employee relations policies. Collective bargaining was considered a good and desirable activity. Union membership was encouraged and such encouragement led to high levels of unionisation in the public sector. Nine out of ten white-collar trade unionists were employed in the public sector. When industries were taken into public ownership, there was an obligation on the public corporation created to recognise, consult and negotiate with trade unions. The state also sought to ensure that its staff received comparable pay and conditions to those doing the same or similar work in the private sector. Comparability was thus the basis of wage claims and adjustments. For example, in the Civil Service the civil servants were given a Pay Research Unit to look at rates of pay, to compare pay with private sector employees, and to provide negotiators with information.

Increasing the supply side

Conservative Governments post-1979 had a different approach to economic management and pursued a twin-track policy to achieve their objectives. They eschewed the prevailing post-war consensus in areas such as the welfare state, UK Government intervention in industry, incomes policy, tripartite discussions, and keeping unemployment in check even at the risk of increasing inflation. Instead, they made clear their intention of letting the market decide.

Monetarist policies were introduced as a means of reducing inflation, which meant sharp increases in interest rates and in indirect taxes (especially VAT) and cuts in public expenditure. The result was large increases in unemployment, especially in the country's manufacturing industries such as shipbuilding, motor cars and steel. By allowing unemployment to rise, the UK Government was making it clear that radical measures were needed if the British economy was to re-establish its competitiveness.

In addition, Conservative Governments sought the encouragement of an enterprise culture by the deregulation of product and labour markets, the privatisation of nationalised industries, and the regulation of trade unions' industrial activities. As Blyton and Turnbull (1994) saw it, 'The objectives of UK Government policy in the 1980s could be simply stated – namely, to encourage enterprise through the deregulation of markets, especially the labour market.' They noted that the foundations of Conservative Governments' policy under Mrs Thatcher can be found in the writings of free-market economists such as Milton Friedman and, in particular, Friedrich Hayek. Of the UK economists who subscribe to the monetarist philosophy, the work of Patrick Minford is a good indicator of why the policy agenda has been developed as it has. Minford argued that trade unions used their power to raise wages above the market rate, which then caused price inflation, which in turn caused further rises in unemployment. This process, he argued, reduced the efficiency of both individual firms and the economy as a whole through the imposition of restrictive practices, demarcation, etc. For the monetarists, then, if employment was to increase, the labour market behaviour of trade unions had to be regulated. Trade unions had to be restrained from abusing market power, and it was for this reason that Conservative administrations over the period 1979–1997 introduced legislation to free up labour markets from trade union, employers' association and government influence.

The restriction on trade union behaviour was two-pronged. The Conservatives made it clear that they were no longer prepared to promote the government's traditional role as a 'model employer'. The idea that the state should be a model to the private sector remained, but the notion of what constituted a 'model employer' changed, and in 1981 the Government ended the Civil Service comparability agreement that had operated since 1951.

The UK Government became less favourably disposed to collective bargaining and instead argued that employees should be rewarded as individuals. They sought to act against the collective voice because they subscribed to the view that it led to overpriced jobs and consequently unemployment. The state ceased to encourage people to become members of trade unions or to take part in collective bargaining. Conversely, they also discouraged the traditional role of employers' federations in national wage bargaining. Comparability of pay for public sector employees was terminated because it was thought that pay increases should be related to the ability to pay and the availability of labour resources. The pay of an occupational group should thus not necessarily be the same in different parts of the country. Differentials should reflect the scarcity of that labour. Wage negotiation at operating unit levels, where the ability-to-pay and the scarcity-of-labour factors could more easily be taken account of, was therefore encouraged and the traditional 'going-rate' argument discouraged.

Outline three main functions of the state in employee relations.

Public expenditure

The UK Conservative Government argued that inflation was the result of the money supplys increasing faster than the increase in output of goods and services in the economy. Money supply is the total spending power in the economy as a whole, but a major component in it is public expenditure. Because the UK Government was responsible directly or indirectly for the wages of one third of the employees in the country, and because pay is an important part of public sector expenditure, UK Governments cannot adopt a neutral stance on public sector settlements. So although the Conservative Government made it clear that a formal incomes policy with norms and enforcement agencies was not on its agenda, it was prepared to ensure effective controls over pay rises for public sector employees by the simple expedient of limiting the rise in public expenditure. This approach brought the UK Government into conflict with a number of public sector unions – for example, schoolteachers, who had their collective bargaining rights removed by Act of Parliament.

The labour market reforms over the past 20 years have seen a progressive diminution of the welfare safety-net for unemployed workers. Governments considered that over-generous welfare provision meant that people had less incentive to work and therefore remained unemployed for longer than necessary. This so-called 'dependency culture' was tackled by changing the basis on which an individual became eligible for unemployment benefit and by reducing the length of time such benefit was payable. Because of the fear of unemployment, such changes in the welfare system meant that employees became less resistant to employer control and were less likely to seek reviews of their terms and conditions of employment for fear of losing their jobs.

Although the present Labour Government has not reversed the policy initiatives of its predecessors, it has, through a series of interventions, sought to make work pay for a greater number of people, thus reducing the dependency culture. A report by the Institute for Fiscal Studies (IFS) assessed government changes to the tax and benefits system and the introduction of the national minimum wage. It concluded that the package of measures would make work pay by between £7 and £13 a week extra. This report, together with the Warwick report referred to above, suggest that we are in the process of creating a labour market in which employers are creating new jobs and people are more willing to take them.

The impact of technology

All organisations operate within certain technological constraints which impact on its size and structure. In turn, the size and structure of an organisation will undoubtedly have an influence on its culture. Because culture affects relationships between people, technology and technological development are evidently important factors in employee relations.

It is important for employee relations professionals to understand the term 'technology'. If it merely implies some form of process or engineering, does it have any relevance outside manufacturing? Technology is more than an engineering process. From the perspective of an organisation it is about the application of skills and knowledge. It is therefore both relevant and necessary to understand it.

In the context of employee relations it is possible to identify three perspectives from which to view the impact of new technology. The first is that new technology, because of its impact on traditional skills, acts as both a de-skilling agent and a creator of unemployment. The second perspective is that new technology is a positive force in that it creates new opportunities for employees who have the chance to learn new skills. A third perspective sees technology as the means whereby previously unpleasant or repetitive tasks can be eliminated. For example, the introduction of robotics into the car industry removed the need for employees to carry out mundane operations, with a consequent improvement in the climate of employee relations in an industry previously dogged by labour problems. Each of these three perspectives is, to some degree, correct, but the impact of new technology varies from industry to industry and from organisation to organisation.

Although most people acknowledge that, in general terms, technological development has reduced the demand for certain types of labour, it is clear that it has presented some significant opportunities also for job creation. One example is the large growth in the use of call centres, particularly in the financial services sector. Call centres now employ nearly 300,000 people in the UK, and this figure is forecast to rise even further. They are clearly technology-driven and rely on a combination of complex computerised communications technologies.

Technological development based on computers, lasers and telecommunications not only has the capacity to de-skill jobs, it can blur demarcation lines, create an alternative lower-paid workforce for an employer, and provide the impetus for changes in work patterns. There is also another role. Earlier in this chapter we examined the part that out-sourcing is likely to play in the changing world of work. Moynagh and Worsley (in *People Management*) believe that:

New technology will make this possible by enabling outsourced networks to be managed through high-speed digital links. If you thought the earth moved with the arrival of the World Wide Web, you ain't seen nothing yet. Driven by the same people who developed the web, 'the grid' – the next generation of the Internet – is destined to make the web a dinosaur over the next decade.

With broadband technology and improved mobile telephony, e-communication will be piped through the equivalent of the Channel Tunnel rather than today's drinking straw. It will be more user-friendly and much faster.

They reported on a firm in the USA who are

already providing a taste of things to come. Made-2-Measure systems can run a small manufacturing company's entire day-to-day operation completely online, with huge efficiency gains. There is great potential for the same provision to be extended to the service sector.

It is important for the employee relations professional to recognise where technology requires changes in working patterns or processes, and to identify appropriate and available training opportunities. A commonly held view about the impact of technological change is that it creates problems, particularly where trade unions are represented in the workplace, and is often resisted. Of course, when change is on the agenda, both trade unions and employees generally will have fears over job losses, de-skilling and increased management control. The skill of the employee relations professional lies in understanding these concerns and seeking ways to mitigate them. Personnel professionals should have a vested interest in the management of change, not just the imposition of change.

Whatever the nature of the technology, its impact, and therefore the response to it by all stakeholders, is inevitably linked to the UK's poor record in skills development and productivity. The Government was so concerned about the lack of skills development that the Performance and Innovation Unit (PIU) at the Cabinet Office set up a task force to examine the problem and recommend policies to overcome it. The task force has now reported, and concluded that 'workforce development' (WfD) can 'help to raise labour productivity and increase social inclusion'. They describe WfD as 'a relatively new term for training and skills development [sitting] between training (which has a narrow focus) and education (which is broad), and is firmly grounded in business need'. The PIU has adopted the following definition:

Workforce development consists of activities which increase the capacity of individuals to participate effectively in the work-force, thereby improving their productivity and employability.

The full report of the task force can be seen on the Web at www.cabinet-office.gov.uk/innovation, but the key points are:

- A relatively high proportion of the UK population of working age lacks basic and intermediate skills.

- The benefits of education and training are, in large part, captured by individuals through increased earnings and by firms through increased productivity.

- Without basic skills – literacy and numeracy – individuals cannot start to develop a career path and may be trapped in a low-pay/no-pay cycle.

So far as productivity is concerned, there continues to be concern over Britain's productivity deficit relative to the performance of other advanced economies. Peter Nolan writing in *People Management* ident-ified how

the government, the TUC and the CBI are now revisiting this long-standing problem. Productivity and the quality of Britain's goods and services have been major concerns for previous gov-ernments, but the Chancellor has put these issues at the centre of his strategy for revitalising the domestic economy. The Treasury, well aware of the superior relative performance of companies in mainland Europe, has started another review of what is preventing businesses in this country from performing to their full potential.

Whatever skills organisations require in the future, the employee relations professional will have to recognise that changes in the balance of skills will have a significant impact on his or her work. In some organ-isations investment in improved technology may lead to both staff devel-opment and redundancies. In some organisations such investment may cause difficulties in recruiting sufficient skilled labour, with the conse-quent pressure that this shortfall can bring, particularly in respect of unit labour costs. Overall, it is important to remember that new tech-nology is inconsistent in its impact because of the number of variables involved, including the nature of the product or service, the type of organisation, the management strategy, and the attitudes of trade unions (where they are represented) and employees.

What changes in technology do you expect to affect your organisation, or the sector in which you operate, in the next five years? What is their likely impact on employee relations behaviour?

The balance of bargaining power

In Chapter 1 we introduced the concept of the 'balance of bargaining power' and said that it was this balance that determines whether employers or employees feel that their interests have been satisfied. We also said that the balance in bargaining power operates at both a macro and a micro level. At the macro level the combination of economic management and political, legislative and technological change influences the overall conduct of employee relations, whereas at the micro level these factors can have totally different impacts.

The macro level

The Government's economic and legal policies have major implications for the outcome of employee relations behaviour. When economic policies are directed towards the creation of full employment and the maximising of economic growth, the relative bargaining power of the employer is weakened but that of the employee is strengthened. A high level of demand for goods and services in the economy as a whole generates demand for labour to produce/provide those goods and services. If the demand for labour services increases relative to their supply (ie shortages develop), the 'price' employers will have to pay to secure those services will go up.

If, on the other hand, Government economic policies give the highest priority to reducing inflation by lowering household and corporate spending and reducing public expenditure, then the demand (spending power) in the economy will fall, and as a consequence so will the demand for labour. The result will be 'labour surpluses', giving rise to redundancies and increased unemployment. The effect of the supply of labour's exceeding demand is downward pressure on the 'price' of labour services – or if labour prices are inflexible downwards, less labour will be employed than previously (unemployment) at the same price. In such situations, the relative balance of bargaining power of the employers will be strengthened and that of the employees weakened.

If a government introduces legislation favourable to employers' interests, the bargaining power of employers relative to employees is evidently strengthened. This is what Conservative Governments did during the period 1980–1997 by introducing a series of labour law reforms. If, conversely, a government introduces legislation favourable to the interests of employees and trade unions, the bargaining power of employees relative to employers is strengthened. Some employers have real fears that the introduction of the statutory recognition procedures contained in the Employment Relations Act (1999) will swing the balance of power towards trades unions, particularly in industries like media and communications. Legislation, by setting standards of behaviour for employers in the regulation of the relationship between an individual employee and his or her employer (for example, in the right not to be unfairly dismissed), also influences the relative balance of bargaining power between employers and individual employees.

The implementation of new technology also impacts on bargaining power. For example, developments in communications have helped to produce global markets which have increased product market competition. This can lead to downward pressure on the 'price' of labour services and a shift in bargaining power towards the employer. The reverse may also be true. By creating new jobs and new skills and by making some industries more capital-intensive, the implementation of technological change has strengthened the bargaining power of employees. One only has to look at the advertised vacancies for a whole range of Information Technology jobs to identify one sector where this is true.

The influence on bargaining power of the wider economic and legal environment surrounding an employee relations system cannot be underestimated, and in this regard the decision-making bodies of the European Union have become increasingly important. The role of the UK Government and the European Union Council of Ministers (see Chapter 4) in this context means that representative bodies of employers and employees must endeavour to participate in the political lobbying process to persuade the political decision-makers to introduce economic and legal policies favourable to their interests.

The micro level

So far, the relative bargaining power between the buyers and sellers of labour services has been analysed on the macro level. However, analysis at this level cannot explain why some groups of employees retain their bargaining power vis-à-vis the employer despite low growth or high unemployment, or why some employers are in a relatively weak bargaining position despite the economic climates being in their favour. In many respects what matters for the employer is their bargaining power relative to particular groups of workers at the enterprise level. This is the relative bargaining power at the micro level.

Consider a situation where the national picture is unfavourable to employees in general. Unemployment is rising steeply, redundancies are occurring every day, employers are seeking to restrict wages and general employment conditions, and new, small firms are replacing more established businesses. However, your organisation could be in a sector where the product or process has a limited shelf-life. If you also have a collective relationship with a well-organised trade union(s), your employers would be aware of how a trade dispute could have an immediate and costly effect on customer confidence or income generation. Alternatively, your company could be non-union but very high-tech and experiencing rapid expansion. It requires highly skilled, highly trained and committed employees to produce its products. However, these skills are in short supply because the major employers in the area are in the information industry and other new companies, seeking the same skilled labour, are continuing to move into the area.

In both these situations employees would perceive that notwithstanding the national (macro) picture, the relative balance of bargaining power was very much in their favour. This situation could be made even worse if the management of the business had no clear employee relations strategy or policies and if procedures were non-existent or out of date.

> Consider the work groups in your organisation. Which have the most potential power to disrupt the organisation? What is the basis of that power? Do they realise they have this power? If not, why not? Do you think they would be willing to use their power?

Bargaining power and management behaviour

In general terms, the balance of bargaining power has been in favour of employers over the past years because of the legislative and economic policies of successive governments. When this is the case it is important that power is exercised in a responsible and not an arbitrary manner.

If the balance of bargaining power favours management, the employers may achieve their objectives despite adopting a management style that is unprofessional and based on an attitude of 'Take it or leave it,' 'If you don't like it, go and work for somebody else,' and 'There are plenty of other people who would be only too willing to work here.' In such situations the workforce complies with, but is not committed to, management's action and policy. The employees are cowed, have no respect for management and store up grievances that will come to the surface with a vengeance when the relative balance of bargaining power turns in favour of the employee. There is some anecdotal evidence that some of the claims for union recognition have gained the support of a majority of the affected workforce as a response to previous (bad) management behaviour.

Managing in such a way that employee commitment is not forthcoming is non-sustainable in the longer term. It inevitably relies on a crude abuse of power, and this in the long-term will be detrimental to the business which, in turn, will experience high labour turnover, low employee morale and depressed productivity levels. The employee relations professional manages on the basis of just cause for action, consults and discusses with employees, and treats them in a fair, reasonable and consistent manner. Managing on this basis, regardless of the relative balance of bargaining between employers and employees, normally gains the respect of the latter even though management invariably gains what it wants.

A further reason why an employee relations professional should not act in an arbitrary manner is that if the bargaining pendulum can swing one way, it can swing back. If you fail to exercise power responsibly when it is your favour, then you should not expect responsible behaviour from employees when they have the advantage. Bargaining power, as we have noted, is influenced by economic policy and legal intervention. If those policies are changed, a number of variables may be affected. For example, if the predicted increase in managerial, professional and technical jobs becomes a reality and employers do not invest sufficiently in skills training, skill shortages will raise the price of certain types of labour. Statutory rights to union recognition could provide employees with greater bargaining power

Can you identify where the relative balance of bargaining power lies in your organisation? Is this balance static, or is there potential for any significant shift in power?

CONCLUSION

This chapter has examined the role of the UK Government as an economic manager in terms of the objectives of macro-economic policy, and how employee relations is affected by the way in which that policy is implemented. In particular we have examined the contrast between the Keynesian and monetarist approaches to economic management, and the impact that the change to monetarism has had on the UK economy since 1979.

We noted how the rise in multi-national companies and the growth of globalisation have had an impact on both economic management and individual organisations, and that globalisation has provided the spur to organisations to take tough decisions, confront performance issues, and create new products so that they compete the world over. However, we also highlighted the insecurity that can be a byproduct of the drive to do things in new and better ways.

We have looked at the role of the UK Government as an employer, and examined the way in which the concept of the UK Government as a 'model employer' has changed over time. In the immediate post-war years there was encouragement of collective bargaining and an attempt to ensure comparability of pay between the public and private sectors. From 1979 the emphasis was on a more individual approach to the employment relationship, with a clear discouragement of national pay bargaining.

Finally, we looked at the impact of technological change on the corporate environment and acknowledged that it influences employee relations in a number of ways. We also examined the need to generate enthusiasm for skills development and to raise UK productivity levels so that they match those of its competitors. We saw that technology can have negative as well as positive effects – it can create unemployment, it can provide the opportunity for employees to learn new skills, and it can generally improve the working environment.

From whatever perspective you view the corporate environment there is no doubt that over the last 20 years there has been a radical change in our system of employee relations. This transformation has manifested itself in changes to working practices and changes in the labour market with an increase in part-time and temporary working. Reward systems have also changed, such factors as performance-related pay, reward for teams and profit-related pay becoming more prevalent.

Changes in legislation, closer ties with our European partners, rapidly changing economic circumstances – all have an impact on the corporate environment and in turn on the established patterns of employee relations.

KEY POINTS

- Changes in economic management and reforms to labour law can cause trade union power and strike activity to decline/increase, and such changes have a marked effect on the balance of bargaining power.

- The role of the state in employee relations has changed: it no longer seeks an active role in promoting particular practices.

- The way in which the economy is managed has a direct impact on employee relations because it influences such things as price stability, growth, investment and employment levels.

- The continuing globalisation of markets will be a major influence on organisational change and thus employee relations.

- Technological innovation will continue to influence the workplace, and will inevitably therefore impact on employee relations practices.

- Management power should be exercised in a responsible manner, and never arbitrarily.

Further reading

BLYTON P. and TURNBULL P. (1994) *The Dynamics of Employee Relations*. London, Macmillan.

DONALDSON P. and FARQUHAR J. (1991) *Understanding the British Economy*. London, Penguin.

EMMOTT M. and HUTCHINSON S. (1998) 'Employment flexibility: threat or promise?', in Sparrow P. and Marchington M. *Human Resource Management: The new agenda*. London, Financial Times/Pitman Publishing.

FARNHAM D. *The Corporate Environment*. (1995) London, Institute of Personnel and Development.

INSTITUTE FOR EMPLOYMENT RESEA*and Employment 1998.*RCH (1999) *Review of the Economy*

INSTITUTE FOR FISCAL STUDIES (1998) *Entering Work and the British Tax and Benefit System*.

KEEGAN W. (1984) *Mrs Thatcher's Economic Experiment*. London, Penguin.

LEWIS D. and SARGEANT M. (2000) *Essentials of Employment Law*. 6th edition. London, CIPD.

LEWIS D. and SARGEANT M. (2002) *Essentials of Employment Law*. 7th edition. London, CIPD.

MOYNAGH M. and WORSLEY R. (2001) 'Prophet sharing', *People Management*, Vol. 7, No.25, December. pp 24–29.

MOYNAGH M. and WORSLEY R. (2001) *Tomorrow's Workplace*. London, CIPD.

NOLAN P. (2001) 'Shaping things to come', *People Management*, Vol. 7, No.25, December, pp 30–31.

NOLAN P. and WALSH J. (1995) 'The structure of the economy and labour market', in Edwards P. (ed.), *Industrial Relations – Theory and practice in Britain*. Oxford, Blackwell.

STREDWICK J. and ELLIS S. (1998) *Flexible Working Practices: Techniques and innovations*. London, Institute of Personnel and Development

3 • The Legislative Framework

CHAPTER OBJECTIVES

When you have completed this chapter you should understand and be aware of:

- the importance of the employment contract
- the legislative process
- the principal function of the law
- how the law impacts on relationships at work
- the nature and jurisdiction of employment tribunals
- recent developments in the law.

Introduction

There has always been a significant role for the law in the conduct of employee relations, but relative to the last 100 years the present employment law regime now imposes itself on every facet of the employment relationship. However, it is important that the employee relations professional does not view the law as simply something that has to be complied with. Good employee relations is not achieved by waving a legal rulebook and stating what people cannot do. Good employee relations is achieved by the positive actions that employers take to win the trust and confidence of their workforce.

Notwithstanding this approach, we have to recognise that from recruitment to departure, every act of the employer is measured against a particular legislative standard. Whether that standard is 'not to discriminate', 'to act reasonably' or to provide a certain level of 'care', it means that employee relations professionals and line managers have to stop and think before taking particular actions. This is because the sheer amount and complexity of employment law can often overwhelm even the most experienced of practitioners, and for this reason the law's range and impact must be clearly understood.

It is not our intention to provide a detailed explanation of every piece of legislation, and we will not do that. Textbooks like Lewis and Sargeant's *Essentials of Employment Law* (CIPD, 2002) and the CIPD Employment Law Service can do that job in a much more effective way. Our purpose is to examine the legislation in the context of employee relations, and to explain how relationships can be influenced by the way in which individual employers apply legislative rules and standards.

The legislative process

There are now two principal sources of employment law that the employee relations professional must be concerned with: legislation that derives from a political decision of the governing Parliamentary party, and legislation that derives from the European Parliament. Notwithstanding this, it is important to recognise that the UK Parliament is the source of most laws with which the employee relations specialist has to be concerned, even though the actual legislation might have been directed by, or influenced by, Europe. In Chapter 4 we describe the process by which European legislation is decided, and give numerous examples of EU Directives that have been, or will be, transposed into UK law and it is not necessary to repeat that detail here. We will however, be looking at some of the developments in European law. Lewis and Sargeant provide a detailed explanation of the 'sources and institutions of employment law', but generally the process by which the legislative is enacted is as follows. The government of the day issues a 'Green Paper', followed by a 'White Paper', followed by a 'bill' which, after the parliamentary process has been exhausted, becomes an 'Act of Parliament'. The first two stages are not obligatory, and governments can bypass them if they so wish. The Green Paper is a consultative document and is used by the government to obtain the views of interested parties on proposed legislation. This can apply irrespective of whether the proposal is prompted by the European Parliament or results from a UK political decision. Views may be submitted by employers' organisations, trade unions and organisations such as the CIPD. Even lay individuals can contribute to the consultative process. Once the consultation is complete, the government usually issues a White Paper, which sets out the government's policy and intentions. A bill is then introduced into Parliament, and, assuming it survives the scrutiny of both the House of Commons and the House of Lords, the agreed bill becomes an Act – eg the Employment Rights Act 1996.

Explain the key stages in the UK legislative process at which employers can attempt to influence the contents of legislation.

Sometimes the distinction between a nationally politically driven development and one that is European-driven is not easily identified; as Bercusson (*European Labour Law*, 1997) says:

The dynamic of national labour laws is no longer determined solely or even mainly by domestic developments. It is not merely that UK labour law is required to incorporate EU norms, EU norms are themselves the reflection of the national labour laws of member states.

It is also the case that legislators often merge these two influences in an attempt to maximise the use of parliamentary time. For example, the Employment Relations Act 1999 contains provisions relating to part-time workers, parental leave, etc, that derived from the European process, as well as provisions that derived from the UK political process, relating for example to trade union recognition and the right to be accompanied at disciplinary and grievance hearings. For HR and personnel practitioners a classic example of how the source of legislation can become confused is demonstrated by the Minimum Wage Act 1998. The proposal for a minimum wage was a clear manifesto commitment of the Labour Party prior to the 1997 General Election, and was in part a product of their close relationship with the trade union movement. Once they were elected, it become one of their priorities for legislation – and yet many practitioners remain convinced that the minimum wage was introduced because of a European Union Directive. Similarly, the current rules concerning statutory union recognition were nationally driven rather than European-driven.

The law and employee relations

Employee relations specialists do not need to be lawyers, but they do need to understand the interaction between the law and employee relations. They must understand that because of the many legal developments over the past 30 years and because we live in a more litigious age, every employee relations decision is potentially capable of legal challenge. In the following part of this chapter we have attempted, by reference to some of the principal areas of law, to identify where these challenges are most likely to occur and how employee relations policies and processes must be capable of dealing with them.

For example, the psychological contract – seen by many as a key element in the employment relationship – can be seriously affected by how existing and new rights are implemented. Simply doing the minimum required might avoid legal challenge, but might leave individual employees feeling vulnerable or undervalued. Equally, using the statutory provisions as a baseline from which to offer enhancements, such as providing paid rather than unpaid parental leave, can, in appropriate circumstances, pay major dividends in employee commitment to the organisation.

The contract of employment

The most important and major instrument in employment law is the contract of employment. The first Contracts of Employment Act was placed on the statute book in 1963. Although that act has now been repealed, its provisions have been incorporated into the Employment Rights Act 1996, and it is vital that the employee relations professional understands its impact. This is because it defines and regulates the relationship between the employer and the employee. Being an 'employee', or in recent years a 'worker', is the key determinant in the types of rights an individual enjoys, and it is an area that has thus given rise to a large amount of litigation and case law.

In any business the categories of workers used may include one or more of the following:

- employees, either full-time or part-time
- independent contractors
- agency workers
- casual workers
- fixed-term contract workers
- homeworkers.

However, in the UK only certain of these individuals are entitled to all the protection afforded by current employment legislation. These distinctions, although they might seem pedantic, are of crucial importance to the management of individuals. 'Workers' might not have all the rights that 'employees' have, but failure to observe good practice in the management of such individuals could be costly if, for example, they allege that they have been unlawfully discriminated against. In many cases it is absolutely clear that a person is an employee, but in between these two specificities there exists a wide variety of relationships that exhibit characteristics of both employment and self-employment, and it is *in respect of* these relationships that the difficulties lie.

Section 230(1) of the Employment Rights Act 1996 defines an 'employee' as an 'individual who has entered into or works under (or, where the employment has ceased, worked under) a contract of employment'. Section 230(2) provides that a 'contract of employment' means 'a contract of service or apprenticeship, whether express or implied and (if it is express) whether oral or in writing'. This definition does not provide any guidance on when an individual may be said to work under a contract of service (as opposed to a contract for services), which means that in order to determine whether a particular relationship is one of employment (contract of service – referred to in the old cases as a 'master and servant' relationship) or self-employment (contract for services or 'independent contractor') it is necessary to refer to precedents in case law.

There have been many attempts by the courts to provide a simple and easily understandable definition, but in *Montgomery v Johnson Underwood Limited*, the Court of Appeal confirmed that in determining whether a contract of employment exists, the 1968 case of *Ready Mixed Concrete (South East) Limited v Minister of Pensions and National Insurance* offers the best guidance. In the *Ready Mixed Concrete* case it was held that a contract of employment exists if three conditions are fulfilled.

The first condition is that there exists a *mutuality of obligation* between the parties. If an individual agrees to provide his or her own work (ie personal service) and skill for the employer when the employer requires him or her to do so, and the employer in return agrees to provide work for the individual and pay a wage or other remuneration for that work, then there exists a mutuality of obligation.

The second condition is that the individual is *under the control* of the employing company. Relevant factors to be considered when determining if an individual is under the control of the employing company include whether the individual:

- is under a duty to obey orders
- has control over his or her hours
- is subject to the company's disciplinary procedure(s)
- is supervised in his or her mode of working
- provides his or her own equipment
- has to comply with the company's rules on the taking of holidays
- works regular hours
- can delegate his or her duties
- can work for others at the same time as working for the particular company
- is integrated into the employer's business – eg is he or she responsible for issuing management instructions, and does he or she have the power to discipline the company's workers?

Finally – and if the first two tests are satisfied – the third condition is that *other provisions of the contract of employment are consistent with its being a contract of service*. Relevant factors include who has responsibility for tax and National Insurance and whether the individual is eligible to receive sick pay/holiday pay.

Notwithstanding that these factors may be present, the first two factors (mutuality of obligation and control) are the 'irreducible minimum' required for a contract of employment. Once these tests have been satisfied and it is clear that an individual is employed under a contract of employment, he or she effectively has the following full rights under all current employment legislation:

- protection from unfair dismissal
- the statutory redundancy payment
- maternity leave and statutory maternity pay
- statutory sick pay
- parental and urgent family leave

- a minimum period of notice

- a written statement of particulars of employment.

Nevertheless, there are occasions when employers will dispute that an individual is an employee, and in such cases it is necessary to look at the prevailing case law. A useful source of reference in such circumstances is the CIPD Employment Law Service.

Unfortunately, such has been the development in individual employment rights that it is now necessary to look beyond the distinction of employee and non-employee to determine what entitlements an individual might have and take into account the relatively new concept of 'worker'. Section 203(3) of the Employment Rights Act 1996 sets out the definition of a 'worker', but a general definition can be broken down in three parts so that a 'worker' is someone who:

- works under a contract

  - to carry out personal services

    - for another party to the contract.

This definition potentially covers a wide range of individuals who provide personal services under a contract. The great majority of agency workers, homeworkers, casuals and freelances are likely to be 'workers'. Someone who falls within the definition of a 'worker' enjoys rights under the following legislation (rights which are, of course, also conferred on employees):

- the Working Time Regulations 1998

- the National Minimum Wage Act 1998

- the Health and Safety at Work Act 1974

- the Public Interest Disclosure Act 1998

- the Part-Time Workers (Prevention of Less Favourable Treatment) Regulations 2000

- the Employment Rights Act 1996, Part 11 (the right not to have unlawful deductions made from wages)

- the Employment Relations Act 1999, Section 10 (the right to be accompanied at disciplinary and grievance proceedings)

- the Race Relations Act 1976, the Sex Discrimination Act 1975 and the Disability Discrimination Act 1995.

How would you explain to a line manager, the importance of issuing employees with a written statement of their terms and conditions of employment?

Aside from the issue of employment status, one area in which the contract of employment is of vital importance is in the management of change. In Chapter 5 we examine change in the context of employee relations strategies – but there is also a legal dimension to this process, in that the desire for change within an organisation might well involve an alteration to an individual's contract, and how this alteration is managed may have a very significant impact on the employment relationship.

In a strictly legal sense neither employer nor employee can unilaterally change the terms and conditions of employment because a contract can be changed only by mutual agreement. In reality, organisations change their employees' terms and conditions quite frequently, and very often there are little or no discussions about the change. Certainly, it would sometimes be hard to identify where and when the 'mutual agreement' on change happened. It is also wrong to believe that such agreement can be implied simply because the employer 'gives notice' of an intent to make changes. The key is consent. Consent can be gained by either individual or collective negotiation or can be implied by the conduct of the parties. Implied consent may be deemed to have occurred if an individual remains at work for a considerable period after a change has been imposed. Where a unilateral change is imposed, and the employee makes it clear that it is unacceptable, he or she is entitled to treat the contract as repudiated. In such circumstances the employee could argue that he or she has been 'constructively dismissed' and seek a suitable remedy from an employment tribunal.

But, as Lewis and Sargeant (2000) state:

Developments in the law of unfair dismissal make it very difficult for an employee to resist a unilateral variation. Suffice to say at this stage that employers can offer, as a fair reason for dismissal, the fact that there was a sound business reason for insisting on changes being put into effect.

Provided that the managers dealing with the change process operate from a 'good practice' perspective, they should find it relatively easy to satisfy a tribunal that they have acted reasonably. This is particularly true if the majority of employees affected had been prepared to go along with the employer's proposals. There is one caveat to this: the amount of consultation that took place. Although it is not possible to specify what amounts to a reasonable amount of consultation, 'good practice' and common sense would indicate that any consultation would require that employees knew what the changes meant to them personally, knew what, if any, impact the changes would have on their remuneration, their working time and working arrangements, and knew what other options were available to them. It might also be expected that they would have sufficient time to consider the proposals and voice any objections. Common sense should tell any manager that presenting somebody with a *fait accompli* is hardly likely to be judged reasonable.

There will nonetheless be unscrupulous employers who, despite current legal realities, believe that imposing change asserts management's 'right to manage'. They could not be more wrong. There is now over-whelming evidence that individuals work harder, and smarter, when the 'psychological contract' is in a state of high maintenance. Forcing change on people may well be possible, but does it pay dividends? We think not. In this book we have emphasised time and again the need for 'good practice' in employee relations. To use the law as a blunt instru-ment to drive through change could never be described a 'good prac-tice'. Then again, neither are we naïve: some individuals will always resist change, no matter how much you seek to negotiate or consult with them. In such circumstances, and as a last resort, change might have to be imposed – but at least the employer may be seen to have acted in good faith and in the interests of the business.

The function of the law

Notwithstanding the fact that the contract of employment underpins the legal relationship between employers and their employees, it is – as we have said – not a legal text. In the context of employee relations we therefore need to consider the law in a much broader framework. Otto Kahn-Freund in his classic book *Labour and the Law* (1972) stated that the 'principal purpose of labour law [was] to regulate, to support, and to restrain the power of management and the power of organised labour', and he outlined three functions of the law in regulating employee relations that would achieve this purpose. They were:

- The auxiliary function by which the law is designed to promote cer-tain behaviour (for example, collective bargaining) towards certain ends, or by which the law, in the last resort, may actually regulate behaviour. The statutory recognition procedures contained in the Employment Relations Act 1999 are a classic example of this function – as the number of voluntary arrangements made since the Act came into force testify.

- The regulatory function by which the law regulates management's behaviour towards its employees and trade union officers' behav-iour towards their members. This is the area of individual employ-ment rights and the rights of individual trade union members.

- The restrictive function by which the law establishes the 'rules of the game' when employers and employees are in the process of making agreements. This type of legislation effectively lays down the circumstances in which employers and trade unions can impose industrial sanctions on each other without the parties having redress to the legal system.

In this section we link these three functions to various pieces of employment law so that you may understand how the legislative framework develops over time.

The auxiliary function

From the end of World War II and throughout most of the 1950s and 1960s there was tacit support, by both the main political parties and through the legislative process, for the principle of collective bargaining. However, from the late 1960s and throughout the 1970s, employers and some politicians began to challenge this principle because of what they considered an excess of trade union power. This recognition that collective bargaining, and its manipulation by some trade unionists, was a factor in our low-productivity, low-output economy was the reason that some people started to lobby for change. The lobby was highly successful. The idea that the law should be used to promote collective bargaining was anathema to successive Conservative Governments from 1979 to 1997. Certainly, the auxiliary function of the law as described by Kahn-Freund did not figure highly in their legislative programme during this period. In fact, the Employment Act 1980 repealed a statutory trade union recognition procedure that had been introduced in 1975 by the Employment Protection Act, and further legislation during this period actively discouraged the process of collectivism. The Employment Relations Act 1999 – which is discussed in more detail in later chapters – with its provisions for statutory recognition and opportunities for trade union representation at discipline and grievance hearings, may well prove to have reversed such an attitude.

The regulatory function

This second function of the law has provided the foundations for a series of statutory rights individual employees have, relative to their employer. Such rights began to emerge in the early 1960s, when Parliament justified providing them on the grounds that private arrangements (for example, by collective agreement) had failed to establish an adequate minimum acceptable level of protection to individual employees against certain behaviour by their employers. Interestingly, the trade unions were initially opposed to such initiatives as the Redundancy Payments Act because they believed it undermined their own role. At the same time, the introduction of individual rights at work sent a clear message to employers that they must act with just cause and be 'fair and reasonable' in the treatment of their employees on those matters in which statutory minimum standards were being established for their employees.

A floor of legal rights was created, which has since been expanded and developed by successive UK governments and the courts, who have been sympathetic to the view that there should be basic levels of employment protection below which no employee should be permitted to fall. These minimum levels can be enhanced by private agreements – for example, via collective bargaining. Or they may simply be introduced by employers who wish to offer a more attractive employment package. For example, many organisations now offer maternity pay and maternity leave that goes beyond the statutory minimum because they need to attract women back to work after the birth of a child. But this is a matter of policy for individual organisations (see Chapter 5) – what is important for the employee relations professional is to understand the range and importance of these individual rights.

Discrimination

Discrimination law in all its guises continues to be one of the most dynamic and complex areas of employment law. With no cap on the level of compensation payable and with potentially damaging publicity arising out of high-profile cases, employers would be wise to regard the eradication of discrimination, harassment and inequality as of high priority – not just because of the high costs involved, but because unlawful discrimination in any form makes it impossible to foster a climate of good employee relations.

In the UK it is unlawful to treat people less favourably on the ground of their sex or their race, or because they have a disability. This applies during the employment relationship (and to a limited extent after employment) and therefore also applies to less favourable treatment in recruitment, performance review appraisal, training, a compensation package, promotion, or selection for redundancy. Unlike claims of unfair dismissal, in which the level of compensation is capped, discrimination claims are unlimited in the potential amount of the financial award. Moreover, employers can, in appropriate cases, be required to pay compensation for injury to feelings and personal (psychological) injury as well as being required to discharge aggravated or exemplary damages. On top of this, interest can be added to the award of compensation.

For this reason the eradication of discrimination requires a knowledge and understanding of the key legal principles, the ability to monitor changes and developments in the law, and the will to take on board the practical lessons to be learned from cases regarded as legal precedents.

The case of *Garry v London Borough of Ealing*, CA 2001, demonstrates this. One of the key elements an applicant must prove if he or she wishes to succeed in a discrimination complaint is the existence of a detriment – a concept that even the courts have sometimes struggled with. Ms Garry, a Nigerian, worked in the housing department of the London Borough of Ealing (LBE) and dealt with housing benefits. In 1996 her manager learned that in a previous employment with another London borough Ms Garry had been investigated for housing benefit fraud. Furthermore, another Nigerian employee had recently been dismissed for housing benefit fraud at the LBE. The Council initiated a covert special investigation into Ms Garry, which she became aware of only in May 1997. This special investigation was a departure from the more usual form of internal investigation.

Ms Garry was interviewed by an audit officer on 30 June, whose findings were reported to the Director of Housing. He decided that there was insufficient evidence to justify disciplinary action but regrettably failed to inform either the 'suspect' or the special investigator. It appears as if the investigator continued the investigation for almost another year until Ms Garry became anxious and asked what was happening with the enquiry – at which point she was informed that no further action would be taken.

Ms Garry then complained of race discrimination on the basis that a special investigation had been commenced and that it had been continued without her knowledge long after the Council had concluded it should have halted. It was held by the tribunal that the special investigation had indeed been initiated because of the applicant's race (the tribunal observed that it was open to the Council to invoke a quicker and more modest form of internal investigation), but the question of whether she had suffered any actual detriment became the subject of an appeal – first to the Employment Appeals Tribunal and then to the Court of Appeal.

The Court of Appeal had little hesitation in holding that it was no defence to say that ignorance is bliss – ie that because she had not known about the continuing investigation the applicant had suffered no distress or concern. The reality was that some of the applicant's colleagues were at the time or subsequently became aware of the continuing investigation, and it was perfectly possible therefore that some stigma or career damage could arisen. Accordingly, the tribunal's finding of discrimination was upheld.

This case underlines the fact that applicants in race (and by implication, in sex and disability) claims have a low threshold to clear in terms of establishing detriment. It also reminds employment relations practitioners that a person's not hearing or knowing of potentially discriminatory words or conduct does not prevent the person from making a claim of discrimination if he or she becomes aware of it at a later date.

It should also be stressed that in other cases the courts have taken a more restrictive approach to what constitutes a detriment, postulating that a physical or economic manifestation of detriment is necessary. Until this apparent disparity is resolved, employment relations practitioners are advised to assume that the low threshold espoused in the *Garry* case is applicable.

The cost of dealing with complaints of discrimination and harassment and resultant tribunal claims can be prohibitive. There are also a number of business risks. Firstly, there is a major risk to the organisation's reputation, particularly if the case is covered by the press. Secondly, a discrimination claim is also likely to be personally embarrassing and, in all likelihood, distressing for those managers named in the claim. If found to have discriminated, harassed or bullied, managers are likely to be subject to disciplinary action, may be dismissed, and may well find that the claim continues to blight their career thereafter. Thirdly, as we stated above, there is no limit on the amount of a financial award for unlawful discrimination. Finally, there is the issue of management time. Frequently in discrimination claims an employer will be served with a discrimination questionnaire. The time taken to respond to these questionnaires together with the time taken to properly prepare for and attend a tribunal hearing can be substantial.

Employers and individual line managers are most at risk of allegations of discrimination when making key decisions that impact on employees on subjective grounds. What this means in practice, of course, is that when making key decisions about employees, employers must as far as possible base them on objective criteria. By far the best means of minimising the risk of claims is to behave proactively and stop claims from being brought in the first place. In order to do this it is naturally essential that employers are sensitive to potential issues of discrimination and harassment within the workplace, and that steps are taken at an early stage when a potential problem arises.

It is therefore particularly important that employers watch out for the warning signs of possible discrimination/harassment, which include:

- grievances (which may themselves seem somewhat petty)
- 'personality clashes'
- high levels of absenteeism
- ill health (particularly any stress-related illness)
- poor performance (particularly where there has been a sudden downturn in performance following some change in the working arrangements)
- negative comments through peer evaluation/appraisal process
- high levels of staff departures
- negative comments during exit interviews.

There are very few employers or individual line managers who do not genuinely want to eradicate discrimination and harassment from their workplace. If asked to pinpoint where employers/line managers with the best of intentions have gone wrong, the majority of employment lawyers would tell you that they have waited too long before obtaining advice and assistance from their own personnel specialist. If line managers are facing a difficult personnel issue, are having to make high-risk decisions or believe they have spotted the warning signs of a potential dispute within their team, then clearly the first action they should take – rather than seeking to resolve it themselves – is to pick up the phone and call for help. But for this to happen, the employee relations specialist must ensure that he or she enjoys the confidence of line manager colleagues – confidence that is gained through offering reliable, consistent advice.

Time and again cases indicate that if action is taken at an early stage, potential problems can be resolved. Often problems can be resolved using an employer's internal grievance procedure, particularly if it allows any grievance to be dealt with confidentially. If, however, potential problems are not dealt with at an early stage, there will be an increasing risk of potentially damaging claims, liability and costs, as already outlined.

Does your organisation have an anti-discrimination policy? What are the business-case arguments you would use to justify such policies?

Dismissal and redundancy

Although discrimination law might be one of the most dynamic and complex areas of employment law, the law relating to unfair dismissal and redundancy continues to provide the bulk of the practitioner's workload. In Chapters 10 (Managing employee performance and behaviour) and 12 (Managing redundancies) we look at the skills that are required to manage these two important issues in much greater detail, but in the context of Kahn-Freund's regulatory function these individual rights are a key area for any employee relations professional.

By virtue of section 94 of the Employment Rights Act 1996, an employee who, at the effective date of termination (EDT) has continuous service of one year or more with his or her employer, has a right not to be unfairly dismissed and is afforded the right also to present a complaint on the matter to an employment tribunal. In order to defend successfully an employee's claim for unfair dismissal, an employer must be able to satisfy an employment tribunal of three things:

- that the real or principal reason for the dismissal was one of the potentially fair reasons set out in section 98(2) of the Employment Rights Act 1996;

  - that it was reasonable to dismiss in all the circumstances of the case; and

    - that the employer followed a fair procedure.

The potentially fair reasons for dismissal (each individually potentially sufficient) are:

- incapability (including ill health) or lack of qualifications
- misconduct
- redundancy
- contravention of statute (eg no work permit for the employee)
- 'some other substantial reason'.

Concerns often arise when employers seek to attach a label to the 'reason' that they are dismissing an employee. This has been especially true in, for example, cases of persistent short-term absences. Where employees have been dismissed on these grounds, some employers have sought to justify their actions by classifying the dismissal as being for incapability arising from sickness, whereas others have classified the dismissal as being on the basis of poor conduct relating to the employee's attendance. Understandably, this has caused employers some concern in that they had difficulty in satisfying themselves that they had a potentially fair reason for dismissal. To their relief, the Employment Appeals Tribunal sought to resolve this difficulty in the case of *Post Office v Wilson*, in which it indicated that employment tribunals should consider whether any of the reasons set out in section 98(2) applied to the facts before them, and if none of these categories fitted the facts, the tribunal should then consider whether the employer had established 'some other substantial reason' for dismissal. The burden of proof in establishing the reason for dismissal lies squarely with the employer, although in most cases this burden is not difficult to discharge.

However, there are a number of circumstances in which an employee's dismissal are held to be automatically unfair. They include situations in which the employee can show that the real reason for dismissal was in fact related to:

- valid health and safety factors

- maternity

- dependant care or parental leave

- the employee's assertion of a statutory right

- the participation by the employee in industrial action within the first eight weeks of that industrial action

- the employee's membership or non-membership of a trade union, or to his or her participation in trade union activities

- redundancy, where the employee was selected for redundancy for any of the reasons set out above

- being a shop worker or betting worker who refused to work on Sundays

- the appointment of the employee as a member-nominated trustee of the employees' pension fund, or to his or her exercising the duties of such a trustee

- the employee's election (or seeking election) as employee representative for the purposes of consultation over collective redundancies or transfers of undertakings, or to the employee's proposing to perform any such functions or activities

- a business transfer to which the Transfer of Undertakings (Protection of Employment) Regulations 1981 apply

- a spent conviction or failure on the part of the employee to disclose it

- a disclosure qualifying under the Public Interest Disclosure Act 1998, or exercising rights under the Working Time Regulations 1998, the National Minimum Wage Act 1998 or the Tax Credits Act 1999.

Individual employees enforce their rights on discrimination, redundancy, unfair dismissal and a range of other matters via employment tribunals We will examine the nature and jurisdiction of tribunals later in the chapter, but suffice to say here that they are independent judicial bodies set up with the objective of dealing with employment disputes quickly, informally and cheaply.

The sheer variety of potentially unfair reasons for dismissal, or claims for discrimination, indicates that for the employee relations professional there is no room for complacency. An incorrectly handled dismissal, a failure to deal with a complaint of discrimination, an ill-advised decision in respect of a business transfer or health and safety issue, can mean an appearance before an employment tribunal. Even when things are done properly, the area of law that deals with individual rights at work can still give rise to a vast amount of litigation. The number of complaints brought by employees continues to rise and is now in excess of 50,000 per annum.

> Some employers believe that the law prevents them from dismissing employees. Does it? If it doesn't, why doesn't it? If it does, how does it?

The rights of union members
As well as the statutory floor of rights for employees, union members have their own additional statutory rights. These rights, which were considerably extended under the post-1979 Conservative Governments, have been justified on the grounds that trade unions had to be made more democratic, more accountable to their members, and to exercise their power more responsibly. As UK industrial relations declined in the 1960s and 1970s, there was a widespread belief that trade union leaders were, without collecting the views of their members, coercing them to undertake labour market activities (for example, undertaking industrial action) that were harmful to their employment security. In short, the notion was current that a large proportion of strike activity was the result of political idealism on the part of trade union officials, rather than the consequence of a breakdown in collective bargaining.

This view resulted in the enactment of a series of measures to provide positive rights for union members to participate in or restrain union decision-making on specific issues. The main trade union member rights are:

- the opportunity to participate in regular secret postal ballots, at least once every 10 years, to decide whether or not the union should establish, or retain, a political fund financed by political fund contribution, independent of the normal union subscription

- to elect all voting members of the union's executive (including its president and general secretary) by secret postal ballot at least once every five years

- to participate in a secret ballot before the union takes organised industrial action against an employer

- not to be called upon to participate in industrial action not supported by a properly conducted secret ballot

- not to be disciplined unjustifiably by the union

- to be able to inspect the union's accounting records.

As a means of helping individual union members to enforce their rights, the Employment Act 1988 provided the means by which they could seek assistance if they were considering or taking legal action against their union.

The restrictive function

Ever since 1871 trade unions have – except when they were undermined by the Taff Vale decision in 1901 – enjoyed immunity from actions for civil damages. That is, they have been protected from being sued simply because they took, or were taking, industrial action. The basic immunity framework was contained in the Trade Disputes Act 1906, and this remained in force until 1971 when the Conservative Government introduced the Industrial Relations Act. This act limited trade union immunity by introducing the concept of 'unfair industrial practices' which, if unions committed them, gave those affected by such activities the right to sue for damages.

The Trade Union and Labour Relations Act 1974 repealed the Industrial Relations Act 1971 and returned the trade unions' immunity position back to that provided by the Trades Disputes Act 1906. The Trade Union and Labour Relations (Amendment) Act 1976 then extended trade union immunity to cover the breach of all contracts for which trade unions were responsible when they called their members out on industrial action. This gave trade unions licence to persuade their members to take secondary industrial action. 'Secondary action' refers to measures taken against an employer with whom the trade union has no dispute but who might, for example, be a key customer of an employer with whom they currently do have an industrial dispute. By taking this type of industrial action the union would hope to provoke the secondary employer into putting pressure on the employer involved in the main dispute to settle the dispute on terms more favourable than currently on offer.

By 1976 trade unions had a very wide immunity from legal action in the case of industrial disputes. They could call, without incurring legal liability, for industrial action in connection with any kind of industrial dispute, no matter how remote those taking the action were from the original dispute. Nobody seriously challenged this union legislative position until 1979 when, as we noted above, there were moves to clamp down on the unions' abuse of their power. Legislation thereafter came at regular intervals, so that between 1980 and 1993 there were seven Acts of Parliament designed to restrict trade union activity and behaviour.

- The Employment Act 1980 removed the unions' immunity if their members engaged in picketing premises other than their own place of work when they took industrial action.

- The Employment Act 1982 narrowed the definition of a trade dispute, outlawed the practice of pressuring employers not to include non-union firms on tender lists, and enabled employers to take out an injunction to restrict industrial action or to sue unions for damages where they were responsible for unlawful industrial action.

- The Trade Union Act 1984 introduced pre-strike ballots.

- The Employment Act 1988 effectively outlawed the closed shop.

- The Employment Act 1990 removed unions' immunity if they organised any type of secondary action in support of an individual dismissed for taking unlawful action.

- The Trade Union and Labour Relations (Consolidation) Act 1992 brought together in one piece of legislation much of the law relating to collective provision.

- The Trade Union Reform and Employment Rights Act 1993 made some amendments to existing legal requirements, most particularly in relation to ballots on industrial action.

These pieces of legislation substantially increased the grounds on which an employer may take legal action against a union. The circumstances in which unions can claim immunity from civil action have been restricted and now include accompanying provisions that require full-time officials to repudiate the actions of lay officials if they take actions contrary to the legislation. If union immunity is to be maintained, such repudiation has to be meaningful, and the courts can require unions to present evidence as to the steps they have taken to bring their members within the law.

> Outline, with appropriate examples, the functions of the law in employee relations

There is now no serious argument over whether these reforms were both necessary and timely. For unions to be required to hold a pre-strike ballot of their members prior to taking industrial action has since become part of the employee relations landscape and is not seriously questioned. Similarly, the requirement that full-time union officials should be subject to periodic re-election has become part of the fabric of trade union organisation.

The nature and jurisdiction of employment tribunals

Employment tribunals are independent judicial bodies – 'inferior courts' within the meaning of the Rules of the Supreme Court. For administrative convenience the country is divided into regions, each of which has its own regional chairman and regional office. Applications to tribunals are made to the appropriate regional office.

The employment tribunal is a statutory body: its composition is governed by the Employment Tribunals Act (ETA) 1996, and the rules for its administration are set out in various regulations together with the Employment Rights (Dispute Resolution) Act 1998.

The tribunal usually comprises three members:

- a legally qualified chairman (a solicitor or barrister of at least seven years' qualification)
- an employer representative
- an employee representative (usually a trade union representative).

An employment tribunal has jurisdiction in a wide range of matters derived from various statutory provisions. Each case is initiated with an application, which is subject to its own time-limit that the employment tribunal usually has a discretion to extend.

The application process

Proceedings are commenced when an employee (the applicant) presents an originating application form ETI, which lists the names and addresses of the persons against whom relief is sought (the respondent), and the grounds (with particulars) on which the relief is sought.

Once the application is received, it is registered and a copy sent to the respondent and another to the Advisory, Conciliation and Arbitration Service (ACAS). To the copy sent to the respondent the tribunal attaches a blank form of 'notice of appearance', form ET3, which the respondent has 21 days to complete. Not all cases proceed to a full hearing, and it is open to either party to request on receipt of notice – or to the tribunal of its own volition to stipulate – that a case be considered in a preliminary hearing.

Either party may apply to the tribunal to order the other party – or the tribunal may of its own volition require both parties – to provide further and better particulars of any grounds upon which they rely, or any facts or contentions that are relevant to their claim. The essence of such further particulars is to enable each party to know in advance the nature of the case that it must meet at the hearing. Failure to provide further particulars can result in the 'striking out' of the ET1 or the ET3. In connection with the requirement to provide further and better particulars, a tribunal can order the disclosure and inspection of documents, and set a time and a place for compliance. As with further particulars, disclosure is an important step in the process of enabling the parties to know the nature and extent of the case to which they have to respond. Revised tribunal rules of procedure, which came into force in 2001, allow tribunals the power to strike out applications, and/or award costs, when a party to the proceedings does not comply with a directions order. This change has meant that the importance of compliance with any directions made is greatly increased. The new rules have also widened the circumstances in which tribunals can award costs: an award can now be made if a party, or its representative, has conducted proceedings vexatiously, abusively or disruptively.

The hearing and the decision

Both parties must ensure that their witnesses are ready and willing to attend the tribunal, and that following any required disclosure of information (known in legal terms as 'discovery') they have in their possession all necessary and relevant documents. Every encouragement is given to the parties to agree on documents – indeed, tribunals much prefer that the parties prepare an agreed 'bundle' of documents for use during the hearing.

Individual applicants may appear before a tribunal without representation or may be represented by a lawyer, a trade union official or any other person of their choice. If they are unrepresented, the tribunal does what it can to assist them while ensuring that there is no bias.

Although there is no specific rule that dictates the order in which evidence is given, it usually depends on who has the burden of proof. In unfair dismissal cases, where dismissal is admitted, the respondent employer begins. If dismissal is not admitted, or it is incumbent upon the applicant to prove his or her case – for example, in constructive dismissal – the applicant begins. In order to speed up the process of evidence-giving tribunals encourage the production of witness statements that can then be read out at the hearing.

Once a witness has given evidence, he or she may be cross-examined by the other side and may also have to answer questions put to them by the tribunal members. When the parties have called all their witnesses they are given an opportunity to make their final submissions. Generally, the party that presented evidence first has the final word. Finally, the tribunal withdraws to consider its decision. Tribunals usually indicate whether they can announce their decision on the day of the hearing, or whether it will be delivered later in writing to the parties. If it is the applicant who is successful, both parties often have to make further submissions in respect of the size of any compensation payment or of the type of relief to be granted.

You are asked by your line manager to explain the procedure used in employment tribunal hearings. What do you tell him or her?

Tribunal reform

The Government has signalled its intention to further reform the tribunal system. The Employment Act 2002 contains a number of changes in relation to tribunals – in particular:

- granting the Secretary of State power to make regulations authorising Employment Appeal Tribunals, in all types of cases, to make awards of costs directly against a party's representative because of the way the representative has conducted the proceedings – and to relieve a party of the duty to pay some or all of their representative's charges; and to order one party to pay the other party's costs of preparing a case for hearing

- granting the Secretary of State power to make regulations to introduce a fixed period of conciliation by ACAS by ordering a stay of proceedings for a defined period

- granting the Secretary of State power to redraft the standard forms used for originating applications (ET1) and notice of appearance (ET3), making their use mandatory for the first time, and the forms for requiring each party to give more information, together with certain documents such as the written particulars of employment

- granting the presidents of employment tribunals in England and Wales and Scotland respectively power to issue practice directions, in order to ensure a consistent approach by tribunals around the country

- making it clear that at pre-hearing reviews, a tribunal has the power not only to require a deposit of £500 to be paid but also to strike out weak cases (a power to be used sparingly and only where there is no need to consider the evidence or where no conflict of evidence exists).

The ACAS scheme

ACAS was empowered by the Employment Rights (Dispute Resolution) Act 1998 to operate an arbitration scheme as an alternative to employment tribunal hearings. The implications of the scheme are far-reaching, so before submitting to arbitration the parties should be aware of the process involved.

The central features of the arbitration scheme are that it is (meant to be):

- voluntary
- speedy
- informal
- confidential
- free from legal arguments.

With these aims, it is thought by many that the scheme heralds a return to the idealism of the original tribunals of the mid-1960s. The scheme is currently only applicable to unfair dismissal complaints, so that where an individual's complaint includes that and another claim, only the unfair dismissal part may be referred to the arbitrator.

Recourse to the scheme must be by mutual consent. Where an ET1 form has already been submitted, the parties can enter this scheme either by means of an initial settlement reached with the help of ACAS or through a separate compromise agreement. In both cases the parties agree that the final claim will be settled by arbitration under the scheme.

On the other hand, if any term within a separate compromise agreement effectively restricts the ACAS arbitrator's freedom of final decision in arbitrating, it is extremely likely that ACAS will refuse to accept the referral. Any agreement by disputant parties to refer the matter to ACAS arbitration should therefore contain a provision to the effect that such referral to the ACAS arbitrator is subject to ACAS's acceptance of the referral. Even the absence of such a provision might cause the ACAS arbitrator to refuse to take up the case for as long as the applicant has agreed to withdraw his or her application (ET1) to the employment tribunal.

Arbitration under the scheme is on standard terms only, which cannot be varied. If the arbitrator, having regard to the ACAS code of practice, finds a dismissal to have been unfair, the remedy set may be reinstatement, re-engagement or compensation.

The hearing

The parties are expected to co-operate with the arbitrator in setting a hearing date. This should be within two months of ACAS's being notified of the agreement to go to arbitration, which is intended to ensure a speedy solution. In agreeing to go to arbitration, the parties also agree that they will co-operate fully in the process leading up to the hearing, such as exchanging copies of documents they wish to rely on, forwarding details of witnesses (at least seven days before the hearing), swapping witness statements, and so forth. Although the arbitrator – unlike a tribunal chairman – has no power to order either party to comply with these requirements, adverse inferences may be drawn from failure to do so.

The arbitrator is responsible for the conduct of hearings. The general principles stipulate that the language of the proceedings is English, there are no preliminary oaths or affirmations, and parties are free to engage representatives and bring witnesses if they wish. No special status is accorded to legally qualified representatives. The arbitrator decides on procedural and evidential matters. His or her approach is inquisitorial, and there is no direct cross-examination. Questions between the parties may only be addressed through the arbitrator.

The applicant may withdraw from the process at any time, provided it is done formally with written documentation to the arbitrator or to ACAS. The parties are also free to reach private agreement to settle the dispute before the end of the hearing. The arbitrator can endorse such an agreement but not interpret it or ratify it in any way. This power is limited to agreements that are in the arbitrator's remit – ie unfair dismissal disputes.

The arbitrator's decision is delivered in writing, includes references to general considerations and reasoning taken into account in reaching the decision, and is sent to both parties at the same time within a three-week deadline. As noted above, the arbitrator has the power only to award reinstatement, re-engagement or compensation. The amount of any compensation awarded will be reasonable in the circumstances, taking into account the established practice of and statutory limits imposed on employment tribunals. The arbitrator's decision will not be published nor lodged with the employment tribunal – which makes the process very attractive if the issue in dispute is of a sensitive nature or if publicity is preferably to be avoided.

There is no appeal on a point of law in respect of the arbitrator's award, which is final and binding on both parties. Appeals in respect of the conduct of the arbitrator – a matter that may occasionally be of concern to some – are possible only on the grounds of serious irregularity.

Any award is enforceable in the county courts in England and Wales and in the sheriff's court in Scotland, with interest payable as appropriate under the rules of such courts. Awards involving reinstatement or re-engagement that are not complied with should be referred to an employment tribunal.

The speed, informality and relative inexpense of the arbitration scheme is of particular attraction, along with the fact that the scheme affords a form of resolution that allows a case to be concluded without undue publicity. However, in the light of the fact that no cross-examination is permitted, no reference made to precedent cases and no forensic approach adopted by tribunals, some may be concerned that the circumstances of a particular case might benefit from rather more intimate scrutiny. Furthermore, there is inevitably an element of the unknown about the scheme, exacerbated by the fact that the arbitrator is not bound by precedent, and it is felt by some that this will lead to novel, potentially inconsistent results and a consequent inability to anticipate the outcome of any hearing.

> Explain *three* advantages *and* disadvantages to an employer in agreeing to have alleged unfair dismissal claims decided by voluntary arbitration through ACAS rather than by an employment tribunal.

Recent developments in the law

For personnel practitioners, dealing with the law should be second nature, and taking account of the law in decision-making ought to be automatic. However, throughout the 1960s, 1970s and 1980s the scope of the law was relatively narrow and could be neatly categorised as 'individual' or 'collective'. Latterly, however, that scope has widened. New pieces of legislation continue to be introduced, requiring the employee relations professional to be particularly vigilant in monitoring them. In the concluding part of this chapter we look at some of these developments and seek to forecast what their impact is likely to be.

Developments in discrimination law

We have already said that discrimination law is one of the most dynamic and complex areas of employment law, and yet its scope and coverage is set to change dramatically over the next five years. The reason for this potentially radical shift can be found in the European Union Anti-Discrimination Framework Directive. The Race and the Employment Directives were adopted under Article 13 of the EC Treaty by the UK and other European member states in 2000. Together, they provide a common framework of protection against discrimination and harassment.

The Employment Directive (2000/78/EC) prohibits discrimination in the context of sexual orientation, religion or belief, disability and age. It applies to conditions for access to employment, self-employment and occupation, including selection criteria and recruitment conditions; to working conditions, including dismissals and pay; to vocational guidance and training; and to the membership of employers' and workers' organisations or professional bodies.

The Race Directive (2000/43/EC) prohibits discrimination on the grounds of race and ethnic origin. It applies to the same areas as the Employment Directive and, in addition, to social protection (including social security and healthcare); to education; to goods and services available to the public, including housing; and to social advantages (which covers things like housing benefit, student maintenance grants and loans, bus passes for senior citizens, etc).

There are a number of important points to note about the scope of the Directives:

- They apply to both the public and private sectors, regardless of the size of the organisation (there is no small firm exemption). The armed forces can, however, be excluded from legislation implementing the provisions on age and disability.

- 'Pay' is likely to include all types of remuneration and fringe benefits such as performance-related pay, group insurance (eg private healthcare insurance provided as part of an employment package) and occupational pensions.

- All state benefits (including state pensions) are excluded from the scope of the Employment Directive. The Directive also allows member states to set specific ages at which occupational pension schemes mature and, in this context, provides that such age criteria in actuarial calculations should not be regarded as age discrimination.

- 'Access to employment' covers employment agencies and bodies that award licences or qualifications needed to carry out a particular job (eg the Public Carriage Office which licenses taxi-drivers in London).

- 'Vocational training' has a wide meaning. It covers not only in-house training provided by an employer but also courses or studies that provide training for jobs or professions, including most university degrees and many other further- and higher-education courses (for example, teacher training courses).

The Government has already indicated that there will be separate items of legislation for each of the strands in the Directives in order for there to be sufficient time for consultation and preparation. Legislation on discrimination for race, sexual orientation and religion will be implemented first, in the second half of 2003, and the other strands follow, so that by 2006 new legislation on disability and age discrimination will also be on the statute-book.

What will the business implications be for your organisation in complying with the European Union Anti-Discrimination Framework Directive? Give reasons for your answers.

Fixed-term employees

The European Community (EC) Directive on fixed-term work was agreed by the European Council in 1999 and has the broad aim of preventing fixed-term employees from being less favourably treated than permanent employees doing similar work. It also aims to limit the scope for using a series of fixed-term contracts to employ the same person in an essentially permanent position, and to improve access to training and to information on permanent jobs for fixed-term employees. The Government is required to implement the Directive by 10 July 2002; in April 2001 the Government issued a set of draft regulations and began a consultation process. The draft regulations and the consultation document indicated that the following provisions for fixed-term employees were likely:

- Fixed-term employees will be defined as employees (or ex-employees) who work under a contract of employment fixed for a term in advance or agreed to terminate upon the occurrence (or non-occurrence) of a specified event.

- A fixed-term employee will have the right not to be treated less favourably than a comparable non-fixed-term employee engaged in the same or broadly similar work, either in connection with the terms and conditions of employment or by being subjected to a detriment. There is a defence of objective justification.

- A fixed-term employee who suspects that he or she is receiving less favourable treatment will be able to ask for written reasons for that treatment. If the employer fails to provide written reasons, a tribunal is entitled to draw an adverse inference.

- An employee working under a fixed-term contract will have a right to be notified by the employer of any suitable 'permanent' (ie non-fixed-term) vacancies that may become available.

- Where an employer renews a fixed-term contract, and the employee has been working for four years (or more) under a series of fixed-term contracts, it will be deemed by law to become an indefinite contract and any attempt to fix the term will be void.

Following the consultation process the government issued revised draft regulations which contained – in the view of the CBI and other employers' organisations – some highly contentious proposals on pay and pensions. In the initial consultative phase the Government took the view that the Directive did not require pay and pensions to count as comparable employment conditions, because Directives brought in under the Social Chapter (see Chapter 4) do not include pay. However, the Government has since announced that in the light of new evidence of pay disparities between fixed-term and permanent employees, it intends to go beyond the strict requirements of the Directive to cover pay and pensions. It remains to be seen whether the lobbying of the CBI and others will influence the Government, but early indications are that it will not.

Employee consultation

In 1998 the European Commission, encouraged by the success of the European Works Council Directive, published a draft Directive on

Information and Consultation of Workers at national level. After some hesitation, the UK Government finally signed up to the Directive in 2001, and some of its provisions could become law by 2004. The precise shape of any new legislation will depend on how the Government intends to transpose the Directive into UK law, but it looks as though the main elements will be that UK companies will be required to consult with employee representatives and provide them with information on:

- recent and future probable development of the business's activities and economic situation

- the situation, structure and probable development of employment within the business, and any anticipatory measures envisaged – in particular, any potential threat to employment

- decisions likely to lead to substantial changes in work organisation or in contractual relations.

This will affect an employer's ability to keep secret mergers, disposals and acquisitions, plans to change terms and conditions of employment and planned reduction programmes.

Some of the practical arrangements for informing and consulting will be left to member states to determine. In the UK this is likely to mean that consultation will take place with trade unions where trade unions are already recognised, and that the election of employee representatives will take place only where there is no existing recognition agreement. It is likely that employers will have the option of reaching voluntary agreements by which they may negotiate arrangements for consulting that differ from those set out in Article 4 of the Directive.

Other legal developments

The developments described above are, or will be, of direct relevance to employers and employees. But one other piece of legislation that does not specifically relate to employment matters has nevertheless impacted upon the work of the personnel professional and must be taken account of and its significance understood.

The Human Rights Act (HRA)

The Convention for the Protection of Human Rights and Fundamental Freedoms ('the Convention') was signed by the UK in 1950, and in 1951 the UK was the first to ratify it, but until recently UK citizens were only able to pursue cases before the European Court of Human Rights in Strasbourg and were not able to rely directly on European Convention rights in UK legal proceedings or to bring a claim for breach of Convention rights in a UK court or tribunal.

The rights provided for within the European Convention on Human Rights include:

- (Article 2) the 'right to life'

- (Article 3) the right not to be tortured (effectively a prohibition on torture)

- (Article 4) the right not to be treated as a slave (effectively a prohibition on forced labour)

- (Article 5) the right to liberty and security

- (Article 6) the right to a fair trial

- (Article 7) the right not to be punished without prior and due process of law

- (Article 8) the right to have one's private and family life respected

- (Article 9) the right to freedom of thought, conscience and religion

- (Article 10) the right to freedom of expression

- (Article 11) the right to freedom of assembly and association

- (Article 12) the right to live with a partner of one's choosing (if available and willing)

- (Article 14) the right not to be discriminated against (effectively a prohibition on discrimination).

One of the present Government's manifesto promises was to incorporate the Convention into UK law. It was this manifesto promise that led to the enactment of the Human Rights Act 1998. The act – which came into force on 2 October 2000 – states in its preamble that it is 'an Act to give effect to the rights and freedoms guaranteed under the European Convention on Human Rights ...'. Although it is not specifically a piece of employment legislation, it impacts on employment law in three ways:

- Courts and employment tribunals are obliged to construe domestic legislation compatibly with the European Convention on Human Rights (ECHR) so far as it is possible to do so.

- Courts and employment tribunals must themselves act compatibly with the ECHR, save where they are prevented from doing so by primary legislation.

- Public bodies must act compatibly with ECHR (specifically in their employment policies and procedures), again save where they are prevented from doing so by primary legislation.

The impact of the Act on different types of employer
The position in an employment context is this. A public authority (such as Central Government or the police) is required to act at all times compatibly with Convention rights. Insofar as an employer has acted in breach of a Convention right in respect of a particular employee, then

that employee can instigate proceedings. Private employers, however, are not required to act compatibly with Convention rights, regardless of the capacity in which they are acting.

The impact of the Act on courts and tribunals

It would be a mistake, though, to assume that the Act does not have implications for a private sector employer or for a public sector employer when acting in a private context. The Act will still be relevant to the actions of such an employer because of its impact on UK courts and tribunals. The Act will affect UK courts and tribunals in the following ways:

- Courts or tribunals are required to act compatibly with Convention rights. (This is because for the purposes of the Act 'public authority' is expressly defined as including courts and tribunals.)

- Courts and tribunals are required to take into account European Court of Human Rights jurisprudence when considering an issue relating to a Convention right.

- Courts and tribunals are required to interpret UK legislation in a way that is compatible with Convention rights *so far as it is possible to do so.*

It is, however, early days in the operation of the Act, and it remains to be seen whether and how its impact will be felt over a much longer period.

Implications of the Act in an employment context

As we have said above, the exact impact of the Act and particular Convention rights remain unclear and will depend upon how UK courts and tribunals interpret their role under the Act, and what they make of particular Convention rights. Notwithstanding this, it is possible to identify potential implications, and there can be little doubt that litigants and their lawyers will seek to link Convention rights with employment rights. For example, Article 6 – which provides for the right to a fair trial – might be used to include the admissibility or otherwise of evidence in tribunal hearings. Tribunals will have to consider whether to admit such evidence as obtained from phone-tapping or searches of a company's e-mail system, where that evidence has been obtained in breach of Article 8, which guarantees the right to have one's private and family life respected.

There is also the issue of legal aid. The philosophy behind employment tribunals is that proceedings should not be overly legalistic, and that it should therefore not be necessary for a party to have legal representation. Consistent with this there is, accordingly, no right to legal aid. In practice, of course, tribunal hearings are frequently complex and require an understanding of statute and case law as well as tribunal procedures. There is a potential issue, logically, as to whether the right to a fair trial necessarily involves real access to legal representation and, consequently, legal aid. This might particularly be a question in complex proceedings or in a harassment case where an unrepresented applicant would have to cross-examine his or her alleged harasser.

Similarly, Article 10 – which guarantees the right to freedom of expression – might be used by employees to sound the death knell for employers' dress codes.

But potentially the most contentious issue might arise over Article 11 – which affords the right to freedom of assembly and association. Article 11's principal significance is in relation to trade unions and their activities. The provisions of the Trade Union and Labour Relations (Consolidation) Act 1992 ('TULRCA'), following the coming into force of the Act, have to be interpreted in a way that is compatible with Article 11 insofar as this is possible – and the general view of commentators is that by and large it should be possible.

One area in which it is felt that Article 11 is especially likely to be relevant is picketing, where the question revolves around whether the existing provisions contained within TULReCA section 220 and the code of practice on picketing – Code of Practice: Picketing (1992) – create a reasonable balance between the right to protest and the interests of those affected by protest. In particular, it has been suggested that although these provisions generally do create a reasonable balance, there may be room for argument that certain provisions – such as, for example, those that limit the number of pickets on site to six – go beyond this.

A further issue concerns the right to be a member of a particular trade union/not to join a trade union: there have already been a number of cases focusing on this issue before the European Court. It has also been argued that because Article 11 gives a right to form and join trade unions for the 'protection of interests', then this must necessarily involve a right to representation. There is, however, European Court of Human Rights case law, which makes clear that there is no right on the part of a union to insist on being consulted on behalf of its members.

Finally, there is the matter of the 'right to strike'. It has been held that the right to strike is one of the rights protected by Article 11. Yet the consensus of commentators is that it is likely to be reasonable for a state to impose significant restrictions on this right.

What is certain is that it is likely that trade unions and their lawyers will seek to use Article 11 in order to extend their rights to picket, strike and represent their members. The extent to which they will be successful in this remains to be seen.

> Has the Human Rights Act made any impact on your organisation (or on one with which you are familiar)?

CONCLUSION

In this chapter we have tried to identify the relationship between good employee relations and the law. We have stressed that employee relations is as much about 'good practice' as it is about legal compliance, but we have recognised that the employee relations professional cannot afford to be dismissive of the law. This is because the law impacts on almost every activity in the workplace. Furthermore, individual employees are very much aware of their 'rights' at work and may not hesitate to use the mechanisms open to them (such as employment tribunals) to assert those rights. We have tried to demonstrate that the legal intervention comes from two sources – from the political choices of the national governing party and from developments within Europe. We have examined the role of employment tribunals and investigated alternatives to the accepted method of dispute resolution. Finally, we have looked at some, but not all, particular legal developments that we believe will impact on the work of the employee relations professional.

KEY POINTS

- Because all employee relations decisions have the capacity for legal challenge, it is important for managements to operate 'good practice'.

- The sheer variety of potentially unfair reasons for dismissal, or of claims of discrimination, indicates that for the employee relations professional there is no room for complacency.

- Union members have rights allowing them to participate in or restrain union decision-making on specific issues.

- The contract of employment is one of the most important legal instruments that affect the employment relationship.

- Discrimination has to be taken seriously, and steps taken to eradicate it.

- The scale of legal development is such that employee relations professionals must constantly monitor changes and endeavour to improve their own knowledge in the area.

Further reading

BERCUSSON B. (1997) *European Labour Law*. Butterworth.

CHARTERED INSTITUTE OF PERSONNEL AND DEVELOPMENT *Employment Law Service*.

Employee Relations Act 1999

Employment Rights Act 1996

Employment Act 2002

IRS (2000) *Employment Review – Policy, Practice and Law in the Workplace*.

KAHN-FREUND O. (1972) *Labour and the Law*. Stevens.

Lewis D *and* SARGEANT M. (2000) *Essentials of Employment Law*. 6th edn London, CIPD.

LEWIS D. *and* SARGEANT M. (2002) *Essentials of Employment Law*. 7th edn. London, CIPD.

O'DEMPSEY D., ALLEN A. BELGRAVE S. and BROWN J. (2001) *Employment Law and the Human Rights Act 1998*. Jordan.

4 • The European Union

CHAPTER OBJECTIVES

After you have read this chapter you should be able to:

- explain the influence of the European Union on employee relations management in the UK

- outline the main developments in the social dimension to the European Single Market

- describe the key institutions of the European Union

- understand the legislative processes of the European Union

- appreciate the unique opportunity for 'social partner' organisations at the inter-professional and sectoral level to shape, draft and determine the scope of all new EU employment and social legislation (the so-called social dialogue process)

- explain the Social Chapter of the European Union

- identify how the Social Chapter of the European Union impinges on the everyday work of the employee relations professional in the fields of equal opportunities, employment protection/working conditions, employee relations and health and safety at work.

The importance of the European Union

The influence of the European Union (EU) on personnel/HR management in the UK is considerable. First, in the areas of employment and social legislation its influence on nearly all areas of the employment relationship has grown dramatically since the mid-1990s. As successive EU employment Directives have been adopted at EU level and then implemented in UK law, there has been a requirement in almost all cases to introduce significant change to existing custom and practice. The extent to which the EU has instigated UK legislation is thus considerable. Collective redundancies, transfers of undertakings, acquired rights, proof of an employment relationship, information and consultation, part-time and fixed-term work, pregnancy and maternity leave and payment, parental leave, transfer of employees to another EU member state, working time and equal opportunities are all areas in which EU legislation now directly impinges on the everyday work of the UK personnel professional.

Implementation of an EU Directive into the UK does not end the changes to previous law, custom and practice. Further changes to personnel/HR policy can occur after implementation. As a result of incorrect implementation, cases can be and have been taken before the European Court of Justice. For example, in 2001 the trade union BECTU argued successfully before the European Court of Justice that the British Government had implemented the Working Time Directive incorrectly. In giving effect to this Directive, the UK Government had imposed a qualifying period for entitlement to paid holidays of 13 weeks. The European Court ruled that this qualifying period was not consistent with the provisions of the Working Time Directive under which workers are entitled, from day 1, to accrue annual paid holiday leave at the rate of one twelfth of the annual entitlement per month actually worked, rounded to the nearest half day.

Second, the decision by the UK to become a signatory to the Social Chapter has involved the UK's allocating a unique role to the 'social partner' organisations, the TUC and the CBI, to shape, draft and determine the scope of all new EU employment and social legislation. The TUC and CBI, as the UK members of the ETUC and UNICE, the trade union and employer organisations at EU level, participate in determining the law which directly affects every employer and employee in the UK. Although the UK Government remains responsible for implementing EU laws that emerge from social partner agreements between the ETUC and UNICE in the traditional way, it can be argued that the CBI and TUC are parties to legally enforceable collective agreements. Such agreements, as we saw in Chapter 1, have been uncommon in the past within the UK. In the longer term, the consequences of this change in legislative power at the EU level could lead to an increase in the influence of the CBI and the TUC in determining the shape of how EU law is implemented in the UK.

Third, the EU does not stand still. Not only do new treaties introduce new areas of competency within which the EU can legislate but the EU process itself creates a steady stream of legislative action requiring implementation at member state level. At present, each member state of the EU holds the EU Presidency for six months. It has become a regular feature of each Presidency, regardless of which member state is holding the Presidency, that action is taken in a wide range of areas. Employment issues are regarded as a key area at an EU political level. There is also the fact that there is an inbuilt mechanism in all EU legislation that creates further change. Each EU law or Directive contains a clause requiring the legislation to be reviewed following its introduction at a member state level. Most reviews occur after four years, but they are often delayed as a result of the need to see how the implemented legislation works in practice.

Fourth, it is likely that in the first decade of this century, the UK will – subject to referendum – join the European Single Currency (the euro). In the UK, there has been considerable debate over the economic and political merits and likely impacts of joining the euro. Little attention has been given to the potential effects on employee relations in the light of the fact that currency transparency should inevitably permit easier comparisons of productivity and labour costs across member states. This is likely to lead to further pressures for harmonisation of minimum employment and social standards across member states, possibly into the areas of social security and supplementary pension and health schemes. As the EU itself enlarges, so inevitably will the range of influences that may affect and change personnel/HR policy. This will certainly be the case with the accession of the newly emerging democracies in central and eastern Europe, which possess a high-skill and lower-cost labour force, as they become full members of the EU in the first quarter of the 21st century.

What arguments would you use to convince a line manager that he or she ought to be aware of employee relations developments at the level of the European Union?

The development of the European Union

The origins of the European Union date back to 1951 and popular revulsion following the devastating World Wars. In that year, under the terms of the Treaty of Paris (1951), Germany, Italy, France, Belgium, the Netherlands and Luxembourg created the European Coal and Steel Community, whose fundamental aim was to allow these six countries jointly to control production, development and distribution of coal and steel which were still then major prerequisites for waging war.

The institutions' powers and procedures of the Coal and Steel Community provided a model for the establishment, via the Treaty of Rome (1957), of two further European Communities – the European Atomic Energy Community, and the European Economic Community (EEC), which was commonly referred to as the 'Common Market' and aimed to develop close co-operation on economic matters.

In 1967 the three Communities and their institutions were united by a Merger Treaty which created the European Communities (EC). The UK, Ireland and Denmark joined the EC in 1973, followed by Greece in 1981 and Spain and Portugal in 1986. The EC became the European Union (EU) in 1993 when the Maastricht Treaty on European Union revised and widened the remit to include intergovernmental co-operation between member states on common foreign and security policy and on justice and home affairs. In 1995 Sweden, Finland and Austria joined the EU. The 15 member states of the EU constitute the largest economic unit in the world, with a total population of over 372 million and a labour force of about 146 million.

In early 1998 the EU began enlargement negotiations with Poland, the Czech Republic, Slovenia, Hungary, Estonia and Cyprus. Further negotiations were started in early 2000 with Bulgaria, Romania, Slovakia, Latvia, Lithuania and Malta, while Turkey was given candidate status but has not yet commenced negotiations. The enlargement of the EU to 27 members is expected to commence in 2004–2005 with the admission of Poland, Hungary and the Czech Republic. If all applicant counties eventually join the EU, it will have a total population of 500 million.

Iceland, Norway and Liechtenstein are part of the European Single Market. They are subject to all EU Single Market legislation under the European Economic Area Agreement (EEAA), including some employment legislation. They are not, however, full EU members.

The aims of the European Union

The principal aims of the European Union are to:

- preserve and strengthen peace in Europe

- enable member states to compete more effectively, both between themselves and together in the world marketplace, by removing barriers to free trade and creating a Single European Market

- bring its members closer together politically, economically and socially

- ensure that wherever joint European action by member states in achieving a common objective would be more effective than separate action, a common approach is taken.

The basic objectives, structure and operation of the EU are defined in a series of Treaties (see below). They are the constitution of the EU and provide a legal basis for legislation and other measures. All members have to abide by these Treaties and the legislation agreed under them.

Any changes to the Treaties have to be ratified by all member states. This is done in two ways. In Denmark, Ireland and Portugal, Treaty changes have to be approved in a referendum of their citizens. In the other 12 member states, ratification is achieved by a majority vote in their national parliaments. In both cases, the people, or their representatives, have the last word. However, there is always a price to democracy – namely, delay. Ratification normally takes about 18 months to two years. Changes brought about by Treaties do not become binding on member states until the ratification process has been completed.

The Treaty of Rome (1957)

The founding treaty of the EU is the Treaty of Rome (the European Economic Community Treaty) of 1957, which provided for the creation of a free trade area by removing barriers to the free movement of goods, labour, capital and services (the so-called four great freedoms) between member states. By integrating the economies of the member states, it was hoped that healthy competition would stimulate innovation, techno-logical development, increased productivity and increased demand. It was envisaged that consumer prices would fall, stimulating even further demand for goods and services. The 'European Economy' would thus be firing on all four cylinders and this 'virtuous circle of prosperity' would result in real benefits for everyone within the Common European Market.

Although most of the Treaty of Rome was concerned with removing the barriers to free trade, it did contain two chapters which related to employment. The 'Free Movement of Workers' chapter enshrines the fundamental right of EU citizens to live and work wherever they wish in the EU without discrimination on grounds of nationality except for limited reasons connected with public security.

The 'Social Chapter' provides for closer co-operation in the 'social and employment field' between member states and has as one of its objec-tives:

> *to promote improved working conditions and an improved standard of living for workers so as to make possible their harmonisation while the improvement is being made.*

The Chapter also enshrines, as one of its principles, the right to equal pay for equal work between men and women.

The founders of the EU were not just creating a free trade area but a community in which there would be harmonisation of social and employ-ment conditions. There would be free competition within the free trade area, but this would be within the constraints of minimum social and employment standards across member states. Unlike any other free trade agreement (for example, the North American Free Trade Agreement), the EU has always had a social dimension.

The Single European Act (1987)

Progress in moving towards a free market was slow, largely because each proposal to achieve this objective required the unanimous agree-ment of all member states. There was always at least one member state which objected, and a way had therefore to be found to prevent any single member state from allowing the rest to get on with the job of completing the establishment of a free trade market. In 30 years, the Council of Ministers (see below) had hardly been able to adopt a single important measure designed to achieve the Single Market.

In 1985 the Commission (see below) proposed that member states should speed up the creation of the Common Market and by 31 December 1992 adopt 282 necessary measures to achieve the free movement of goods, capital, labour and services between member states. To achieve this, the Single European Act amended the Treaty of Rome in three important ways.

First, a deadline – 31 December 1992 – was set for finally achieving the 'four great freedoms'.

Second, it introduced a new legal basis to allow member states to agree measures by 'qualified majority vote' (QMV) rather than by unanimous vote. Under this system member states were allocated a number of votes relating to their populations:

- France, Germany, Italy and the UK each have ten votes

- Spain has eight votes

- Belgium, Greece, the Netherlands and Portugal each have five votes

- Sweden and Austria have four votes

- Denmark, Finland and Ireland have three votes

- Luxembourg has two votes.

A 'qualified majority' is 62 of the total 87 votes available. To 'block' proposals, a member state must gather together 26 votes. Put another way, there must be opposition from at least three member states to block a proposal. Two large states (for example, France and Germany together) cannot veto proposals. In the absence of at least 26 votes against, a proposal becomes accepted, and even the member states who abstained or voted against it have to implement it into their national law.

Third, the Act introduced another innovation by formalising the EU's commitment to involve the 'social partners' (employers and trade unions) in its decision-making machinery (see below).

The Single European Act also brought changes to the Social Chapter. It provided that health and safety regulations across the EU member states could be harmonised on the basis of qualified majority voting. This health and safety 'fast track' has been used lavishly (see CIPD *Europe: Personnel and Development*, December 2000) and was the basis of the Working Time Directive (1993), which was then transposed into UK employment law via the Working Time Regulations 1998 (see below).

The impact of the Single European Act cannot be overestimated. By removing the veto of a single member state to proposals, it was radical and revolutionary. It meant Europe would never be the same again. It meant the EU law-making mechanisms could actually start to work as envisaged by the authors of the Treaty of Rome. Above all in our context, it meant employee relations professionals had to take Europe seriously because it was now possible to influence the drafting of new EU laws in a way unthinkable within national parliaments.

The Treaty on the European Union (1993)

In December 1991 the heads of member states met in Maastricht to agree further steps on the road to greater political, economic and monetary integration among member states. The eventual outcome was the Treaty on the European Union 1993, which formally changed the name of the European Communities or Community (EC) to the European Union (EU) and provided for the creation of a common currency (the euro) from 1 January 1999, and the abolition of national currencies by the year 2002. The Treaty also reaffirmed the principle of 'subsidiarity' in EU legislation. Although the principle is interpreted in different ways, it basically provides that the EU should only take legislative action when the objectives of such legislation can be achieved solely or at least better at the EU level than at national level. Not surprisingly, however, there is little agreement on when this criterion is met.

The Treaty on the European Union also made two important changes to the Social Chapter. First, all member states (excluding the UK) accepted proposed extensions of issues in employment and social legislation to be harmonised by QMV. Because the UK objected, no new 'social provisions' were incorporated into the main Maastricht Treaty. However, a compromise agreement was reached whereby member states other than the UK could use EU institutions to introduce additional binding legislation within the social field, although any such legislation could not be applied in the UK. This was done under a separate Social Policy Agreement which listed the specific social issues upon which the rest of the member states could legislate. The agreement was attached to the Social Protocol annexed to the main Treaty.

The second innovation was the formalisation of the EU's commitment to involve the 'social partners' directly in its decision-making machinery. It provided for compulsory consultation with the 'social partners' on EU Commission social and employment proposals, and permitted them to agree voluntarily to negotiate a framework agreement on the issue and for that agreement then to be made binding on member states by the Council of Ministers' issuing a Directive.

The Treaty of Amsterdam (1999)

This Treaty introduced changes thought necessary to help prepare the EU for eventual enlargement by the admission of the applicant countries of central and eastern Europe, to take account of changing political priorities, and to give effect to the need for stronger EU action in areas such as employment, social policy and the environment. The key provisions of the Treaty are:

- It develops further the principles of democracy and individual rights and for the first time establishes a clear procedure to be followed in the event of 'serious and persistent' breaches by member states.

- The Council of Ministers is provided with new powers to take more effective action to combat discrimination based on sex, ethnic origin, religion or belief, disability, age or sexual orientation.

- It pledges to remove all remaining restrictions on the free movement of labour between member states by 2004, the only exemptions being the UK and Ireland, which will be allowed to retain frontier controls.

- It introduces a new Chapter which relates exclusively to employment.

- The Agreement on Social Policy is incorporated into the Treaty and thus becomes applicable to all member states.

For the personnel/HR professional, the Treaty is thus significant for four reasons. First, the UK's Labour Government agreed to opt into the Agreement on Social Policy annexed to the Treaty of Maastricht. As a result, the provisions governing this area were fully incorporated into the Treaty proper, and the UK again takes full part in social policy-making and is fully bound by EU legislation in this area. The UK also had to adopt those Directives – on parental leave and on European Works Councils – which had been adopted under the Social Policy Agreement.

Second, the principle of equal pay for equal work was extended to 'work of equal value'.

Third, the Treaty provided the EU with competencies to take action to combat any form of discrimination whether based on sex, racial or ethnic origin, religion or belief, disability, age or sexual orientation. Legislation in this field will, however, be subject to the agreement of all member states.

Fourth, the Treaty contained an Employment Chapter committing the EU to taking into account the need to achieve high and sustainable employment opportunities when making decisions related to its commercial and economic objectives. This was the first time the promotion of a high level of employment had been written down as one of the main objectives of the EU. It is to be achieved by co-ordinating the employment policies of the member states to develop a common strategy.

The Employment Chapter
The Chapter is designed to restore balance in the EU by creating a counterweight to its economic and monetary provisions. It asserts that:

- Employment is a matter of common concern.

- The objective of generating high employment is to be taken into consideration when implementing all other common policies.

- The achievement of this objective is to be closely monitored.

- The EU is to consider the employment situation in each member state and in the Union as a whole on an annual basis, and to conduct a detailed examination of the steps taken by individual governments to promote employment.

- An employment committee is to promote co-ordination of national measures and to encourage dialogue between employers and employees.

The Employment Chapter is important because it makes the EU and its institutions for the first time the guardians of an overall employment policy. It is ambitious in the sense that it provides for permanent and regular collaboration within the EU framework.

The Treaty of Nice (2000)

In March 2000 the EU embarked on another round of treaty revisions to see whether agreement could be reached on a major reform of the way the EU institutions operate. The previous meeting in Amsterdam had largely ignored the very real reforms necessary to operating practices if the EU was to expand and meet the challenges of enlargement. The outcome was the Treaty of Nice, which extended further the issues that could be harmonised on the basis of qualified majority voting, changed the future size and composition of the European Commission, and introduced enhanced co-operation.

Qualified majority voting is to be extended to 39 additional issues, one of which is the harmonisation of anti-discrimination measures in employment. The Treaty also re-weights member states' voting powers in the Council of Ministers to reflect their larger population size. Under the Nice Treaty, a qualified majority will consist of 255 of the total 342 votes. This will raise the threshold majority from 71 per cent to just below 75 per cent. In addition, a qualified majority will also have to carry 62 per cent of the total EU population.

The Treaty also will limit the maximum size of the European Commission (see below) to 27 Commissioners, the five large member states therefore giving up their second Commissioner in 2005. It was further agreed that should the EU eventually expand beyond 27 member states, a rotation system would be agreed at that time.

It was also agreed at Nice that where there are at least eight member states who wish to proceed further and faster on an issue, they will be able to request a formal proposal from the Commission and – subject to the agreement of the Council of Ministers acting by qualified majority voting as well as to the approval of the European Parliament – to introduce such a measure. When receiving a request for enhanced co-operation, the Commission will have to ensure that such co-operation aims to achieve the objectives of the Union, that those objectives could not otherwise be achieved, and that the proposed enhanced co-operation will not undermine the functioning of the Single Market. Opting in to enhanced co-operation will require each new member state to adopt all decisions previously taken under enhanced co-operation.

The Treaty of Nice currently has still to be ratified by all member states.

The rejection of the Treaty by Ireland, in a referendum in 2002, will result in some delay in this regard.

> Explain the difference between qualified majority voting and unanimous decision-making in the European Union.

How the EU works

The Treaty of Rome set up four key institutions to achieve its objectives. These were:

- the European Commission
- the Council of the European Union
- the European Parliament
- the European Court of Justice

The European Commission

This is the EU's executive body, whose main role is to propose measures and ensure their implementation. There are currently 20 Commissioners comprising the President, two Vice-Presidents and 17 members. Commissioners, who are usually senior and distinguished politicians, are nominated by the governments and serve for a period of five years. The President is chosen by agreement between the 15 heads of state. The President enjoys considerable power and influence, and sets the agenda for the weekly Commission meetings where new initiatives for making European law are discussed. The larger member states (the UK, France, Germany, Italy and Spain) nominate two Commissioners whereas the others nominate one, although this will change, as we have seen, when the Treaty of Nice becomes operative. The Commissioners think EU-wide and not in national terms. All policy proposals made by a Commissioner must have the support of a simple majority of all Commissioners before they can be launched officially.

Each Commissioner has a personal 'cabinet' of advisory staff and each is also in charge of one or more of the policy divisions in the Commission called Directorates-General (DGs). These are subdivided into Directorates. They are responsible for drawing up proposals for EU action and monitoring implementation of agreed measures. The Commissioner for Employment and Social Affairs is responsible for employment (including employee relations), social affairs and equal opportunities.

The Council of the European Union

The Council comprises 15 members – one representing each member state. It is the EU's decision-making body. Its main function is to adopt measures proposed by the Commission for enactment in the member states. The Council has several levels. There is the European Council level, which comprises the heads of government or state of the EU member states and which meets four times a year to discuss major issues and decide on broad areas of policy.

There is then the level of the Council of Ministers, which comprises a Minister from each member state according to the subject under discussion. Although each country has a permanent seat in the Council, the personalities who fill these seats therefore change in accordance with the subject in hand. For example, if the Council is discussing employee relations matters, the seats are filled by the respective employment/labour Ministers from each of the member states.

There is also the level of Presidency of the Council which is held by each member state for a period of six months. As President of the Council, the member state sets Council agendas and can therefore determine, to some extent, which Commission proposals are progressed and given priority. Member states normally run a programme of high-profile events during their Presidency. All Council meetings are chaired and negotiations co-ordinated by the representative of the presiding member state.

The European Parliament

The European Parliament is the EU's main consultative body. It has 626 members, directly elected since 1979, distributed among member states in proportion to their populations. Germany is the largest with 99 seats, and Luxembourg the smallest with 6. The UK has 87 seats. Elections to the Parliament are held at five-yearly intervals. Members of the European Parliament (MEPs) take up their seats according to their trans-national political group rather than their nationality. UK MEPs are elected by proportional representation. Labour MEPs sit as part of the European Socialist Group whereas UK Conservatives sit with the European People's Party (EPP) group.

The Parliament has 20 specialist committees – such as the Employment and Social Affairs Committee and the Women's Rights Committee – which examine issues in depth. The committees draft opinions on Commission proposals and on other issues within their remit which are debated at the monthly plenary session of the Parliament.

The European Parliament approves the appointment of the 20 European Commissioners, determines the EU budget and proposes amendments to measures initiated by the Commission. Initially, the European Parliament had few powers and was regarded as nothing more than a talking-shop. However, over the years it has acquired greater influence, and its powers to influence the legislative process vary according to the procedures governing decision-making in any given area (see below). For example, since the introduction of the co-decision procedure by the Treaty on the European Union, the Parliament has significant co-legislative powers – for example, in the areas of training and the free movement of labour. Although the Parliament can reject the annual budget prepared by the Commission, it has only exercised this power on two occasions since 1957.

The Parliament can dismiss the 20 Commissioners, but only *en bloc*. It cannot dismiss a lone Commissioner: it is 'all or none'. This power had never been exercised until spring 1999, when President Santer and his team of Commissioners resigned *en bloc* – preferring to 'go voluntarily' rather than be 'pushed' into going by the powers of the Parliament, which on this occasion would most certainly have been used. Santer's Commission collapsed as a result of six cases of mismanagement and petty corruption.

The European Court of Justice

This Court is the supreme custodian of the laws enacted by the EU, and its decisions take precedence over any laws or judicial decisions taken in the member states. It comprises 15 judges, one from each member state, appointed for a six-year term, plus a sixteenth appointed by the larger member states in rotation. They are assisted by six Advocates-General – one from each of the five larger member states and a sixth appointed by the smaller states in rotation – who deliver preliminary opinions on cases before they are put to the Court. A subsidiary court, the Court of First Instance, hears many of the more routine cases. Even so, the average time for a case to be heard is 18 months, and the full procedure can take several years.

The European Court of Justice acts as the final arbiter in disputes over the interpretation of the Treaties, and over the failure of member states to implement EU laws. It can quash any measures introduced by member states that are incompatible with the Treaties.

The Court has been used by UK individuals, groups and organisations to challenge UK employment legislation on the grounds that it contravenes EU law. For example, the UK Equal Pay Act 1970 was challenged. The Act allowed for equal pay for work of equal value where this was shown to be the case by a job evaluation scheme. Claims by women employees were being rejected after the use of job evaluation. However, a complaint was laid before the European Court of Justice that such claims were failing because the job evaluation schemes that UK employers were using contained gender-bias factors. The complaint was upheld, and in 1983 the Equal Pay Act 1970 was amended to permit the undertaking of job evaluation by independent job evaluators in the case of a claim for equal pay for work of equal value.

Explain the differences in the functions of the European Commission, the Council of Ministers, the European Parliament and the European Court of Justice.

Legislative instruments

Most EU employment and social legislation comes in one of three forms, all of which have important differences from each other:

- Regulations
- Directives
- Decisions.

Regulations are the highest and most rigorous form of EU legislation. They comprise detailed instructions which are immediately applicable throughout the European Union once adopted by the Council of Ministers, and are 'directly binding' upon all member states. In other words, Regulations have the same direct status as laws passed by the UK Parliament and must be enforced by the UK courts in the same way. Failure to apply Regulations results in the European Commission making a complaint to the European Court of Justice.

Decisions are more specific in their application (to particular member states, sectors or industries) and are immediately binding on those to whom they are addressed. Decisions that impose financial obligations are enforceable in national courts. Decisions are used when the EU wants the full force of European law to apply to individuals, to particular firms or enterprises, or to specific member states.

However, in the employment and social field, Directives are the main legislative instrument. Directives set out specific objectives and each member state is given time (usually two years) to enact legislation within its own parliament to ensure that the objectives are achieved. Directives, while being less rigid and allowing more flexibility than Regulations or Decisions, are still binding in all member states. In itself a Directive does not have legal force in the member states – but particular provisions may take direct effect if the Directive is not duly implemented. In the UK Directives have been implemented either by being incorporated as they stand into national law or by means of secondary legislation drawn up by the relevant government department or by an Act of Parliament, formulated in the usual way through a Parliamentary bill.

Softer instruments

In addition to Regulations, Directives and Decisions which are 'hard legislation' enforced by the EU, there are other 'softer instruments' which attempt to regulate behaviour in the EU. These are:

- recommendations
- opinion
- resolutions
- declarations
- communications
- memoranda.

They might all sound dauntingly formal but in fact they are not legally binding. They have a moral rather than a legal force – although they can be used as evidence in court. Probably the best-known declarations in the employee relations field are the Community Charter on the Fundamental Rights of Workers – commonly known as the Social Charter – and aspects of the Charter of Fundamental Rights of the European Union (see below).

Implementation of the instruments

Of the three categories of European law with real teeth, the most widely used is the Directive. Since 1957, more than 50 Directives have been adopted in the social policy field. Over half of these relate to health and safety at work, while the others deal with employment protection/working conditions, equal opportunities, freedom of movement and public health. At the time of writing, 48 of these 50 Directives have been transposed into UK legislation.

If a member state fails to transpose Directives into domestic law by the target date or if EU law is infringed, complaints may be made to the European Commission. Such complaints can be made by individuals, companies, other member states, the European Parliament or pressure groups. The Commission investigates the complaint and asks the member state(s) concerned for an explanation. If this is unsatisfactory, the Commission orders the member state(s) to put the matter right within one month. If the infringement continues, the matter is referred to the European Court of Justice. If this Court finds against the member state(s), it passes a judgment with which each offending member state has to comply. If failure to comply results in a denial of individual rights, the European Court of Justice may require the member state to pay compensation to the individual. The important thing about the European Court of Justice is, as we have already seen, that it takes precedence over all the courts within member states. It has the power to overrule the UK judiciary, including the House of Lords. When issues and disputes reach the European Court of Justice, it is the end of the road. Once that Court make its judgment, there is no further appeal.

Outline the difference between a European Union Directive and a Regulation. Which is the more important in employee relations terms?

The social partners

Following the ratification of the Treaty of Maastricht, the EU-wide representative bodies of employers and employees (referred to as the social partners) now have a role to play in the EU legislative process. There are three main social partners at the inter-sector level of the EU:

- the European Trade Union Confederation (ETUC)

- the Union of Industrial and Employers' Confederations of Europe (UNICE)

- the European Centre of Enterprises with Public Participation (CEEP).

The European Trade Union Confederation

The European Trade Union Confederation (ETUC) has a dual structure. Apart from the member states' leading national trade union confederations, which are affiliated to the ETUC as full members, it also comprises 14 European sectoral trade union organisations that until 1995 were called European industry committees but are now known as European Industry Federations (EIFs). These federations represent individual trade unions from a particular sector. They are accepted by the EU institutions as the sectoral (industry) employees' social partner.

The Confederation was formed in 1973, and today its full members include 62 national trade union confederations from 28 countries in Western, Central and Eastern Europe, plus the 14 European sectoral trade union organisations. All in all, the ETUC represents the interests of some 57 million trade union affiliates at European level. There are three decision-making bodies which determine ETUC policy – Congress, the Executive Committee and the Steering Committee. The Congress, the highest body, is held every four years and decides the organisation's policy priorities. The Executive Committee generally meets every three months and takes the policy decisions required to implement the priorities laid down by the Congress. The Steering Committee normally meets every two months to decide on urgent action required to implement the strategies laid down by the Executive Committee. The ETUC secretariat is in Brussels and carries out tasks assigned to it by the Congress, the Executive Committee and the Steering Committee.

The Union of Industrial and Employers' Confederations of Europe

The Union of Industrial and Employers' Confederations of Europe (UNICE) is the official voice of European business and industry in contact with European institutions, and was established in 1958. It comprises 33 central industry and employers' federations from 25 European countries, with a permanent secretariat based in Brussels. Its aims are: to keep up with issues that interest its members by maintaining permanent contacts with European institutions; to promote a framework which enables industry and employers to secure European policies and proposed legislation and prepare position papers; to promote its policies and position at European and national level and to persuade European legislators to take these into account and represent its members in the dialogue between social partners provided for in the European Treaties as outlined above. It operates through its Council of Presidents and an Executive Committee which assists in policy formation and suggests actions to be taken.

The European Centre of Enterprises with Public Participation

The third social partner at the inter-sectoral level is the European Centre of Enterprises with Public Participation and of Enterprises of General Economic Interest (CEEP). It represents the interests of public sector employers. It was formed in 1961, and has some 200 member organisations.

The legislative process

The Treaty of Amsterdam streamlined the EU's decision-making procedures so that there are now two main procedures for adopting EU legislation: the so-called co-operation procedure and the co-decision procedure. In addition, in the social and employment field, a third procedure is used, known as a social dialogue process (see below). What was once called the consultation procedure now only applies in very limited cases, such as those involving discrimination on the grounds of racial or ethnic origin, religion or belief, disability, age or sexual orientation.

Common to all procedures is that the initiative is taken by the European Commission. Indeed, as we have already seen in examining the Treaties, the Commission has the sole right of initiative. In practice, however, many Commission proposals emanate from direct requests or indirect pressure from member states, other EU institutions or interest groups.

The co-operation procedure

Under the terms of the co-operation procedure, legislation may be adopted by qualified majority vote (QMV) in the Council, following two readings by the European Parliament. After the Parliament's first reading, the Council adopts a so-called common position. Parliament may then propose amendments to this common position or reject it outright. If the Council wishes to maintain its common position, despite Parliament's objections, it may only do so unanimously. After the Parliament's second reading the Commission will re-examine its original proposal along with the Council's common position and the Parliament's amendments. If the Council wishes to make amendments to this re-examined proposal, it may do so only by unanimous agreement. If it does not wish to do so, the proposal may be adopted by QMV.

The co-decision procedure

Under the terms of this procedure the Parliament's legislative powers are significantly enhanced, in that the Council can only adopt legislation jointly with the Parliament. The procedure is considerably longer than the co-operation procedure and it includes a final stage in which an attempt is made to reconcile potentially diverging positions of the Council and the Parliament.

The framework agreement procedure

Inter-sectoral

Under the Social Chapter, the European Commission must consult with the social partners (ETUC, UNICE and CEEP) about both the direction and the content of the EU legislation in the social and employment field and, should they wish so, may seek to negotiate framework agreements as a substitute for legislation. The social partners may also engage in negotiations on their own initiative. This process is known as 'social dialogue' (see Table 6). It operates as follows:

- When considering proposed legislation, the Commission must first consult the social partners on whether there is a need for legislation. The social partners typically have six weeks within which to submit their views.

- If the Commission, after consultation with the social partners, concludes that a need for legislation exists, it then consults the social partners for a second time with a view to establishing their views on the possible scope of such legislation. The social partners are given the opportunity to negotiate an agreement as a substitute for Commission legislation. This second period of consultation lasts normally for a six-week period.

- If the social partners reject the negotiations option, the Commission can decide to initiate the normal legislative process. If, however, the social partners opt for the negotiations route, they have up to a period of nine months, with the possibility of extension, within which to negotiate a framework agreement.

- If the social partners successfully negotiate a framework agreement, they have to submit that agreement to the Commission with a recommendation that it be put forward as a formal legislative proposal to be adopted as a decision by the Council of Ministers.

- Should the social partners agree not to negotiate a framework agreement, or indeed fail to reach a voluntary agreement, then a fall-back position comes into play. The Commission may submit its own proposals under the co-decision procedure and under which the Council of Ministers takes decisions on the basis of QMV.

The negotiation of a EU-wide framework agreement has already happened successfully in the cases of parental leave (the Parental Leave Directive), part-time work (the Part-Time Workers' Directive) and fixed-term contracts of employment (the Fixed-Term Contracts Directive). However, on three issues – European Works Councils, the burden of proof in sex discrimination cases, and information and consultation at the national level – the social partners were not able to agree to enter into negotiations on these issues. The social partners opted in 2000 to attempt to negotiate a framework agreement to provide minimum protections throughout the EU for temporary (agency) workers. The negotiations broke down in May 2001, however. The Commission has now committed itself to bringing forward a proposed Directive to cover such workers.

Framework agreement negotiations are arranged and appropriate venues and interpreters provided by the Commission, which also provides a chairperson to facilitate the negotiations between the social partners. All the costs associated with the negotiations – for example, those of travel, accommodation, etc – are met by the Commission. The employer and trade union sides usually negotiate against very tight mandates from their respective constituents. Once agreement is reached, the social partners' affiliated organisations must ratify the agreement.

Table 6   Summary of the framework agreement procedure

The European Commission
identifies an area for possible regulation and consults
the EU social partners – UNICE, CEEP and the ETUC,
who discuss the contents of the proposal and the need for EU-level action. The social partners

decide to negotiate an EU-level collective agreement on the issue over a nine-month period, to be implemented through collective agreement at national level, and/or to form the basis for a proposal by	or	suggest that the
the European Commission for adoption as a legally binding instrument by		**European Commission** drafts its proposal for debate and possible amendment by
the Council of the EU by unanimous vote or qualified majority vote, depending on the subject*		**the Council of the EU,** which finally adopts an EU Directive (or other legal instrument) via the consultation procedure or the co-operation procedure, depending on the legal basis of the proposal*

* Proposals that require a qualified majority vote and that involve the co-operation procedure relate to: working conditions, employee involvement, equal opportunities for men and women, integration of those excluded from the labour market, and health and safety. Under the social protocol, qualified majority voting requires at least 52 of the available 77 votes to be in favour.

Proposals that require a unanimous vote and that involve the consultation procedure relate to: social protection, termination of employment, and the terms and conditions of employment.

No harmonisation is envisaged on issues related to pay, the right of association, the right to strike or the right to impose lock-outs.

Sectoral

The same social dialogue process as exists for inter-sectoral purposes is also available to the social partners within the EU industrial sectors to establish minimum social and employment standards for a particular sector. The social partners at a sectoral level are the relevant European industry federation on the employees' side and on the employers' side their appropriate employers' federations for various sectors – for example, transport, engineering, coal mining, agriculture, etc.

To date, three sector-wide framework agreements have been negotiated. In March 2000 the social partners in the civil aviation industry signed an agreement limiting annual working time in the industry to 2,000 hours and flying time to 900 hours. This was the third agreement of its kind in the transport industry. The other two agreements were negotiated in 1998 and related to sea transport and the railways.

Framework agreements have been negotiated at a European level. Briefly explain:
- who the parties are that negotiate such agreements
- how long the parties may take to reach such an agreement
- how such agreements are enforced throughout the member states of the EU.

The social dimension of the EU

The Social Chapter

The founders of the European Union did not just create a free trade area in which people, goods, services and capital could move freely. They were establishing a political and economic community in which there would be social regulation/protection. Product and service market competition would take place on a 'level playing-field' of minimum social and employment conditions in all member states. To this end the Treaty of Rome contained a Social Chapter (Title III, Social Policy), subsequently amended by the Single European Act 1987 and the Treaty on the European Union 1993 and regrouped under Title XI of the Treaty of Amsterdam. The objectives of the Social Chapter are:

the promotion of employment, improved living and working conditions, proper social protection, dialogue between management and labour, the development of human resources with a view to lasting employment, and the combating of social exclusion.

It also commits member states, as a condition of membership, to ensure and maintain the application of the principle that men and women should have equal pay for equal work or work of equal value. The UK became fully covered by the Social Chapter on 1 May 1999 when the

Treaty of Amsterdam came into force. That treaty also empowers the EU to take action to combat any form of discrimination based on sex, racial or ethnic origin, religion or belief, disability, age or sexual orientation. Finally, when making social policy, the EU may draw inspiration from the Social Charter (see below), which has now been incorporated into the Treaty of Amsterdam.

The Social Chapter is not a set of detailed regulations. It is a mechanism which allows the member states to make new rules and legislation at the EU level on a wide range of social and employment issues. As we have seen, it allows common rules to be introduced by the Council of Ministers by one of three methods –

- a unanimous vote

- a qualified majority vote

- a framework agreement negotiated by UNICE, CEEP and the ETUC and/or their sectoral equivalents

– which are then issued as a Directive and transposed into national legislation.

The framework agreement procedure limits the power of the European Parliament or member states in the Council of Ministers to make any amendments. This ability of collective bargaining to shape both the direction and content of legislation is considerable and unique. The CBI and the TUC are the UK members of UNICE and the ETUC respectively. As a result, they have acquired a new and special significance as organisations in the UK. Both organisations respectively represent the interests of UK companies and employees in the drafting of legislation that then becomes legally binding in the UK and applies equally to unionised and non-unionised companies/establishments.

Qualified majority vote issues
Under the Social Chapter (see Table 7) procedures, legislation in any of the following areas can be adopted by qualified majority voting:

- improvements in the working environment to protect workers' health and safety

- working conditions

- giving information to and consulting with workers

- equality between men and women with regard to labour market opportunities and treatment at work

- the integration of persons excluded from the labour market.

The European Works Council Directive 1994 was adopted under this procedure, as was the Parental Leave Directive 1996 after the social partners had negotiated a framework agreement on the issue.

Unanimous vote issues

The Social Chapter mechanisms can be used to introduce European Union-wide legislation on the basis of unanimity amongst member states in the following areas:

- social security and the social protection of workers

- the protection of workers once their employment contract is terminated

- the representation and collective defence of workers' and employers' interests, including co-determination

- conditions of employment for third-country nationals legally resident in the EU

- financial contributions for employment promotion and job creation.

Excluded issues

Certain subjects – namely, pay, the right of association, the right to strike and the right to impose lock-outs – are formally excluded from harmonisation by legislation based on Social Chapter procedures.

However, critics of the EU point out that the fact that some areas are formally subject to unanimity or even excluded altogether is by no

Table 7 Summary of the bases on which specific Social Chapter issues can or cannot be decided

Qualified majority voting	<ul><li>health and safety</li><li>working conditions</li><li>informing and consulting with workers</li><li>equality between men and women with regard to labour market opportunities and treatment at work</li><li>the integration of persons excluded from the labour market</li></ul>
Unanimous vote	<ul><li>social security and the protection of workers</li><li>the protection of workers once their employment is terminated</li><li>the representation and collective defence of the interests of workers and employers, including co-determination</li><li>financial contributions for the promotion of employment and job creation</li></ul>
Excluded issues	<ul><li>pay</li><li>the right of association</li><li>the right to strike</li><li>the right to lock out</li></ul>

means a secure safeguard. They argue that such terms as 'working conditions' and 'health and safety' are open to wide differences in interpretation. They point out, for example, that the European Court of Justice ruled in another context that the British social security benefit, Family Credit, is a working condition. EU critics contend that past experience suggests EU institutions will seek to apply the broadest possible interpretations in order to maximise the scope for adopting measures by qualified majority vote despite possible objections from individual member states. The Social Chapter mechanisms are seen as risking the imposition of costly, far-reaching and unforeseeable legislation on the UK. It is viewed by its opponents as mirroring the more interventionist approach common in much of the EU and as contrary to a deregulated approach to the operation of labour markets.

The Social Chapter in practice

There are four areas of employee relations management in which EU laws have had, and will continue to have, a direct impact on the work of the UK personnel/HR specialist:

- equal opportunities
- employment protection/working conditions
- employee relations
- health and safety at work.

Employee relations professionals should obtain copies of the actual Directives in these areas rather than depend on summaries. They should also bear in mind that many Directives are not simply implemented into UK law by one piece of legislation. For example, in areas such as equal opportunities, the requirements of a Directive have been transposed into several separate legal instruments within the UK (see Table 8).

Equal opportunities

Equal pay
The 1975 Equal Pay Directive sought to improve the effectiveness of measures to ensure equal pay for men and women as laid down in the Treaty of Rome by reducing differences between member states in the application of this principle through approximation (ie general standardisation) of member state laws on the subject. The Directive stated that the principle of equal pay required the elimination of all discrimination on the grounds of sex with regard to all aspects and conditions of remuneration for the same work or for work to which equal value is attributed. It also stipulated that any job classification (evaluation) system used for determining pay must be based on the same criteria for both men and women and must be drawn up so as to exclude discrimination on grounds of sex.

Table 8   Summary of areas of employment in which European Union-wide legislation impacts on the work of the UK personnel/HR professional

Equal opportunities	• equal pay (1975) • parental leave (1996) • equal treatment (1976) • the burden of proof in sex discrimination cases (1997)
Employment protection/ working conditions	• redundancy (1975 and 1992) • transfers of undertakings (1977 and 1998) • insolvency (1980) • contracts of employment (1992) • the posting of workers (1996) • part-time working (1997) • fixed-term contracts (1999)
Employment relations	• informing and consulting with workers (1994 and 1997) • employee involvement in the 'European company' (2001) • informing and consulting at the national level (2002)
Health and safety	• the Health and Safety (framework) Directive (1989) • the health and safety at work of workers with a fixed-duration employment relationship or a temporary employment relationship • health and safety at work for pregnant employees and new mothers • the organisation of working time (1993) • the Young People at Work Directive (1994)

In 1983 the Equal Pay (Amendment) Regulations were introduced in the UK to comply with this Directive. These regulations introduced, *inter alia*, provision for 'independent experts' to undertake job evaluation exercises independently of the employer in the case of claims for equal pay based on work of equal value.

Parental leave
In 1996, the Social Partners (UNICE, the ETUC and CEEP) concluded a framework agreement on parental leave which was then issued as the Parental Leave Directive. This provides an individual right for parents to take up to three months' unpaid leave after the birth or adoption of a child before its eighth birthday. Employees are protected from dismissal for asking for the leave, and have the right to return to work on the same conditions as before. The Directive also entitles individuals to a

certain number of days off work for urgent family reasons in the case of sickness or accident. The UK Government translated this Directive into national legislation via the Employment Relations Act 1999.

Equal treatment

The Equal Treatment Directive (1976) was designed to give effect to the principle of equal treatment for men and women with respect to access to employment, promotion, vocational training and working conditions, including the conditions governing dismissal. As a result of this Directive, the UK had to introduce legislation to equalise the retirement ages for men and women, to remove the difference whereby men could receive statutory redundancy payments up to the age of 65 but women upto 60, and to ensure that occupational pensions were equal for men and women.

The burden of proof

Measures to lift the burden of proof in cases of discrimination based on the Sex Discrimination Directive (1997) sought to improve the effectiveness of national implementation of the principle of equal treatment by enabling all persons to have the right to equal treatment asserted by judicial process after possible recourse to other competent bodies. The Directive provides that where a complaint to a tribunal establishes 'facts from which it may be presumed that there has been direct or indirect discrimination', the employer has to prove 'that there has been no breach of the principle of equal treatment'. The Directive effectively thus provides a reversal of the burden of proof. It was implemented in the UK in October 2001 by means of the Sex Discrimination (Indirect Discrimination and Burden of Proof) Regulations.

Employment protection/working conditions
Redundancy

The Collective Redundancy Directive (1975) introduced the requirement for consultation, in good time, between employers and employee representatives on mass redundancies with a view to reaching an agreement. The consultations must cover ways and means to avoid collective redundancies or to limit the number of workers affected, and to mitigate the consequences through help in redeploying or retraining workers made redundant. The employer must provide the workers' representatives with certain information – for example, the reason for the redundancies, the number and types of workers to be made redundant, and the criteria proposed for the selection of workers to be made redundant.

The Directive was translated into UK legislation within the Employment Protection Act 1975. It was amended slightly by a further Directive (1992), which was implemented in the UK in June 1994 within the Trade Union Reform and Employment Rights Act 1993. This ensured that consultation takes place at the workplace affected even if the redundancy decision has been taken by a controlling body in another country.

Transfer of undertakings

The Transfer of Undertakings/Acquired Rights Directive (1977) sought to protect employees in the event of a change of employer. It introduced the principle that when a business is sold, employees should transfer to the new owner on the same basic terms and conditions of employment, and may not be dismissed for reasons connected with the transfer. In implementing the Directive into UK law (via the Transfer of Undertakings and Protection of Employment Regulations – TUPE), the Government excluded the public sector.

However, in 1992 the European Court of Justice confirmed that the Directive applied to employees in both the private and non-profit sectors. The UK law was therefore amended by the Trade Union Reform and Employment Rights Act 1993 to include public sector employees. In 1998 an amendment to the 1977 Directive was introduced to clarify and limit existing law and stated that transfer of undertakings legislation applied only when an 'economic activity' which retains its identity is transferred, rather than simply a name or marque. The UK implemented this amendment in July 2001.

Insolvency

The Insolvency Directive (1980) requires member states to set up insolvency funds to guarantee reimbursement of outstanding pay to employees if a business collapses. It was implemented in the UK without change to existing law, which was already established by the then Employment Protection (Consolidation) Act 1978.

Contracts of employment

The Proof of an Employment Relationship Directive (1992) imposed an obligation on an employer to inform employees of the conditions applicable to the contract or employment relationship. By doing so, it is hoped to provide employees with improved protection against possible infringements of their rights and to create greater transparency in the labour market. The Directive required all employees who worked more than eight hours per week for more than one month to receive written confirmation of the main terms and conditions of their employment within two months of starting work. Changes to written particulars must be notified in writing within one month. It also required conditions for overseas postings to be provided in writing. Implementation of the Directive in the UK was via the Trade Union Reform and Employment Rights Act 1993.

Posting of workers

The Posting of Workers Directive (1996) aims to ensure minimum protection for workers posted temporarily to a member state other than the one in which they normally work. It is also designed to ensure fair competition and to provide minimum employment conditions for these employees. A posted worker is guaranteed such terms and conditions as are laid down in the law and in applicable collective agreements in the member state to which he or she is posted – in particular, maximum work periods and minimum rest periods; minimum paid annual holidays; minimum rates of pay, including overtime rates; health and safety; the conditions of hiring out workers, particularly by temporary employment agencies; protective measures concerning the employment of pregnant women, new mothers, children and young people; equality of treatment between men and women; and other non-discrimination measures.

Member states are required to establish adequate procedures to allow workers and/or their representatives to enforce the provisions of the Directive. A posted worker can bring a claim under the Directive in the host country without affecting any right to do so elsewhere. The UK introduced regulations to give effect to this Directive in December 1999.

Part-time workers

In 1997 UNICE, the ETUC and CEEP negotiated a framework agreement on part-time workers designed to remove discrimination against part-time workers, to improve the quality of part-time work, to facilitate the development of part-time work on a voluntary basis, and to contribute to the flexible organisation of working time in a manner that took into account the needs of employers and workers. A part-time worker is defined as a worker whose normal average weekly hours of work calculated over one year are less than those of a comparable full-time worker. If no comparable full-time worker exists within the same establishment, reference is made to applicable collective agreements or national law.

The social partners agreed that part-time workers should be treated no less favourably with regard to employment conditions except where justified on objective grounds. Employers are to facilitate the transfer between part-time and full-time work by providing information on available work within the establishment and by greater access to vocational training. Member states and national social partners were urged to identify and eliminate obstacles to part-time work. The framework agreement was translated into a Directive with an implementation deadline of 20 January 2000. In April 1998 this Directive was extended to the UK and came into force in June 2000 under the Part-Time Workers (Prevention of Less Favourable Treatment) Regulations.

Fixed-term contracts

In 1999 the EU social partners concluded a framework agreement on fixed-term contracts. The negotiations had been initiated by UNICE who in February 1998 had proposed that the social partners negotiate on the subject. This was unique in that it was the first UNICE-proposed, and -initiated, legislation in the social and employment field. The agreement generated an EU Directive discouraging the promotion of fixed-term contracts and limiting their use. Fixed-term employees are:

- to be treated no less favourably than permanent employees who do similar work for the same employer at the same establishment

- protected against unfair dismissal without a qualifying requirement

- no longer able to waive their right to claim redundancy pay when their contract expires

- entitled to terms and conditions equivalent to permanent staff, on a *pro rata* basis.

The UK gave effect to this Directive in 2002 via the Fixed-Term Employees (Prevention of Less Favourable Treatment) Regulations.

Employee relations
The European Works Council Directive
This Directive (1994), through its extension in the UK in 1998, provides for a European-level information and consultation system to be set up in all organisations with more than 1,000 employees in member states or employing more than 150 people in two or more member states. A 'works council' (or an alternative system) has to be agreed between the central management of the organisation and a 'special negotiating body' (SNB) of employee representatives. If no agreement is reached within three years, a fall-back system applies. This requires the establishment of a European Works Council of employee representatives with the right to meet central management at least once a year for information about and consultation on the progress and prospects of the company, and to request extra consultation meetings before certain major decisions are taken that affect more than one EU member state.

European information and consultation systems already in place before the set deadline implementation date of 22 September 1996, or 15 December 1999 in the case of the UK, were exempted. Effect was given in the UK to the European Works Council (UK Extension) Directive (1997) by the Transnational Information and Consultation Regulations 1999.

Informing and consulting at national level
The aim of the Information and Consultation Directive (2002) is to establish a general framework setting out minimum requirements for the right of employees to be informed and consulted in undertaking or establishments within the European Community. Its requirements apply to undertakings that employ at least 50 employees in any one member state or establishments that employ at least 20 employees in any one member state. The right to information and consultation covers information on the recent and probable development of the undertaking's or the establishment's activities and economic situation; on the situation, structure and probable development of employment within the undertaking, and on any anticipated measures envisaged, in particular where there is a threat to employment; and on decisions likely to lead to substantial changes in work organisation or in contractual relations. This information is to be given at such time, in such fashion and with such

content as is appropriate to enable employees' representatives to conduct an adequate study, and, where necessary, to prepare for consultation.

Under the Directive, consultation should take place at the relevant level of management and employee representation and in such a way as to enable employees' representatives to meet with the employer and obtain a response – and the reasons for that response – to any opinion they might formulate. In addition, consultation must take place with a view to reaching an agreement on decisions within the scope of the employer's powers likely to lead to substantial changes in work organisation or in contractual relations.

Member states also have to provide for appropriate measures in the event of non-compliance by employers or employees' representatives with the provisions of the Directive, and ensure that adequate administrative or judicial procedures are available to enable the obligations deriving from the Directive to be enforced. Member states must also provide for adequate penalties to be applicable in the event of infringement of the Directive. Such penalties are to be proportionate in relation to the seriousness of the offence.

Member states have until early 2005 to implement the requirements of this Directive. Implementation of the required provisions by a voluntary negotiated agreement between labour and management is permissible. In member states such as the UK and Ireland where there is no general, permanent and statutory system for informing or consulting, nor for employee representation at the workplace, the Directive can be introduced in stages as follows:

- Undertakings with at least 150 employees (or establishments with at least 100 employees) are to be covered no later than two years from the implementation date (ie by early 2007).

- Undertakings with at least 100 employees (or establishments with 50 employees) and undertakings with 50 employees (or establishments with 20 employees) are to be covered no later than one year later. In short, full implementation of the Directive in the UK and Ireland can be no later than early 2008.

The European Company Statute

In October 2001 the EU adopted a Regulation establishing the European Company Statute (ECS) and an accompanying Directive on the involvement of employees in the 'European company'. In terms of the development of EU social and employment legislation, this event was historic, bringing to fruition after 31 years what was probably the longest legislative process ever experienced in this field. It was in 1970 that the European Commission first proposed giving companies the option of forming a European company, which could operate on a European-wide basis and be governed by Community law directly applicable in all member states (rather than by national law). For many years the proposal failed to gain approval in the Council of Ministers largely owing to disagreement over the worker-involvement provisions to apply in a European company.

The European Company Statute gives companies the option of forming a European company which can operate on a Europe-wide basis and be governed by Community law directly applicable in all member states. A European company may be formed by two or more EU companies through merger or formation of a joint subsidiary or holding company, or by the transformation of a single existing EU company. Employee-involvement arrangements – information and consultation, plus board-level employee participation in some circumstances – must generally apply in all types of European companies.

Companies' participation in the formation of a European company must negotiate with the employee via a special negotiating body (SNB) made up of employee representatives. The negotiations are expected to result in a written agreement on the employee-involvement arrangements. If these arrangements include a reduction of existing board-level participation rights that cover a certain proportion of employees, that reduction must be approved by a two-thirds majority of SNB members (from at least two member states). The SNB may decide not to open talks or to terminate talks in progress – in which case existing national information and consultation rules will apply. Where the SNB and the management reach an agreement, it should essentially result in the setting up of a works council-like 'representative body' or an information and consultation procedure. If the parties so decide, the agreement may also set out rules for board-level participation. SNB negotiations must be completed within a six-month period. This may, however, be extended by annual agreement to a total of one year. If no agreement is reached, or if the parties so decide, a statutory set of 'standard rules' may apply, providing for a standard 'representative body'. The standard rules also provide for board-level representation in certain circumstances where such representation existed in the participating companies.

Health and safety at work

Several Directives were adopted in the 1970s and 1980s that set minimum standards for the control of levels of noise, vibration, and asbestos and other agents, as well as Directives to harmonise safety signs and symbols. Today, over 30 Directives have been adopted making health and safety at work the most regulated area of EU social policy. These Directives have largely been incorporated into UK law via the control of substances hazardous to health (COSHH). However, the majority of these Directives are so-called 'daughter Directives', aimed at implementing, in specific areas, the provisions laid down in the 1989 framework Directive which aims to encourage improvements in the health and safety of workers at in their workplaces.

An important EU measure in the health and safety area is the Working Time Directive (1993), translated into UK law via the Working Time

Regulations, which became operative on 1 October 1998. The Conservative Government (1992–1997) mounted a challenge to the Directive in the European Court of Justice, on the grounds that working time was a health and safety matter. They argued that as an industrial issue it should be considered under the 'Social Chapter' mechanism providing for agreement by the Council of Ministers on the basis of qualified majority voting – from which the UK Government was, at that time, exempted.

The Working Time Regulations introduce a range of significant new rights and entitlements, such as a minimum of four weeks' paid annual leave (that can include Bank Holidays). There is significant scope in the Regulations for employers and employees to enter into agreements on how the working time rules will apply in their own particular circumstances. Collective agreements can be made with an independent trade union, whereas 'workforce agreements' can be made with workers who are not covered by collective bargaining. Certain activities, or sectors of activities, are excluded from the Regulations. These include the activities of those whose working time is necessarily extremely flexible – for example, managing executives, family and religious workers, domestic servants and trainee doctors.

Broadly, worker entitlements under the Regulations (eg rest periods and paid annual leave) are enforced by an individual complaint to an employment tribunal. In the case of the mandatory limits on working time (such as on weekly working time and night-work), employees' rights are enforced by health and safety authorities (the Health and Safety Executive and local authorities). However, workers have protection against detrimental treatment or unfair dismissals for, *inter alia*, refusing to work in breach of an acceptable working time limit. Employers are required to keep adequate records, going back two years, to show that working time limits have been honoured.

Explain, with appropriate examples, the impact of at least three pieces of European Union-derived law on your organisation. What implementation problems did they give rise to? How were these overcome?

European Union Declarations

In the field of employee relations, there are two major Declarations. These are the so-called 'Social Charter' of 1989 and sections of the 'Charter of Fundamental Rights' (2000).

The Social Charter

The Community Charter on the Fundamental Rights of Workers, commonly known as the Social Charter, was adopted by all member states except the UK in December 1989. It was introduced as a result of political pressure to provide benefits for employees as a balance to what was seen as the advantages for companies provided by the Single European Act (1987) and the coming into force of the Single Market on 1 January 1993. The Charter is a Declaration and has no legal force in itself. It is in essence a 'wish list' of social objectives.

The Charter proposes a floor of basic common employment rights and objectives which should be established and implemented without discrimination at appropriate levels across all member states to ensure that:

- The right of free movement in the EU becomes a reality.

- Workers are paid a sufficient wage to ensure a decent standard of living.

- Adequate social security protection is provided by all member states.

- Basic law on working time, provision of contract, treatment of part-time and temporary workers, and collective redundancies is improved and harmonised.

- All workers have the right to join or not to join a union, negotiate collective agreements and take collective action, including strike action.

- All workers have access to continuous vocational training throughout their working lives.

- Equal treatment and equal opportunities between men and women are developed, particularly to enable men and women to reconcile family and work responsibilities.

- Information and consultation are developed along appropriate lines taking into account national practices, particularly in European enterprises.

- Health and safety protection is improved.

- Young workers are given access to training and fair treatment.

- The elderly are guaranteed an adequate income.

- Measures are taken to improve the social and professional integration of people with disabilities.

The Charter emphasises that the implementation of these 12 principles would contribute not only towards the improvement of living and working conditions provided in the Treaty of Rome (1957) but would also lead to a more effective use of human resources across the EU and therefore improve economic competitiveness and job creation. Although not in itself a legally binding document, the Charter has nevertheless formed the basis for a good deal of EU activity in the area of social policy – for example, the Working Time Directive, the European Works Council Directive and the Part-Time Workers Directive. The Charter's incorporation into the Treaty of Amsterdam strengthens its standing as an important basis for EU social and employment policy.

The Charter of Fundamental Rights of the European Union
This Charter, commonly known as the Charter of Fundamental Rights, was adopted by all member states in 2000. It is a Declaration of rights for all EU citizens. It sets out 54 rights, of which those relevant to employee relations professionals are:

Article 12	The freedom of assembly and of association, which covers the right of everyone to form and join trade unions for the protection of his or her interests.
Article 23	The right to equality between men and women, which covers areas such as employment work and pay.
Article 27	Workers' rights to be consulted and informed within the undertaking.
Article 28	The right of collective bargaining and action, which requires that workers and employers have, in accordance with Community law and national laws, the right to negotiate and conclude collective agreements at the appropriate levels, and, in cases of conflict of interests, to take collective action to defend their interests, including strike action.
Article 30	The right to protection in the event of unjustified dismissal.
Article 31	The right to fair and just working conditions, which requires working conditions that respect a worker's health, safety and dignity.

Some member states – although the UK is not among them – wish this Charter to become incorporated into the EU Treaties rather than to remain, as at present, a statement of political intent. This issue of incorporation is to be raised again at the inter-governmental conference to be held in 2004. What has been noticeable, however, is that the Charter was quoted in the opinion given by the Advocate-General of the European Court of Justice in the case brought by the trade union BECTU against the British government in regard to the way the Government had implemented the Working Time Directive. The fact that the UK legislation included a 13-week qualifying period was judged to have been an unlawful translation of the Directive, which clearly specified that all workers had a right to four weeks' paid leave regardless of how long they had been employed. It is expected that this citing of the Charter of Fundamental Rights will set a precedent for future cases.

CONCLUSION

This chapter has:

- traced the development of the European Union since its inception, formally marked by the Treaty of Rome in 1957 (see Table 9)

- measured the growing influence of the European Union on employee relations management in the UK

- explained how the European Single Market in which groups, services, people and capital can move freely (the four great freedoms) also has a social dimension, known as the Social Chapter, to provide for the harmonisation of minimum social and employment conditions between member states

- outlined the main role and function of the legislative institutions of the European Commission, the Council of Ministers, the European Parliament and the European Court of Justice

- pointed out how the introduction of the qualified majority voting (QMV) procedure in 1987 removed the veto of member states over Commission proposals in certain areas and meant that Europe could never be the same again and that its law-making mechanisms could actually start to work as envisaged in 1957

- explained how the Treaty of Maastricht (1993) provided for compulsory consultation by the European Commission with the social partners (both at the inter-sectoral and sectoral levels) on any social and employment proposals, and gave the social partners the option to agree voluntarily to negotiate a framework agreement on any such issue and for that agreement to be made binding on member states via its transcription into a Directive

- noted that framework agreements collectively bargained by the inter-sectoral social partners and then issued as a Directive and then translated into UK legislation have been concluded in three areas – parental leave, part-time work and fixed-term contracts

- elaborated on the fact that European Union social and employment legislation comes mainly in the form of Directives which set out specific objectives, and each member state is given time (usually two years) to enact legislation within its own

Table 9 The development of the European Union

1957	The Treaty of Rome	• created a 'Common Market'
		• contained two social measures
		  – freedom of movement for workers
		  – harmonisation of social conditions (the Social Chapter)

1987	The Single European Act	• introduced the qualified majority voting (QMV) procedure • declared that health and safety were to be harmonised on the basis of QMV
1993	The Treaty on the European Union	• provided for a common currency (the euro) from 1 January 1999 • formalised a Social Policy Agreement containing a Social Protocol that extended the social issues to be decided/ harmonised by QMV • stipulated greater involvement of the social partners in the EU decision-making machinery
1999	The Treaty of Amsterdam	• introduced an Employment Chapter • incorporated the Social Policy Agreement fully into the Treaty as the Social Provisions Chapter • formalised further measures to combat discrimination based on sex, sexual orientation, disability, age, religion or belief, and racial or ethnic origin • required EU institutions to encourage social dialogue on such issues as employment, the right to work, training, etc
2000	The Treaty of Nice	• extended the issues to be decided/harmonised on the basis of QMV • changed the size and composition of the EU Commission • enhanced provisions for members' co-operation

Parliament to ensure that the objectives are achieved

- explained how, under the Social Chapter procedures, some issues (eg working conditions, informing and consulting with workers) can be harmonised by qualified majority voting, others (eg the protection of workers once their employment contract is terminated, co-determination) can be harmonised on the basis of unanimity among member states, and yet others (eg the right to association, the right to strike, and the right to lock out) are formally excluded from harmonisation procedures

- spent time outlining how, and where, European Union laws have had, and will continue to have, a direct impact on the work of the employee relations professional in the UK

- noted that UK legislation arising from the European Union exists in the following areas – equal opportunities (equal pay, parental leave, equal treatment, and the burden of proof in cases of sex discrimination); employment protection/working conditions (redundancies, transfers of undertakings, insolvency, part-time work, fixed-term contract workers); employee relations (informing and consulting with employees in multi-national companies within the EU, in European companies and in foreign companies based in member states); and health and safety (Working Time Regulations).

Further reading

CHARTERED INSTITUTE OF PERSONNEL AND DEVELOPMENT (2000) *Europe: Personnel and Development*. London.

CHARTERED INSTITUTE OF PERSONNEL AND DEVELOPMENT *European Update*. This appears 10 times a year and provides invaluable information on EU developments in employment and related areas.

CHARTERED INSTITUTE OF PERSONNEL AND DEVELOPMENT *People Management*, a fortnightly journal for CIPD members which covers major developments in employment and social matters in the EU. Legislative matters concerning employment that arise from EU Directives are covered in its 'Law at work' section.

DEPARTMENT OF TRADE AND INDUSTRY (1996) *The Social Chapter – The British and Continental Approaches*.

EUROPEAN UNION COMMISSION (2000) *Industrial Relations in Europe*.

INDUSTRIAL RELATIONS SERVICES and Industrial Relations Research Unit, Warwick Business School *European Works Council Bulletin*. This is a regular bulletin dealing with developments in European Works Councils.

JENSON C. S., MADSEN J. S. *and* DUE J. (1999) 'Phases and dynamics in the development of EU industrial relations regulation', *Industrial Relations Journal*, Vol. 30, No.2, June.

KELLER B. and SORRIES B. (1998) 'The new social dialogue: procedural structuring, first results and perspectives', in Towers B. and Terry M. (eds) *European Annual Review, 1997*. *Industrial Relations Journal*.

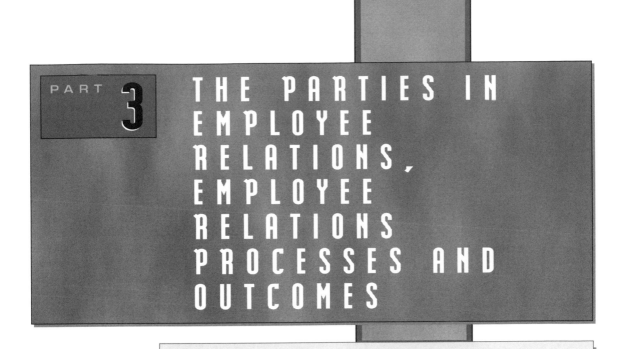

PART 3

THE PARTIES IN EMPLOYEE RELATIONS, EMPLOYEE RELATIONS PROCESSES AND OUTCOMES

• Employee Relations Institutions

Introduction

This chapter is concerned with the institutions of employee relations – employers' associations or federations, trade unions and staff associations, umbrella organisations such as the CBI and the TUC, their international and European equivalents (see Chapter 4), and state organisations such as the Advisory, Conciliation and Arbitration Service (ACAS), the Central Arbitration Committee (CAC) and the Certification Officer. This list demonstrates that both employers and employees have a range of options open to them by way of external organisations which might be useful to them, and about which they have to make choices. For example, should employers join their industry association or a federation? Should they join umbrella organisations such as the Confederation of British Industry (CBI) or the Institute of Directors (IoD)? If they do decide to join their industry or sector organisation, do they – assuming that the organisation they are thinking of joining is one that gets involved in collective bargaining in the first place – allow that organisation to bargain on their behalf? Does becoming a member bind them to particular courses of action? Even if the reasons for contemplating membership are nothing to do with collective bargaining, what sort of services are available to employers – and how are they to be paid for?

On the other side of the coin there is a need for employers to hear the voice of their employees so that there is a two-way dialogue that enables staff to influence what happens at work. This in turn raises the question of what institution embodying the employee voice might be appropriate. Is it a trade union? A works council? Or should employee voice not be viewed any longer in terms of collective representation? And again in turn this raises issues such as why employees join or do not join trade unions.

Employers' organisations

Employers' associations are voluntary, private bodies which exist to provide information and co-ordination in areas of common interest. There are many different associations, covering overlapping areas of geographic spread and industrial sector, and grouping larger and smaller organisations. The *Annual Report* of the Certification Officer (2001) lists 98 employers' associations with a total membership of 268,568 separate enterprises. In 2000 the gross income of employers' associations was £281 million, and gross expenditure was £274 million. Employers' associations vary in size and influence from the very small with no full-time staff to large and highly influential organisations like the Engineering Employers' Federation (over 5,000 member organisations), the Road Haulage Association (9,700 members) and the Retail Motor Industry Federation Ltd (12,500 members).

The largest UK employers' associations

Engineering Employers' Federation
Electrical Contractors' Association
Heating and Ventilating Contractors' Association
Road Haulage Association
British Printing Industries Federation
Chemical Industries Association
National Federation of Retail Newsagents
Construction Confederation
Newspaper Society
Federation of Master Builders
British Clothing Industry Association Ltd
Paper Federation of Great Britain Ltd
Building Merchants' Federation

The 1998 Workplace Employee Relations Survey showed that employers' association membership in industry and commerce fell during the 1980s from 22 per cent of workplaces in 1984 to 13 per cent in 1990. The 1998 results, however, suggested a modest recovery, in that 18 per cent of workplaces then reported membership. The recovery was complete among the largest workplaces – those that employed 500 or more workers – for whom membership levels in 1998 had retuned to the level of 1984.

In common with trade unions, employers' associations who wish to have their legal status confirmed must be registered on a list kept by the

Certification Officer (see below). Employers' associations are required to keep proper accounting records, to establish and maintain a satisfactory system of control over their accounting records, and to submit an annual return to the Certification Officer. An employers' association must submit its annual returns and accounts to this Officer before 1 June each year. The Certification Officer can investigate the financial affairs of an employers' association.

Is your organisation a member of an employers' association? If not, why not? If it is, what does it get out of being one?

The importance of employers' associations

Employers' bodies, whether in the public or private sector, organise themselves in different ways. The priority each gives to employee relations, as opposed to trade matters, differs according to tradition, the nature of the industry it represents and the degree of unionisation in its particular sector. Generally, it remains true that those associations that are most concerned with employee relations are those involving companies that make use of semi-skilled and skilled labour in areas where there is a high concentration of a single industry, such as engineering or printing.

There are three types of employers' associations: national federations to which local employers' associations are affiliated – eg the Engineering Employers' Federation (EEF), which is a federation of 13 autonomous organisations; single national bodies. such as the British Printing Industries Federation (BPIF), which is divided into six regions for administrative and representational purposes; and single associations with a national membership like the British Ceramic Confederation.

Employers' associations consist of companies of different sizes, from the very small to the very large. The largest are sometimes organised into either autonomous local associations (for example, the EEF West Midlands Association, EEF South and EEF Lancashire) or non-autonomous district associations, like the British Printing Industries Federation. Some employers' associations have a similar organisational structure to trade unions such that its ultimate decision-making authority is a national council or the equivalent. The basis of representation on such a council varies from association to association. Except for those with local autonomy, in most employers' associations local and regional associations are consultative, rather than decision-making, bodies.

Although organisations of employers have existed for a very long time, there is some evidence that in recent times their prominence and influence over employment issues has declined. The 1998 Workplace Employee Relations Survey reported, for example, that in their role as sources of advice and information and as the employers' side of industry-wide or regional negotiating bodies, employers' associations had diminished in importance since the 1980s, indicating that more and more managements seemed to be assuming responsibility for their own employee relations. Nevertheless, there are still a significant number of employers' associations, which continue to negotiate agreements at national level. In the private sector national agreements still exist, for instance, in electrical contracting, paper-making, construction, road haulage and general printing. In the public sector national pay arrangements still exist for doctors and nurses, and the National Association of Health Authorities and Trusts – an employers' body – provides evidence to the appropriate pay review body. Yet in many industries national agreements have become less extensive as the percentage of employees covered by collective bargaining has fallen from 70 per cent of employees in 1994 to 41 per cent in 1998. National agreements tend to remain in industries dominated by small companies that operate in very competitive labour markets. For these companies, which usually do not have the resources to establish a personnel function, the national agreement is still regarded as significant in taking labour out of competition and in providing an infrastructure to the industry via the procedures (eg disputes and grievances) contained in the agreement.

The social dialogue procedure at the inter-professional and sector level of the European Union (see Chapter 4) has given an added importance to the collective bargaining role of employers' associations. Employer enterprises that wish to influence the social regulation of the labour market in the EU can do so only by joining an employers' association and then trying to shape the policy of that association so that in turn that body attempts to get that policy adopted as the view of its EU-wide equivalent either at the sector or inter-professional level. If British companies wish to influence the position of UNICE (which is the only EU-wide inter-professional employer voice recognised by the EU Commission) on the social regulation of the single market, they have to be members, directly or indirectly, via the Confederation of British Industry (CBI). If UK engineering companies wish to shape EU social regulation of the EU-wide engineering industry, they have to be members of the EEF, which in turn affiliates to the Western European Metal Trades Employers' Organisation, which represents the only EU-Commission-recognised EU-wide engineering sector employer voice for consultation and negotiating purposes.

National and other representative bodies

The best-known national employers' organisation in the UK is the Confederation of British Industry (CBI) whose roots go back to 1915 with the formation of the National Union of Manufacturers, later renamed the National Association of British Manufacturers (NABM). Within five years two further organisations – the Federation of British Industries (FBI) and the British Employers' Confederation (BEC) – were formed. The CBI as an organisation was the result of a merger in 1965 between these three bodies. Its membership includes individual companies, and national and regional trades and employers' associations. It sees as its overall task the promotion of policies for a more efficient mixed economy. It is estimated that around half of the total workforce are employed in organisations affiliated to the CBI. An important political lobbying organisation, the CBI's major function is to provide for British industry the means of formulating, making known and influencing general policy in regard to industrial, economic, fiscal, commercial, labour, social, legal and technical questions.

However, although it does not specifically engage in employee relations activities, the CBI's lobbying activities can (and do) have an impact on issues that affect workplace employee relations. In recent years, the CBI has lobbied successfully on behalf of employers on issues such as the national minimum wage, statutory trade union recognition procedures and the reform of the employment tribunal system. As an organisation the CBI does not engage in negotiations with employee representatives, but it does maintain a direct working relationship with the Trades Union Congress (TUC) as well as an indirect one via joint membership of bodies such as ACAS and the Health and Safety Executive.

Outline the main services the CBI provides for its members.

The activities of employers' associations

Employers' organisations have traditionally offered their members services in five areas:

- collective bargaining with trade unions
- assisting in the resolution of disputes
- providing members with general advice
- representing members' views to political decision-making bodies
- representing member companies at employment tribunals.

Collective bargaining

Collective bargaining services carried out for members have declined. Multi-employer bargaining, which had greatly diminished in importance in the 1980s, became – according to the 1998 Workplace Employee Relations Survey – even more of a rarity during the 1990s. In workplaces with recognised trade unions, multi-employer negotiations affected the pay of some or all employees in 68 per cent of workplaces in the 1980s. By 1990, this had fallen to 60 per cent – but in 1998 it was down to 34 per cent. Over three broad sectors of the economy, the fall over the period 1980–1998 was substantial. In public services, the drop was from 81 to 47 per cent, while in private manufacturing the fall was from 57 to 25 per cent. The most dramatic fall, however, was in private services. In 1984, in this sector, 54 per cent of workplaces were affected by multi-employer negotiations. By 1998 the figure had fallen to just 12 per cent.

The Workplace Employee Relations Survey (1998) reports that when the falling proportion of workplaces with recognised unions is taken into account, the demise of multi-employer collective bargaining is even more apparent. Among all workplaces with 25 or more employees, multi-employer bargaining directly affected 43 per cent of workplaces in 1980, 31 per cent in 1990, and just 14 per cent in 1998. The public sector emerged as the only major sector of the economy in which multi-employer bargaining remained common – in 1998, 41 per cent of public sector workplaces were affected by it. In the private sector, the proportion in 1998 was a mere 4 per cent of workplaces, down from over 25 per cent in 1980. Private sector employers have effectively abandoned acting jointly to regulate the terms and conditions of employment.

Dispute resolution

The provision of dispute resolution services has links with national bargaining arrangements in that most national agreements provide access to an established dispute procedure. Such procedures tend to stipulate a number of stages through which a dispute is to be processed. Stage one may include the involvement of a local employers' association representative, a union branch secretary, lay union officials from within the organisation in dispute and the organisation's management. If the dispute is not resolved at this stage, it may – depending on the employers' association and the union involved – move up to a district or regional level. Some of the players will stay the same as for the first stage, but the full-time officials will probably differ. The third stage involves national officials of the employers' association and the appropriate trade unions. If there is no resolution of the differences at this stage, some disputes procedures provide for the involvement of an independent third party whose decision will be binding. Such dispute procedures usually contain provisions stating that 'no hostile action' is to be taken by either side, or that the status quo must prevail while the dispute is going through its various stages.

Advisory and information services

During the years when national collective bargaining was in the ascendancy, many employer organisations became bureaucratic and unimaginative. They had a captive audience and paid little attention to membership retention or to the range of services that they offered members. All this changed as companies began to prefer bargaining at a more local level. This in turn led employers to examine what else they were receiving from their associations in return for not insignificant subscriptions. Some employers' organisations quickly realised that if they were to continue to have an employee relations influence, they had to provide their members with a package of benefits and services that would be seen to add value to businesses. In this context many employers' associations widened their existing advisory services on good practices and model procedural agreements on issues such as disciplinary, dismissal and redundancy. Their ability to market such services was helped by the growth – particularly in the 1970s and 1980s – of employment legislation that added to employees' 'rights at work': unfair dismissal, health and safety, and equal pay are just three examples. In the 1990s the advent of legislation from the European Union added to the advisory and information services that employers' associations can now provide for their members.

The recruitment literature of any of the larger employers' associations places greatest emphasis on the employment advice and support services they can offer to members. For example, the Construction Confederation offers its members advice and support on wage rates and conditions of employment, disciplinary procedures, redundancy procedures and representation at employment tribunals, and provides a regular bulletin outlining relevant developments in employment law. Most employers' organisations also provide employee relations information services. Prominently featured in such information are pay and benefits data based on regularly conducted surveys, which are useful for salary and pay comparisons and for use in local negotiations. However, such surveys can be problematic, because the associations have no means of enforcing individual returns. Nevertheless, provided that the employee relations professional recognises these limitations, such surveys can be a valuable tool. Other topics on which employers' associations provide information include labour productivity and Government and EU policy developments in employee relations.

The representation of members' interests
A major growth area of activity has been the representation of members' views before a range of other organisations, particularly political bodies – UK Government departments, local authorities, the institutions of the European Union, and political parties. These political lobbying activities may be of particular interest to a large company whose inclination might otherwise be to leave an association if its only purpose was the negotiation of a national agreement. Now that many large organisations operate in a European and worldwide market, they know that their only means of influencing UK Government or European Union policy is through a collective voice. In its 2001 review the EEF reported on its representations to the major political parties to try to ensure that the employment policies that they develop meet the needs of the engineering industry (EEF *Annual Review* 2001). UK Governments and the EU Commission find employers' organisations useful in obtaining a collective employer view on a wide range of consultative documents. Examples include reform of the employment tribunal system, possible pension reform, and the removal of any limits to the compensation to be awarded to individuals unfairly dismissed. Employers' associations also play an important role in representing the interests of their members (especially small companies) at employment tribunal hearings.

Why might organisations wish to be members of an employers' association?

Non-membership of employers' associations

Some companies view employers' associations as too restrictive and see membership as an obstacle to independent action to introduce innovation in employee relations policies and practices. Such companies regard innovation, whether in operational matters or in people issues, as an essential managerial activity in today's economic climate. They therefore feel the need to be responsible for, to co-ordinate and to control their own employee relations activities. Nevertheless, it is important to remember that even those companies which bargain unilaterally, or independently of the appropriate employers' association, cannot ignore when deciding their own employee relations policies and practices what is happening more generally in the sector in which they are operating. An important part of the employee relations function is to take account of other wage settlements, particularly within the sector in which their organisation operates. Not being aware of such settlements, many of which affect their competitors, could seriously weaken their own bargaining position and impact adversely on their competitiveness.

There are businesses, which, despite their feelings, join employers' organisations because of their more traditional trade association activities. A number have arbitration schemes to resolve differences between supplier and customer, whereas others have the ability to remove an organisation from membership if it does not meet agreed standards on, for example, the quality of service or product provided for the customer. This can be an effective sanction for a company which relies on the 'badge' of the trade association to help secure business, such as some of the building trades or electrical contractors.

Trade unions

Purpose and objectives

Trade unions are organised groups of employees who

consist wholly or mainly of workers of one or more description and whose principal purposes include the regulation of relations between workers and employers.
— *Section 1 of the Trade Unions and Labour Relations (Consolidation) Act*

The primary purpose of trade unions is to protect the jobs of their members and to seek to enhance their pay and the conditions of employment mainly by the process of collective bargaining and the lobbying of political decision-making bodies. The core business of a trade union is therefore interest representation to employers, to other trade unions and to the political decision-makers.

UK trade unions are bodies that defend sectional economic interests rather than working-class interests as a whole. In Flanders' (1968b) view, unions are job-conscious, not class-conscious, organisations. He also argued that the value of a union to its members lies in its capacity to protect their dignity at the workplace by establishing worker rights – for example, not to be discriminated against – by establishing rights to paid holidays and by establishing a standard working week. Unions thus participate in job regulation by establishing with employers a body of jointly agreed rules for jobs or a set of minimum employment standards for jobs established by law. Trade unions are thus best seen as economic, social and political agents.

Union methods

Trade unions attempt to achieve their objectives by a number of different methods. The most common are collective bargaining, which results in a collective agreement setting out minimum standards to apply to those members covered by the agreement; joint consultation; the providing of such services for members as representation in grievance and disciplinary matters and the obtaining of sickness, accident and unemployment benefit; the providing of employee relations training and development opportunities and legal assistance for both work-related and work-unrelated matters; and influencing national and local government and inter-governmental political institutions such as the European Union and the International Labour Office (which is a United Nations agency) to achieve legal regulation of employment conditions.

The European Union is influenced via the activities of the European Trade Union Confederation (ETUC) and the International Labour Office by the International Confederation of Free Trade Unions (ICFTU) which was formed in 1949. ICFTU membership consists of 141 affiliated organisations in some 97 countries and totals 86 million members. Its objectives include promoting the interests of working people throughout the world, reducing the gap between rich and poor, defending fundamental human and trade union rights, and helping workers to organise themselves and to secure the recognition of their organisations as free bargaining agents. It also has close relationships with the International Labour Organisation (ILO) which is a UN body made up of government, employer and worker representatives. The ILO has established many international minimum labour standards (known as Conventions) to protect workers' rights, and which all governments in membership of the UN are expected to enact in their national legislation.

Union resources

The major financial resources of trade unions in the UK come from membership subscriptions and from interest payments from investments.

Some unions charge their members a flat-rate subscription paid either weekly or monthly, whereas others – particularly those representing the interests of relatively high-paid non-manual employees – charge members a subscription rate on the basis of a percentage of their pay. The Certification Officer's *Report* for 2001 stated that the gross income of trade unions in 2000 was £754,100,000, of which £593,200,000 was from members' subscriptions. The TUC estimates that the average union subscription is £6 to £8 per month.

What are the main purposes of trade unions?

Trade union membership levels

Overall

Table 10 shows trends in UK trade union membership over the period 1978–2000. Total union membership in the UK peaked at an all-time high of 13.2 million members in 1979, made up of 12.1 million members in TUC-affiliated unions and just over 1 million in non-TUC unions. In 2000 the total trade union membership, as reported by the Certification Officer, was 7.9 million. Although over the past 20 years trade union membership in the aggregate declined in many organisations, there are now signs that membership is starting to increase again. Unions still play an important part in the process of employee relations in particular sectors. In the manufacturing sector there is still a significant union presence, especially among skilled manual workers, but the number of people employed in this sector has declined dramatically over the last two decades. Unions still have a large presence in the public sector, particularly in the health service, local government and central government.

Trade union membership remains low, however, in private sector services (financial, retail), among private sector non-manual employees, in small firms, and in foreign-owned firms. In the private sector of the economy today only some 17 per cent of employees are members of a trade union. The 1998 Workplace Employee Relations Survey estimated that 47 per cent of workplaces had no trade union members, as opposed to 30 per cent in 1980.

The period of decline, 1979–1999

The decline in trade union membership over the period 1979–2000 can be explained by a number of factors, many of which reflect changes in the economy. The last 20 years has seen changes in the structure of employment which have been problematic for trade unions. Employment distribution shifted from manufacturing (a heartland of trade unions) towards the private service sector where trade union membership has traditionally been low. The size of employing unit has also fallen. It was easier, and cheaper, for unions to organise in large workplaces than in smaller ones. In the past, trade unions have always found it relatively

Table 10 UK trade union membership 1978–2000

Year	Membership of the TUC	Number of TUC-affiliated unions	Membership of non-TUC unions
1978	11,865,390	112	1,188,206
1979	12,128,078	112	1,084,276
1980	12,172,508	109	463,847
1981	11,601,413	108	709,821
1982	11,005,984	105	738,406
1983	10,510,157	95	789,406
1984	10,082,144	89	691,809
1985	9,855,204	91	963,745
1986	9,580,502	91	1,017,506
1987	9,127,278	87	1,236,853
1988	9,127,278	83	1,259,960
1989	8,652,318	78	1,391,288
1990	8,405,246	78	1,404,773
1991	8,192,662	74	not available
1992	7,786,885	72	1,142,017
1993	7,647,443	70	1,018,501
1994	7,117,436	69	1,113,109
1995	6,894,604	67	1,136,722
1996	6,790,339	73	1,147,874
1997	6,756,544	75	1,044,771
1998	6,638,986	74	1,212,918
1999	6,749,481	77	not available
2000	6,745,907	76	1,151,612

Sources: TUC Annual Reports, Certification Officer, Annual Reports

more difficult to organise women than men. Over the last 20 years an increasing number of women, relative to men, have entered the labour force. Non-manual employees, particularly in the private sector, have been another occupational group that has been traditionally reluctant to join trade unions. Their share of employment in the last 20 years, relative to manual work employment, has increased significantly and is set to rise further. Employees in foreign-owned firms have also been difficult groups for recruitment for trade unions. The share of total employment accounted for by such firms has increased significantly since 1979.

However, structural factors do not tell the whole story. The Conservative Governments between May 1979 and May 1997 enacted public policy initiatives in the employee relations field that created an environment unfavourable to trade union membership retention and advancement For example, statutory trade union recognition procedures were repealed in 1980 and legal protection for the closed shops (ie where union membership was a condition of gaining and/or remaining in employment) was progressively removed. Public policy initiatives also weakened trade union bargaining power relative to the employer by restricting severely the circumstances in which a trade union could impose industrial action on an employer without that employer having the right to resort to the courts for redress.

During the 1980s the private sector employers faced increasingly competitive product market pressures whereas the public sector was privatised, deregulated or 'contractorised'. These increased competitive pressures led employers to introduce more flexible employment policies. The result was, *inter alia*, a significant growth in the number of workers employed on the basis of a fixed-term contract, of part-time working and of temporary hiring. Employees brought in on such terms have always proved more difficult to organise than full-time workers. This was another factor that contributed to the decline in trade union membership.

Competitive pressures also resulted in some employers' de-recognising trade unions and ending the associated collective bargaining institutions and procedures. De-recognition was particularly prominent in situations where the trade union only represented a small proportion of the workforce and was therefore limited its representative capacity. Other policies introduced by management over the period 1980–1999 that made organising workers more difficult included the introduction of employee empowerment, involvement and participation schemes, and the introduction of dual communication-channel systems by which the employers still communicated with their employees indirectly through trade union representatives but more often communicated directly with them.

Increased membership levels?
During 2000–2001, the total union membership recorded by the Certification Officer stood at 7.9 million – up from 7.8 million in the previous year. This represents an increase of some 0.6 per cent. Membership of the TUC has also increased. In 2000 the total membership of its affiliates stood at 6.8 million, compared with 6.7 million in 1999. This increase has been explained by two major factors – the willingness of trade unions to enter into partnership agreements with employers (see Chapter 8) and the trade union recognition provisions of the Employment Relations Act 1999.

At the workplace level, partnership means employers' and trade unions' working together to achieve common goals such as fairness and competitiveness. This more co-operative attitude on the part of trade unions, it is argued, has made employers more willing to recognise them and have a relationship with them. The Union of Shop, Distributive and Allied Workers claims to have recruited some 23,000 additional members at Tesco following its signing of a partnership deal with that company in 1998.

The trade union recognition provisions of the Employment Relations Act 1999 began operating on 6 June 2000. The Trades Union Congress

(2002) reported that over the period November 2000 to October 2001 inclusive there were more than 470 new trade union recognition agreements signed, representing almost three times the 159 concluded in the corresponding period for 1999–2000. As a result, over 120,000 more workers became represented by a recognised trade union. The overwhelming majority of trade union recognition agreements in 1999–2000 and 2000–2001 were voluntary agreements for recognition covering at least pay, hours and holidays. The introduction of a legal framework governing trade union recognition appears to have helped to boost the profile, power and coverage of unions in the modern world of work.

However, it is perhaps too early to say that trade unions are enjoying something of a renaissance. Many of the sectors in which trade unions have recently gained recognition – the printing and newspaper industry and parts of the financial services sector – are areas in which unions were de-recognised in the 1980s, so unions may merely be regaining some lost ground. With only a few exceptions, there is little evidence that unions have been able to make serious inroads into gaining members in sectors of the economy where they have been traditionally weak – retailing, hospitality and services – and where recently much of the employment growth has occurred.

> What do you think will be the trend in total trade union membership over the next five years? Why do you think so?

Trade union structure

Union 'structure' refers to the particular way unions organise themselves and their coverage in terms of industry and occupations. The UK trade union structure is characterised by a small number of very large trade unions co-existing with a large number of small trade unions. In 2001 the *Annual Report* of the Certification Officer reported that the 16 unions with a membership of 100,000 or more accounted for 82 per cent of total trade union membership but accounted for only 7 per cent of the 237 trade unions on the list of independent unions. The largest 11 unions had a total membership of 5.7 million out of a total of 7.9 million; 115 unions had memberships of less than 1,000 but accounted for 49 per cent of the total number of unions and only 0.5 per cent of the total membership of trade unions (see Table 11). The largest 16 unions in 2000 are shown in Table 12.

Table 11 Trade unions: distribution by size

Number of members	Number of unions	Membership (000s)	%	Number of unions Cumulative %	Membership of all unions %	Membership of all unions Cumulative %
Under 100	44	1	18.6	18.6	0	0
100–499	49	12	20.7	39.3	0.2	0.2
500–999	22	14	9.3	48.6	0.2	0.4
1,000–2,499	34	58	14.3	62.9	0.7	1.1
2,500–4,999	23	83	9.7	72.6	1.1	2.2
5,000–9,999	12	92	5.1	77.7	1.2	3.4
10,000–14,999	4	53	1.7	79.4	0.7	4.1
15,000–24,999	10	181	4.2	83.6	2.3	6.4
25,000–49,999	18	618	7.6	91.2	7.8	14.2
50,000–99,999	5	304	2.1	93.3	3.8	18.0
100,000–249,999	5	788	2.1	95.4	10.0	28.0
250,000 and over	11	5,693	4.6	100	72.1	100
TOTAL	237	7,898	100		100	

Source: *Annual Report of the Certification Officer, 2000–2001*, p20

Table 12 Trade unions with memberships of 100,000 and more in 1999–2000

Union	Membership
UNISON, the public services union	1,272,350
Transport and General Workers' Union (T&GWU)	871,512
Amalgamated Engineering and Electrical Union (AEEU)	727,369
GMB, the 'general' trade union	694,174
Manufacturing Science and Finance Union (MSF)	404,741
Royal College of Nursing (RCN)*	326,610
Union of Shop Distributive and Allied Workers (USDAW)	309,811
National Union of Teachers	294,672
Communication Workers' Union (CWU)	281,472
Public and Commercial Services Union	258,278
National Association of Schoolmasters and Union of Women Teachers (NASUWT)	252,021
Graphical, Paper and Media Union (GPMU)	200,676
Association of Teachers and Lecturers (ATL)*	183,144
Union of Construction, Allied Trades and Technicians (UCATT)	171,249
UNIFI, the financial services union	122,579
British Medical Association (BMA)*	110,206

* Non-TUC affiliate

Types of union

The UK trade unions have a complex structure in terms of their recruitment and membership base. When unions began to come to prominence in the mid-nineteenth century they developed, principally, as organisations of skilled workers whose main objective was to secure employment for themselves; they did little or nothing for labourers and other unskilled workers. As a result, in the late nineteenth century the labourers' unions came into being by combining labourers in the craft-dominated industries with workers from previously unorganised industries and services.

From these beginnings, union structure in the UK developed to the point where it has been conventional to divide trade unions into three types – occupational (or craft), industrial, and general. However, today few occupational unions exist, and those that do are relatively small in size. Examples include the British Air Line Pilots Association (BALPA), the Associated Society of Locomotive Engineers and Firemen (ASLEF) and the Professional Footballers Association (PFA). Such unions recruit members selectively, on a job-by-job basis, irrespective of where they work. It is the worker's occupational status, job skills and qualifications or training that determine whether or not individuals qualify for membership, not the industry or the organisation that employs them.

Industrial unions will organise any workers, regardless of their status and skills, who are employed in a particular industry. They recruit vertically within an industry but will not recruit from groups working in much the same way in a different industry. In short, they recruit members vertically from among all employment grades, normally including both manual and non-manual workers, within a single industry. However, in the UK because of the constantly changing and evolving structure of industry, it is not a simple matter to define the boundaries between industries. Examples of industry-based unions in the UK are few. The best examples are the National Union of Mineworkers, the Iron and Steel Trades Confederation, the Ceramic and Allied Trade Union. The Graphical, Paper and Media Union (GPMU) seeks to organise all workers except journalists in the general print, newspaper and paper-making industries.

General unions will recruit any workers (both manual and non-manual) horizontally across industries and vertically within industries. Such unions seek to regulate labour markets by trying to establish a monopoly over the supply of all employees. The two best examples of general unions in the UK are the Transport and General Workers' Union and the GMB.

Mergers

Changing product and labour markets and the implementation of technological change have recently nevertheless caused unions to alter their recruitment and membership-base. Loss of membership, continuing employer opposition in key economic sectors, difficulties in financial viability and inter-union competition for members has made trade unions attempt to widen their membership-base. The net result has been a series of union mergers in the form of amalgamation and/or a transfer of engagements. A merger involves the creation of a new union, with a new rule-book, which is approved in a ballot by both sets of members. A tranfer of engagements involves one union transferring its membership and financial assets into another, and in doing so accepting the constitution and industrial policies of the union into which the membership is being transferred. Over the last 20 years, as a result of trade union mergers, the number of trade unions affiliated to the TUC has fallen from 112 in 1979 to 76 in 2000.

Job-centred unionism

Despite all this merger activity, the job an individual performs still effectively determines the union he or she joins. Although in theory individuals have a legal right to join any union of their choice, the reality is somewhat different. Where unions exist in a workplace and are recognised by the employer, most individuals who choose to join a union will want to join one that has a significant membership within their work group.

There are downsides to job-centred unions. It has resulted in an unwieldy trade union structure in which multi-union disputes occur. It can result in unions competing to recruit the same employees (membership jurisdiction), and in unions having different wage policies. Inter-union disputes were very much a feature of the 1960s and 1970s employee relations scene and often resulted in strike action, leaving the employers unwilling victims of a problem outside their control. Such disputes have decreased over the past two decades – partly as the result of legislative interventions and partly as a consequence of union mergers. They can, however, still be an issue, and the employee relations professional cannot afford to ignore their impact on employment relationships.

Job-conscious trade unionism also has implications for trade union solidarity. There is a tendency to think – especially among left-wing political romantics – that unions automatically support each other. In reality, that happens almost solely when the job interests of the different trade unions coincide. Then and only then do they show support and solidarity for each other.

> Explain the term 'job-conscious trade unionism'. Outline its implications for management, giving examples.

International comparisons

Job-centred trade unionism is also found in the USA, Canada and Australasia, and is thus a central feature of trade union recruitment in English-speaking countries. In Japan, most trade unions are organised not by occupation, job or industry but by enterprise or establishment. An enterprise union consists solely of regular employees of a single firm, regardless of their occupational status. About a third of all Japanese employees expect life-long employment at the same company until their mandatory retirement age, unless they are made redundant or leave voluntarily (Bamber and Lansbury, 1998).

In Germany, trade unions are organised along industrial lines. This industrial principle means that one trade union represents all organised employees at a workplace, irrespective of their individual occupation. It is, however, a system that is being superseded by the growth of the service sector and the blurring of traditional industry boundaries. In France, trade unions are general unions with divisions – though not absolutely rigidly or consistently – along political and religious lines. There are five major, and competing, trade union confederations in the private sector, each with a larger or smaller number of affiliated unions, organised by each sector. Each also has a white-collar affiliate. The CFDT is the largest union confederation recognised by the government at national level. It was established in 1964 and its affiliates have a socialist orientation. The CGT is associated with the Communist Party of France. Its membership is grounded in the manufacturing sector. The CGT-FO, formed in 1948, is particularly strong in the public sector, commerce and finance, and its affiliates are Social Democrat in political orientation. The CFTC organises mainly in health, teaching and engineering, and is a Christian trade union confederation. The CGC affiliates organise engineers, executives, supervisors and technicians. Union confederations and their industrial affiliates play a role in collective bargaining at the industry level but their strength at the workplace is patchy. Trade union density in France is less than 10 per cent, and falling.

The Trades Union Congress

The TUC was established in 1868. In 2000 it had 76 affiliate unions with a total membership of 6.8 million. It performs two broad roles. First, it acts as the collective voice of the UK trade union movement to governments and international trade union bodies. Second, it attempts to influence the behaviour of its affiliated unions. However, the sanctions it possesses to influence its affiliates are limited. When the TUC was established it was very much the voice of the craft unions which jealously guarded their autonomy. As a result, in devising the TUC constitution, they were not prepared to devolve much power or resources to it or to allow it to interfere in their activities. This limitation still remains, and the autonomy of affiliated unions is still regarded as paramount, particularly in the area of wages and employment conditions. The TUC has limited authority over its affiliates and few resources. It has to persuade its affiliates of the rightness of its decisions. It is not always successful.

The supreme authority in the TUC is its annual Congress, which is held in September, and to which affiliated organisations send delegates on the basis of one for every 5,000 members or part thereof. Congress policy is decided on the basis of motions submitted by affiliated unions, that are accepted by a majority vote of delegates. The implementation of policy decided at Congress is the responsibility of the General Council, which is overseen by the General Secretary. Unions over a certain size of membership have automatic representation on this Council. There is also reserved representation for women and black unionists.

The role of the TUC

The TUC has authority from its affiliates to act in three areas – industrial disputes, inter-union disputes, and the conduct of affiliates. In the case of a dispute between an affiliate union and an employer, the TUC does not intervene unless requested to do so by the affiliate involved. However, if negotiations break down (or are likely to break down) and if the nature of the dispute is such that the members of the affiliate or of another affiliated union might be laid off, the TUC General Secretary can intervene to try to effect a settlement.

The TUC can intervene in the case of disputes between affiliated unions over membership and job demarcation issues. A complaint by one affiliate against another is investigated by a Disputes Committee which may, for example, recommend that a union that has poached members from another affiliate must give those members back. If the union fails to comply with recommendations of a Disputes Committee, the General Council can suspend the union from membership until the next Congress, at which it may be expelled from membership.

The TUC can also investigate complaints that an affiliated union is engaging in conduct detrimental to the interests of the trade union movement or contrary to the declared principles or declared policy of the Congress. Should such a complaint be upheld, the General Council will make recommendations to the union concerned on what it must do to put the matter right. Should the union fail to do it, the General Council will recommend its suspension from membership until the next Congress, at which it will be expelled unless in the meanwhile it complies with the recommendation.

Outline the main functions of the TUC.

Staff associations

Staff associations are usually established within a single organisation and for a particular group of employees. Their funding and/or office accommodation is therefore often dependent on the employer. They are not regarded as trade unions in the traditional sense, and stand apart from mainstream trade unionism even if they are not actually hostile to it. Staff associations included on the Certification Officer's list of independent trade unions have historically been strongest in banking and insurance. However, such staff associations are small in membership size in that more than half have fewer than 500 members. The main causes of the formation of independent staff associations relate to the employees' wish to:

- respond concertedly to a specific event (eg threatened redundancies)

- have their own rather less formal type of 'union'

- replace an existing consultative body by one with negotiating powers

- establish collective representation where no representative system previously existed.

They also include employer desires for a management-dominated consultative body or a management-inspired association.

Independent staff associations are characterised by high membership density. For example, the coverage rate within the top 10 building societies typically averages around 70–80 per cent. They typically represent all white-collar employees of a company, from managers to clerks and word-processor operators. However, a substantial minority limit their membership to specific groups, the two most common being managers and executives, and agents, representatives and salesmen.

Although the largest staff associations may act as independent unions, the effectiveness of the smaller ones is limited by their narrow membership-base and weak financial resources. Many operate from a modest financial base. The majority of the staff associations are recognised by employers for negotiating and representational purposes. Most agreements they conclude follow the normal pattern and cover such issues as recognition, provision of facilities, joint negotiating machinery, consultation, and grievance and disciplinary procedures.

The ability of independent staff associations to represent the interest of their members may be questioned. An organisation of which membership is confined to the employees of a single employer is exposed to pressures that are much less effective against a broadly based organisation. It will also find it difficult to bargain on equal terms with that employer, particularly if the size of the undertaking places strict limits on its membership and financial resources. The fact that senior managers can, and do, belong to a staff association, leads some to question their genuine independence from employer interference.

In addition to staff associations which have a Certificate of Independence from the Certification Officer (see below), there are a much larger number of bodies which bear the title of 'staff association' and which make no claim to be a trade union even in an informal sense. Such bodies usually have a consultative rather than a negotiating function, and little or nothing in the way of independent resources. Membership is usually automatic for all non-manual employees, and there is often no membership subscription since the employer meets any expenses incurred by the association.

Explain the difference(s) between a staff association and a trade union.

Professional associations such as the British Medical Association or the British Dental Association often represent the interests of their members in negotiation with the relevant employers but also function as organisations responsible for the education and certification of practitioners and the maintenance of professional standards among members. The dual role of negotiators and professional standard-bearers can sometimes conflict, as the medical and nursing professions have found. It can be difficult to take legitimate action in support of an industrial dispute without coming into conflict with a professional code of conduct.

State agencies

In this section we look at those state agencies that have a statutory role in employee relations, whether that role is in respect of individual or of collective issues. In the UK there are three major agencies of this kind: the Certification Office for Trade Unions and Employers' Associations, the Advisory, Conciliation and Arbitration Service (ACAS), and the Central Arbitration Committee (CAC).

The Certification Office

The post of Certification Officer was established in 1975. The Officer is appointed by the Secretary of State for Trade and Industry after consultation with ACAS. The office performs the following functions:

- maintaining a list of trade unions
- determining that a trade union is independent of employer control, domination or interference – The principal criteria used by the Certification Officer for this purpose are history, membership-base, organisation and structure, finance, employer-provided facilities and negotiating record.
- dealing with complaints by members that a trade union has failed to maintain an accurate register of members or failed to permit access to its accounting records; seeing that trade unions keep proper accounting records, have their accounts properly audited and submit annual returns; investigating the financial affairs of trade unions; ensuring that the statutory

requirements concerning the actuarial examination of members' superannuation schemes are observed; and dealing with complaints that a trade union has failed in its duty to ensure that positions in the union are not held by certain offenders

- handling complaints by members that a trade union has failed to hold secret ballots for electing members of its executive committee, its president and general secretary

- monitoring observance by trade unions of the statutory procedures governing the setting up, operation and review of political funds; and dealing with complaints about breaches of political fund rules or about the conduct of political fund ballots, or the application of general funds for political objects

- seeing that the statutory procedures for trade union amalgamations, transfers of agreements and changes of name are observed; and dealing with complaints by members about the conducting of merger ballots

- maintaining a list of employers' associations; ensuring that the statutory requirements concerning accounting records, annual returns, financial affairs, political funds and the statutory procedures for amalgamation and transfers of engagements in respect of employers' association are observed.

The Employment Relations Act 1999 extended the Certification Officer's power to deal with:

- complaints by trade union members that there has been a breach, or that a breach is threatened, of the rules of a trade union relating to the appointment, election or removal of an office-holder

- disciplinary proceedings

- ballots of members other than in respect of industrial action

- the constitution or proceedings of an Executive Committee or decision-making meeting.

The Advisory, Conciliation and Arbitration Service (ACAS)

The state provided third-party intervention in industrial disputes long before ACAS was established (Mumford, 1996). Such measures were previously the responsibility of the Department of Employment and its predecessor Ministries (eg the Ministry of Labour). The credibility of third-party intervention depends on the two disputant parties being confident that the third party is independent of government (or any other political) influence and therefore totally impartial.

In the 1960s and 1970s the credibility of government-provided third-party intervention services became seriously compromised. This came about because Ministers – often as a condition of making the third-party services available to the disputant parties – made it clear that they expected the independent arbitrator to have due regard to the government of the day's incomes policy. Indeed, on occasions the Minister refused joint requests from employers and unions for third-party intervention on the grounds that the employer's offer was already in excess of the limits of the government's incomes policy. The clash between the government's role as an industrial peace-keeper and its role as an economic manager became most acute in 1968, when the newly created Department of Employment and Productivity – which was responsible for the provision, *inter alia*, of third-party intervention services – was also given responsibility for ensuring that the government's incomes policy was applied effectively.

The early 1970s therefore saw increased demands by unions and employers for a third-party intervention service that was formally independent of the state, and, in particular, of the whims of different governments' prices and incomes policies. The strength of this feeling was seen when the TUC and CBI established their own private third-party arrangements. In September 1974 the then Labour Government set up the Advisory, Conciliation and Arbitration Service (ACAS) as a Royal Commission. It was established as a statutory body on 1 January 1976 under the provisions of the Employment Protection Act 1975.

ACAS is independent of direct ministerial intervention although its sponsoring Ministry is the Department of Trade and Industry. ACAS is governed by an executive body known as 'the Council', which originally consisted of a chairperson and nine ordinary members – three chosen in consultation with the CBI, three in consultation with the TUC, and the remaining three independent people with specialist knowledge of employee relations. In 1992 the Council became 11 ordinary members, the additional two members representing the interests of small businesses and non-TUC unions.

ACAS seeks to:

- promote good practice
- provide information and advice
- conciliate in complaints to employment tribunals
- conciliate in the case of collective disputes
- prevent and resolve employment disputes.

Promoting good practice
ACAS organises conferences and seminars on topical employment and industrial relations issues. For small businesses, ACAS also runs self-help workshops where employment policies and procedures are discussed. Unlike the other services provided by ACAS, which are free, there is a charge for conferences, seminars and small-firm workshops. ACAS also sells a range of booklets offering practical guidance and advice on employment and industrial relations topics – for example, on

discipline, job evaluation, recruitment and induction, employee appraisal, hours of work, teamworking, and employee communications and consultation. During 2000 ACAS organised over 540 conferences, seminars and workshops. These make an important contribution to ACAS' objective of disseminating good practice and assisting in the formulation of sound policies for the employment relationship.

ACAS also has issued three Codes of Practice. Its Code of Practice on Disciplinary and Grievances Procedures was formally published on 4 September 2000, from which date the Code – which relates to all aspects of grievance and disciplinary procedures – has been obligatorily taken into account by arbitrators appointed by ACAS to determine cases brought under the ACAS Arbitration Scheme (see Chapter 11).

The ACAS Code on the Disclosure of Information to Trade Unions for Collective Bargaining Purposes sets out good practice in this area, and its Code on Time Off for Trade Union Duties and Activities provides guidance on time off for trade union duties, time off for training of trade union officials and time off for other standard trade union activities. It also covers the responsibilities which employers and trade unions share in considering reasonable time off, and outlines the advantages of reaching formal agreements on time off. These Codes impose no legal obligations on an employer. Failure to observe the Code does not, by itself, render anyone liable to proceedings – but their provisions are to be taken into account in proceedings before an employment tribunal (disciplinary and grievance procedures) and arbitration hearings under the ACAS Arbitration Scheme (unfair dismissal) and Central Arbitration Committee Hearings (informing and consulting with employees, and time off).

Providing information and advice
ACAS provides information and guidance on a wide range of employee relations matters. It does this primarily through a network of Public Enquiry Points (PEPs) which can be contacted by anyone. The service is free, confidential and impartial, and is designed to assist employers and people at work. PEPs provide a particularly useful and cost-effective service for small firms and individuals to help clarify the range and increasing complexity of employment legislation, avoid difficulties at work, or understand the options available for their possible resolution. Most enquiries are dealt with by telephone, but a small number are answered by letter or personal interviews, usually by prior appointment.

In 2000–2001 PEPs received 760,000 calls. Of these, 56 per cent came from individual employees and most of the rest from employers of different types and sizes, trade unions and other organisations. There were high volumes of questions on contract of employment matters, including wages and holiday pay, discipline and dismissal issues, redundancy and transfer of undertakings and maternity rights. For many, PEPs are often the first point of contact with ACAS. Sometimes their enquiry raises issues that cannot readily be answered by telephone, and in such cases the problem is addressed by face-to-face contact with ACAS field staff.

Clarifying individual employment rights

ACAS provides individual conciliation in cases which are, or could be, the subject of complaints by individuals to employment tribunals about an alleged infringement of employment rights. Individual conciliation is voluntary, impartial, confidential, free of charge and independent of the employment tribunals. ACAS has a duty to act as conciliator in a wide range of individual employment rights complaints, including unfair dismissal, breach of contract (eg non-payment of termination payments or commission, or discrimination on the grounds of sex or race or in terms of equal pay) or failure to provide statutory benefits. The number of complaints handled by ACAS concerning alleged breaches of employment rights is shown in Table 13.

When making a complaint to an employment tribunal, a person must first complete form ET1 and send it to the appropriate employment tribunal office, which then passes a copy to ACAS. The case is then allocated to a conciliation officer whose responsibility it is to attempt to help the parties settle the complaint without the need for a tribunal hearing, if that is their wish and if both parties are willing to accept conciliation. The officer's role is to help in a neutral and independent way, and involves making both parties aware of the options available to them so that they may reach informed decisions on how best to proceed. The conciliation officer explains tribunal and voluntary arbitration procedures as well as relevant law, but does not make decisions on the

Table 13 Individual complaints concerning employment rights 1987–2000

Date	Complaints of unfair dismissal	Total number of complaints received
1987	34,572	40,817
1988	36,340	44,443
1989	37,324	48,817
1990	37,654	52,071
1991	39,234	60,605
1992	44,034	72,166
1993	46,854	75,181
1994	45,824	79,332
1995	40,815	91,568
1996	46,566	100,399
1997	42,771	106,912
1998	40,153	113,636
1999	52,791	164,525
2000	50,065	167,186

Source: ACAS Annual Reports, 1985–2000/01

merits of the case or impose or recommend a particular settlement. Any settlement terms are the responsibility of the parties concerned. The conciliation officer conveys the views of one party to the other. If there is information one party wishes to keep from the other, then so long as the party explains that to the conciliation officer the information will not be passed on. Where a case is not settled before the date fixed for the tribunal hearing, the employment tribunal will resolve the matter.

Conciliation is available also when an individual claims that he or she is having to put up with a situation about which a formal complaint to an employment tribunal could be made. If both parties agree to ACAS involvement, the conciliation officer can conciliate in the same way as if a formal complaint had been laid to an employment tribunal. If conciliation does not result in a settlement, the individual may then carry the complaint on to the employment tribunal.

In unfair dismissal cases, the conciliation officers have the statutory duty to explore first the possibility of reinstatement, or of re-engagement on suitable terms, before seeking to promote a monetary or other form of settlement. The Employment Rights (Disputes Resolution) Act 1998 empowers conciliation officers – if both parties agree – to draw up binding settlements in which both parties opt out of the employment tribunal system in favour of resolving the employee's complaint of unfair dismissal through voluntary arbitration (see Chapter 11). The underlying principle behind the Act is to make the resolving of unfair dismissal claims by this procedure as similar as possible to the arbitrations currently undertaken by ACAS in settling trade disputes.

ACAS's role is to attempt to settle cases without the need for a tribunal hearing – although it is evident that not all disputes are capable of such a settlement and that some parties may wish to have their cases decided in a legal setting. The proportion of employment rights breaches claims settled by ACAS has remained fairly constant over the years, and in 2000–2001 amounted to 35 per cent of the cases cleared. In addition, ACAS conciliation also influences the proportion of cases withdrawn, which comprised some 30 per cent in 2000–2001. ACAS' involvement is normally welcomed by the disputant parties because it provides a means of settling their differences without the need for what can be expensive, stressful and lengthy legal hearings. An important part of the conciliation officer's job is to defuse the tension and reduce the acrimony that often exists between the parties so as to enable them to focus realistically on the options open to them.

> How and why has ACAS been so successful in preventing individual complaints against employers' allegedly unprofessional behaviour from going to employment tribunals?

Conciliating and mediating in collective disputes

Employment disputes are very costly both to the employers and to the employees, so it is sensible to resolve workplace problems before they develop into disputes. ACAS employs two principal methods to help organisations avoid costly disputes:

workshops in which employer and employee representatives discuss and agree on potential barriers to the achievement of long-term organisational goals. Such workshops are useful for exploring problems where the underlying causes are not clearly known. Once these are identified, courses of action can be agreed to rectify the problems.

joint working-parties in which employer and employee representatives work together to devise and implement practical solutions to specific problems by, for example, collecting and analysing information and evaluating options.

ACAS staff normally chair a working-party. However, although prevention is better than cure, employment disputes inevitably occur. When this happens, ACAS can help the parties by offering:

- conciliation,
  - mediation, or
    - arbitration.

Conciliation

Requests for conciliation normally come from employers, trade unions or employee representatives in organisations where there are no trade unions. Before it agrees to conciliate, ACAS checks that the parties have exhausted any internal dispute resolution procedures they may have. In coming to conciliation, no prior commitment is required from the parties, only a willingness to discuss the problem(s) at issue. Conciliation is an entirely voluntary process, and it is open to either party to bring discussion to an end at any time – although effectively management remains in control, deciding whether to continue with the process or to withdraw from it.

ACAS conciliators help the parties in dispute settle their differences by agreement, and, if possible, in a long-term way. The conciliator remains impartial and independent, makes constructive suggestions to facilitate negotiations, provides information at the request of the parties, and gains the trust and confidence of both parties so that a sound working relationship is developed. The first step in conciliation is to discover what the dispute is about, a fact-finding process that usually requires the conciliator to meet with both sides separately, although occasionally information may be obtained at joint meetings. Almost all conciliations involve a mixture of side-meetings, at which the conciliator explores issues separately with the parties, and joint meetings, at which the parties can explain their position face to face. The exact mix of side- and joint meetings is determined by the conciliator in discussion with the parties. Where it is clear a settlement might be achieved, the conciliator seeks to secure a joint agreement, usually in the form of a signed document, which finalises the terms of the settlement. Any agreements reached in conciliation are the responsibility of the parties involved: ACAS has no power to impose or even to recommend settlements. There is no time-limit to the conciliation process, and ACAS continues to assist the parties so long as they wish and there appears a chance of reaching an agreed settlement. The role of the conciliator is to keep the two sides talking and to help facilitate an agreement.

Mediation

If a settlement is not reached through conciliation, ACAS can arrange for the issue to be resolved through mediation. In this case, both parties agree that an independent person or a Board of Mediation should mediate between them. The process of mediation involves each side setting out its case in writing, followed by a hearing at which the two sides present, in person, their evidence and arguments. Hearings are usually held at ACAS offices or at the premises of the employer or the trade union. The mediator (or the Board of Mediation) makes formal, but not binding, proposals or recommendations to provide a basis for settlement of the dispute. The parties are free to accept or reject the mediator's proposals or recommendations. In mediation, as in conciliation, the employer effectively remains in control of the situation. A settlement cannot be imposed by a third party. The employer remains free to accept or reject.

Arbitration

In arbitration, a single arbitrator is normally appointed to consider a dispute and to make a decision to resolve it. Occasionally, arbitration may be by a Board of Arbitration with an independent chairperson and two side-members drawn from employer and trade union representatives. It is the arbitrator who makes the award resolving the dispute, and not – as many seem to think – ACAS. Unlike conciliation and mediation, in arbitration the employer has no effective control because before ACAS will facilitate arbitration, both parties must agree to accept the arbitrator's decision as a binding settlement of the dispute. This is a long-established principle, and in practice arbitration awards are invariably accepted and implemented.

> Explain the difference(s) between conciliation, mediation and arbitration.

What issues go to the arbitrator?

Table 14 shows the extent to which conciliation, mediation and arbitration has been used in the UK in collective disputes since 1979. A significant fall is evident in the use of all three processes. The types of issues that are the subject of arbitration are what are often referred to as disputes of rights, which are issues arising from the parties' rights under collective agreements. Arbitration is rarely used in what are referred to as disputes of interest – issues that arise from the negotiation of new or revised collective agreements.

An analysis of the types of issues under dispute at arbitration in the last 20 years shows a dominance of three – job grading, dismissal, and pay and conditions of employment (especially discipline, but not annual pay increases). This demonstrates that employers have been prepared to go to arbitration on issues:

● that are important to them – but not so important that they are prepared to impose industrial sanctions on the union

Table 14 The use of third-party intervention in industrial disputes

Date	Completed collective conciliations	Number of successful mediations	Number of arbitration hearings
1979	2,284	31	394
1980	1,910	31	281
1981	1,716	12	245
1982	1,634	16	235
1983	1,621	20	187
1984	1,448	14	188
1985	1,337	12	150
1986	1,323	10	174
1987	1,147	12	133
1988	1,053	9	129
1989	1,070	17	150
1990	1,140	10	190
1991	1,226	12	144
1992	1,140	7	155
1993	1,118	7	156
1994	1,162	8	148
1995	1,299	5	136
1996	1,197	4	113
1997	1,166	11	60
1998	1,214	8	42
1999/2000	1,247	1	63
2000/2001	1,226	5	55

Source: ACAS Annual Reports, 1979–2000/01

- where the cost of losing is bearable

- where there is unlikely to be adverse publicity from the arbitrator's award.

Why is arbitration so little used?

Arbitration is the accepted instrument of the last resort, but employers – whether in the private or public sector – continue to be sceptical about the principle of arbitration even on disputes of rights, let alone disputes of interests. Trade unions essentially remain pragmatic in their approach to accepting arbitration. They are in the bargaining business and are suspicious of anything that impedes their ability to gain by whatever means the best possible deal for their members. Although many trade unions profess to love 'free and unfettered' collective bargaining, their objections to arbitration are as much pragmatic as principled. However much they might be opposed to it in other circumstances, trade unions whose bargaining power is weak sometimes propose arbitration if and when they sense they could not secure approval for industrial action. In the 1980s and 1990s unions anxious to maintain or expand their membership-base showed a willingness to enter into so-called 'new-style' agreements in which pendulum arbitration was provided as the basis of avoiding the need for strike action.

Employers can also be similarly guided by pragmatism. Despite the principal argument of companies that they should negotiate within their procedure agreements and then, if there is a final 'failure to agree', stand up to the consequences without third-party intervention, the fact remains that many companies, faced with the prospect or reality of industrial action, themselves seek the conciliation – and even at times the arbitration – route.

However, a major reason for employers' reluctance to resort more readily to arbitration is the reputation of the arbitration process itself – that the employer loses control of events and must accept whatever the arbitrator may award, and that the arbitrator will 'split the difference' between the parties. Arbitration is first and foremost a process that transfers the ultimate responsibility for certain key business decisions from management to an independent third party. This is in contrast to collective bargaining, conciliation and mediation, in which each side retains considerable authority over events. Either party can exercise the prerogative of walking away at any time. There is little evidence to support the view that in disputes of interests the arbitrator always 'splits the difference'. Yet however undeserved it is, arbitrators have this reputation. Until ACAS (and the CAC) can effectively nail this misconception, any extension of the arbitration process into disputes of interests is unlikely to be achieved.

In disputes of interest there is also the criticism that the arbitrator usually improves upon the final offer made by the employer in direct negotiations. In doing this, arbitrators are likely to be acting on two assumptions. First, that the union would not be coming to arbitration unless it felt it could secure more for its members; second, that in agreeing to arbitration, the employer is anxious to avoid the alternative of industrial action and all its associated costs. The employer might well therefore be willing to pay a little more if such action can be avoided. An award handed down by an independent arbitrator holds out greater certainty of this than an improved offer by the employer.

Arbitration will remain a vital and indispensable instrument of last resort in dispute resolution. It can never be ignored – but it is unlikely to become more extensively used.

> Explain the circumstances in which an employer might be prepared to go to arbitration to resolve a dispute with the employees. What are the main dangers to an employer of using arbitration to resolve collective and/or individual disputes with employees?

The Central Arbitration Committee (CAC)

The Central Arbitration Committee's roots go back to the Industrial Courts Act 1919, which established the Industrial Court as a permanent and independent arbitration body. In 1971 the Industrial Relations Act changed its name to the Industrial Arbitration Board, which in turn became the Central Arbitration Committee under the Employment Protection Act 1975. CAC's main functions are:

- to rule on complaints by a trade union that an employer has failed to disclose information for collective bargaining purposes

- to rule on claims and complaints regarding the establishment and operation of European Works Councils in Great Britain

- to adjudicate on applications for the statutory recognition or de-recognition of trade unions for collective bargaining purposes when such recognition or de-recognition cannot be agreed voluntarily

- to provide voluntary arbitration in industrial disputes.

The Committee consists of a chairperson, nine deputy chairpersons, 16 members experienced as representatives of employers, and 16 members experienced as representatives of workers. All members of the Committee are appointed by the Secretary of State for Trade and Industry after consultation with ACAS. Decisions are made by panels of three Committee members appointed by the chairperson, one member whose experience is as a representative of employers and one member whose experience is as a representative of workers.

In the case of the trade union recognition procedure, the CAC has powers to decide which groups of workers will be included in any recognition agreement, and to establish the arrangements for ballots on recognition. The CAC arbitrates on disputes between employers and trade unions over what is the appropriate bargaining unit compatible with effective management. If there is a CAC-imposed bargaining unit and the union still wishes to proceed to obtain recognition for itself, the CAC has to decide whether the union has majority support. Except where the union has already recruited the majority of employees in the bargaining unit, the CAC will arrange for a secret ballot, which can – at the discretion of CAC – be held at the workplace or be by postal ballot via the employees' homes. If the union has a majority or a vote of at least 40 per cent of the whole bargaining unit, the CAC declares the union recognised. If the employer persists in failing to recognise the trade union, the CAC can impose trade union recognition for collective bargaining purposes by means of an 'agreement' that then becomes legally binding on the parties. The CAC also plays a similar role in the trade union de-recognition procedure contained in the Employment Relations Act 1999.

The CAC's first *Annual Report* published in June 2001 showed that 57 trade union recognition applications had been received by March 2001: 27 were accepted and three rejected, 21 were withdrawn before acceptance, and seven resulted in statutory recognition being confirmed. Only one case had been received concerning the establishment and operation of European Works Councils in Great Britain.

Explain the differences between ACAS and the CAC in terms of their roles and functions.

CONCLUSION

- The main services that employers' organisations offer to their members are assistance in the resolution of disputes, representation at employment tribunals, advisory and information services ('good practice', model agreements, salary data, etc) and the representation of members' views to political and other decision-making bodies.

- The primary purpose of trade unions is to protect the jobs of their members and to enhance their pay and conditions of employment principally by the use of collective bargaining and political lobbying.

- The UK trade union organisation is characterised by a small number of very large unions and a large number of very small unions.

- Over the last 20 years trade union membership has declined due, *inter alia*, to structural factors (eg a switch of employment from manufacturing) and public policy initiatives unsupportive of trade union organisation.

- Although there are those who believe trade unions are in terminal decline, the early 2000s have seen an increase in total trade union membership.

- Staff associations are usually established within a single organisation and are characterised by proportionately high membership.

- The majority of large staff associations are recognised by employers for negotiating and representational purposes, and most agreements to which they are a party cover such matters as recognition, provision of facilities, consultation, and grievance and disciplinary procedures.

- In addition, there are a much larger number of staff associations which are employer-dominated and have only a consultative function.

- The Certification Officer performs a number of functions including determining that a trade union is independent of the employer, dealing with complaints by members, seeing that unions' merger procedures are observed and monitoring trade union political funds.

- ACAS promotes good practice (via Codes of Practice), provides employee relations information and advice, conciliates in individual complaints before employment tribunals, and in cases of collective disputes conciliates and facilitates mediation and arbitration.

- The Central Arbitration Committee arbitrates on industrial disputes, on complaints from trade unions of an employer's failure to disclose information for collective bargaining purposes, on complaints over the establishment and operation of European Works Councils in the UK, and on disputes over trade union recognition and de-recognition.

Further reading

ADVISORY, CONCILIATION AND ARBITRATION SERVICE, Annual Reports.

BAMBER G. and LANSBURY R. D. (1998) International and Comparative Employment Relations. Australia, Allen & Unwin.

BROWN W. and TOWER B. J. (2001) Employment Relations in Britain: 25 years of the Advisory, Conciliation and Arbitration Service. Oxford, Blackwell.

CENTRAL ARBITRATION COMMITTEE, Annual Reports.

CERTIFICATION OFFICER, Annual Reports.

FLANDERS A. (1968a) 'Collective bargaining: a theoretical analysis', in Flanders A. (1970) *Management and Unions*, London, Faber & Faber.

FLANDERS A. (1968b) 'What are unions for?', in Flanders A. (1970) *Management and Unions*, London, Faber & Faber.

GENNARD J. (1998) 'The Labour Government: changes in employment law', *Employee Relations*, Vol. 20, No.1.

INDUSTRIAL RELATIONS SERVICE (1995) 'Staff associations: independent unions or employer-led bodies?', *Publication*, No.575, January.

INDUSTRIAL RELATIONS SERVICE (2002) 'Gaining recognition: latest round-up of union deals', *Publication*, No.745, February.

MUMFORD K. (1996) 'Arbitration and ACAS in Britain: a historical perspective', *British Journal of Industrial Relations*, Vol. 34, No.2.

TRADES UNION CONGRESS, General Council Reports.

WADDINGTON J. *and* HOFFMAN R. (eds) (2000) *Trade Unions in Europe*. European Trade Union Institute.

Workplace Employee Relations Survey (1998) PSI, ACAS, ESRC and DTI.

• Employee Relations Strategies and Policies

Introduction

The preceding chapters identified and described the main components of employee relations. In Chapter 1 we noted that the balance of bargaining power is affected by the economic, legal and technological environments, and that this in turn can influence prevailing management style. In Chapters 2, 3 and 4 we developed these issues further as we examined the corporate environment, the legislative framework and the European Union and their importance to employee relations professionals. In this chapter we look at the importance of employee relations strategies and the type and style of employment policies that flow from such strategies.

The management of people is one of the most challenging areas of business management, but it is, in many organisations, the poor relation in terms of importance and profile. This is despite the large amount of research and analysis that shows how significant it is in contributing to individual organisational performance.

Yet, as Simon Caulkin (*People Management*, 30 August 2001) points out:

more than 30 studies conducted in the USA and the UK since the early 1990s leave no room for doubt: how organisations manage and develop people has a powerful – perhaps the most powerful – effect on overall performance, including the bottom line.

Reviewing the evidence on behalf of the CIPD, Caulkin states that:

it would be hard to overestimate the importance of this finding. The empirical results that prove the business case slot the final piece into a new business model that has people squarely at its centre. It completes a historic transition from a [mechanical] view of the company to one that sees it as a living system where Tayloristic task management gives way to knowledge management; the latter seeking to be cost-efficient by developing an organisation's people assets, unlike the former, which views labour as a cost to be minimised.

Caulkin believes that:

for individuals and firms, it is clear that the findings open up huge opportunities for competitive improvement through learning, managing and developing people more effectively. The same goes for the UK economy as a whole, where people management has the potential to turbo-charge investment in skills, R&D and new technology, offering a way to jolt the economy out of its low-skills/low-quality equilibrium and claw back the productivity advantage held by its competitors.

And yet, one of the most difficult tasks facing the personnel professional is to open the minds of his or her management colleagues to adopting different, but proven, approaches to managing people. That is why, in this book considerable stress is laid on gaining commitment from colleagues to employee relations initiatives. Nevertheless, in order to obtain this commitment it is important to ensure that a proper business case is made for the adoption of new techniques or new approaches. It is easy to be critical of managers for not embracing new ideas, but if they are simply invited to buy into them as an article of faith, they will not make available the necessary investment in time and resources.

So, before seeking to change things within the organisation, there has to be a business case made that will demonstrate that such change is necessary. In making this business case it is important to show that there is a link between business performance, human resource management generally, and – in the context of this book – employee relations specifically.

To be successful, the business case must flow from the organisation's overall strategy, and to understand this connection we must look at the whole concept of strategy – a subject that has, in recent years, become a topic of intense discussion and debate, and become increasingly more important to managers in both the public and private sector. This has happened because although organisations have always had strategies, 'only since the 1960s has it been common to address explicitly the question of what their strategy should be' (Kay, 1993). One of the reasons for the change in emphasis is, as we noted in Chapter 2, that economic fluctuations and intense competition have forced organisations to face a continuing process of change. This change has to be managed, and requires that organisations develop clear business strategies that will then drive functional strategies, one of which is employee relations. However, it is not only senior managers who need to concern themselves with the strategic direction of an organisation – it is essential for all levels of management.

If the last two decades have taught us anything, it is that the pattern of employee relations has been constantly evolving, and this is likely to continue. This process of evolution has, quite clearly, been driven by the pace of change to which most businesses have been exposed, and has created a need for directors and senior managers to look more carefully at their approach to strategic employee relations management. They have come to accept that there are advantages to be gained in re-shaping employee attitudes. This attitudinal change is of particular importance as organisations, in both the public and private sectors, have sought to maximise efficiency as a means of securing competitive advantage. Such advantage is now as important an issue for the public sector as it is for the private sector. Public sector organisations have had competition forced upon them as successive governments have insisted on their being more customer- and quality-focused, while private sector organisations have had their own challenges. As we saw in Chapter 2, these are very often linked to new technology or the growth of the global economy. Whatever the challenge, it will impact on and dictate the type of employment policies that the management of an organisation will seek to implement.

What is strategy?

The overall purpose of strategy is to influence and direct an organisation as it conducts its activities. It may be described as the attempt by those who control an organisation to find ways to position their business or organisational objectives so that they can exploit the planning environment and maximise the future use of the organisation's capital and human assets (Tyson, 1995). Clearly this is but one definition of strategy and many writers have attempted to offer their own variants, but two writers stand out for having sought to define strategy in a way that is relevant to all tiers of management.

Johnson and Scholes (2002) have identified a number of characteristics commonly associated with the terms 'strategy' and 'strategic decisions', and these are:

- Strategic decisions are likely to be concerned with or affect the long-term direction of an organisation.

- Strategic decisions are about trying to achieve some advantage for the organisation – for example, over the competition.

- Strategic decisions are sometimes therefore conceived of as the search for effective *positioning* to give such advantage in a market or in relation to suppliers.

- Strategic decisions are likely to be concerned with the scope of an organisation's activities.

- Strategy can be seen as the matching of the activities of an organisation to the environment in which it operates.

- Strategy can be seen as building on or stretching an organisation's resources and competences to create opportunities or capitalise on them.

- Strategies may require major resource changes for an organisation.

- Strategic decisions are likely to affect operational decisions.

- The strategy of an organisation is affected not only by environmental forces and resource availability but also by the values and expectations of those who have power in and around the organisation.

Overall, Johnson and Scholes would say that if a definition of strategy is required, the above characteristics provide the basis for the following one:

Strategy is the direction *and scope of an organisation* over the long term: *which achieves* advantage *for the organisation through its configuration of* resources *within a changing* environment, *to meet the needs of* markets *and to fulfil* stakeholder expectations.

If Johnson and Scholes are correct in listing these as characteristics, it means that the whole process has become very complex. This is particularly true if the organisation operates in a wide geographic area – as a multi-national, for example – or has a wide range of products. Throughout this text we make the point that employee relations cannot stand alone – that it has to be integrated with other management and personnel functions. The same is true of strategy: it too requires, as Johnson and Scholes point out, an integrated approach to managing the organisation.

> *Managers, therefore, have to cross functional and operational boundaries to deal with strategic problems and come to agreements with other managers who, inevitably, have different interests and perhaps different priorities.*

Strategic formulation

To further understand the nature of strategy it is helpful to examine the process of strategy formulation. We can identify a number of different approaches. One of the oldest and most influential regards strategy as a highly rational and scientific process. The approach is based on one of the characteristics identified above – the importance of the 'fit' between an organisation and its environment. Analyses are made of a firm's environment to assess likely opportunities and threats, and of its internal resources to identify strengths and weaknesses. This process is often referred to as a SWOT analysis, and it is argued that through rigorous planning senior managers can predict and shape the external environment and thus the organisation itself.

A different approach to strategy formulation argues that the complexity and volatility of the environment may mean that a SWOT analysis is both difficult and inappropriate. This evolutionary approach believes that organisations are at the mercy of the unpredictable and hostile vagaries of the market. The environment in which they operate may be changing so frequently that any data they use, either historical or current, may be worthless.

Some writers argue that it is not possible to apply either a rational or an evolutionary label to the process of strategy formulation, but that what is fundamental is behavioural – that strategic choice results from the various coalitions that are to be found within organisations. The most dominant of these coalitions will be at senior management level, and that it is those coalitions which have to 'create a vision of the organisation's future' (Burnes, 1996).

The extent to which managing people is given a high profile within the organisation is driven by the values, ideologies and personalities of those in positions of power and influence and those individuals who formulate strategy and the long-term direction of the organisation. When we talk about the organisation in strategy terms, we are very often actually talking about the chief executive because it is his or her values and beliefs that will ultimately shape the culture of the organisation and consequently decide the type and style of employee relations policies that it tries to follow. In essence the point here is leadership: it is through leadership that strategy is moulded by the personality of an individual or individuals, through the way in which he, she or they are able to motivate people to change.

Similarly, the values and beliefs of such a chief executive will have a significant impact on the long-term direction of a business, and there are those who believe that leadership is a key success factor. Some writers

(Blakstad and Cooper, 1995) have examined this in the context of particular businesses. In one case, British Petroleum, they concluded that without the personal vision and change programme initiated by Robert Horton, the then chief executive, there is some doubt as to whether BP could have survived the recession of the early 1990s as well as it did.

However, not everybody takes this view. David Butcher and Mike Meldrum (*People Management*, 28 June 2001) question whether leadership is really important in business. They note that 'where chief executives do preside over successful businesses, it is sometimes because they are the beneficiaries of decisions taken long before they landed the top job'. Sometimes this issue of leadership is linked to particular organisations that are the flavour-of-the-month and are perceived to be doing something different. As Butcher and Meldrum point out:

> *The reason that companies such as Virgin, Cisco Systems, Dell, easyJet and other 'different' enterprises have been so keenly observed is that each has, in its own way, pioneered a new business and organisational model. They have eschewed tried and tested industry practices and ignored the rules of the game. That is why these companies are celebrated by management gurus.*

From this brief description it is clear that there is no one right way of formulating strategy. There are a number of approaches that can be adopted by an organisation, but it is important to understand that whichever one is adopted, it will be constrained by societal, environmental, industry-specific and organisational factors, many of which will conflict with each other. To take societal factors as an example: there can often be significant national differences in the way people approach work, and with the growth in multi-national companies and internationalisation, this can have a major impact on workplace culture.

The environment within which any organisation operates will, without doubt, constrain strategic choice. It may be a relatively stable and predictable environment in which planning and predicting the future is not a particularly hazardous exercise. Alternatively, it may be a hostile, unpredictable and uncertain environment in which planning is almost impossible. Whatever the environment, most organisations have to operate in a constantly changing world, and it is this change process that provides the link between business strategy and employee relations strategies. Although environmental considerations may provide the stimulus for change, there is a clear consensus that the success or otherwise of individual change programmes is governed by the people in each organisation.

Consider the environment in which your own organisation has to operate. How would you describe it?

Levels of strategy

It is important to consider not only the sort of strategic choices that organisations can make, but also the levels of strategic decision-making. There are three levels with which we should concern ourselves (Burnes, 1996):

- corporate-level strategy, which concerns the overall direction and focus of the business

- business unit strategy, which is concerned with how to compete in a particular market

- functional-level strategy, which is concerned with individual areas such as personnel, marketing, etc.

These levels are all interrelated, but equally, each of them has its own distinctive strategic concerns. We now look at them in a little more detail.

Corporate-level strategy

Corporate-level strategy concerns itself with a number of questions and is usually formulated at board level. One of these questions will be about the overall mission of the organisation – what is the game plan? How should the business portfolio be managed? Should you make acquisitions or dispose of parts of the business? What priority should be given to each of the individual parts of the business in terms of resource allocation? How is the business to be structured and financed?

Whatever the mission, it is worthless unless it is capable of being achieved. To do this, three things are necessary. Firstly, the mission must be expressed in language that is understandable to the great majority of employees. This means paying attention to the communications process (see Chapter 7). Secondly, it must be attainable. That is, employees must recognise that the organisation has some chance of achieving the objectives it has set itself. Thirdly, the mission must be challenging. All those involved in its achievement must be stretched – the effort they put into their individual performances must be a condition of the mission's overall success.

> If the organisation in which you work has a declared mission, how does it fit with the criteria we have described? If it doesn't fit, how would you re-express the mission so that it meets the need to be understandable, attainable and challenging? Alternatively, if no mission has been articulated, what do you think your organisation's mission should be? (Make it match our declared criteria.)

Business unit-level strategy

Competitive or business unit-level strategy is concerned with the way a firm or business operates in particular markets, with what new opportunities can be identified or created, and with which products or services should be developed. In this context strategy has mainly to do with gaining an advantage over the competition. Porter (1985) sees it as seeking to obtain a sustainable competitive advantage – which markets should the organisation attempt to compete in, and how does it position itself to achieve its objectives? How does it achieve some form of 'distinctive capability' (Kay, 1993)? What should its product range or mix be? Which customers should it aim for? Decisions about products, markets and customers were central to some of Porter's (1985) theories about strategy. He argued that there are only three basic strategies that dictate the choice to be made. These are:

- cost leadership, which aims to achieve lower costs than the competitors' without reducing quality

- product differentiation, based on achieving industry-wide recognition of different and superior products and services compared with those of other suppliers

- specialisation by focus – in effect, seeking out a niche market.

This type of distinction is fine in the private sector, but what about the public sector? All the decisions Porter says are important have an effect on employee relations in that they impact on the way that the organisation structures itself internally and on the way that relationships are managed. For this reason it is important for public sector organisations to adapt these principles to their own service in order to create their own business strategies.

Functional-level strategy

Functional-level strategy is, in a sense, fairly straightforward. At this level strategy is concerned with how the different functions of the business (marketing, personnel, finance, manufacturing, etc) translate corporate- and business-level strategies into operational aims – as Johnson and Scholes describe it:

how the component parts of the organisation in terms of resources, processes, people and their skills are pulled together to form a strategic architecture which will effectively deliver the overall strategic direction.

In Figure 3 we demonstrate diagrammatically how employee relations strategy is formulated. Business strategy drives HRM strategy, which in turn drives employee relations strategy – and from this process are derived the practices and policies that influence the employment relationship. Once this level of functional strategy is reached, it is important that the various functions organise themselves with care, in order not only to achieve their aims but to ensure synergy with the rest of the business.

Figure 3 Strategic employee relations management: an overview

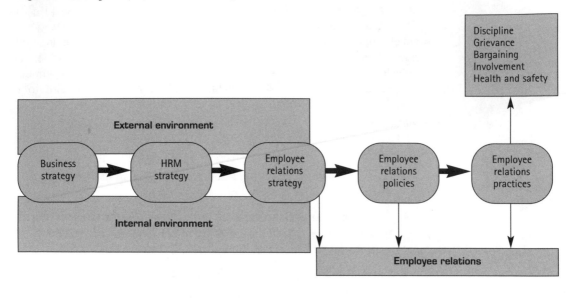

What external factors over the next five years are likely to impact on corporate strategy, both in the wider business context and in the specific challenges that your own organisation is likely to face? How will these impact on your employee relations strategy, if at all?

We now turn specifically to the strategic issues concerning the management of people.

People strategy

One aspect of strategy concerns the match between an organisation's activities and its resources. These resources can be inanimate (equipment, buildings, etc) or they can be people. Strategies in respect of inanimate resources may require decisions about investment or even about the ability to invest. Strategies about people also require decisions to be made about investment – but it is a different type of investment decision, not the type that fits easily into the process usually reserved for capital expenditure. It is more likely to be the sort of investment that we discussed in Chapter 2 – investment in skills development, for example.

Research carried out by the Institute of Work Psychology and the Centre for Economic Performance, and published by the IPD (1997) and by Deloitte & Touche (1998), shows a clear link between the adoption of human resource management practices and improved business performance. This demonstrates how much of the variation between companies in change in productivity and profitability is attributable to focusing on key people management issues. That significant improvement in both productivity and profitability can be achieved by focusing on:

- ensuring that people are satisfied with their jobs, rewards, working conditions and career prospects

- developing commitment by encouraging people to move beyond the contractual obligations to emotional commitment, where they develop a strong sense of loyalty to the organisation, its customers and clients, and not only see what needs to be done for the benefit of the organisation but initiate action and urge action from colleagues

- managing organisational culture through concentrating on all the key cultural dimensions

- adopting an integrated approach to human resource management programmes and processes that will develop satisfaction and commitment.

The research then goes on to show that the use of human resource management practices and effective job design can have more impact on productivity and profitability than other fundamental business activities.

This research is of some significance in that it provides very clear evidence that concentrating on people is one of the keys to success. An effective strategy for people management is therefore a key requirement for any business.

But what makes an effective strategy for managing people?

The Deloitte & Touche survey in 1998 identified 12 key factors in five main areas of management activity that differentiate between high-growth businesses and low-/no-growth businesses. The five main areas of management activity are:

- taking a strategic view of managing people

- involving people in the business

- investing in communication

- managing people's performance

- focusing on employees as individuals.

Some of these activities are covered in much greater detail in Chapter 7, 'Employee involvement', but because they are key features in the development of strategy we summarise them here too.

In 'taking a strategic view of managing people' it is imperative that people are at the centre of strategic planning for the organisation. Key questions about the organisation's people must be addressed in planning business strategy. Are the right knowledge, skills and competencies available within the organisation, and if not can they be acquired? Are people capable of taking forward new directions in business strategy? Can the knowledge, skills and competency available be deployed in a way that opens up new business opportunities?

It is also important in developing strategy to take account of company culture. This is a complex area, says the Deloitte & Touche survey, and requires a focus on:

- the artefacts and symbols of the organisation, such as the layout of the working environment, the technology used, the use of information and reporting

- the stories and myths that are commonly shared in the organisation and that indicate success and failure

- the rites and rituals that reinforce behaviour patterns and demonstrate the organisation's values

- the rules, systems and procedures that set the parameters for behaviour and action

- the organisational heroes and heroines that act as role models for people

- the beliefs, values and attitudes that are expressed and displayed in everyday activity

- the ethical standards that guide the boundaries of what is acceptable and not acceptable

- the basic assumptions that are made about human behaviour, human nature, relationships, reality and truth.

'Involving people in the business' requires careful job design with a particular emphasis on teamworking by which teams have a high degree of autonomy and freedom for self-management. To be effective, teams need clear objectives and targets and the autonomy to plan and undertake work, acquire resources, and improve processes, products and services. Parameters must be specified so that integration with the organisation as a whole is not compromised, but these must be as wide as possible.

There are very few managers who would disagree with the third main activity, 'investing in communication'. Successful businesses invest heavily in communications, and there are three aspects of communication that distinguish high-growth businesses from the less successful. These are:

- communicating business strategy to all employees

- regularly giving feedback on performance measures to all employees

- using a wide range of communication methods.

The fourth activity, 'managing people's performance', is also self-evident – but failing to pay sufficient attention to this area can cause significant employee relations problems. People perform best if they know what they have to do, how well they are doing it, what they have to improve, and how the improvement is going to be achieved. Setting clear, individual objectives for employees is a critical element in any successful organisation. For people not to know what is expected of them can lead to dissatisfaction, low morale, high labour turnover and high levels of absenteeism – all classic employee relations problems.

The final activity is 'focusing on employees as individuals', and in that the use of such terms as 'human resources' and 'human capital' encourages a view of an organisation's employees as a homogeneous group, they can diminish the view of employees as individuals. Yet high-performing organisations do focus on people as individuals and use techniques of involvement that are designed to encourage satisfaction and commitment (see Chapter 7).

All the activities identified by Deloitte & Touche are important in formulating strategy, but they must not be viewed in isolation. The necessity is to ensure that the whole range of people management activities – recruitment and selection, reward and recognition, training and development, and employee relations – are integrated into the strategic planning process. This is important for any manager concerned with business performance because the research and evidence from companies that are achieving the best results in productivity, profitability and growth show that good people management strategies make the real difference. Such evidence was compelling in 1998 but, as we noted above, the review of all the research conducted by Simon Caulkin leaves little room for doubt. It allowed Geoff Armstrong, Director-General of the CIPD to write to all the Institute's members and say that 'In the global, knowledge-based economy it is the ability of the leaders in organisations to elicit the willing contribution of resourceful, continuously learning, customer-focused people at all levels that makes the difference between success and failure.'

Strategy and employment policies

Having examined the process of strategy formulation we now turn to look at how it links into employee relations in particular, not forgetting that there must be a link with other aspects of the employment relationship – employee resourcing, employee reward, employee development.

Whatever method an organisation chooses for formulating its strategy, either at corporate or business level, maximising the organisation's competitive advantage has to be a major issue. This inevitably means that an organisation must constantly re-evaluate itself in order to be able to sustain any necessary improvements. Organisations are therefore concerned with the design and management of employment policies and processes that will deliver and sustain business improvement. The process of change, and its impact on the development of strategy, presents many challenges for the employee relations professional. For example, as we discuss later, there is the issue of trade unions and the provisions on recognition. Where trade unions already exist and are recognised within an organisation, the trends towards individualism – as opposed to collectivism – means that strategic choices have to be made about whether those unions are encouraged or marginalised. Where they do not exist and requests for recognition are received, strategic choices have to be made about whether such requests are resisted or voluntarily accepted.

Overall, strategies and policies on employee relations must have a direct relationship with the business strategy and must be imaginative, innovative, clear and action-oriented. They must be formulated by a continuing process of analysis to identify what is happening to the business and where it is going. In this context, the relevance of clear business objectives, as expressed through the medium of a mission statement, cannot be overstated. The key is to develop an employee relations strategy that is responsive to the needs of the organisation, that can provide an overall sense of purpose to the employee relations professional and assist employees in understanding where they are going, how they are going to get there, why certain things are happening and, most importantly, the contribution they are expected to make towards achieving the organisational goals.

Once it is clear what the overall philosophy of an organisation is, the employee relations specialist can use this knowledge to put together the employee relations policies for the business. The needs of an organisation in terms of its employee relations policies are potentially infinite, but could emanate from two specific areas. First, 'the management of change' could encompass issues as diverse as improving productivity, greater employee involvement, changing reward systems or introducing teamworking. The second is the organisation's attitude towards trade unions.

Future challenges

If we examine some of the challenges facing the personnel specialist both now and in the future, we can identify some of the important links between the various personnel disciplines. In the area of employee resourcing, organisations are confronted by continuing challenges in developing policies on recruitment and selection. In employee reward there are constant challenges to the personnel practitioner. Stimulating employee commitment, motivation and enhancing job performance are matters to be examined in Chapter 7, but among the issues that should be considered here is the balance between pay and non-pay rewards and individual as opposed to collective bargaining. Reward policies must however be 'developed and managed as a coherent whole . . . They need to be integrated with one another and, importantly, with the key business and personnel processes of the organisation' (Armstrong, 1996).

So far as employee development is concerned, the personnel practitioner faces three challenges, all of which impact on employee relations. Firstly, is it in the company's interests to buy in staff or to develop its own in-house people? Where do the long-term interests of the business lie? If you get the balance wrong and buy in too much labour, there is a risk that existing employees will become disillusioned and assume that the organisation is not interested in investing in their future.

Secondly, what sort of employees are required? Generalists or specialists? Personnel professionals have a significant role to play in helping to identify what value there is to the organisation in particular types of employee. Although it is popular to support the idea of multi-skilling, the concept does not always serve an organisation's best interests. Too many people may want to be trained in specific skills, some of which may never be fully utilised. This can then lead to resentment or resistance to further training interventions.

Finally, if investment is to be made in employee development, is it simply a question of training people to carry out the current tasks that they are required to fulfil, or is it strategically valuable to create a learning environment, as many organisations have done?

All of these challenges are strategic issues that are interlinked and have an impact on employee relations. Each one will be conditioned in its scope and its impact by the type and size of the organisation.

What challenges will your organisation face over the next five years, and how will these impact on employee relations strategy?

In answering the second part of this question you should have looked at any trends in your organisation's business strategy that might have an impact, such as:

- *plans for expansion*
- *proposals for new investment*
- *the need to improve profitability or productivity.*

You should also have considered the impact of changes to your employee relations strategies on the other policy areas – for example, resourcing, reward, health and safety, and development. Finally, you should additionally have considered the impact of external influences such as political influences (a change of UK Government, or even Prime Minister), economic influences (interest rates, inflation, joining the euro, unemployment), societal influences (demographic trends, the age profile of the population), new technology, and any possible changes in legislation, particularly European influences.

Management style

We said above that an organisation's attitude to trade unions could have a significant impact on employee relations strategy. We have already discussed the impact that the values and preferences of the organisation's dominant management decision-makers have on strategy formulation. These values and perceptions will in part be determined by whether the organisation adopts a unitary or pluralist approach to its employee relations. The unitary approach sees organisations as harmonious and integrated in such a way that all employees share the organisational goals and work as members of one team. The pluralist approach recognises that different groups exist within an organisation and that conflict can, and does, exist between employer and employees.

These are broad definitions, and it must be noted that although an organisation may describe itself as unitarist, the management and the employees do not necessarily share the same agenda. Unitarist organisations can be either authoritarian or paternalistic in their attitudes, and this distinction can have a major impact on management style. Pluralism – a term generally used to describe an organisation that embraces collective relationships – can emphasise co-operation between interest groups, not just conflict. It is this distinction in approach to the management of people that leads to variations in employee relations policies, ranging from the paternalistic no-union approach of Marks & Spencer through the single-union, no-strike philosophy of Japanese firms like Nissan, to the multi-union sites of companies like Ford.

Whereas external constraints on employee relations policy formulation are an important factor, the internal constraints are probably of greater significance. Factors that often determine management style are organisational size, ownership and location. Style can be an important determinant in defining an employee relations policy, and is as much influenced by the organisation's leader as is business strategy. Since Fox (1966) first categorised management and employee relations as unitarist or pluralist, others have sought to define the topic in greater detail. In particular, Purcell and Sisson (1983) identified five typical styles:

- authoritarian
- paternalistic
- consultative
- constitutional
- opportunist.

The authoritarian approach sees employee relations as relatively unimportant. Although policies and procedures may exist, they are often there because of some legislative necessity (eg grievance and disciplinary procedures), and as a consequence people issues are not given any priority until something goes wrong. Typically, firms with an authoritarian approach might be small owner-managed businesses, and it is not unusual to find that the things that go wrong centre on disciplinary issues. In many of the small firms that we have contact with, complaints against them of unfair dismissal are a common problem. For example, an employer who has paid little attention to setting standards of performance dismisses an employee who makes a mistake – and then finds that the dismissed employee wins a tribunal claim for compensation. This is usually because no previous warnings were issued and no formal disciplinary procedure was followed. An analysis of the size and ownership of organisations that appear in tribunal cases would support this view.

Paternalistic organisations share many of the size and ownership characteristics of the authoritarian type, but they tend to have a much more positive attitude towards their employees. Employee consultation takes a high priority, irrespective of whether unions are present in the workplace, and staff retention and reward are perceived as key issues.

The type of constitutional organisation described by Purcell and Sissons assumes a trade union presence. Although sharing some of the characteristics of the previous types of organisation, management style in employee relations is often more adversarial than consultative.

In the opportunist organisation management style is determined by local circumstances. On these circumstances rest whether it is appropriate to recognise trade unions or not, or the extent to which employee involvement is encouraged.

Purcell (1987) moved the analysis of management style forward and redefined it as:

> *the existence of a distinctive set of guiding principles, written or otherwise, which set parameters to and signposts for management action in the way employees are treated and particular events handled.*

This principle of setting parameters is of vital importance in the management of people. Hilary Walmsley (*People Management*, April 1999) argued that 'to get the most out of people, managers need to adapt their styles to fit different situations'. However, she went on to say that:

> *Managers typically use the same personal style to handle a range of situations. Usually they do this out of habit. Some are not clear about the array of potential styles available to them. Even those who are aware that there are, for example, different ways of developing and motivating people, or of approaching problem-solving, often fail to apply this knowledge to their day-to-day activities. Those who do want to apply new styles can feel confused about where and when they should try them.*

Our own research would suggest that the Purcell definition is still valid, but that very often the 'guiding principles' to which he refers are those of the chief executive. The style employed by these individuals is very closely linked to the issue of leadership.

The individual and collective dimensions

Purcell suggested that management style has two dimensions, individualism and collectivism, and that each dimension has three stages. Individualism is concerned with how much policies are directed at individual workers and whether the organisation takes into account the feelings of all its employees and 'seeks to develop and encourage each employee's capacity and role at work'. The three stages in the individual dimension are:

- commodity status
- paternalism
- resource status.

In the first the employee is not well regarded and has low job security; in the second, the employer accepts some responsibility for the employee; in the third, the employee is regarded as a valuable resource.

The collectivist dimension is, in a sense, self-explanatory. It is about whether or not management policy encourages or discourages employees to have a collective voice and collective representation. The three stages in this dimension are:

- unitary
- adversarial
- co-operative.

At the unitary stage management opposes collective relationships either openly or by covert means. The adversarial stage represents a management focus that is on a stable workplace, where conflict is institutionalised and collective relationships limited. The final, co-operative, stage has its focus on constructive relationships and greater openness in the decision-making process.

Can you identify the management style that operates within your organisation? Do you think that it changes to meet different needs or is it static?

Remember, identifying a particular management style is not simply a question of labelling an organisation 'individualist' or 'collectivist'. Purcell points out that the interrelationship between the two is complex, and that for an organisation to be seen to encourage the rights and capabilities of individuals should not necessarily mean that it is seeking to marginalise any representative group.

Selecting employee relations policies

The ability to identify which policies are suitable and which are unsuitable for particular types of organisations is a skill that it is important for the employee relations professional to develop. Two issues that must be taken into account in drafting employee relations policies, and then implementing them, are the distinctive influences of external and internal factors. We identified what some of the external factors were in earlier chapters – in particular, existing and future legislative constraints – but there are others. It is important to be aware of the type of policies other employers in your sector or industry are pursuing. These may have an impact on your own organisation if, for example, those employers have taken a particular stance on employee involvement as a means of retaining key employees. This could affect your own organisation's ability to retain staff. Thirdly, another major factor is the identification of precisely what is considered to be the prevailing 'good practice'. In this context 'good practice' means those acts or omissions that distinguish the good employer from the perceived 'bad' employer. For example, if you fail to operate your disciplinary procedure in line with natural justice, you may find that your ex-employees constantly file complaints against you at tribunals, and not only that, but they win compensation as well. Many employers when drafting policies and procedures only 'scratch the surface'. They either do not consider how the policy might operate in practice and whether it will meet the needs of their employees, or they are careless in its operation, with the result that it fails to meet the criteria of 'good practice', which is a standard that we pursue throughout this book. Whatever the policy, therefore, it is important to incorporate monitoring mechanisms within it so that checks can be made on its effectiveness.

All organisations must have policies on grievance, discipline, health and safety, pay and benefits and sickness absence, and these should always be written down and consistently applied. It is also important to acknowledge that although each of the policies mentioned above might differ in scope and depth from one organisation to another, no one – irrespective of the type of organisation that he or she works in – would seriously question their selection in the range of employment policies adopted.

However, where we do need to examine seriously questions of selection is in respect of those policies that have a clear impact on corporate and business strategies and that can seriously affect relationships at work. An organisation's approach to strategy formulation, and thus its approach to employee relations, will continue to be influenced by UK Government actions and also by consumer preferences; such considerations will inevitably impact on an organisation's decisions over the way that it manages people and the policies that underpin these management processes.

In Chapters 2 and 3 we explained that for well over a decade the main thrust of industrial, economic and legislative policy has been to create a market-driven economy, and that 'from an industrial relations perspective, the most telling feature of this policy has been the successive pieces of legislation designed to limit the role and rights of trade unions' (Guest, 1995). Because the question of why some firms willingly recognise trade unions and others do not is so important to employee relations, it is dealt with separately within this chapter. For the moment we will concentrate on policy choices in other areas.

For many organisations that try to link policy choices in employee relations to their business strategies, the real issue is not about individualism or collectivism but about ensuring that their workforce is committed to the organisation. Obtaining employee commitment is one of the principal ways organisations can position themselves in order to achieve a competitive advantage – one of the necessary prerequisites of a successful business. However, employees will only give their commitment if they feel secure, valued and properly motivated – a sense of wellbeing that will, in part, be derived from the type of employment policies that are adopted. Such policies must be capable of 'adding value' to the business – and for the employee relations professional who may be trying to decide on the advice he or she gives in respect of a particular policy, this is of some importance.

In respect of trade unionism, the question is not about pro- or anti-union stances, it is whether entering into a relationship with an appropriate trade union can add value to the business. It would be wrong to assume that the answer to this question will always be No. The search for competitive advantage and employee commitment are key issues and are linked to the management of change in an organisation.

Managing change may require variations in organisational culture, the introduction of flexible working practices, empowerment, or some form of teamworking. If any of these routes, or a combination of them all, is followed, the devising and implementation of policies to support it/them will be required. This is where the involvement of the employee relations professional can be of crucial importance – and before we examine the subject of change, it is important to recognise that the process of designing and implementing policies to support change requires the employee relations professional to have developed certain skills. When asked to do so by the board, an employee relations professional must be able to establish whether a particular initiative will be suitable for the organisation. It will do neither your organisation nor you much good if it invests in new ideas that are not suited to it.

Managing change

The management of change is something that most organisations have to undertake at some time or other. During the change process, employee relations can be under tremendous stress. In most change programmes it is safe to assume that no more than 25 to 30 per cent of people will be in favour of the proposed alterations, that up to 50 per cent will probably sit on the fence to see what happens, and up to another 25 per cent of people will actively resist any change at all. That is why, as Machiavelli said:

> *There is nothing more difficult to plan, more doubtful of success, nor more dangerous to manage than the creation of a new system. For the initiator has the enmity of all who profit by the preservation of the old institutions, and merely lukewarm defenders in those who would gain by the new ones.*

In view of the importance of people to the change process it is essential that management is able to articulate a clear vision of the objectives of the change programme. To gain commitment to change, that vision has to be expressed clearly and unambiguously. Such commitment can be obtained if management takes the right steps in managing the process.

Those steps would include an endeavour by managers to persuade employees of the need for change. In Chapter 3 we acknowledged that a consensus cannot always be achieved when change becomes necessary, but it is a basic principle of good employee relations that consent, however grudgingly given, is better than force. In this context managers might have to accept that change will sometimes have to be negotiated, with or without trade unions. Even without negotiation, it is absolutely vital to realise that seeking to ascertain employee feelings about the change is much more likely to lead to effective implementation than a management attitude of 'We know best.'

Organisations of all shapes and sizes are embroiled in change, and increasingly this includes changing the established culture. That means asking such questions as 'How can we get our people to be more innovative, more focused, more assertive, more in line with our values?' In some cases a whole new culture is needed in order to fit a new set of values to parallel the organisation's intentions.

There are a number of means at an organisation's disposal to change culture (by which we really mean behaviour and perspective). These include:

- Training, mentoring and coaching – All these can help people see where they are not meeting the requirements or values of the company, and help them to change.

- Performance measurement – If we start to measure the things that demonstrate the right behaviours or culture, that deliver the right results, then people will pay them more attention; and if the measurement is brought into performance reviews, the associated actions will gather momentum.

- Reward and recognition – If in addition we allocate rewards according to key behaviours and actions, then we are bound to affect the culture. A word of warning about those clever people who are bound to find ways of extracting the maximum reward for the least effort should be inserted here, however!

- Recruitment and retention – If we build in processes which favour key capabilities and behaviours, we can stimulate what we need in terms of culture change.

However – as with many of the issues covered in this chapter – managing change, altering behaviour and creating a new culture requires clear leadership. An article in *The Director* magazine summarised some research on leadership conducted by Alan Hooper of Exeter University. Five key themes emerged from the research:

- Effective leaders create an understanding in the company about why change is necessary. They are clear thinkers and highly effective communicators, able to define a clear strategy, but with the flexibility to adapt to changing circumstances. Very good listeners, they are aware of the importance of unlocking others' potential and are passionate and motivating.

- They set a personal example, demonstrating integrity, truth, openness and honesty. When Archie Norman took over as chief executive of the struggling supermarket chain Asda in 1992, he adopted an open communication policy and always spoke his mind. During the early days of restructuring this won him grudging respect and then a growing momentum of support.

- Good leaders ensure good succession. Jack Welch spent 15 to 20 per cent of his time on leadership development at GE.

- They share their experiences with their people. Ken Keir, for example, the managing director of Honda UK, spends three and a half days a week in the factory with his workforce.

- Effective leaders are self-pacing, more akin to a marathon runner rather than to a sprinter. This means good time management, discipline, effective delegation and a good work–life balance. They are also sensitive to the effect of change at work on the people they are responsible for.

It seems clear that the way in which an organisation is led has a major impact on the management of change. In the same way, the decision-making process is also important. Because the introduction of most new initiatives is an evolutionary process, overseeing the pace of change is an increasingly important issue for successful management – and this requires effective decision-making. Decision-making in this context is both an end to achieve and a mechanism that can be used deliberately to shift people's behaviour and perspective over time.

Unfortunately, in many organisations, the expectation of change creates an uncertainty regarding the immediate and long-term future that can be difficult to manage or placate. If left to manage itself, this uncertainty can quickly fester to become an institutionalised insecurity that can undermine effective decision-making and create a range of employee relations problems. We are not suggesting that a focus on decision-making alone will mean the effective management of change, but clear decision-making with specific decisions allocated to relevant roles should underpin the support employees need to cope with it.

A further factor to be taken into account is that during the change process responsibilities might have to be altered and the boundaries of jobs clarified. Even the overall organisational structure may have to be scrutinised anew because some change programmes challenge traditional hierarchies – the sort of change that can give rise to considerable resentment and individual resistance. It is also important to ensure that other policies which might be required to underpin change are themselves in place – for example, policies in relation to equal opportunities or a single-status workforce. With any new policy there will always be those who oppose it, sometimes openly and sometimes covertly, and the employee relations professional will recognise this. He or she will not assume that the process is complete just because an initiative has been properly evaluated and then properly communicated to all employees. He or she will monitor implementation and seek ways to reinforce the initial communication about the policy change.

Management and trade unions

Although the influence of trade unions has been declining steadily since 1978, the subject of trade unionism *per se* is very important to the employee relations professional in trying to determine policies and procedures for his or her own organisation. Some companies seem to manage extremely well by being 'non-union'; some organisations appear to be happy to embrace unions; some actively resist them. So, as we have already seen, one of the policy choices an organisation has to make is over its relationship, or its lack of a relationship, with a trade union. As acknowledged elsewhere in this chapter, management style and philosophy will cause different managers to have different approaches to the role and the involvement of unions. Such approaches will range from encouragement to active resistance and refusal, but the Employment Relations Act 1999 now makes it more difficult, if not impossible, to say No.

However, before making the assumption that some existing non-union firms will become unionised we must understand what is meant by the term 'non-unionism'. Salamon (1998) explains that the expression can be used to describe two different types of organisation:

- Type A, in which an organisation has a policy not to recognise unions for any employees or for particular groups of employees (such as managers) and in which it is therefore a distinct aim or element of management's employee relations strategy to avoid any collective relationship (ie non-unionism results from a management decision).

● Type B, in which union membership within the organisation or group of employees is low or non-existent, and unions are therefore not recognised because of the absence of employee pressure for representation (ie non-unionism results from the employees' decision not to join unions).

Clearly, Type B organisations have little to fear from current union recognition legislation unless something happens in the working environment that fundamentally alters the status quo. Unless the company has a history of treating its employees badly and those employees suddenly succumb to the blandishments of a union recruiting drive, something will have to change abruptly for the worse in the employment relationship for unions to make an impact. If it is possible to identify some causal act, might something other than union recognition remedy it? If, in a Type B organisation, there was a sudden rush to join a trade union, the organisation would have to ask itself some very searching questions. Have recent redundancies created a climate of uncertainty? Has there been a change in management style? Have grievances been ignored or badly handled? Any of these could trigger a change in employee attitudes to collective representation – and in that situation if management wants to remain non-union it will have to consider how such issues are managed (Judge, 1997).

Non-union organisations

One of the unsubstantiated myths in employee relations has been the idea that non-unionism is the panacea for business success, for which organisations such as Marks & Spencer and IBM are put forward as prime examples of the concept. There will always be a debate between those who see trade unions as a negative influence and those, like most of our European partners, who see rights at work (including trade union membership and collective bargaining) as part of an important social dimension to working relationships. It is this polarisation that results in the antagonism of many politicians and business leaders towards the social dimension of the European Union. Post-war industrial relations has allowed some commentators the opportunity to promote non-unionism as the ideal state to which all businesses should aspire, and the stated belief that to allow interventions from Europe would be a massive step backward.

Although the debate about unionism versus non-unionism continues, the real question tends to be ignored. That is – is it easier to manage with unions or without unions? Personal prejudice should not to come into the process of effective management, but many managers' attitudes towards trade unions have been conditioned either by their own negative experiences during the 1970s and 1980s – a period when the unions contributed to their negative image with some self-inflicted wounds – or by a perception that unions somehow stop managers managing. In some cases the negativity is a result of union representatives' being allowed to take the initiative because of poor management. There were two reasons for this:

- poor training in core skills like negotiation, communication and interviewing

- a lack of clear policy guidance.

It is because this lack of skills can have such a negative impact on the whole process of employee relations that the second part of this book concentrates on the development of such skills as bargaining, negotiating, managing grievances and handling discipline.

As personnel practitioners ourselves, we have received many requests for help from organisations who are having difficulty in managing their employee relations in a collectivist environment. In almost all these cases blame is laid at the door of the union, and there is no recognition that poor management might also bear some responsibility. When appropriate training interventions have been agreed and implemented, we find that there is a complete turnaround. Not only do managers seize responsibility but they find that they are able to do so with little or no union resistance. In truth, union representatives had merely been filling a vacuum that nobody else was interested in. These experiences have caused a good number of managers to become very biased against unions, and many of those that we have spoken to believe genuinely that without the unions business success would be guaranteed.

Such faith in managing without unions has meant that some of the larger non-union firms within the UK have become the focus of attention for developments in employee relations. Companies like Marks & Spencer and IBM have always been held up as exemplary non-union employers, but now others have joined the list. At the risk of over-generalisation, the generic characteristics of these non-union companies tend to be (Blyton and Turnbull, 1994):

> *a sense of caring, carefully-chosen plant locations and working environments, market leadership, high growth and healthy profits, employment security, single status, promotion from within, an influential personnel department, competitive pay and benefit packages, profit sharing, open communications, and the careful selection and training of management, particularly at the supervisory level.*

How many of the companies who yearn for non-union status would be prepared to make the investment in people management that the organisations that they envy have done? The real issue is how well a business is managed – *that* is what determines success.

Notwithstanding the influence of large organisations, data from the 1990 Workplace Industrial Relations Survey (WIRS) found that non-union establishments are more likely to be small single-plant establishments in the private services sector. This is not that surprising, given the great encouragement that the small firms sector has received and continues to receive. The number of business start-ups has risen, and many of the new organisations have not been able to see the relevance of trade unions. Their employees may have been the victims of redundancy in older, traditionally unionised, industries, and a reluctance to embrace the supposed cause of industrial decline (trade unions) may be understandable.

Yet one must also question how active trade unions have been in trying to recruit from new industries and the new workforce. Have the unions been so busy defending the interests of their existing members that they have not been able to devote sufficient resources to recruitment? Another question that should be asked is whether employees' feelings of insecurity about their long-term job prospects will provide a useful catchment area for trade union recruiters.

These and other questions link back to the matter of policy choice. If a business wishes to be, or to remain, non-union, then it needs to be clear about the relationship it will have with its employees. To be a Marks & Spencer you must be very people-oriented, placing great importance on respect for employees. This means highly developed and effective leadership skills – and that requires an investment in people. Gaining commitment and becoming a harmonious and integrated unitary workplace requires more than words – it can mean changing the established order.

Alternatively, a business can be a Type A organisation as identified by Salamon. Such organisations have to be prepared to deal with a request for union recognition. Although the idea might be anathema to an anti-union organisation, having an identifiable policy relating to trade unionism and trade union recognition could be very helpful. We are certainly aware of organisations that have been traditionally non-union but that are taking steps to prepare for a recognition claim – by training their managers in bargaining skills, for example.

Union recognition

The 1998 Workforce Employee Relations Survey (WERS) found that in 47 per cent of workplaces there were no union members at all – 'a substantial change from 36 per cent of workplaces in 1990'. The survey found that there are 'strong associations between the type of union presence and workplace employment size' but, as we have noted elsewhere, 'even stronger associations with management attitudes towards union membership'.

By the end of the 1990s trade union recognition had fallen to the point where only 45 per cent of workplaces recognised trade unions, compared to 66 per cent in 1984 and 53 per cent in 1990. But, as we have remarked elsewhere (particularly in Chapter 2), the decline in union membership seems now to have been halted. For some, this is as a consequence of the Employment Relations Act 1999, but Gregor Gall (*People Management*, 14 September 2001) considers that 'the industrial relations landscape had already begun to change' before the ERA became law. Noting that between 1995 and mid-2000 there were nearly 800 recognition agreements signed, Gall points out that this is not simply a numbers game. For him,

> *the kinds of new deals being signed – and where, by whom and under what conditions – are also important. They will influence not only the conduct of industrial relations in those organisations themselves, but also the behaviour of other organisations.*

Clearly, the number of recognition deals that have been signed owes something to the influence of the ERA, but according to Gall,

> *Increasing numbers of employers are realising that there is a positive business case for dealing with their workforces through unions, and that it is more efficient, effective and democratic than treating employees as a collection of atomised individuals.*

Taking such a stance is clearly a strategic choice for many businesses, who recognise that signing a voluntary deal allows them much more influence over the content of the agreement and saves a damaging confrontation with their workforce.

What is clear is that membership gains have been achieved and unions are now poised to take advantage of the provisions of the ERA in order to reassert their influence in the workplace. How employers respond will be a mixture of strategic choice and policy formulation.

Obtaining union recognition

The Employment Relations Act 1999 sets out the basis on which employees can obtain recognition. In summary, those provisions are:

- An independent trade union (or more than one independent trade unions) seeking recognition must apply to the employer in writing requesting that it be recognised. The employer has 10 working days in which to respond. If by the end of the 10-day period the employer has not responded or has rejected the request, the union may apply to the Central Arbitration Committee (CAC) for a decision on the 'appropriate bargaining unit' and/or whether a majority of the workers support recognition for collective bargaining.

- If, however, the employer indicates during the 10-day period that, while not accepting the request, the company is prepared to negotiate to agree the bargaining unit and recognition for it, a negotiation period of 20 working days (or longer, if mutually agreed) is available. If these negotiations fail, the union may apply to the CAC as above, but may not apply if it has rejected or not responded within 10 days to an employer's proposal for ACAS to assist.

- Once a recognition claim is referred to the CAC, it must try to help the parties reach agreement within 20 working days (or such longer appropriate period as it may determine). If agreement is not reached within that period, the CAC then has 10 days (or a longer period where it specifies the reasons for extension) to decide the appropriate bargaining unit.

- In respect of an application to decide the appropriate bargaining unit and whether the union(s) has the support of the majority of the workers in it, the CAC must not proceed unless it decides that:

  - members of the union (or unions) constitute at least 10 per cent of the workers constituting the proposed bargaining unit, and

  - there is *prima facie* evidence that a majority of the workers constituting the proposed bargaining unit would be likely to favour recognition of the union(or unions) as entitled to conduct collective bargaining on behalf of the bargaining unit.

- In deciding the appropriate bargaining unit, the CAC must take these considerations into account:

  - the need for the unit to be compatible with effective management

  - 'the matters listed in sub-paragraph (4), so far as they do not conflict with that need'.

The matters listed in sub-paragraph (4) are:

- the views of the employer and of the union (or unions)

- existing national and local bargaining arrangements

- the desirability of avoiding small, fragmented bargaining units within an undertaking

- the characteristics of workers falling within the proposed bargaining unit and of any other employees of the employer whom the CAC considers relevant

- the location of workers.

If the union(s) shows that a majority of the workers in the bargaining unit are members of the union(s), the CAC must declare the union(s) recognised, *unless* one of the following three conditions applies:

- The CAC is satisfied that a ballot should be held in the interests of good industrial relations.

- A significant number of the union members within the bargaining unit inform the CAC that they do not want the union (or unions) to conduct collective bargaining on their behalf.

- Membership evidence is produced which leads the CAC to conclude that there are doubts whether a significant number of the union members within the bargaining unit want the union (or unions) to conduct collective bargaining on their behalf.

If the union (s) cannot show majority membership, or can, but one of the three conditions above applies, the CAC must arrange (through a qualified independent person) a secret ballot of the workers in the bargaining unit, asking whether they wish the union(s) to conduct collective bargaining on their behalf.

If the ballot result shows that the union is supported by a majority of those voting and at least 40 per cent of those in the bargaining unit, the CAC will declare the union(s) recognised.

Note that the CAC must not proceed with a recognition application from more than one union unless:

- the unions declare that they will co-operate with each other in a manner likely to secure and maintain stable and effective collective bargaining arrangements, and

  - the unions make it clear that if the employer wishes, they will enter into arrangements under which collective bargaining is conducted by the unions acting together on behalf of the workers constituting the proposed bargaining unit.

Where the CAC declares a union(s) recognised, the parties have a negotiating period of 30 working days (or longer if mutually agreed) to agree a method for conducting collective bargaining. If they have not reached agreement then, they can seek CAC assistance during a further period of 20 working days (or longer if mutually agreed with the CAC). If they still cannot agree, the CAC will specify the method by which the parties must conduct collective bargaining (which they can vary by written agreement) and which will be a contract legally enforceable through the courts, by orders for specific performance, failure to comply with which will constitute contempt of court.

Employer concerns
Writing in *People Management* (January 1999), Mike Emmott, IPD policy adviser on employee relations, stated that 'One thing is clear beyond any doubt: most employers are opposed to the idea of a law on trade union recognition.' Many of their anxieties centred on the timescales within the recognition procedure, but they have become less of an issue given the overwhelming number of voluntary recognition deals that have been struck. Of more concern is the perception that many organisations have of the CAC – that it may or may not adopt an

even-handed approach to union recognition claims. The fact that its approach in some disputed cases has been criticised is not necessarily surprising – organisations that have resisted union claims are unlikely to be favourably disposed to the body that granted the disputed recognition. Whether the CAC does give trade unions preferential treatment is largely a matter of perception, but if it is to maintain the confidence of organisations, it must ensure that its independence is clearly maintained.

The Government, as is to be expected, takes a much more benign view of the legislation. It sees unions, 'where they are run efficiently along modern lines, as important partners for employers in promoting competitiveness and good practice' (Ian McCartney, *People Management*, 17 September 1998). This view is supported by Gall, who believes that 'the Labour Government has helped to engender a climate in which many employers are less inclined to behave unilaterally, and this has legitimised a union role in organisations'. Of course that may have little to do with the Government but may instead represent a more pragmatic reaction on the part of employers who realise that the legislation on union recognition is here to stay, at least for the foreseeable future.

Notwithstanding this, negative views of the CAC will not necessarily diminish, and as Gall and Cooper report (*People Management*, 12 July 2001), the 'unequivocal legal backing [given to the CAC in the first disputed case to reach the courts] may deter other aggrieved employers from going down this costly avenue'. There is certainly a danger that employers will grant recognition in the belief that the CAC is pro-union – and that this will have a consequentially negative effect on employee relations.

Employers and their use of the law

The laws that are now on the statute-book impact on employee relations in a number of ways, and changes in legislation have meant that trade unions are much more responsible for the actions of their members than they used to be. It is potentially much easier for employers now to seek a legal remedy when industrial action is taken against them. There is a much stricter definition of what constitutes strike action, which can only be lawful if it follows a properly conducted ballot, relates wholly or mainly to matters such as pay and conditions, and takes place only between an employee and his or her direct employer. This is intended to rule out sympathy or secondary action by those not involved in the main dispute.

Other provisions in the legislative package include restrictions on the numbers of people that can mount a picket outside a workplace, and compulsory ballots to test union members' support for contributions to a political fund. The law has also outlawed the closed shop – which is not to say that *de facto* closed shops do not still exist, because they do, most notably in the printing industry.

Against this background we should consider the employers' use of such laws. Why do some employers seek legal assistance in the resolution of disputes, and others do not? Much has been made of the rights that employers now have to take legal action against their employees, either to sue for damages caused by industrial action or to seek injunctions prohibiting the action from taking place.

Although the occasional high-profile case hits the headlines, there is no evidence to suggest that employers seek to exercise their legal rights every time they are faced with disruptive action. Indeed, there is probably more evidence to suggest that most employers resist the temptation to use the law. This is because they enjoy reasonably good employee relations and are more interested in maintaining those relations in the long term than they are in short-term victories. That is not to say that some organisations, in industries such as transport, set out deliberately to alienate their workforce. It is simply that there are often other considerations. If they were not seen to challenge 'unnecessary' strikes, they would run the risk of losing, perhaps permanently, many of their customers. For this reason, any employer faced with the threat of industrial action would have to take seriously concerns voiced by their customers and seek to balance these against the long-term relationship with its workforce.

The circumstances in which an employer might have to consider using the law usually follow a breakdown in negotiations with a recognised union. Such a breakdown could lead the union to seek a formal mandate from their members supporting industrial action, or there could be some form of unofficial industrial action encouraged by lay officials. The response that an employer makes in such circumstances is extremely important and can have a critical effect on employee relations.

Consider how you would respond to a ballot for industrial action in your organisation, and what factors you would take into account.

Industrial action ballots

If, for whatever reason, negotiations with a recognised union break down, there is every possibility that the union will seek to organise a ballot of its members. It may do this not because it has a burning desire to take industrial action but because a positive vote can be a very useful means of forcing the employer back to the bargaining-table. At the same time, if you – as the employer – are faced with a ballot for industrial action, there are a number of steps to be taken to check that it complies with all the legal requirements. Firstly, was the ballot conducted by post? Before any form of industrial action can commence, all those employees who it is reasonable to believe will be called upon to take part in the action must have been given a chance to vote. Secondly, were you as the employer given seven days' notice before the ballot took place?

Thirdly, has the union appointed independent scrutineers to oversee the ballot? Finally, did you receive notice of the result, and was this at least seven days before any proposed action?

Let us assume that all the legal requirements have been complied with. What are the legal options? Can any action be taken against the union? Not really, unless it can be demonstrated that the proposed action would not be a lawful trade dispute within the meaning of the legislation. There used to be a right to take sanctions against individuals, but the Employment Relations Act 1999 has changed that. The legislation makes it automatically unfair to dismiss workers who take part in protected (lawful) action within eight weeks of the action's beginning. Furthermore, after eight weeks it will still be unfair to dismiss if the employer has not followed an appropriate procedure for the resolution of the dispute. An 'appropriate procedure' is one established in a collective agreement. But the employer can do something about it if the union is, or its members are, in breach of an agreed procedure.

Now let us examine a second scenario – one in which the ballot for industrial action was not conducted properly. In these circumstances, and before seeking a legal remedy, it is important to consider all the options. Decisions on using legal intervention should never be taken without a full and extensive evaluation. Firstly, it might be appropriate to sit down with those who organised the ballot to discuss concerns about its validity. It is possible that they are already aware of its flaws, but are merely seeking to demonstrate the depth of feeling about a particular issue in order to get a resumption of negotiations. Alternatively, it might be appropriate to talk to those who might have been excluded from a ballot. They may be prepared to back the company in any dispute, and it is possible that their votes, in a re-run ballot, might overturn the original result. The third option is to seek an injunction against the union restraining it from taking any action until a proper ballot is conducted. Again this can be a high-risk strategy because in a re-run ballot those who previously voted against the union might this time vote with them on the basis of solidarity.

Ultimately, as with many aspects of employee relations, whether particular employers choose to seek a legal remedy to constrain the actions of their workforce will depend on management style and on how strong is the desire to maintain good working relations.

CONCLUSION

In this chapter we have looked at the link between corporate and business strategies and functional activities such as personnel. This has enabled us to see the relationship between the decisions of the board and the role of line managers in translating those decisions into active policies. We have looked at the process of strategy formulation and have seen that a number of different approaches are available. The methodologies employed will, inevitably, differ, but as we saw in our review of types of environment, the markets that an organisation operates in will have a clear impact on strategic choice. We also pointed out that employee relations, like every other function within the business, does not operate in a vacuum: it is insolubly linked with employee development, reward, and resourcing.

The chapter has also examined some of the issues that have to be taken into account when drawing up an employee relations policy and managing change, and we looked at the skills required in selecting and applying particular policies to the organisation and the skills needed to manage change effectively. In the context of gaining commitment we highlighted a number of core skills that we feel are an absolute necessity for the professional personnel practitioner.

We noted that different organisations have different approaches to the role and involvement of unions, and we examined the causes and effects of non-unionism. We looked at some examples of non-union firms and at whether their success was due to good management or the fact that they kept unions at arms' length. We concluded that good management was the most important factor. We identified the role that the law can play in management–union relations, and the factors that employers must consider before they use the legal processes against trade unions or trade union members.

KEY POINTS

There has to be a clear link between business strategy and employee relations strategies and employment relations policies.

- It is important to incorporate monitoring mechanisms into employee relations policies so that checks can be made on their effectiveness.

- It is important to evaluate new initiatives and ideas and gain overall commitment to particular policies before seeking to implement them.

- Management style has a major role to play in the determination of an employee relations policy in respect of trade unionism, union recognition, or non-unionism.

- Decisions on whether, and when, to use the law against trade unions or trade union members can be quite complex and should not be taken lightly.

Further reading

ARMSTRONG M. (1996) *Employee Reward*. London, Institute of Personnel and Development.

ARMSTRONG M. (2002) *Employee Reward*. London, Chartered Institute of Personnel and Development.

BLAKSTAD M. *and* COOPER A. (1995) *The Communicating Organisation*. London, Institute of Personnel and Development.

BLYTON P. *and* TURNBULL P. (1994) *The Dynamics of Employee Relations*. London, Macmillan.

BURNES B. (1996) *Managing Change: A strategic approach to organisational dynamics*. London, Pitman.

BUTCHER D. *and* MELDRUM M. (2001) 'Defy gravity', *People Management*, Vol. 7, No.13, June.

CAULKIN S. (2001) 'The time is now', *People Management*, Vol. 7, No.17, August.

DELOITTE & TOUCHE (1998) *Business Success and Human Resources*. Management survey.

EMMOTT M. (1999) 'Collectively cool', *People Management*, Vol. 5, No.2, January.

GALL G. (2001) 'In place of strife', *People Management*, Vol. 7, No.18, September.

GALL G. *and* COOPER C. (2001) 'Court upholds CAC recognition award to steel union', *People Management*, Vol. 7, No.14, July.

GUEST D. (1995) 'Human resource management, trade unions and industrial relations', in Storey J. (ed.). *Human Resource Management: A critical text*. London, Routledge.

INSTITUTE OF PERSONNEL AND DEVELOPMENT (1997) *The Impact of People Management Practices on Business Performance*. London, IPD.

JOHNSON G. *and* SCHOLES K. (2002) *Exploring Corporate Strategy*. 4th edition. London, Prentice Hall.

JUDGE G. (1997) 'United firms stand, but divided they fail', *The Guardian*, 29 April.

KAY J. (1993) *Foundations of Corporate Success*. Oxford, OUP.

MARCHINGTON M. *and* WILKINSON A. (1996) *Core Personnel and Development*.London, Institute of Personnel and Development.

MARCHINGTON M. *and* WILKINSON A. (2002) *People Management and Development*. London, Chartered Institute of Personnel and Development.

MCCARTNEY I. (1998) 'In all fairness', *People Management*, Vol. 4, No.18, September.

MILLWARD N., STEVENS M., SMART D. *and* HAWES W. R. (1992) *Workplace Industrial Relations in Transition: The ED/ESRC/PSI/ACAS surveys*. London, Gower.

PORTER M. (1985) *Competitive Advantage: Creating and sustaining superior performance*. New York, Free Press.

PURCELL J. (1987) 'Mapping management styles in employee relations', *Journal of Management Studies*, Vol. 24, No.5. p535.

SALAMON M. (1998) *Industrial Relations Theory and Practice*. 3rd edition. London, Prentice Hall.

TYSON S. (1995) *Human Resource Strategy: Towards a general theory of human resource management*. London, Pitman.

WALMSLEY H. (1999) 'A suitable ploy', *People Management*, Vol. 5, No.7, April.

Introduction

Employee involvement covers a wide range of practices. As defined by Marchington *et al* (1992), these practices are initiated principally by management and are designed to increase employee information about, and commitment to, the organisation. Employee involvement concentrates on individual employees and is designed to produce a committed workforce more likely to contribute to the efficient operation of the organisation. By introducing employee involvement mechanisms, management seeks to gain the consent of the employees to its proposed actions on the basis of commitment rather than control (Walton, 1985).

Employee *participation*, on the other hand, concerns the extent to which employees – often via their representative – are involved with management in the decision-making machinery of the organisation. This includes joint consultation, collective bargaining and worker representation on the board.

It is management, however, who makes the final decision as to whether employees are to be involved, and to participate, in management decision-making. Employee involvement, unlike collective bargaining and worker representation on the board, is not about employees' sharing power (jointly regulating) with management. The decision whether to accept, or reject, the views of the employees rests with management alone.

Explain the difference between the terms 'employee involvement' and 'employee participation'.

Why involve employees?

The control-oriented approach to workforce management associated with F. W. Taylor took shape in the early part of the twentieth century in response to the extending division of labour into jobs for which individuals were considered accountable. To monitor and control effectiveness in these jobs, management organised itself into a hierarchy of specialised roles supported by a top-down allocation of authority and status symbols to positions within the hierarchy. At the centre of this workforce control method was the desire to establish order and to inculcate efficiency in the employee – who was expected to obey, and not to challenge management instructions.

However, increasing international competition and technological change in the last 25 years have meant that higher skills and far greater flexibility are required of the employee. According to Walton (1985), in this environment a commitment strategy towards the workforce is required. Following this strategic approach to managing the workforce, jobs are designed to be broader than before (job enlargement), to combine planning and implementation and to include efforts to upgrade operations, not just to maintain them. Responsibilities of individual employees are expected to change as conditions change (functional flexibility), and teams – not individuals – are accountable for employee performance. The teams control how they deliver their output objectives. Employees are thus said to be 'empowered'. A commitment strategy therefore involves dispensing with whole layers of management and minimising status differentials so that control depends on shared goals and expertise rather than on a formal position that carries influence with it.

Under an employee commitment strategy, according to Walton, performance expectations are high and serve not to establish minimum standards but to emphasise continuous improvement and reflect the requirements of the marketplace. As a result, pay and reward strategies reflect not the principles of job evaluation but the importance of group achievement and concerns for gain-sharing and profit-sharing. Equally important, argues Walton, is the challenge of giving employees some assurance of security by offering them priority in training and re-training as old jobs are destroyed and new ones created, and providing them with the means to be heard on such issues as production methods, problem-solving and human resource policies.

Underlying all these policies is a management philosophy that accepts the interests of an organisation's multiple stakeholders – owners, employees, customers, and public. At the heart of this approach is an acceptance that growing employee commitment will lead to improved performance. No organisation in today's modern world can perform at peak levels unless each employee is committed to the corporate objectives and works as an effective team member. Employees want to use and develop their skills, enhance their careers and take pride in their work. The commitment strategy involves employees' contributing their own ideas on how their performance and the quality of product or service they provide can be improved. There is clear evidence that employees want to be part of a successful organisation which provides a good income and an opportunity for development and secure employment.

Harnessing this potential enthusiasm requires an investment of time and resources to build up mutual trust and understanding. The potential rewards are said to be great. Many organisations have publicised the benefits employee commitment has brought. An Industrial Relations Services survey (1999) of 49 organisations' experiences with employee involvement practices over the period 1992–1999 reported that:

- around three quarters believed it had enhanced employee commitment and motivation

- a similar number considered that their employee relations had improved

- approximately six in ten said the quality of products manufactured had improved

- over half claimed there had been advances in labour productivity

- just under a half believed that their employees' job satisfaction had increased

- the same proportion claimed that their organisational profits or performance had increased.

- one third said that involving employees had reduced absence rates

- just under 30 per cent believed switching to more participative working arrangements had improved their capacity to attract and retain employees.

The aims of employee involvement and particip

The involvement of and participation by employees in any organisation should aim to:

- generate the commitment of everybody to the success of the organisation

- enable the organisation better to meet the needs of its customers and adapt to changing market requirements

- help the organisation to improve performance and productivity, and adopt new methods of working to match new technology

- improve the satisfaction employees get from their work

- provide all employees with the opportunity to influence and be involved in decisions which are likely to affect their interests.

Employee involvement practices, by giving employees greater influence and control over their own work and involving them in workplace decisions, are designed to increase employees' commitment to the organisation and thereby – to mutual advantage – improve the economic performance of the enterprise. However, commitment is a two-way process. Management must also demonstrate a commitment to its employees in terms of:

- job security

- pay and other employment conditions (single status)

- access to training and re-training

- the provision of a safe working environment

- a balance between the work and the employees' wellbeing.

The objectives of employee involvement and participation practices

Modern management theory emphasises the benefits of involving employees in the organisation's decision-making processes. Teamworking, flatter managerial structures and participative working arrangements – such as briefing groups and business-oriented consultation and information-giving bodies – are now common in UK employing organisations, while de-layering – which normally results in reducing the number of middle managers – has resulted in the cascading down through the ranks of a wide range of tasks and decision-making responsibilities. As employing organisations face the demands of increased product market competition and downward pressures on costs, there is a high probability that this trend will continue into the future.

The case for employee involvement and participation stems from economic efficiency arguments. It is said to make business sense to involve employees because a committed workforce is likely to understand better what the organisation is trying to achieve and to be more prepared to contribute to its efficient operation. It is argued by the supporters of employee involvement practices that by encouraging a greater understanding of, and commitment to, the goals of the organisation among employees, such practices improve wider corporate performance, provide better working relationships and give employees greater ownership ('empowerment') of their day-to-day work.

Advocates of employee involvement also argue that employees have the opportunity to contribute to organisational success, and that because they are close to the work situation they may be able to recommend improvements which management can then decide whether or not to implement. They also argue that involving employees in management decision-making increases workers' job satisfaction and reduces labour turnover because employees feel more committed to organisational goals. In addition, empowering workers is said to reduce the need for complex systems of control and hence to improve efficiency. There is an assumption behind employee involvement theory that employees are an untapped resource with knowledge and experience that can be used by employers if they provide opportunities and structures for worker involvement. As Wilkinson (2001) points out, it is also assumed that participative decision-making is likely to lead to better management decisions so that empowerment represents a win/win situation with gains available to both employers (increased efficiency) and employees (job satisfaction).

Ramsay (1996) points out that the means of achieving the aims of employee involvement and participation practices lie in management's acting on five areas: changing attitudes, increasing business awareness, improving employee motivation, enhancing employee influence/ownership, and involving trade unions (see *Management objectives* box below). This is not an exhaustive list but does demonstrate the need for careful definition of objectives. Vague and general terms like 'changed attitudes' or 'greater incentives' are inadequate for evaluating whether employee involvement and participation practices are operating as management intends. The list also illustrates the potential conflict, or at least strain, between employee involvement schemes. As Ramsay (1996) remarks:

> *To exemplify this last point, a general sense of unity and belonging may sit poorly with the need to sharpen individual competition and incentive, and it may be advisable to use distinct kinds of scheme to achieve each if both require enhancement ...*

Management objectives in introducing employee involvement practices

Attitudes

- Employees' morale is improved
- Employees' loyalty and commitment are increased
- Employees' sense of involvement is enhanced
- Employees' support for management is increased

Business awareness

- Employees are better, more accurately informed
- Employees take greater interest
- Employees have better understanding of reasons for management action
- Employees evince support for/reduced resistance to management action

Incentive/motivation

Passive

- Employees accept changes in working practices
- Employees accept mobility across jobs
- Employees accept new technology
- Employees accept management authority

Active

- Employees improve quality/reliability
- There is increased productivity/effort
- Costs are reduced
- There is enhanced co-operation and team spirit

Personal

- Employees gain greater job interest
- Employees gain greater job satisfaction
- Employees gain enhanced opportunities for development

Employee influence/ownership

- Employees feel they have better job control
- Employees contribute suggestions
- Employees feel ownership in the company
- Employees feel increased ties to company performance and profitability

Trade unions

Anti-union

- Keeps union out of company
- Representative needs are met outside union channels
- Wins hearts and minds of employees away from union

With union

- Gains union co-operation
- Draws on union advice
- Restrains union demands

> *Source*: Ramsay H. (1996) in B. J. Towers (ed.) *The Handbook of Human Resource Management*, 2nd edn, Oxford, Blackwell

Trade unions

In organisations where trade unions are recognised and membership is high, it is important that management brings trade union representatives in on developing employee involvement and participation arrangements and procedures. In some cases, especially where trade union density is high, their co-operation, support and advice is likely to be an important factor in establishing employee involvement methods. The 1999 Industrial Relations Services Survey of employee involvement experiences showed that trade unions are generally in favour of the introduction of employee involvement initiatives. Of the 49 organisations in the Survey that recognised trade unions, more than six in ten reported a positive response, a quarter of them stating that unions were either neutral or indifferent to employee involvement schemes; 10 reported a negative union reaction. In many of the organisations surveyed by the IRS, trade unions had played a key role in the establishment and development of employee involvement initiatives. Nevertheless, more respondents to the Survey (33 per cent) believed that the introduction of employee involvement practices weakened the role of unions than believed strengthened it (17 per cent).

If the management already recognises unions, to use employee involvement practices to reduce a union's influence over the company's employees is a high-risk strategy. If the union has a high degree of membership, controls its members, has bargaining power and delivers on agreements, then an employee relations professional is unlikely to introduce employee involvement practices as an alternative to dealing with a trade union. But where a union has a low membership, cannot control its members, has little bargaining power and cannot keep to agreements, management will, in any event, have little difficulty in introducing employee involvement practices and joint consultative schemes as a means of bypassing what is a weak trade union presence.

Increased business awareness

If the businesses awareness of employees can be improved, they are more likely to be better and more accurately informed, the 'rumour grapevine' will be reduced, and there is a higher probability that they will enjoy greater job interest, have improved knowledge and understanding of the reasons for management decisions, and evince greater support for (or resistance to) to management action. The *Management objectives* box (above) suggests that by using employee involvement schemes to increase employee influence/ownership, management is more likely to provide its employees with greater job control and at the same time, via financial participation schemes, create increased employee ownership in the company and enhanced employee ties to company performance and profitability.

Ramsay (1996) argues that if management can change employee incentive and motivation in a positive direction, it may have passive, active and personal impacts. The employees may benefit from greater job interest, enhanced job satisfaction and increased opportunities to develop themselves. Active advantages may arise for the organisation stemming from improved quality/reliability of the product or service, increased labour productivity and effort, reduced costs and enhanced co-operation and team spirit. Among the probable passive advantages accruing to the organisation that Ramsay notes are a greater willingness on the part of employees to accept changes in working practices, flexibility across jobs, the implementation of new technology and enhanced front/first line management authority.

Increased commitment

As we have seen, if management can achieve a positive change in employee attitudes, it is likely to improve not only the morale of employees but also their loyalty and commitment to the organisation. Their sense of belonging and involvement is also likely to be enhanced. In addition, there will be greater probability that employees will give greater support to management's position. Employee involvement practices are thus an important means by which management can bring about organisational cultural change. However, such cultural change can only be achieved in any organisation on an incremental basis – the full benefits to the organisation from cultural change arising from the successful implementation of involvement methods will not accrue immediately. The attitudes of every employee, or manager, will not change in a positive direction at the same moment in time. Some will take longer than others to develop a positive change in attitude towards the actions of management. Management must be aware of this phenomenon of *incremental* cultural change when reviewing and monitoring the impact of the introduction of employee involvement practices.

> Outline the business case for introducing employee involvement practices into an organisation.

Employee involvement practices

The different practices

Marchington *et al* (1992) talk of direct and indirect employee participation practices. Direct participation consists of:

- downward communication practices
  - team briefing
  - workplace-wide meetings
  - staff newsletters
  - cascading of information down via the management chain

- upward problem-solving communications practices
  - suggestion schemes
  - employee/staff attitude surveys
  - employee groups established to solve specific problems or discuss aspects of performance or quality

- financial participation
  - profit-related bonus schemes
  - deferred profit-sharing schemes
  - employee share ownership schemes.

The main form of indirect employee participation is through some form of employee representative structure such as a joint consultative committee (JCC) or in some multi-national companies a European Works Council.

The Industrial Relations Services Survey of employment involvement undertaken in 1999 divided employee involvement initiatives into three broad categories:

- communication – which includes company journals and newsletters, team briefings, video presentations, e-mails, employee attitude surveys and employee reports which usually communicate financial information and details of business performance to the workforce

- participation – which includes team meetings, customer care initiatives, quality initiatives, suggestion schemes and recognition programmes

- representation – which covers joint consultation committees, company councils, works councils and European Works Councils.

Ramsay (1996) divides employee initiatives into four broad types, however:

- communications and briefing systems – which include downward and upward communications systems

- task and work group involvement – which includes teamworking, quality circles and total quality management programmes

- financial participation – which embraces profit-sharing, profit-related pay and share ownership schemes

- representative participation.

In this chapter, the Ramsay classification is used.

The distribution of employee involvement practices

The main sources of information about the overall distribution of employee involvement practices are the Industrial Relations Services Surveys of 1993 (62 participating organisations), 1996 (26 organisations surveyed) and 1999 (49 participating organisations), and the Workplace Industrial Relations Survey series which relate to 1980, 1984, 1990 and 1998.

The Industrial Relations Services surveys

These surveys (see Table 15) show that the incidence of team-based employee involvement initiatives rises as the frequency of collective bargaining falls. In 1993, the most common type of practice included company newspapers (used by over 80 per cent of respondents) and collective bargaining (89 per cent). Three years later, team meetings (mentioned by 88 per cent) were the most frequently used employee involvement strategy, team briefings (81 per cent) also featuring strongly, reflecting the growth of teamworking and more direct, participative working cultures. In common with 1993, company journals (81 per cent) and collective bargaining (77 per cent) emerged as popular employee involvement strategies.

Tables 16, 17 and 18 show the distribution of communications, participative and representational forms of employee involvement in the 1999 survey of 49 organisations. Taking the overall picture, team meetings (92 per cent), company letters (92 per cent) and team briefings (86 per cent) broadly repeat the trends of 1996. However, collective bargaining had slipped down the employee involvement pecking-order. Just 39 per cent reported using it, suggesting that traditional union-based representative forms of employee involvement are becoming rarer. The general conclusion from Table 15 is that over the period 1993–1999 there was a shift away from collective representation towards direct participation and involvement practices.

Table 15 Employee involvement practices: emerging trends 1993–1999

Practice	Percentage of respondents		
	1993 $n = 62$	1996 $n = 26$	1999 $n = 49$
Company newspaper	80	81	92
Team meetings	–	88	92
Team briefings	–	81	86
Collective bargaining	89	77	39

Source: Industrial Relations Services Surveys on Employee Involvement

Table 16 Employee involvement: communications

Mode of communication	Percentage *n* = *49*
Company journal	92
Team briefings (top-down)	86
e-mail	82
Attitude surveys	49
Employee reports	43
Video presentations	18

Source: Industrial Relations Services, *Employment Review*, No.683, July 1999

Table 17 Employee involvement: participation

Mode of participation	Percentage *n* = *49*
Team meetings	92
Suggestion schemes	45
Customer care initiatives	45
Quality initiatives	39
Recognition programmes	22

Source: Industrial Relations Services, *Employment Review*, No.683, July 1999

Table 18 Employee involvement: representation

Mode of representation	Percentage *n* = *49*
Joint consultative committee	49
Collective bargaining	39
Works council	12
Company council	10
European Works Council	8

Source: Industrial Relations Services, *Employment Review*, No.683, July 1999

The 1999 Survey also revealed that the average number of employee involvement practices operating in the 49 organisations surveyed was 7.2. In addition, it indicated that:

- Employee involvement practices tended to be found mostly in large manufacturing companies that had a tradition of consultation and some form of worker participation in the production process.

- Employee reports and employee attitude surveys were deployed by only about half the organisations in the sample.

- Respondents used a multitude of communications techniques, no single employer using fewer than two different approaches.

- Some 25 per cent of respondents did not use any form of employee representation.

- Unions are generally in favour of the introduction of employee involvement initiatives.

The Workplace Industrial Relations Survey series

Joint consultative committees were the principal channel of employee voice during World War II and the years immediately afterwards. In 1980, 34 per cent of all workplaces had a joint consultative committee – but by the time of the 1998 Survey the proportion had fallen to 29 per cent. These figures include some committees that meet rarely and which provide only limited opportunities for employees to communicate with management. If attention is confined to joint consultative committees that meet at least once every three months, the proportion of all workplaces in 1998 with an effective joint consultative committee was 23 per cent, compared with 31 per cent in 1990. The proportion of employees in workplaces with an effective joint consultative committee fell from 50 per cent in 1984 to 34 per cent in 1998. Such committees were most prevalent in the public sector and least common in the private services sector. Managements in organisations with a number of different establishments often prefer to consult with their employees on a multi-site basis rather than have a consultative committee for each establishment. In 1998, 56 per cent of workplaces belonging to a larger organisation reported a higher-level committee in their organisation, compared with 48 per cent in 1990 and 50 per cent in 1984. The increase since 1990 has been entirely within the private sector where the proportion rose from 35 to 48 per cent.

There is no doubt that profit-related pay became much more widespread during the 1980s. In 1984, 19 per cent of workplaces in industry and commerce belonged to enterprises that operated a scheme. By 1990 this percentage had risen to 44, and eight years later to 46. During the 1990s there were significant increases in profit-related pay in the manufacturing sector that brought its overall distribution up to the level in the private services sector. Profit-related pay also increased in foreign-owned workplaces and in a small number of publicly owned establishments in the commercial sector. In 1980, 13 per cent of all workplaces in industry and commerce had employees who were participating in a share-ownership scheme. This figure had increased to 22 per cent by 1984 and to 30 per cent in 1990. By 1998, however, the figure had fallen back to 24 per cent.

Turning to upward communication channels, the Workplace Surveys revealed an increase in the proportion of workplaces that held a regular meeting (at least once a year) between senior managers and all sections of the workforce from 34 per cent in 1984 to 49 per cent in 1998. With respect to the existence of problem-solving groups which met at least once a month to discuss aspects of performance, the proportion of all workplaces with such groups increased from 35 per cent in 1990 to 49 per cent in 1998. Briefing groups (team briefing) in which junior managers or frontline managers met at least once a month with all employees for whom they were responsible existed in 1998 in 65 per cent of all workplaces, compared to 48 per cent in 1990 and 36 per cent in 1984. The increase in the use of briefing-groups practices during the 1990s was confined solely to the private sector, to workplaces without union representation and to those without an effective joint consultative committee.

Table 19 shows the provision of information by managements to their employees over the period 1990 to 1998. It indicates that workplace managers have taken on board the need for increased efforts to inform employees, in that during the 1990s there was a marked increase in the number of items of information they disseminated to employees and/or their representatives. Increases in the amount of information provided were most noticeable in the public sector.

What employee involvement practices operate in your organisation (or one with which you are familiar)? How, and why, have the various practices been introduced? Has the distribution of the employee involvement practices changed over time? Why has it changed/not changed?

General principles

In implementing employee involvement practices there are a number of basic principles to bear in mind. Among the most important are:

- The arrangements and procedures should be appropriate to the needs of the organisation.

Table 19   The provision of information by managements to employees or their representatives, 1990–1998

Information about:	Percentage of all workplaces							
	Private manufacturing		Private services		Public sector		All sectors	
	1990	1998	1990	1998	1990	1998	1990	1998
The financial position of the establishment	55	58	51	61	67	83	56	67
The financial position of the enterprise	55	56	58	64	51	62	55	62
Investment plans	48	53	38	50	33	65	39	54
Staffing and manpower plans	52	36	49	58	77	84	57	61
None of the above	23	27	28	19	12	4	22	16

Source: Millward N., Bryson A. and Forth J. *All Change at Work?*, Routledge, 2000, p69

- Agreement on arrangements should normally be arrived at jointly with the employees.

- The arrangements should involve trade unions where the unions are recognised by the organisation.

- The lead in establishing, operating and reviewing arrangements should be taken by management.

- All employees in the organisation should be covered by the arrangements.

- Education and training should be provided to enable those participating in the arrangements to perform effectively.

- Management should retain full responsibility for business decisions.

- Employees' rights and trade unions' responsibilities should not be prejudiced.

Principles underlying employee involvement schemes

- A scheme should be capable of general application to all organisations in which people are employed.

- Arrangements and procedures should be appropriate to the organisation. There is no one best scheme.

- There should be joint employer–employee agreement on participation.

- Where trade unions are recognised there should be involvement of trade unions.

- Leadership in the scheme should be taken by management.

- The scheme should be inclusive of all employees.

- Education and training should be given to enable participants to fulfil their role in a constructive manner.

- Management must retain the responsibility for business decisions.

- Employees' rights and trade unions' responsibilities may not be prejudiced.

The needs of the organisation

The employee involvement and participation practices selected by the management should be compatible with the characteristics of the organisation, including the nature of its activities, structure, technology and history. Processes and structures appropriate to older industries do not necessarily match the needs of newer organisations formed in a different social, industrial and commercial context. There is no one way of implementing employee involvement and participation practices, and a guiding principle is that the practices proposed for introduction are compatible with the organisation's circumstances. It is not essential, for example, to introduce employee involvement practices to help improve product and/or service delivery quality if the organisation operates in a product market where competitive advantages rests with price and not the quality and reliability of the product.

Joint agreement

Employee involvement and participation arrangements in organisations are best developed by joint agreement between management and the employees. If arrangements are introduced on a jointly agreed basis, employees have some ownership of them and have a greater commitment to ensuring the success of the schemes. If management imposes the arrangements, the employees have no ownership of them and therefore no stake in ensuring their success. Joint agreement by management and employees means joint commitment to operate the arrangements in good faith and as intended. Both parties have an interest in ensuring that they succeed. It is something they have jointly created. In addition, employees see advantages in their representatives' being involved in the management decision-making processes, if for no other reason than to act as the custodians of their interests and to ensure management accountability. Employees desire that all levels of management take notice of their views and concerns.

It makes sense on the basis of the joint agreement/joint commitment argument that good practice in introducing employee involvement and participation schemes into organisations where trade unions are recognised is that union representatives be involved in deciding the appropriate arrangements and in their operation. This helps to reassure the trade unions that management's real agenda is not to undermine their influence. In initiating the necessary action to implement effective schemes the lead must come from management. Employee involvement and participation will not occur or develop of their own accord.

Training and development

Two other key principles are that opportunities must be available to all employees, including managers, to participate in employee involvement and participation schemes, and that appropriate training and education should be provided for such participants. The former principle involves all employees having confidence that their views (which are being actively sought) will be taken into account by management before a final decision is made, and not afterwards. An important consideration in this regard is the quality of relationships between individual employees and their immediate superiors and managers. If the quality of decisions made by management is to be improved, they must obtain information by listening to what their employees have to say and by asking them appropriate questions. By the same token, employees require information from employers. Both employees and employers require training in communications, presentational and meeting-chairing skills.

Employee involvement and participation arrangements do not relieve management of its responsibility for making business decisions falling within the area of its own accountability, or for communicating such decisions, with relevant background information, to the employees. The quality of management business decisions is likely to be improved if it takes into account, before making a final decision, the views of the work-force. However, the employees do not have a veto on management decisions. The prerogative to make business decisions continues to lie with management.

Selecting employee involvement practices

Context
There is no single model for the successful implementation of employee involvement and participation practices. Many considerations have to be taken into account by management in deciding which practice(s) to select (see *Factors to be considered* box below). Individual organisations have to develop and adapt arrangements to fit their own needs. These can vary over time as the organisation's size, structure and activities change. There is no single blueprint for success. Consideration has to be given to the context in which the arrangements will be introduced and operated. If they are to be introduced as part of a coherent and consistent strategy to improve the performance of the enterprise, the proposed arrangements should be the result of a full evaluation of all the possible practices. On the other hand, if they are being introduced to deal with a crisis situation, then it is likely the arrangements selected will have been ill-thought-out and possibly rationalised on the flimsy basis that the proposed employee involvement arrangements have been suc-cessfully implemented in other organisations. Without any detailed assessment and evaluation, the management will be assuming that the arrangements can be transplanted successfully into their own organis-ation. Arrangements introduced without proper analysis and evaluation are unlikely to be successful or to provide management with the advan-tages that might be expected from the implementation of employee involvement and participation schemes.

Factors to be considered in the selection of appropriate employee involvement and participation practices

Context
The practices should be introduced as part of a coherent and consis-tent strategy.
The practices should preferably not be introduced as 'crisis management'.

Single v multiple arrangement(s)
The mix can vary.
A greater mix does not necessarily mean a greater quality of arrangements.

Integration
There should be integration between the mix of arrangements (horizontal integration).
There should be integration with the strategic objectives of the organisation as a whole (vertical integration).

Success elsewhere
Why have such practices been successful elsewhere?
Could they be transplanted successfully?

Legal requirements
The Companies Act 1989
- requires a statement in the Directors' report describing action taken to introduce, maintain or develop information/communication consultation, financial participation and economic awareness

The European Works Council Directive (1994)
- makes available European Union-wide information and consultation systems in pan-European companies

The National Information and Consultation Directive (2002)
- requires employers with 50 or more employees to inform and consult with employees about employment prospects and decisions likely to lead to substantial changes in work organisation and contractual relations.

Multiple arrangements
Research by Marchington (1993) into the operation of employee involvement and participation practices revealed that single measures designed to enhance employee commitment to the organisation are much less likely to succeed than the existence of a multiplicity of practices. Nevertheless, whatever the mix of employee involvement and participation practices adopted, they must be appropriate to the organisation's needs as revealed by a thorough assessment and evaluation. Marchington (1993) found, for example, that in some small companies the mix of employee involvement arrangements was no more than one or two different practices, whereas in some larger manufacturing organisations there were as many as eight or nine different schemes for enhancing employee involvement and participation. However, he warns that it is dangerous to assume that the greater the number of employee involvement and participation arrangements an organisation introduces, the greater will be their overall quality. He points out that multiple techniques can lead to potentially conflicting pressures and confusions or communication overload for the staff subject to these arrangements.

Integration

If a multiplicity of different employee involvement and participation schemes is appropriate, then not only must they integrate with each other (horizontal integration) but they must be integrated with the strategic objectives of the organisation as a whole (vertical integration). This may require schemes to be customised so that they are relevant and appropriate to the organisation's needs and practices (see below). Since a wide range of employee involvement and participation practices are available to organisations, giving careful consideration to all of them before attempting to implement them is common sense. If employee involvement and participation arrangements are to make an impact, integration with business objectives and consistency with other management practices is essential.

Success elsewhere

Just because employee involvement practices have proved to be successful in one organisation, there is no guarantee that they will work as successfully in another organisation which is operating in a quite different context. Copying those arrangements that are perceived to be successful elsewhere is a poor basis for selection. A full analysis and investigation of their appropriateness to another organisation is essential. Information is required on what factors made them successful in that organisation. Do these factors exist in the 'copying' organisations? Are there factors at one organisation that would prevent the practice from being successfully transplanted in another organisation?

Legal requirements

There are also legal considerations that might influence a management's choice of which involvement and participation practices to introduce. The Companies Act 1989 requires any organisation that employs more than 250 employees to include a statement in its annual Directors' report describing the action taken in the previous financial year to introduce, maintain or develop arrangements in the following areas:

- information/communication – providing employees systematically with information on matters of concern to them as employees

- consultation – consulting employees or their representatives on a regular basis so that the views of employees can be taken into account in making decisions likely to affect their interests

- financial participation – encouraging the employees in the company to improve its performance through an employee share scheme or some other means

- economic awareness – achieving a common awareness on the part of all employees of the financial and economic factors that affect the performance of the company.

The European Works Council Directive (1994) and the European Works Council (UK Extension) Directive (1997) provide for a European

Union-wide information and consultation system to be set up in all organisations with more than 1,000 employees in European Union member states and/or employing more than 150 people in each of two or more member states. A pan-European Works Council (or alternative system) must be agreed between the central management of the company and a 'special negotiating body' (SNB) of employees elected from the various EU countries in which the company has productive capacity.

The Directive requires the establishment of a European Works Council of employee representatives with the right to meet central management at least once a year for information and consultation about the progress and prospects of the company on a pan-European basis. At this annual meeting the employees' representative is to receive information and be consulted about the enterprise's structure, economic and financial situation, any probable developments in the business and in production and sales, the employment situation and likely trends, investments, and any substantial change concerning the organisation, new working methods of production processes, transfers of production, mergers, cutbacks or closures of undertakings, establishments or important parts thereof, or collective redundancy. Employees also have the right in exceptional circumstances to call an additional meeting with management in order to be informed and consulted on 'measures significantly affecting employees' interests'.

The European Works Council Directive was transposed into UK law via the Transnational and Consultation of Employees Regulations, which became operative on 15 January 2000. Disputes arising between management and employees over the establishment and operation of works councils are, in the last resort, settled by the Central Arbitration Committee (see Chapter 5).

The National Information and Consultation Directive (2002) requires employers with 50 or more members of staff to inform and consult employee representatives about employment prospects and decisions likely to lead to substantial changes in work organisation or contractual relations. The Directive provides for a six-year transition period in the UK. Organisations with at least 150 employees are covered from spring 2005, with an additional two years allowed for those employing between 100 and 150 people, and a further year for those with at least 50 employees. The Directive does not make the setting up of employee representative committees compulsory, but that may prove necessary to meet its requirements – which include evidence of a procedure. The Directive is very open in leaving matters to be determined at member state level. It is silent on a range of subjects. For example:

- There is no default information and consultation structure as there is with the EWC Directive.

- No provision is specified for the negotiating process under which agreements can be reached.

● There is no information on how the process is to be initiated.

However, there is a mechanism by which a voluntary agreement may be made to ascertain a pre-implementation date (similar to that stipulated by Article 13 of the EWC Directive).

Outline the likely impact of the National Information and Consultation Directive on your organisation. Include how any implementation problems might be overcome.

Communications and briefing systems

Communication systems

Employee communications involves the provision and exchange of information and instructions which enable an organisation to function effectively and its employees to be properly informed about developments. It covers the information to be provided, the channels (both upwards and downwards) along which it passes, and the way in which it is relayed. Communication is concerned with the interchange of information and ideas within an organisation.

Whatever the size of an organisation, and regardless of whether it is unionised or non-unionised, employees only perform at their best if they know their duties, obligations and rights and have an opportunity of making their views known to management on issues that affect them. With the trend towards flatter management structures and the devolution of responsibilities to individuals, it is increasingly important that individual employees have an understanding not only of what they are required to do and why they are required to do it but also have the opportunity to influence what happens to them at work. Marchington *et al* (2001) have shown that companies are increasingly rating the views of their employees as a critical business issue and are establishing mechanisms for listening to their employees – not because they are being forced to do so but because it seems essential if they are to meet business objectives. These mechanisms engender a two-way dialogue which gives employees the opportunity to influence what happens at work.

Good communication and consultation are central to the management process. All managers have to exchange information with other managers, which necessitates lateral or inter-departmental communications. Failure to recognise this need is likely to result in inconsistency of approach or application. The ACAS Advisory booklet on *Employee Communications and Consultation* lists the advantages of good employee communications as:

● Improved organisational performance – Time spent communicating at the outset of a new project or development can minimise subsequent rumour and misunderstanding.

- Improved management performance and decision-making – Allowing employees to express their views can help managers arrive at sound decisions that are more likely to be accepted by the employees as a whole.

- Improved employee performance and commitment – Employees perform better if they are given regular, accurate information about their jobs such as updated technical instructions, targets, deadlines and feedback. Their commitment is also likely to be enhanced if they know what the organisation is trying to achieve and how they as individuals can influence decisions.

- Greater trust – Discussing issues of common interest and allowing employees an opportunity to express their views can engender improved management–employee relations.

- Increased job satisfaction – Employees are more likely to be motivated if they have a good understanding of their jobs and how they fit into the organisation as a whole, and are actively encouraged to express their views and ideas.

Employee communications strategy

When devising an employee communications strategy, the following questions should be addressed:

- Why should the company communicate?

- What is to be communicated?

- Who are the audience(s)?

- How is communication to be handled?

- Who is responsible?

- How will success be measured?

A variety of communication methods (spoken and written, direct and indirect) are available for use by management. The mix of methods selected will be determined by the size and structure of the organisation. Two main methods of communication can be distinguished. First, there are face-to-face methods that are both direct and swift, and they enable discussion, questioning and feedback to take place. However, it is often advantageous to supplement these methods with written materials, especially if the information being conveyed is detailed or complex. The main formal face-to-face methods of communications are:

- group meetings – meetings between managers and the employees for whom they are responsible

- cascade networks – a well-defined procedure for passing information quickly, used mainly in large or disparately widespread organisations

- large-scale meetings – meetings that involve all the employees in an organisation or at an establishment, with presentations by a director or by senior managers; these are a good channel for presenting the organisation's performance or long-term objectives

- inter-departmental briefings – meetings between managers in different departments that encourage a unified approach and reduce the scope for inconsistent decision-making, particularly in larger organisations.

Second, there are written methods. These are most effective where the need for the information is important or permanent, the topic requires detailed explanation, the audience is widespread or large, and there is a need for a record of it. The chief methods of written communications include company handbooks, employee information notes, house journals and newsletters, departmental bulletins, notices and individual letters to employees. Electronic mail is useful for communicating with employees in scattered or isolated locations, and audio-visual aids are particularly useful for explaining technical developments or financial performance.

Communications strategies, policies and techniques need senior management support, and they require discipline to follow them through. Industry and commerce are littered with communications schemes that have been introduced with the best of intentions before other matters became priorities and a briefing session or a newsletter was missed. The outcome is the development of cynicism among employees. It is also true that strategies, policies and tools tend not to be effective without the support and interest of staff. Think of it this way:

If I am not a big enthusiast, preferring to laze around the house at weekends, the existence of a toolbox in the house is unlikely to persuade me to put in a couple of shelves. However, if I am very enthusiastic about DIY and very keen to put up the couple of shelves, the fact that I have no toolbox will not deter me. I will simply borrow or buy a toolbox. It is my enthusiasm that is the driver, not the toolbox. ....

Monitoring

It cannot be taken for granted that communications systems are operating effectively, nor can it be assumed that because information is sent it is also received. The communications policy and its associated procedures need regular monitoring and review to ensure that practice matches policy, the desired benefits are accruing, the information is accepted, received and understood, and the management communicators know their roles. Monitoring is largely dependent on feedback from employees through both formal and informal channels, although other indicators include the quality of decision-making by management, the involvement of senior management and the extent of employee co-operation. In monitoring and reviewing an organisation's communication policy, the criteria for assessing its effectiveness are related to the outputs from the operation of the policy. For example, has employee morale improved? Has productivity increased? Is there a greater willingness to accept change on the part of employees and managers? Do the employees have an improved understanding of the company and business generally? Review and monitoring should take place on a regular periodic basis – for example, quarterly or annually – depending on the size of the organisation.

Explain the criteria you would use to assess whether an organisation's communications strategy is operating effectively in management's interests.

Briefing groups

The dangers of the use of such groups, from a management perspective, are that as the information cascades down, it becomes *watered* down, hedged around with rumour, out of date, and imprecise. Many communications policies are less effective than they might be because a lot of information passed down from the top to the bottom of the organisation concentrates on the wider perspective, with the result that the local receivers of the information do not take note of it because it relates to issues which to them are remote and marginal to their interests and concerns.

Of all the communication methods in use, team briefing is perhaps the most systematic in providing employees with top-down information. Information cascades down through various management tiers, being conveyed by each immediate supervisor or team leader to a small group of employees, the optimum number being between four and 20. In this way employee queries are answered. This takes place throughout all levels in the organisation, the information eventually being conveyed by supervisors and/or team leaders to shopfloor employees. On each occasion the information received is supplemented by 'local' news of more immediate relevance to those being briefed. Meetings tend to be short but designed to help develop the 'togetherness' of a workgroup, especially where different grades of employee are involved in the team.

Each manager is a member of a briefing group and is also responsible for briefing a team. The system is designed to ensure that all employees from the managing director to the shopfloor are fully informed of matters affecting their work. Leaders of each briefing session prepare their own brief, consisting of information that is relevant and task-related to the employees in the group. The brief is then supplemented with information passed down from higher levels of management. Any employee questions raised which cannot be answered at once are answered in written form within a few days. Briefers from senior management levels are usually encouraged to sit in at briefings given by more junior managers, while line managers are encouraged to be available to brief the shopfloor employees. The employee relations professional will explain management's view to the employees in a regular and open way, using examples appropriate to each workgroup. Although team briefing is not a consultative process and is basically one-way, question-and-answer sessions can take place to clarify understanding. Feedback from employees is very important.

There are, however, practical problems to be borne in mind in introducing team briefing. First, if the organisation operates on a continuous shiftworking basis, is it technically feasible for team briefings to take place since the employees are working all the time except for their rest breaks? Second, management has to be confident it can sustain a flow of relevant and detailed information. Third, if the organisation recognises unions, the management must be careful not to act in such a manner that the union(s) believes management is attempting to undermine its influence. Team briefing is highly unlikely to succeed if relations between management and the representatives of its employees are distrustful.

Employee attitude surveys
Surveys are an important upward channel of communication from the employees to management. The 1998 Workplace Employee Relations Survey provides evidence of a steady rise in the use, by employers, of employee attitude surveys. In 1998, 45 per cent of workplaces that employed 25 or more people said they had conducted an employee attitude survey within the previous five years. This is a sharp rise from the 17 per cent recorded in the 1990 Workplace Industrial Relations Survey. The increased popularity of employee attitude surveys indicates that they are viewed as an effective tool for assessing both employee morale and commitment.

Management usually uses an employee attitude survey to obtain specific data on employee perceptions of fairness, pay systems, training opportunities and awareness of an organisation's business strategy and long-term goals. Employee attitude surveys can:

- provide managers with early warning of issues of concern before they lead to major employee relations difficulties

- help managers to make internal comparisons of employee morale and behaviour across a number of departments and sites

- provide employee views on specific personnel/HRM policies such as the operation of the discipline and grievance procedure

- provide data that can be used in problem-solving, planning and decision-making.

Many organisations use the information gained from employee attitude surveys to benchmark employee morale and satisfaction against other organisations. Such information is only likely to be helpful, however, if it is used in conjunction with other information, obtained in a different way, and not used in isolation.

Task and work group involvement

The objective of these employee involvement and participation practices is to tap into employees' knowledge of their jobs, either at the individual level or through the mechanism of small groups. These practices are designed to increase the stock of ideas within the organisation, to encourage co-operative relations at work and to justify change. Task-based involvement encourages employees to extend the range and type of tasks they undertake at work. It is probably the most innovative method of employee involvement in that it focuses on the whole job rather than concentrating on a relatively small part of an employee's time at work. Such employee involvement practices include job redesign, job enrichment, teamworking and job enlargement. Job enrichment involves the introduction of more elements of responsibility into the work tasks. Job enlargement centres on increasing the number and diversity of tasks carried out by an individual employee, thereby increasing his or her work experience and skill.

Teamworking is seen by its advocates as a vehicle for greater task flexibility and co-operation, as well as for extending the desire for quality improvement. Geary (1994) remarks that:

> *In its most advanced form, teamworking refers to the granting of autonomy to workers by management to design and prepare work schedules, to monitor and control their own work tasks and methods – to be more or less self-managing. There can be considerable flexibility between different skills categories, such that skilled employees do unskilled tasks when required and formerly unskilled employees receive additional training to be able to undertake the more skilled tasks. At the other end of the spectrum, management may merely wish employees of comparable skill to rotate between different tasks on a production line or the integration of maintenance personnel to service a particular group of machines. It may not result in production workers' undertaking tasks which were formerly the preserve of craft people, or vice versa. Thus, flexibility may be confined within comparable skills groupings. In between, there is likely to be a diversity of practice.*

The two most advanced forms of teamworking are semi-autonomous groups and fully autonomous groups. In fully autonomous groups the team members work with one another, have responsibility for the specific product or service, jointly decide how the work is to be done and appoint their own team leader. In 1998 only 3 per cent of the workplaces surveyed in the Workplace Employee Relations Survey corresponded to this model. Semi-autonomous groups are characterised by members' working with one another, having responsibility for a specific product or service and jointly deciding how the work is to be done. In 1998, 35 per cent of workplaces operated teams that approximately corresponded to the model. The 1998 Workplace Employee Relations Survey found, however, that in 54 per cent of the workplaces it surveyed, there were teams where members worked with one another and had responsibility for a specific product or service. In 62 per cent of workplaces, there were teams where members only worked with one another and had no responsibility for products or services, for deciding how tasks would be done or for selecting their team leader.

Team size is usually seven to ten, although some teams are much larger. Task flexibility and job rotation can, however, be limited, partly by the sheer range of tasks and partly by the nature of the skills involved. Organisations that operate teamworking arrangements see major training programmes as a necessary accompaniment. Teamworking provides a management with the opportunity to remove and/or amend the role of the supervisor and to appoint team leaders. However, research by Grapper (1990) indicates that management time saved in traditional supervision and control may be more than offset by the need to give support to individuals and groups.

> What is the extent of teamworking in your organisation? Why?

Quality circles
A quality circle aims to identify work-related problems that are causing poor service or productivity in a section of the workplace, and to recommend solutions to those problems. It provides opportunities for employees to meet on a regular basis (once a month, fortnightly) for an hour or so to suggest ways of improving productivity and quality, and reducing costs. A quality circle typically involves a small group of employees (usually six to eight) in discussions under the guidance of their supervisor. The members select the issues or problem they wish to address, collect the necessary information, and make suggestions to the management on ways of overcoming the problems.

In some cases, the group is itself given authority to put its proposed solutions into effect, but more often it presents formal recommendations for action, which the management then considers whether or not to implement. Quality circles encourage employees to identify not only with the quality of their own work but also with the management's objectives of better quality and increased efficiency throughout the organisation. Members of a quality circle are not usually employee representatives but are members of the circle by virtue of their knowledge of the tasks involved in their jobs. They are under no obligation to report back to their colleagues who are not members of the circle.

If quality circles are to be effective, a strong commitment from management is necessary. Management does not supply members to a quality circle but allows time and money for its members to meet and provides the members with basic training in problem-solving and presentational skills. A professional management always treats all recommendations from a circle with an open mind, and if it rejects a proposal will explain the reasons for that decision to the circle. If the organisation recognises trade unions, it would be well advised to consult the workplace union representatives on the establishment of quality circles and to encourage their to support for a device, which if operated properly, will contribute to constructive employee relations.

After a dramatic increase in their number such that by the mid-1980s more than 400 such circles were known to be in existence, the popularity of quality circles declined rapidly. Quality circles fail either at their introduction or after a short period of operation mainly because of a lack of top-management commitment, because of the absence of an effective facilitator to promote and sustain the programme, because of management reluctance to bear the costs of operating circles in terms of time – including training time for participants, when employees are inevitably off the job – and/or because of the lack of any follow-up or action by management on suggestions put forward by the circles.

Total quality management (TQM)

Total quality management programmes derive from a belief that competitive advantage comes from high and reliable quality achieved through the associated welding of more stable and mutual relationships between suppliers and customers. The total quality ethic is a philosophy of business management, the aim of which is to ensure complete customer satisfaction at every stage of production or service provision. Although TQM was initially driven by the demands of external customers, the concept was evolved into a more wide-ranging principle to encompass internal operations. TQM programmes are designed to ensure that each level and aspect of the organisation is involved in continuously improving the effectiveness and quality of the work to meet the requirements of both internal and external customers.

Where quality issues were traditionally assigned to specific departments, TQM requires that the quality of products and services be the concern of every employee. Quality management offers service management an effective way of organising and increasing employees' responsibility while meeting the interests of employees at every level, offering them an opportunity to become more involved in the decision-making process. The Prudential Assurance Company claimed in the mid-1990s that TQM had yielded it many benefits, including a reduction of 45 per cent in the average time spent in dealing with a life assurance claim.

Geary (1994) points out that TQM places considerable emphasis on enlarging employees' responsibilities, reorganising work and increasing employee involvement in problem-solving activities, and that this search for continuous improvement is a central thrust. He further notes:

> *The manufacture of quality products, the provision of a quality service and the quest for continuous improvement is the responsibility of all employees, managed and manager alike, and all functions. TQM requires quality to be built into the product and not inspected by a separate quality department. Where employees are not in direct contact with the organisation's customers, they are encouraged to see their colleagues at successive stages of the production process as internal customers. Thus, a central feature of TQM is the internalisation of the rigours of the marketplace within the enterprise.*

A second feature of TQM follows on from the first. Because each employee and department is an internal customer to another, problem-solving necessitates the formation of organisational structures designed to facilitate inter-departmental and inter-functional co-operation. A consequence of this is that problems are best solved by those people to which they are most immediate. Employees are to be encouraged and given the resources to solve problems for themselves. Employees, it is contended, will embrace such job enlargement and undertake activities conducive to an improvement in the organisation's efficiency.

Ramsay (1996) argues that total quality management subsumes quality circles or teamworking arrangements into a more integrated approach and concentrates on stressing change throughout the entire organisational system. It is essentially a top-down management-driven process. If total quality management is to succeed, again top-management commitment is essential. Departments have to be persuaded that resistance to integration is self-defeating, and the employees must have it clearly demonstrated to them that total quality management is not a cover for job rationalisation and redundancies. In short, the employees require evidence that there is a 'stake' for them in the total quality management 'world' – that is, that the TQM world is superior to their current world.

Financial participation

Offering employees a direct stake in the ownership and prosperity of the business for which they work is one of the most direct and tangible forms of employee involvement. By giving employees the chance to participate in financial success, employees can acquire and develop a greater sense of identity with the business and an appreciation of the business needs. Employers also benefit. It is argued that a financial stake gives employees increased enthusiasm for the success of the organisation and often for a voice in its operation. In its most developed form employee share ownership means that employees become significant shareholders in the business, or even their own employer.

Financial employee involvement and participation schemes link specific elements of pay and reward to the performance of the unit or the enterprise as a whole. They provide an opportunity for employees to share in the financial success of their employing organisation. The main forms of financial participation are:

- deferred profit-sharing schemes, by which profits are put in a trust fund to acquire shares in the company for employees

- profit-related pay

- employee share ownership plans.

Profit-sharing

These schemes aim to increase employee motivation and commitment by giving employees an interest in the overall performance of the enterprise. In this way management hopes to raise employee awareness of the importance of profit to their organisation, and to encourage teamworking by demonstrating that rewards accrue from co-operative effort even more than from individual effort. Profit-sharing schemes ensure that employees benefit from an organisation that makes profits.

However, there are practical problems to be addressed if profit-sharing schemes are to have the desired effect. A scheme has to contain clearly identifiable links between effort and reward. Individuals must not feel that no matter how hard they work in any year, that effort is not reflected in their share of the company's profits. There is also the issue of whether there is a clearly understood formula for the sharing of any profits so that employees can calculate their share. Profits cannot be assessed quickly enough to secure early movements in pay in response to rapidly changing market conditions. Due account has to be taken of employees or there is a risk of inter-group dissatisfaction in that some employees might believe that other groups have received the same profit-share payment but have made less effort.

Profit-related pay

Profit-related pay is a mechanism through which employers can reward employees for their contribution to the business. It works by linking a proportion of employees' pay to the profits of the business for which they work. Employees are encouraged in this way to strive for commercial success. Employers who have introduced such schemes argue that as well as helping to create a more motivated and committed workforce, profit-related pay provides greater flexibility in the negotiation of pay settlements.

Share ownership

Share ownership takes financial involvement a step further by giving employees a stake in the ownership of the enterprise. It grants them shareholder rights to participate in decisions confined to shareholders voting at the annual general meeting. Employee share-ownership schemes seek to give individual employees a long-term commitment to the organisation and not just a short-term financial gain from a sharing of profits. Such schemes are usually linked to profit but the employees' portion is distributed in the form of shares, either directly to each individual or indirectly into a trust which holds the shares on behalf of all employees. Distributing shares to employees involves them in a tax liability that has restricted the development of employee share ownership schemes. One way to avoid this tax liability is an employee share ownership plan (known as an ESOP) – such plans were given a boost when the UK Government in the late 1980s provided important tax concessions for investment in such schemes.

In employee share ownership plans the company shares are initially bought, using borrowed money, by a trust representing the employees. They may not be required to put down a cash stake. The transfer of a portion of the company profits to the trust over subsequent years, as laid down in the initial agreement, enables the trust to pay off the loan and to allocate shares to individual employees.

Employee share ownership plans are clearly a means of promoting employee involvement in ownership. They give individual employees democratic control over significant holdings of company shares. They also have limitations. Employees may view the shares as simply a source of income and so lose the thread of the 'shared ownership' concept. Financial participation shares money, and on its own is unlikely to give rise to a greater commitment on the part of the individual employee to the interests of the organisation.

> Do you have any financial participation schemes in your organisation? If you do, why were those particular schemes chosen? To what extent and why are they effective? If your organisation does not have any financial participation schemes, why doesn't it?

Representative participation

The main form of representative participation is joint consultation, which is a process by which management and employees or their representatives jointly examine and discuss issues of mutual concern. It involves seeking acceptable solutions to problems through a genuine exchange of views and information. Consultation does not remove the right of management to manage – management must still make the final decision – but it does impose an obligation that the views of employees will be sought and considered before that final decision is taken. Employee communication is concerned with the interchange of information and ideas within an organisation. Consultation goes beyond this and involves managers' actively seeking and then taking account of the views of employees before making a decision. It affects the process through which decisions are made in so far as it commits management first to the disclosure of information at an early stage in the decision-making process, and second to taking into account the collective views of the employees.

Consultation does not mean that employees' views always have to be acted on – there may be good practical or financial reasons for not doing so. However, whenever employees' views are rejected, the reasons for rejection should be explained carefully. Equally, where the views and ideas of employees help to improve a decision, due credit and recognition should be given. Making a practice of consulting on issues upon which management has already made a decision is unproductive and engenders suspicion and mistrust about the process among employees.

Consultation requires a free exchange of ideas and views affecting the interests of employees. As such, almost any subject is appropriate for discussion. However, both management and employees may wish to place some limits on the range of subjects open to consultation – because of trade confidences, perhaps, or because some topics are considered more appropriate for a negotiation forum. But whatever issues are agreed upon as being appropriate for discussion, it is important that they are relevant to the group of employees discussing them. If consultation arrangements are to be effective, discussing trivialities is to be avoided. This is not to say that minor issues may be ignored. Although the subject matters of consultation are a matter for agreement between employer and employees, there are a number of laws and regulations that specifically require an employer to consult with recognised trade unions and other employee representatives. These include:

- The Health and Safety at Work Act 1974 places a duty on employers to consult with safety representatives appointed by an independent recognised trade union.

- The Transfer of Undertakings (Protection of Employment) Regulations 1981 provide for trade unions to be consulted where there is a transfer of a business to which the regulations apply. This consultation must take place with a view to reaching agreement on the measures taken.

- The Trade Union and Labour Relations (Consolidation) Act 1992 requires employers to consult with trade unions when redundancies are proposed. Such consultation must be undertaken by the employer with a view to reaching agreement, and must be about any possibilities of avoiding the dismissals, reducing the numbers to be dismissed, and mitigating the consequences of any redundancies.

- The Social Security Pensions Act 1975 requires employers to consult with trade unions on certain matters in relation to the contracting out of the state scheme of an occupational pension scheme.

- The Transnational Information and Consultation of Employees Regulations (2000) permit employee representatives the right to meet central management at least once a year for information and consultation about the progress and prospects of the company on a pan-European basis.

Joint consultative committees

Joint consultative committees (JCC) have long been used as a means of employee consultation. They are composed of managers and employee representatives who come together on a regular basis to discuss issues of mutual concern. They usually have a formal constitution which governs their operations. The number of members of a JCC varies depending on the size of the organisation. Managements in organisations that operate over a number of different establishments sometimes prefer to consult with employees on a multi-site basis rather than have a consultative committee for each establishment. These are referred to as 'higher-level committees'. The 1998 Workplace Employee Relations Survey reported a higher incidence (56 per cent) of such committees than in previous surveys.

However, as a general rule the size of the committee should be as small as possible still to be consistent with ensuring that all significant employee groups are represented. It is necessary, in order to demonstrate management's commitment to consultation, that the management representatives on the committee include senior managers with authority and standing in the organisation and who attend its meetings regularly.

Every meeting of the JCC should have as its focus a well-prepared agenda, and all members should be given an opportunity to contribute to the agenda before it is circulated. The agenda is normally sent out in advance of the meeting so that representatives have a chance to consult with their constituents prior to the committee meeting. The JCC must be well chaired if it is to be run effectively. It is important that employee representatives know exactly how much time they will be allowed away from their normal work to undertake their duties as committee members, and the facilities to which they are entitled. Employee representatives should not lose pay as a result of attending committee meetings. If joint consultation is to be effective, the deliberations of the committee must be reported back to employees as soon as possible. This can be done via briefing groups, news-sheets, noticeboards and the circulation of committee minutes.

In some organisations institutions established to inform and consult with employees have titles other than 'joint consultative committee'. Such alternative titles include 'works council' and 'employee representative council'. In Marks & Spencer, consultation arrangements are referred to as Business Involvement Groups. There is such a Group in each store and area of business, and the number of representatives on the Group reflects the size of the business unit/area/store. Each Group is made up of representatives elected by employees and has a clear remit and support across the business. In addition, there are Regional Business Involvement Groups made up of the chairpersons for each local group. They meet periodically to share and debate issues and ideas that have a wider impact on the business. Marks & Spencer sees its system of Business Involvement Groups as an important part of the communication and involvement process, a means for ensuring that employees are up to date with key issues and events, an opportunity for employees to contribute ideas that might improve business performance and a forum to discuss issues that impact on the employees' working lives. In short, the Business Involvement Group system enables employees to become involved in the way Marks & Spencer develops its business in the future.

Do JCCs exist in your organisation? If so, what forms do they take – and are they successful? How could they be improved? If there are no JCCs, what mechanisms are in place to consult with the workforce? Would a JCC be useful? Why/why not?

The introduction of employee involvement schemes

In implementing employee involvement practices, employee relations professionals must remain mindful that different organisations operate under very different environmental circumstances, and that what is good for one may not necessarily be appropriate for another. There are a number of necessary conditions to be met if employee involvement and participation practices are to be successfully implemented and operated.

First, a good employee relations climate is essential. Second, if a strong commitment to the introduction and operation of the practices is not forthcoming from top management, there is little likelihood that the practices will have much chance of survival beyond their initial establishment. If such commitment is forthcoming, there is a greater likelihood that there will be a free flow of information up, down and across the organisation, that employee involvement mechanisms appropriate to the organisation's needs will be selected, and that the impact of the operation of the practices on the value and credibility of other employee relations institutions and procedures will be protected. A management that is prepared to commit resources in terms of time, lost wages, training, facilities and lost output/service to support the operation of employee involvement practices is increasing the probability that the practices will be successful. Appropriate mechanisms to review and monitor the operation of employee involvement and participation arrangements to ensure that they are achieving their objectives are also a necessary condition. However, they are not sufficient on their own to improve the chances of success. Management requires the skills of oral and written communication, interviewing, listening and teambuilding. It also needs negotiating skills to gain the commitment of managerial colleagues and the workforce to the implementation of the employee involvement and participation practices selected. Without management and employee commitment, employee involvement and participation schemes will not survive for very long. Let us now look at these conditions in more detail.

Good employee relations

Employee involvement schemes are more likely to be effective if there is a willingness on the part of both management and employees to be open in their attitude and behaviour. Employee involvement and commitment will not be gained in an atmosphere where there is little trust or motivation. Schemes cannot operate effectively in a background of disputes and confrontation. Insufficient motivation on the part of management and employees to make involvement and participation practices work, or insufficient mutual trust to allow them to work, is more likely to be the cause of their failure than the substance of the practices. If management introduces employee involvement and participation schemes but shortly afterwards changes its style to one that is less open and participative, the employees are likely to regard this behaviour as an attempt by management to undermine the schemes. Employee scepticism towards the employee involvement and participation practices under which they worked will emerge, and the schemes will be less effective.

Good employee relations is thus a necessary precondition for the effective working of employee involvement and participation schemes. An open style of management in which employee support for proposed action is gained by consent, and not by coercion, is essential. However, by itself a good employee relations environment is not a sufficient condition for the successful implementation and operation of involvement and participation schemes. It also requires unquestioning commitment from top management.

Commitment by top management

This is a key condition, but again is not sufficient on its own to deliver involvement and participation schemes that operate effectively. Such schemes are unlikely, however, to be effective unless top management, by its own behaviour, demonstrates a belief in such schemes. Top management's commitment requires not only to be felt positively but also to be seen to be so by employees. All managers should accept the value of employee involvement and participation schemes and not give the impression that they are supporting a mere fad in management practice or are speaking rhetoric behind which there is no substance. Whereas a good committee structure may be important for some involvement and participation schemes to be effective, it is totally irrelevant if individual managers are not committed to the schemes' success. Support for introducing employee involvement and participation schemes requires to be secured throughout the whole management structure. If management is not committed to their success, employees will view the arrangements as 'tokenism' and disregard attempts to gain their commitment, loyalty and support.

If managers wish employee involvement schemes to succeed, there must be no loss of momentum following the initial enthusiasm engendered at their introduction. Management commitment has to last longer than for just the introduction of the schemes, since many are costly in management time if they are not run properly. Nothing destroys employee involvement initiatives more quickly than management action that is inconsistent with the philosophy of worker involvement. This is particularly so when management's behaviour strongly suggests to the employees that it really considers employee involvement and participation of little significance and something to be quickly dropped when there is short-term production/service provision pressure to meet the customers' needs. Care must be exercised by management in deciding the timing of meetings. If they are scheduled late on a Friday afternoon and there is little opportunity to explore issues in sufficient depth, for example, employees will question management's commitment to employee involvement initiatives as a means of improving management decision-making. The same applies if employees feel their views do not really count since their contributions are dismissed without serious examination.

Two important causes of failure of employee involvement and participation practices are the attitudes of middle and lower managers to such schemes, and what Marchington (1993) calls the 'lack of continuity caused by the dynamic career patterns of managers who are the driving force behind the schemes'. Middle and frontline management often lack commitment to, and fail to support, the development of employee involvement and participation initiatives. Some regard them as mechanisms by which senior/top managers 'pander' to the employees and at the same time undermine frontline managers' authority over employees. They perceive top management's support for the continuation of employee involvement and participation practices as being 'soft' on employees who they perceive as only too pleased to be paid while not working, and who, as a result, will always have issues they want to discuss with employers.

Frequently in large multi-plant/multi-product firms senior managers expect to stay at an establishment only for a short period of time, and their duration there is regarded as part of their development package en route to even more senior management positions elsewhere. Marchington (1993) refers to this type of character as the 'mobile champion', reflecting a picture of the manager who introduces a scheme then moves on to other duties, generally at another site, or to employment elsewhere. His or her successor often has different priorities and the employee involvement initiatives that were the 'baby' of the predecessor lapse because of operational difficulties or because the successor expects no praise from his or her senior managers for administering another individual's creation.

The introduction of employee involvement and participation arrangements on the basis of fashion and fad quickly creates feelings of disillusionment among employees and a suspicion that management has no real focus to its current and future activities. However, a management committed to the introduction and successful operation of employee involvement initiatives is highly unlikely to select arrangements on the basis of fads over what is genuinely appropriate to the organisation's commercial and business needs. Proper analysis of the objectives desired from any employee involvement and participation arrangements before their introduction prevents any possible confusion or conflict between the different practices introduced. This is particularly important when the organisation is introducing a multiplicity of practices. Rather than just select any scheme, it can be helpful if management gives extremely careful consideration over how it will apply and modify any schemes introduced to the needs of the workplace. Schemes that are 'customised' (see above) offer better prospects for success than those that are lifted down from the shelf and which may clash with production or service provision considerations.

An all-too-common mistake by management in introducing involvement and participation scheme initiatives is to become seduced by the prevalence of public relations accounts into believing that any scheme introduced will be a panacea to solve all their product market problems. The impact of employee involvement and participation in securing a positive change in employee attitudes and behaviour is less profound and permanent than is often claimed if the schemes selected turn out to be inappropriate to the organisation's needs. An inappropriate choice of systems is most noticeable, Marchington (1993) claims, among companies which bring in consultants to advise them on how to implement a new scheme without establishing its relevance or purpose. A company might decide to introduce a system of monthly team briefings, for example. However, it is a waste of time to do so without having assessed whether there will be sufficient information to sustain it on that basis or whether the frontline manager has the necessary skills or motivation to make it work. This difficult problem becomes further complicated when different management functions or levels in the management structure have a responsibility for introducing employee involvement initiatives, often at the same time and with conflicting objectives. It is a situation particularly current in service sector companies where the issue of customer care often falls within the province of both the personnel and the marketing departments.

A management fully committed to the successful operation of employee involvement and participation practices ensures that those participating in such practices have access to a free flow of information to enable them to operate effectively. This flow of information is most effective if it is up, down and across the organisation. A ready willingness to listen, evaluate and act on views expressed by employees is a sensible approach. There are many pitfalls into which a management can fall with respect to the information it makes available in the workplace to participants in the employee involvement schemes. Managements must strike a balance between providing too little information and providing too much information, or employees may become confused. Managers have to avoid too much 'tell and sell', since this triggers employee mistrust of involvement and participation schemes, especially if most information is perceived as bad news and is accompanied by rallying calls for belt-tightening and restraint.

The effective operation of employee involvement and participation practices involves two-way communication. To focus only on downward communication carries the risk that employees and/or their representatives might feel they are being informed of changes or decisions only after the event rather than before. This may seem an obvious statement, but unfortunately for many managers common sense is not common practice. A further problem management faces is the tendency for employee involvement and participation schemes once implemented to regress, rather than grow and develop, from their original position with respect to their anticipated objectives. Several employee involvement and participation practices that have been successful in one organisation have come apart in another because in the latter their scope collapsed to the level of 'canteen tea discussions'. When the subjects discussed become non-controversial or less interesting, employee indifference, if not scepticism, develops. And so despite the fact that employees are the principal objects and recipients of many employee involvement and participation practices, this is potentially the most common cause of failure. A management fully committed to involvement and participation initiatives, introducing it for the right reasons, and having selected the schemes appropriate for its business objectives, is unlikely to provide opportunities for employee scepticism to arise.

A professional management is motivated to ensure that involvement and participation schemes do not become ineffective because their operation produces adverse impacts on the workings of other employee relations institutions in the organisation. Some of the most successful involvement and participation practices have been established in unionised companies with the joint involvement of management and unions. In contrast, arrangements set up independently of trade unions, where they are recognised and are fully representative of their members' views, have often led to difficulties. This can happen because unions – especially those that are weakly organised – regard the introduction of an independent system of employee involvement as an attempt to bypass them and to undermine its relationship with its members. In strongly unionised organisations employee involvement and participation practices are unlikely to be used to undermine the normal bargaining process with the unions. Attempts to bypass or undermine established trade union channels are likely to backfire and founder on union opposition taken to the point of withdrawal – for example, a refusal to sit at the same table as non-unionists. In non-union companies the danger that employee involvement schemes may adversely affect other employee relations institutions is less likely to be a potential hazard for management.

A management committed to the effective operation of employee involvement and participation adopts an open and participative style of management, selects appropriate schemes tailored to the organisation's needs, ensures that there is a full flow of information up, down and across the organisation, and commits the necessary resources in terms of time, finances, people and equipment to support the operation of the employee involvement and participation schemes.

Is the management in your organisation fully committed to the successful operation of the employee involvement and participation schemes? Give full reasons for your answer.

Resources

If employee involvement and participation schemes are to operate effectively, resources are required to meet the direct and indirect costs (time lost, production/service foregone, meetings, training, paid leave, etc) associated with introducing, operating and monitoring them. An uncommitted management is likely to regard them as a cost without any benefit, and to seek to ensure that there is insufficient business to be discussed by those participating in the schemes. The employee relations professional has an obligation to persuade his or her colleagues to view employee involvement and participation practices that operate in the organisation in a positive light, and to demonstrate to them the value the practices add to the business if they are embraced fully by all levels and functions of management.

The effectiveness of employee involvement practices is often diminished by a lack of skills or knowledge on the part of the participants. It is important for both managers and employees to be provided with training in the skills required to manage employee involvement and participation practices effectively. This involves acquiring and developing the skills of chairing meetings so that members keep to the agenda and put forward suggestions that are appropriate to the subject matter under discussion. Managers also require training in presentational skills to present information by word of mouth or in writing and by the use of visual aids. In addition, they require interviewing skills to question employees in order to gain information and/or seek clarification of employees' views. Listening skills are essential, for consultation involves management's listening to what the employees have to say. In participating in employee involvement practices managers should endeavour to limit their contributions and allow the employees to do most of the talking. By listening, employers acquire additional information. Managers also require the skills of negotiation to gain the commitment of their managerial colleagues at all levels and in all functions, and of the workforce to the effective operation of employee involvement and participation mechanisms. If the organisation's management does provide training for its managers and employees to prepare them to participate in employee involvement practices, it is sound business sense periodically to evaluate the effectiveness of the training provided.

Spending resources on training for all involved in the operation of employee involvement and participation practices represents an investment by management. It demonstrates openly to all concerned its commitment to the schemes. To do otherwise invites employee disillusionment with the schemes. A serious and continuing commitment to employee involvement practices is not easy to achieve and requires significant support from the highest levels of management. The gaining of employee commitment, via employee participation and involvement initiatives, is a time-consuming process. It is much easier to undermine the operation of the schemes than to continue them. Financial resources are necessary to ensure that training is executed effectively and efficiently and that sufficient time – balanced against production and customer service needs – is set aside for joint consultation meetings, briefing groups and regular management walkabouts.

Managements must be aware of the potential problems that face employees working under involvement and participation arrangements. For example, employees may lack knowledge of the subjects under discussion and may have problems coping with the social situation of 'rubbing shoulders with' top management. They may also experience undue pressure from their constituents who have an unreal expectation as to what employee involvement and participation initiatives can achieve in protecting and advancing the interests of the employees. An employee relations professional should assist employee representatives and individual employees to overcome these problems by providing the necessary facilities for them to keep communication channels open between themselves and their constituents. It will add little value to an organisation committed to the successful operation of employee involvement practices to have employee representatives who are unable to represent their members or to report back to them, or to have union representatives that suspect management is really opposed to their activities.

Monitoring and reviewing arrangements

The establishment of mechanisms for the regular monitoring and reviewing of the operation of employee involvement and participation practices is essential. Monitoring is a means of assessing whether the schemes are producing the desired outputs of improved efficiency, productivity, quality of service, a greater willingness on the part of employees to accept change, etc. The effectiveness of employee involvement and participation mechanisms is measured against the outputs of their operation in terms of contributing to the achievement of the overall objectives of the organisation. The outcomes of the operation of the schemes are the important criteria against which to judge their effectiveness.

Assessing effectiveness in this way avoids the simple acceptance by management and employees of a public relations story describing the alleged success of the operation of one or a group of employee involvement practices. Nevertheless, it is not easy to quantify the contribution of employee involvement and participation practices to the achievement of corporate objectives. There are problems, *inter alia*, of identifying appropriate benchmarks and isolating the influence of other factors.

The results of any monitoring exercise are best discussed with employee representatives and, where appropriate, recognised trade unions. If the monitoring process exposes weaknesses, remedial action can be taken. Regular monitoring and reviewing also enables an organisation to assess the cost-effectiveness of its employee involvement and participation schemes.

CONCLUSION

- By the introduction of employee involvement initiatives, a management seeks to gain consent from its employees for its proposed actions on the basis of commitment rather than control.

- Employee involvement covers a wide range of practices initiated mainly by management to increase employee information about, and commitment to, the organisation and thereby produce a knowledgeably enthusiastic workforce more likely to contribute to the efficient operation of the organisation.

- It is management, however, which makes the final decision as to whether employees are to be involved and how much they are to participate in organisational decision-making.

- Employee involvement and participation practices are designed to change the attitudes of employees, enhance their business awareness, improve their motivation, and enhance their influence/ownership in the business.

- Employee involvement and participation practices may be described as either direct (communications, problem-solving groups and financial participation) or indirect (via some employee representative structures).

- The incidence of employee involvement initiatives has risen as the frequency of collective bargaining has fallen.

- In implementing employee involvement practices a number of general principles apply, requiring consideration of the needs of the organisation, joint agreement, the provision of education and training, the multiplicity of arrangements, integration, and legal strictures.

- Important initiatives on employee involvement and participation requirements have come from the European Union, notably the National Information and Consultative Directive (2000).

- Employee communications mechanisms involve the provision and exchange of information and instructions which enable an organisation to function effectively and its employees to be properly informed about developments.

- Task and work group involvement schemes encourage employees to extend the range and types of tasks they undertake at work: teamworking is the best example of such schemes.

- The increasing popularity of employee attitude surveys indicates that they are viewed as an effective tool for assessing both employee morale and commitment.

- Total quality management is designed to ensure that each level and aspect of the organisation is involved in continuously improving the effectiveness and quality of the work to meet the requirements of both internal and external customers.

- Financial participation schemes (profit-related pay, share ownership, etc) enable employees to acquire and develop a greater identity with the business and its needs.

- The main form of representative participation is joint consultation, which is a process by which management and employees (or their representatives) jointly examine and discuss issues of mutual concern.

- From management's perspective there are a number of necessary conditions to be met if employee involvement and participation practices are to be successfully implemented and then to operate effectively – a good employee relations climate, strong commitment from top management, sufficient resources of the right quality, and practicable monitoring and reviewing arrangements.

Further reading

ADVISORY, CONCILIATION AND ARBITRATION SERVICE (1995) *Employee Communications and Consultation*.

GAPPER J. (1990) 'At the end of the honeymoon', *Financial Times*, 10 January.

GEARY J. F. (1994) 'Task participation: employees' participation enabled or constrained', in K. Sisson (ed.) *Personnel Management*, 2nd edition. Oxford, Blackwell.

INDUSTRIAL RELATIONS SERVICES (1999) 'Trends in employee involvement', *Employment Trends*, No.683, July.

MARCHINGTON M., GOODMAN J., WILKINSON A. and ACKERS P. (1992) 'New developments in employee involvement', *Employment Department Research Series*, Employment Department Publication, No.2.

MARCHINGTON M., WILKINSON A., ACKERS P. and DUNDON T. (2001) *Management Choice and Employee Voice*. London, Chartered Institute of Personnel and Development.

RAMSAY H. (1996) 'Involvement, empowerment and commitment', in B. Towers (ed.) *The Handbook of Human Resource Management*, 2nd edition. Oxford, Blackwell.

TOWNLEY B. (1994) 'Communicating with employees', in K. Sisson (ed.) *Personnel Management*, 2nd edition. Oxford, Blackwell.

WALTON R. E. (1985) 'From control to commitment in the workplace', *Harvard Business Review*, Vol. 63, No.2, March-April.

WILKINSON A. (2001) 'Employment', in T. Redman and A. Wilkinson (eds) *Contemporary Human Resource Management: Text and cases*. Financial Times/Prentice Hall.

CHAPTER

8 • Other Employment Relations
Processes

CHAPTER OBJECTIVES

When you have completed this chapter you should be able to:

- explain the dimensions of collective bargaining in terms of its coverage, scope and level

- describe the main types of bargaining arrangements – for example, single-table, multi-union

- outline the main advantages and disadvantages to employers of partnership agreements

- assess the importance of collective bargaining as a pay determination mechanism

- justify the use of conciliation, mediation and arbitration as mechanisms to resolve disputes

- explain the processes of conciliation, mediation and arbitration

- outline the strategies and policies a management might adopt to minimise the likely effects of the imposition of industrial sanctions against their organisation.

Introduction

This chapter begins by analysing the employee relations process that is collective bargaining. Secondly, it examines the options available to a management should it become involved in a collective dispute with its employees. This entails looking at the operation of such conflict-resolution mechanisms as disputes procedures, and of such third-party-intervention employee relations processes as arbitration, mediation and conciliation. Thirdly, the chapter considers possible strategies and policies a management might implement, if a dispute cannot be resolved, to minimise the likely disruption to the organisation should the employees decide to impose industrial sanctions.

Collective bargaining

Collective bargaining is a mechanism for:

- determining pay and other conditions of employment

- involving employees in managing the business jointly with their employer in relation to the control of labour costs and the establishment of minimum standards

- managing people.

For collective bargaining to exist at any level (see below) four conditions must be met. First, there must be organisation on the part of the buyers and sellers of labour services (see Chapter 5). Second, there must be a substantive agreement. Third, there must be a procedural agreement (see Chapter 1). Finally, both the buyers and sellers of labour services must be able to impose sanctions (costs) upon each other so that they can reassess their positions towards each other in terms of the demands they make of each other (see Chapters 1 and 9).

Coverage

Table 20 shows that the overall level of collective bargaining coverage fell from 70 per cent in 1984 to 54 per cent in 1990, and still further to 40 per cent in 1998. Millward *et al* (2000) show that the fall accelerated in the 1990s, increasing from an annual rate of decline of 2.9 per cent between 1984 and 1990 to an annual rate of fall of 3.3 per cent between 1990 and 1998. The table also shows that whereas in the late 1980s private manufacturing, private services and the public sector experienced similar rates of change, there was a divergence of experiences in the 1990s. Private manufacturing experienced a relatively modest fall from 51 per cent of employees to 46 per cent. Collective bargaining coverage in the private sector declined more rapidly from 78 per cent to 62 per cent. And private sector services witnessed even greater falls – in this sector, the percentage of employees covered by collective bargaining fell by over a third, from 33 per cent in 1990 to 21 per cent in 1998, a rate of decline of almost 5 per cent per annum.

Why do you think the coverage of collective bargaining has declined in the last decade? What has happened to collective bargaining coverage in your organisation (or one with which you are familiar)?

Table 20 Overall collective bargaining coverage, by broad sector and union recognition, 1984–1998

	Proportion of employees covered by collective bargaining			Percentage change	
	1984	1990	1998	1984–1990	1990–1998
All workplaces	70	54	40	−2.9	−3.3
Broad sector, private manufacturing	64	51	46	−2.6	−1.3
Private services	40	33	21	−2.3	−4.7
Public sector	95	78	62	−2.3	−2.6
Any recognised unions	90	81	69	−1.3	−2.1

Source: Millward N., Bryson A. and Forth J. *All Change at Work?*, Routledge, 2000, p197

Dimensions of bargaining

The level of bargaining

An important decision for a management which recognises and negotiates with one or more unions is to decide the level at which bargaining is to take place. There are a number of bargaining levels available from which to make a strategic choice:

- multi-employer level

- single-employer-level (ie company level)

- enterprise level

- a combination of all three levels.

Multi-employer bargaining has conventionally combined two levels – bargaining on the establishment of framework terms and conditions at industry level, with bargaining on other matters left to individual companies. The actual distribution of responsibility between the two tiers varies between industries and also changes over time. Company bargaining is where all terms and conditions of employment are negotiated at the central company level. Bargaining at this level enables pay and conditions to be related to the economic circumstances of the company as a whole, and provides standardised conditions across the company for similar jobs.

Enterprise bargaining (or plant bargaining) is where terms and conditions are negotiated between management and union representatives at each plant or business unit of the company. Such bargaining tends to be either autonomous to each plant or co-ordinated across all plants. In the former case, each plant has the authority to settle all terms and conditions locally. In the latter case, bargaining is co-ordinated at plant level within limits set by the corporate centre. Enterprise bargaining has the attraction of enhancing management's ability to respond flexibly to employee relations policies by introducing pay, conditions and incentives related to local conditions. On the other hand, it requires management to have a competency in negotiation skills which might not exist at plant level and can increase the danger of claims for wage priority by different groups of workers.

Over the past 25 years, the trend in bargaining levels has been towards decentralised bargaining within organisations. The 1998 Employee Relations Workplace Survey reported that in the latter half of the 1980s some 1 million employees had been moved out of the coverage of industry-wide agreements. Most noticeable in this regard was the collapse of the national agreement between the EEF and the Confederation of Shipbuilding and Engineering Unions in 1990. Today in most of the private sector collective bargaining takes place at either the company or workplace level. The public sector has also witnessed a decentralisation of collective bargaining. The 1984 Industrial Relations Workplace Survey showed that 82 per cent of employees were covered by multi-employer bargaining. By 1998 the percentage had fallen to 39 per cent, or about two workers in every five.

Towers (1996) argues that the choice of bargaining levels can be guided by well-established criteria. He points out that multi-employer bargaining is an attractive option in industries which are geographically concentrated (for example, the ceramics industry), are dominated by a large number of companies of relatively small size (for example, the general printing industry), are faced by strong competitive pressures, have a high degree of trade union membership, and have high labour costs. Small employers with limited time, resources and expertise are attracted to bargaining arrangements which secure negotiating skills, limit the influence of the union in the workplace, reduce vulnerability to competitive pay pressures in circumstances of labour intensity, and set industry-wide standards. Towers suggests that more generally company-level (corporate-level) bargaining is most likely to be chosen where all or most of the following are present:

- a single product market
- a stable product market
- a centralised organisational structure
- a preference for centralised functions
- standardised terms and conditions across operations
- a preference for negotiating with national union officials.

In contrast, enterprise bargaining is likely to be favoured in the opposite set of conditions – for example, in a multi-product company, in the face of unstable product markets, with a multi-divisional organisational structure, and with a preference for decentralised functions. The decentralised organisational form allows organisations to respond with sensitivity to different market changes across its product range.

> What arguments would you use to convince a line manager that the level of the enterprise (establishment) is the right level at which to conduct collective bargaining?

The scope of bargaining

In 1984, the Workplace Industrial Relations Survey reported that collective bargaining determined pay rates for an average of 90 per cent of employees in unionised workplaces. By the 1990 Survey the figure had fallen to 75 per cent – and the 1998 Employee Relations Workplace Survey estimated the percentage to be 67. However, the 1998 Survey also reported that there were 14 per cent of workplaces in which unions were recognised but no workers were covered by collective bargaining for pay determination purposes. These workplaces were mainly in the private services sector of the economy. This non-pay scope of collective bargaining probably reflects two trends. First, some employers respond to falling or low union density by unilaterally setting employment conditions that treat the union recognition agreement as irrelevant. Second, it may also reflect the employees' quitting a union when management begins to set wages unilaterally even though the management still formally continues to recognise the union.

Table 21 shows that there has been relatively little change in the scope of bargaining over non-pay issues among establishments that recognise trade unions. Although there has been a substantial increase in the proportion of unionised workplaces where pay bargaining does not take place, no such trend applies to non-pay issues. The table also demonstrates that the percentage of workplaces that bargained over none of the six non-pay issues listed remains small. The mean number of items subject to negotiation fell from 3.8 in 1990 to 3.6 in 1998. It reveals some changes on some items, with reductions in the number of workplaces where recruitment and working hours are regularly on the bargaining agenda, and an increase in the proportion who bargained over the amount of redundancy compensation. Millward *et al* (2000) in their study of British employment relations over the period 1980–1998, as portrayed by the Workplace Industrial Relations Survey series, show that the scope of bargaining over non-pay issues declined in private manufacturing and private services but remained the same in the public sector.

Bargaining agreements

Number of unions
Multi-unionism is a feature for a significant number of unionised workplaces although today the existence of a large number of unions in a workplace is comparatively rare. In 1990, 34 per cent of workplaces with

Table 21 The scope of bargaining in workplaces with recognised unions in 1990 and 1998

Items subject to negotiation	Cell percentages and means	
	1990	1998
Physical working conditions	80	79
Staffing levels	57	51
Recruitment	44	34
Re-employment within the establishment	70	66
Size of redundancy payments	46	57
Reorganisation of working hours	88	75
None of these	5	7
Mean number of items	3.8	3.6

Source: Millward N., Bryson A. and Forth J. *All Change at Work?*, Routledge, 2000

union members had a single union present, 27 per cent had two unions present, 12 per cent had three, and over a quarter (27 per cent) had four or more present. A trend towards single-union representation continued during the 1990s such that by 1998, 43 per cent of unionised workplaces had a single union. However, more than half of unionised workplaces had two or more unions present. Between 1990 and 1998 the mean number of unions at unionised workplaces fell from 2.7 to 2.4. Even so, a quarter of unionised workplaces had four or more unions present.

Multi-unionism is said by some to have contributed to the UK's labour productivity deficit relative to its major international competitors. Others have argued that it is not multi-unionism as such that has a negative productivity effects but fragmented bargaining structures. In the last 25 years many organisations – especially when opening a 'green-field site' – have adopted a policy of dealing with one union only or a number of unions collectively. The main planks of this tidying up of bargaining arrangements have been:

- single-union arrangements
- single-table bargaining arrangements.

Single-union arrangements

Single-union arrangements are those that occur where a company recognises only one union for collective bargaining purposes. In workplaces which recognise only one union, this situation has arisen through a formal single-union agreement rather than happening simply by chance. The 1998 Employee Relations Workplace Survey reported that about a fifth (17 per cent) of all unionised workplaces had a multiple-union presence and negotiated separately with each union. In 25 per cent of all workplaces and in 41 per cent of all unionised workplaces single-union bargaining arrangements existed.

Single-union arrangements have existed in the UK retail sector for many years. In the 1980s their growth was most prominent on 'green-field sites'. During this period their growth was also controversial, especially in circumstances where an employer sought to achieve single-union bargaining arrangements by de-recognising existing unions and it turned out that the employer's preferred union was chosen after a so-called 'union beauty contest'. In some cases the selected union had no tradition of membership in the company or industry, and in extreme cases had no members employed at the establishment concerned. Single-union arrangements are particularly beneficial in organisations that aim at teamworking, product/service quality, and flexibility among its workforce, since the presence of one union reduces the likelihood of employee opposition to the introduction of such practices on the grounds that they threaten the job territory claimed by trade unions.

Single-table bargaining arrangements

In single-table bargaining, all trade unions recognised by the management come together to discuss and agree their position before sending a single team representing all the unions' interests to the bargaining table to meet with the employer. This team negotiates on behalf of all employees from each union. Such arrangements save management time and resources, and minimise inter-union strife. All this makes for a more efficient operation and for a more effective management of the enterprise. All employees are likely to end up having similar employment deals or single-table arrangements cannot work. Terms and conditions must be at least close in terms of pay, sick leave, holidays, pensions and other fundamentals. Single-table bargaining shortens the communications chain and can be used to unify and to harmonise working conditions, as well as to make the introduction of new practices – for example, flexible working – more easy to achieve.

However, single-table bargaining is not always the right practice to introduce. There has to be commitment to the concept from top management. In addition, it must be remembered that there are specific levels of negotiation which have to be maintained for particular groups below the level of the single table. Managers have to be prepared to open up all employee issues – for example, prize benefits, which might previously have been restricted to one or two groups.

In 1998, among workplaces which recognised two or more unions, the Employee Relations Workplace Survey found that around three fifths (or 26 per cent of all unionised workplaces) conducted joint negotiations with all of the unions. Among workplaces where collective bargaining was the dominant form of pay-setting the percentage with single-table bargaining arrangements increased from 40 per cent in 1990 to 77 per cent in 1998. By sector, the corresponding figures were:

- private manufacturing up from 57 per cent to 80 per cent

- private service up from 57 per cent to 90 per cent

- public sector up from 23 per cent to 70 per cent.

Among unionised workplaces, single-union agreements and single-table bargaining arrangements were equally common but found in different types of workplaces. Single-table bargaining arrangements were over three times more likely in the public sector than in the private sector (40 per cent, compared with 12 per cent). Over half the unionised workplaces in the wholesale and retail and financial services and the community services had a single-union agreement. The distribution of single-table bargaining arrangements was more evenly distributed, except for the public utilities, where they were especially high.

From the viewpoint of a management that recognises more than one union, what are the advantages of insisting on single-table bargaining?

Partnership agreements

In the face of increasing global competition, thriving business depends upon improving conditions and upon constant change. To achieve this, the co-operation of all those involved in the enterprise is required. It was shown in Chapter 1 that the idea of management, employees and trade unions working together for their mutual benefit and to secure the future of the enterprise is the very essence of employee relations. In the mid-1990s some trade unions, in an effort to reverse the decline in their membership and to gain the acceptance of employers, began to give greater emphasis to the notion of working together with employers to achieve common goals. This took the form of negotiating partnership agreements with employers.

Principles of partnership

Such agreements are a sophisticated form of employee relations in which management and trade unions commit themselves to shared responsibility for meeting business objectives within a framework for jobs, pay security and good conditions of employment. There are six key principles that underpin partnership agreements at the workplace. These are:

- Principle 1: commitment to success of the enterprise – Effective partnership agreements are based on a shared understanding of, and commitment to, business goals of the organisation and of/to its lasting success, including support for flexibility and a willingness to embrace 'good practice' ideas from outside. In some instances, the operation of this principle may mean the replacement of a previously hostile and adversarial atmosphere of employee relations.

- Principle 2: recognising legitimate interests – This principle demands a recognition that at any one time there might be quite legitimate differences in interests and priorities between the partners to the agreement, and an acceptance that ultimately each party will respect others' needs to do their best for their own constituencies. Partnership agreements, if working effectively, should build up trust between the parties and should assist the resolution of differences between the parties.

- Principle 3: commitment to employment security – This principle is usually embodied in partnership agreements by a combination of measures to maximise employment security within the enterprise (for example, limiting the use of compulsory redundancies, joint agreement on staffing levels) and measures designed to improve the employability of staff beyond it (for example, by improving the transferability of skills and qualifications).

- Principle 4: focus on the quality of working life – This principle is a recognition that successful enterprises should invest in the personal development of their employees by strengthening the talent pool of the enterprise and by opening up opportunities for personal growth (including vocational and non-vocational development) that have hitherto been unavailable to employees.

- Principle 5: transparency – If partnership agreements are to be meaningful and not a sham exercise in participation, they must be based upon a real sharing of hard information and on openness to discussing plans about the future when they are at the formulation stage. The process of consultation must be genuine, and the management committed to listen to business cases from the employees for alternative plans.

- Principle 6: adding value – This principle is a recognition by the parties to partnership agreements that they should access sources of motivation, commitment and resources that were not accessed by previous employee relations institutions at the workplace. For example, this may involve adding value beyond the immediate workplace through providing the hub of a training process that meets the enterprise's skill requirements but also puts something back into the wider talent pool of the sector.

There are other factors that are essential for successful partnership agreements. One is leadership on both sides. Successful partnerships are often based virtually on the personal leadership skills of a few individuals who often take significant risks in moving relationships on to a new footing. Another factor is a clear understanding of the case for change. Whether the spur is a shift in product markets, the advent of new business goals or the impossibility of continuing a tradition of adversarial employee relations, it has to be closely understood. Building a relationship requires both employees and managers to invest time and effort. Partnership agreements are by definition based on high-trust relationships, and where they supersede antagonism there is no way to shorten this lengthy process.

Benefits

Partnership agreements operating within the unionised context vary in content and style. However, some common issues are covered in all partnership agreements. These include:

- business-focused consultation and communications arrangements

- joint working groups

- employee commitment to business goals

- long-term pay deals

- employment security

- sharing of information

- training and development

- focus on local problem-solving activities

- harmonisation of employment conditions and single status.

Those who favour the partnership approach to employee relations point to a number of advantages to employers. Involving employees in a partnership arrangement gives them greater say in decision-making and therefore a greater commitment to the enterprise. This in turn should improve the morale of employees and so help employers to achieve the higher work performance employers desire. In both the private and public sectors organisations cannot rise to the challenge of increased competition and demands for improved products and services unless all those working for the organisation feel they have a stake in the success of the business. It is argued, therefore, that partnership agreements will help employees to deliver better products and services.

Advocates of partnership agreements also claim they are an advantage to unionised employers in that they mean that simply saying 'No' cannot be the first response of the workforce to employer proposals for change. They point out that when entering into a partnership, unions must recognise that change is inevitable, that change is not necessarily a threat, and they must associate themselves with good practice, continuous improvement, high productivity and enhanced competitiveness. Supporters of partnership-based employee relations also point to research which shows that workplaces with partnership agreements are one third more likely than others to achieve average financial success and labour productivity (see the TUC's *Partnership Works*; further information available at www.tuc.org.uk/partnership/tuc).

Partnership agreements present employers with important challenges, however. The greatest is that partnership agreements allow unions to exercise much greater influence over strategic decisions. Partnership also requires some rethinking of management roles – in particular, the responsibilities of middle managers. The partnership approach is designed to give workers more autonomy, and this must mean some relinquishing of control by immediate managers, supervisors and team leaders. There is always the danger that some managers may see these developments as a threat rather than as a need to move from a culture of direct intervention in relatively simple tasks to a culture of coaching, problem-solving and facilitation.

Extent

Partnership agreements and arrangements are now well-established in organisations in every sector of the economy. They exist in many organisations that are household names, including Tesco, the Co-operative Bank, Scottish Power, Legal and General, United Distillers and Vintners, the Inland Revenue, British Gas, UNISYS and Alstom. It would, however, be wrong to give the impression that partnership is the defining characteristic of a majority of organisations. Partnership agreements and arrangements do not mean the end of conflicts of interests between employers and employees. Conflicts of interests will inevitably remain – but where partnership arrangements exist at the workplace, some would argue that such conflicts will be much easier to resolve in that employee relationships are more likely to be based on trust and mutual respect than on hostility and suspicion.

> Explain the principles that underpin partnership agreements and arrangements at the workplace. Which do you think is the most important – and why?

Collective bargaining as a mechanism for determining pay

As has been noted previously, collective bargaining has ceased to be the dominant means of pay determination in the economy as a whole. Table 22 overleaf shows the main mechanisms used in 1998 for determining the pay of non-managerial employees, by sector and workplace size. Just under half of all employees had their pay unilaterally set for them by management, either at a higher level in the organisation or by workplace management. Individual negotiations over pay covered some 2 per cent of non-managerial employees. Of the 36 per cent of non-managerial employees whose pay was determined by collective bargaining, most were covered by arrangements that were organisation- or workplace-specific. The 1998 Workplace Employee Relations Survey revealed that only one in five private sector workplaces engaged in collective bargaining, whereas four out of five had pay unilaterally set by management. One in ten employees in the private sector negotiated with his or her employer on an individual basis, whereas in the public sector two out of every five workplaces surveyed did not engage in collective bargaining.

Tables 20 and 23–26 show that the percentage of workplaces in which collective bargaining was the dominant mechanism for pay determination fell by a half over a period of 14 years from 60 per cent in 1984 to 42 per cent in 1990 and 29 per cent in 1998. There was also a substantial change to the nature of bargaining in such workplaces, as seen by the decline in the influence of national, regional and industry-wide agreements. In 1984 multi-employer agreements were a feature of pay determination in over two thirds of workplaces where most employees pay was set by joint negotiation. By 1998 the percentage had fallen below a half (46 per cent). In general terms, this means the percentage of all workplaces in which multi-employer agreements formed some part of the dominant arrangement for pay decreased by about two thirds from 41 per cent in 1984 to 13 per cent in 1998. The proportion of workplaces in which pay was determined unilaterally and influenced to some extent by higher management increased from 16 per cent in 1990 to 25 per cent in 1998.

Table 22 Method of determining pay for non-managerial employees, by sector and workplace size in 1998

| Sector workplaces | Percentage of employees | | | | | | |
| | Pay set by collective bargaining | | | Pay set by management | | | |
	multi-employer	single employer	at the workplace	at the workplace	at a higher level	Pay set by individual negotiations	Pay set by other method
Private sector							
24–49 employees	4	5	2	41	39	5	3
50–99 employees	4	9	3	45	30	5	4
100–199 employees	10	11	7	35	29	1	6
200–459 employees	5	13	14	30	29	2	6
500+ employees	2	25	16	37	17	0	2
All private sector	5	14	9	37	28	2	4
Public sector							
24–49 employees	30	11	0	3	16	0	40
50–99 employees	30	19	0	3	10	1	36
100–199 employees	37	15	1	3	11	0	33
200–459 employees	43	20	1	2	8	2	24
500+ employees	35	16	6	2	4	0	38
All public sector	35	16	3	3	8	0	35
All workplaces	14	15	7	26	22	2	14

Table 23 Locus of pay determination in all sectors of the economy, 1984–1998

Level of pay determination	Percentage decision-making		
	1984	1990	1998
Collective bargaining	**60**	**42**	**29**
Multi-employer bargaining	41	23	13
Multi-site employer bargaining	12	14	12
Workplace bargaining	5	4	3
Don't know	1	1	n/a
Non-collective bargaining	**40**	**58**	**71**
External to the organisation	7	9	14
At a higher level of the organisation's management	11	16	25
Workplace management	21	30	30
Don't know	1	3	2

Source: Millward N., Bryson A. and Forth J. *All Change at Work?*, Routledge, 2000

Table 24 Locus of pay determination in the private sector, manufacturing and extraction, 1984–1998

Level of pay determination	Percentage decision-making		
	1984	1990	1998
Collective bargaining	**51**	**33**	**23**
Multi-employer bargaining	21	12	6
Multi-site employer bargaining	11	6	5
Workplace bargaining	17	14	12
Don't know	2	1	n/a
Non-collective bargaining	**49**	**67**	**77**
External to the organisation	4	7	3
At a higher level of the organisation's management	11	11	24
Workplace management	33	47	48
Don't know	1	2	2

Source: Millward N., Bryson A. and Forth J. *All Change at Work?*, Routledge, 2000

Table 25 Locus of pay determination in the private sector, services, 1984–1998

Level of pay determination	Percentage decision-making		
	1984	1990	1998
Collective bargaining	**36**	**29**	**14**
Multi-employer bargaining	17	8	3
Multi-site employer bargaining	14	19	10
Workplace bargaining	3	2	1
Don't know	1	n/a	n/a
Non-collective bargaining	**64**	**71**	**86**
External to the organisation	13	5	10
At a higher level of the organisation's management	19	24	36
Workplace management	31	41	39
Don't know	1	1	2

Source: Millward N., Bryson A. and Forth J. *All Change at Work?*, Routledge, 2000

Table 26 Locus of pay determination in the public sector, 1984–1998

Level of pay determination	Percentage decision-making		
	1984	1990	1998
Collective bargaining	**94**	**71**	**63**
Multi-employer bargaining	82	58	39
Multi-site employer bargaining	11	12	23
Workplace bargaining	n/a	n/a	n/a
Don't know	1	1	n/a
Non-collective bargaining	**6**	**29**	**37**
External to the organisation	3	16	29
At a higher level of the organisation's management	1	6	6
Workplace management	n/a	n/a	2
Don't know	n/a	6	0

Source: Millward N., Bryson A. and Forth J. *All Change at Work?*, Routledge, 2000

The proportion of private manufacturing establishments in which pay was determined mainly by collective bargaining fell by nearly a half between 1984 and 1998. In 1984, collective bargaining dominated pay determination arrangements in half of all establishments in private manufacturing. By 1990 this had fallen to one third, and by the turn of the millennium to less than one quarter (23 per cent). In the private services sector, collective bargaining has historically been less extensive than in the manufacturing sector. In the mid-1980s in the private services sector, collective bargaining dominated pay determination in over one third of workplaces. However, in the 1990s the sector witnessed a sharp decline in the joint regulation of pay so that by 1998 only 14 per cent of workplaces negotiated the pay of the majority of their employees with trade unions. Between 1984 and 1998, in the public sector, the proportion of public sector workplaces where pay was mainly determined by collective bargaining declined from 94 per cent to 71 per cent. This is mainly explained by the government's abolition of collective bargaining arrangements for many health service professionals and for schoolteachers in England and Wales. Collective bargaining for these groups was replaced by the establishment of a Pay Review Body. In addition, the privatisation of many public utilities in the 1980s and 1990s removed from collective bargaining several important groups of non-manual workers, particularly those employed in middle to higher managerial grades.

Mechanisms for resolving conflict

If agreement cannot be reached in the collective bargaining process and negotiations break down, there are a number of choices available to the employer and the employees. First, the matter can be referred to the dispute procedure (sometimes called an 'avoidance of disputes' procedure) which sets out several stages available to attempt to resolve a dispute. If a settlement can be reached using the collective disputes procedure, that procedure may have a final stage providing for third-party intervention in the form of conciliation, mediation and arbitration. These processes were explained in Chapter 5. What happens then if the parties decide to take their dispute to conciliation and/or arbitration?

Conciliation

ACAS conciliators try to help the parties settle their differences by agreement if possible for the longer term. The conciliation staff of ACAS remain impartial and independent at all times, understand the dispute and the attitude of the parties to it, gain the trust and confidence of both parties, make constructive suggestions, if appropriate, to facilitate negotiations, and provide information at the request of the parties. The first step for the conciliator is to find out what the difference between the parties is about and to ascertain the attitude of the parties to that difference. This fact-finding stage usually involves the conciliator's meeting each of the sides separately, although occasionally he or she may gather information at a joint meeting.

Although the details of conciliation vary from case to case, the process normally proceeds via a series of 'side-meetings' in which the conciliator explores the issues with each party, and joint meetings at which the two sides can explain their position face to face. No time-limits are set and the ACAS conciliator continues to help the parties as long as they wish and there is some chance of achieving an agreement. When it appears clear that a settlement might be achieved, the conciliator looks to secure an agreement, usually in the form of a signed statement. Once an agreement is reached, it is the responsibility of the parties to implement it. ACAS has no powers to enforce the agreement.

If conciliation fails, the parties may agree to settle their differences by arbitration. If they opt for arbitration, how do events unfold?

Arbitration

Terms of reference

If both parties voluntarily agree to arbitration, the first task is to agree terms of reference for the arbitrator. ACAS will assist the parties in this task. The terms of reference are important because they tell the arbitrator what it is the parties wish the arbitrator to do. It sets limits to the arbitrator's powers, which are usually constrained to within the range of the parties' claims. It prevents the arbitrator from wandering into issues that the parties do not wish the arbitrator to get into – for example, commenting on deficiencies in the procedures. In arbitration the terms of reference are usually worded in a simple manner. Typical terms of reference are:

To decide the daily rate of pay for short-term supply schoolteachers.

The terms of reference give the arbitrator flexibility within limits.

However, in the case of pendulum (or final-offer) arbitration, the terms of reference confine the arbitrator's award to either the employer's final offer or the employees' (the union's) final claim. The arbitrator must make an 'either/or' decision, and no other settlement can be awarded. This is made clear in the terms of reference.

An example of the terms of reference in a pendulum arbitration case is as follows, in a dispute that arose between the Isle of Man Post Office and the Communications Workers' Union (CWU):

> The arbitrator is asked to decide between the following differences in the employer's offer and the CWU claim.
>
> *The Isle of Man Post Office offer:* From 1 January 1999, a 3.1 per cent increase in basic pay, bonuses, overtime and all allowances.
>
> *The CWU claim:* From 1 January 1999, a 4.6 per cent increase in basic pay, bonuses, overtime and all allowances.

Pendulum arbitration has been favoured by electronics firms where a strike would run the risk of losing markets because adjustments cannot be made quickly enough to product/services in the light of rapidly changing customer demand and technology. Manufacturing companies whose main customers are the large supermarket chains have also favoured pendulum arbitration, believing that a strike runs the risk of a permanent loss of business to what is the company's main customer. Pendulum arbitration is usually written in as the final stage of an agreed disputes procedure. It is argued by those who favour pendulum arbitration that prohibiting arbitrators from occupying the middle ground between a final employer offer and final union claim encourages the parties to make more reasonable offers and claims, since the alternative is to enter a win-all-or-lose-all situation. Indeed, it is argued that eventually both sides draw so close together that the gap becomes bridgeable in negotiation so that arbitration becomes unnecessary. In other words, the main theoretical advantage of pendulum arbitration is that it puts such pressure on the employer and trade union to make an agreement that the process is unlikely ever to be used.

A great disadvantage of pendulum arbitration lies in the assumption that one side is 100 per cent right and the other is 100 per cent wrong. Why should compromise be an acceptable and justified principle in the collective bargaining processes and yet be ruled out in the arbitration process? Second, there are longer-term employee relations consequences if one side is found to be comprehensively right and the other just as comprehensively wrong. There are further disadvantages. An arbitrator may be faced with two complicated packages and, unless he or she is very lucky, he or she may well find *both* packages unsatisfactory. If the arbitrator cannot select the best items from each package and award accordingly, he or she has to weigh the two packages and choose the least objectionable.

> What do you consider to be the advantages and disadvantages to an employer of favouring pendulum arbitration over conventional arbitration?

The choice of arbitrator

The next stage in the process is for the two sides to agree jointly the name of the independent person to arbitrate on their differences. Again, ACAS facilitates this by making available to the parties its 'panel of arbitrators', but it does not provide any information about previous cases to disputant parties. Sometimes the parties are content to allow ACAS to appoint the arbitrator. Mumford (1996) reports that the vast majority of individuals on the ACAS panel are academics (or retired academics), over 45 years of age and grammar school-educated but interested in the practicalities of industry and employee relations. In short, they do not 'live in ivory towers'. ACAS strives to maintain long tenure among its arbitrators in order that they accumulate experience which helps them develop the skills in conflict management that greatly aid dispute resolution. The parties thus jointly determine the independent person to whom they are prepared to hand over the decision on how to resolve their differences.

The written submission to the arbitrator

After the terms of reference have been clarified and the independent person has been selected, the next step in the process is the setting of the date and the venue for the arbitration hearing.

This is agreed between the parties and the arbitrator, although it is ACAS which implements the actual arrangements. Before the hearing date, both sides submit to the arbitrator a written statement of their case and arguments. The parties also exchange their respective written cases with each other before the date of the hearing. It is essential that all the information given to the arbitrator is known to the other side. Written statements, together with any supporting documents and a list of those attending the hearing, are submitted to the arbitrator at least one week before the hearing.

Arbitrators reach their conclusion only after considering all the facts and arguments put to them by the parties, and they always study the written statements very carefully. The written statement normally covers the background information about the company and its products; union representation, etc; an explanation of the history and background of the dispute, including an account of the sequence and outcome of any relevant meetings or discussions; the arguments supporting or opposing the claim; and a brief summary of the case which brings together the essential points the arbitrator is being asked to consider. Relevant agreements, procedures or rules are attached as appendices. In the case of a job-grading dispute, for example, full details are given of the grading scheme in operation, whereas in a disciplinary case, details of any relevant rules or procedures are provided.

In certain circumstances, before the hearing date, there may also be a site visit. This is highly likely in the case of differences between parties concerning the degree of skill required by a job, the physical conditions under which the work is carried out, or the assessment of piece-work, prices or times. In all these cases it is of value for the arbitrator to see the work in progress.

The arbitration hearing

The hearing is informal and confidential, the parties usually being represented by those responsible for conducting normal negotiations. The hearing is ordinarily completed in two to three hours, is held in private, and the procedure to be followed is a matter for the arbitrator. However, the stages of a typical arbitration hearing are:

1. The arbitrator explains his or her role and then reads out the terms of reference to ensure that both parties place the same interpretation on their scope or meaning.

2. The arbitrator checks that the parties have exchanged their written statements and have had sufficient time to give the statements proper consideration.

3. The arbitrator normally invites the party making the 'claim', or seeking to change the status quo (say, Party A) to put its case uninterrupted, and to include a critique of the written submission of the other party (say, Party B). This is usually done by one person, but other members of the team may be called upon to give supporting statements.

4. The arbitrator then invites Party B to ask questions on Party A's statement. Such questioning can be effected either directly by the leader of Party B to Party A or through the arbitrator.

5. The arbitrator invites Party B to put its case uninterrupted and to include a critique of the written submission of Party A. This again will be carried out by one person but with other members of the team supplying supportive statements.

6. The arbitrator then invites Party A to ask questions on Party B's statement. Again such questioning can be effected directly to the other party or via the arbitrator.

7. The arbitrator will then ask questions of each party in turn or put the same questions to both parties. The party to whom the question is directed may respond through the team leader or nominate another member of the team to respond. The person who answers the question may call upon another member of the team to make a supporting statement. Each time one party responds to a question, the other party is given the opportunity to comment on the response. One party can ask questions of the other through the arbitrator.

8. Before inviting the parties to make their closing statements, the arbitrator normally obtains a formal assurance from each party that everything it wished to say has been said and that it has had sufficient opportunity to comment on or attempt to rebut what has been said by the other side.

¶ The arbitrator will then invite each side to make its closing statement. These are taken in reverse order to the opening presentations. The formal (or closing) statement is a summary of the main points the party wishes the arbitrator to take into account in reaching his or her decision and should contain no new material. The arbitrator cannot accept any further evidence after the hearing.

The award

The arbitrator does not announce the award on the day of the hearing. The arguments of the parties are taken away and given serious consideration. The parties receive the award, via ACAS, usually within two to three weeks of the hearing. All awards are regarded as confidential to the parties and are not published unless the parties agree otherwise. A typical award is presented as follows:

The Award
Having given careful consideration to the arguments very well presented to me, both orally and in writing, I award that:
THE JOB OF CLERICAL OFFICER IS CORRECTLY GRADED AT LEVEL 4.

Arbitrators do not give reasons for their decisions because to do so could give rise to further dispute between the parties. They do, however, indicate the factors (or considerations) they took into account in reaching their decision (award). Those factors may be complex and manifold, and include the need for the parties to continue in a working relationship after the award, the need to bring the dispute to a final conclusion, the potential knock-on effects of an award on other groups of workers, the ability of the employer to finance the award, and the credibility of the negotiators, particularly where the employers' pay offer has been rejected in a vote of the employees concerned. In short, these collapse to three major considerations – equity, economics and expediency (pragmatism).

A wise arbitrator (C. W. Guillebaud) once stated about arbitration that:

If at all possible, neither side should be left with a strong feeling of resentment so that the dispute continues to rankle – for the arbitrator will not then have achieved the objective of settling the matter satisfactorily and improving relations for the future.

In other words, the arbitrator's award should seek to minimise aggregate dissatisfaction. In addition, the parties are not always interested in the rationale behind the arbitrator's decision since they have come to arbitration after a long process and by this time are just relieved that the matter has been resolved and satisfied that they have been able to state all the arguments in favour of their position.

The award of the arbitrator is not legally binding – but it is virtually unknown for an award not to be implemented by the parties. It would be difficult (or require very exceptional circumstances) for one of the parties not to want to implement the award. They are morally bound to do so. After all, they have gone to the arbitration of their own violation, shaped the terms of reference for the arbitrator, selected the arbitrator, and had every opportunity to state their case to the arbitrator.

Coping with industrial action

Although every employer's focus is on steps that may be taken to avoid disputes turning into industrial action with sanctions, such disputes can and do happen. In this event it is essential that management implements a strategy and policy that maintains as much normality as possible. There is a set of strategic options available to management to minimise the likely disruption from the application of industrial sanctions to the organisation. However, not every one applies in every case to every organisation. They are to:

- keep materials and supplies coming in

- find alternative sources of labour

- maintain output or a level of service to satisfy demand

- maintain the distribution of the product or service to the customer.

Management must evaluate critically each of these choices. In the case of a retail organisation that needs to keep supplies coming in, the critical questions that have to be answered are:

- Will a picket be mounted?

- Who will unload and store the goods?

When considering an alternative supply of labour, the critical questions are whether the organisation can get other staff and new part-timers. With respect to the maintaining of a minimum level of service, the vital considerations are:

- Can orders be advanced or dealt with cumulatively?

- Is there any current overstocking that can be used up first?

As regards the distribution of the goods, operation issues include whether customers could themselves come to the organisation, and if so, whether they would be met by pickets. Could customers be telephoned when deliveries are being despatched? Could working hours be temporarily altered to expedite matters?

Imagine you are the manager of a transport operation. You believe that current negotiations with your employees are going to break down and that the employees are going to impose industrial sanctions upon you. What key questions would you ask yourself with respect to the strategic options open to you?

Making sure that supplies keep coming and going is critical. If a business cannot continue to service the market or continue to receive materials, the organisation will have difficulties in maintaining output or some level of service. Recruiting an alternative workforce is more than just getting in extra people. It may be that the alternative workforce is already in your organisation. Managers and team leaders/frontline managers may be able to do the work of the potential strikers. Perhaps the work to be done can be covered by other workers who are members of other trade unions not involved in the dispute or who are not unionised at all. Maintaining output to satisfy demand is often possible in the period before the dispute starts. Overtime can be increased, production switched to other plants or companies, and priority tasks be tackled first.

CONCLUSION

- The distribution of collective bargaining in the UK fell from 70 per cent in 1984 to 40 per cent in 1998.

- A strategic choice for a management involved in collective bargaining is the level at which bargaining takes place – multi-employer-level, company-level, enterprise-level, or some combination of these levels.

- Over the past 25 years the trend in bargaining levels has been towards decentralisation within organisations.

- There has been relatively little change in the scope of collective bargaining over non-pay issues among establishments that recognise trade unions.

- There has been a substantial increase in the proportion of unionised workplaces where pay bargaining does not take place.

- Untidy bargaining structures have been shown to have an adverse effect on the efficiency of organisations. Managements have tried to overcome this by introducing single-union arrangements or single-table bargaining arrangements.

- Partnership agreements are a sophisticated form of employee relations in which management and trade unions commit themselves to share responsibility for meeting business objectives within a framework for jobs, pay security and good conditions of employment.

- The key principles underpinning partnership agreements are: a commitment to the success of the enterprise, recognising legitimate interests, a commitment to employment security, a focus on the quality of working life, transparency, and adding value.

- Partnership agreements are said to bring benefits to employees, employers and trade unions, and they are now well established in organisations in every sector of the economy.

- Collective bargaining has ceased to be the dominant form of pay determination in the economy as a whole: in 1998 just under half of all employees had their pay unilaterally set for them by management, either at a higher level in the organisation or at the workplace.

- If agreement cannot be reached in the collective bargaining process and negotiations break down, there are a number of choices available to the employer – notably, to refer the matter to the disputes procedure and/or seek third-party intervention in the form of conciliation, mediation or arbitration.

- Although the details of conciliation differ in each case, the process usually proceeds via a series of side-meetings in which the conciliator explains the issues with each party, and a joint meeting at which the two sides can explain their positions face to face.

- Arbitration involves the parties' determining the terms of reference for the arbitrator, selecting the arbitrator, presenting submissions to the arbitrator, attending an arbitration hearing, and receiving and implementing the arbitrator's award.

- In jointly agreeing to go to arbitration, the parties may decide to opt for pendulum arbitration in which, unlike conventional arbitration, the terms of reference confine the arbitrator's award to the employer's final offer or the employees' final claim, and in which, therefore, no other settlement can be awarded.

- If the breakdown of the collective bargaining process cannot be rescued by the use of the disputes procedure or by the use of third-party intervention, and the employees impose industrial sanctions, then it is important for management to implement a strategy and associated policies that will minimise the impact of such sanctions on the organisation.

Further reading

CULLY M., WOODLAND S., O'REILLY A. and DIX S. (1999) *Britain at Work as Depicted by the 1998 Workplace Employee Relations Survey.* London and New York, Routledge.

INDUSTRIAL PARTNERSHIP ASSOCIATION (1996) *Towards Industrial Partnership: A new approach to relationships at work.* London, IPA.

INDUSTRIAL PARTNERSHIP ASSOCIATION (1997) *Towards Industrial Partnership: New ways of work in British companies.* London, IPA.

INDUSTRIAL RELATIONS SERVICES (2002) 'When all else fails', *Employment Review*, No.719, January. pp12–16.

MILLWARD N., BRYSON A. and FORTH J. (2000) *All Change at Work?* London and New York, Routledge.

TOWERS B. J. (1996) 'Collective bargaining levels', in B. J. Towers (ed.) *A Handbook of Industrial Relations Practice.* London, Kogan Page.

TRADES UNION CONGRESS (1997) *Partners for Progress.* TUC.

TRADES UNION CONGRESS (1998) *Partners for Progress: New unionism in the workplace.* TUC.

PART 4

EMPLOYEE RELATIONS SKILLS

9 • Negotiating (Including Bargaining)

CHAPTER OBJECTIVES

After you have read this chapter you will be able to:

- describe each of the different negotiating situations in which management may find itself

- explain how employee relations negotiations differ from commercial negotiations

- identify the different stages in the negotiating process

- understand what is involved in preparing for bargaining

- justify the activities involved in conducting and concluding bargaining

- describe what is involved in writing up an agreement.

Introduction

The purpose of negotiation

Negotiation involves two parties (such as individuals, companies, employers, trade union representatives, employee representatives) coming together to confer with a view to concluding a jointly acceptable agreement. It is a process whereby interest groups resolve differences between, and within, themselves. The term can therefore apply to a number of situations ranging from, at one extreme, resolving a difference between two managers as to how a problem might be best solved to, at the other extreme, a meeting with the trade union to determine the year's annual pay increase.

If both parties to an agreement do not have the same understanding of what they have agreed, they run the risk of spending time – time that could be used for more fruitful purposes – in resolving disputes between themselves over whether one or other side is behaving in accordance with what was agreed. Making an agreement commits the parties to behaving within its parameters until they agree jointly to change the terms of the agreement. So what has been agreed must be capable of effective implementation and operation.

Common elements

Negotiation involves two main elements:

- purposeful persuasion

- constructive compromise.

Figure 4   A definition of 'negotiation'

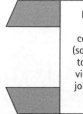

NEGOTIATION
is two parties
coming together
(social interaction)
to confer, with a
view to making a
jointly acceptable
agreement

Negotiation involves –
  – purposeful persuasion
  – constructive compromise

Each party attempts to persuade the other to accept its own case (request) by marshalling arguments backed by factual information and analysis. However, the probability that one party can persuade the other to accept its case (requests) in full is extremely low. If an agreement is to be reached, both parties must attempt to accommodate their demands of each other. To do so they must identify parameters of common ground within, and between, their requests of each other. Constructive compromise can then be made within these parameters. Compromise is only possible if sufficient common ground exists between the two parties. The overriding objective of any negotiation is for the parties to reach a mutually acceptable agreement and not to continue their differences nor to score debating-points off each other. Negotiation is a problem-solving technique.

So we can define negotiation as :

> *two parties coming together to confer, with a view to making a jointly acceptable agreement by the use of purposeful persuasion and constructive compromise.*

See Figure 4 above.

This definition does not confine negotiation to set-piece bargaining situations. It demonstrates that a negotiating situation arises where any two parties have a difference but have a common need to reconcile it, and so have to meet together and through persuasion and compromise find an acceptable solution to that difference.

Different types of negotiating situations

Figure 5 opposite identifies four main types of negotiating situations in which managers may find themselves:

- between managers – This involves a negotiated settlement to an issue usually confined to an individual (for example, establishing at an appraisal interview a manager's objective for the coming year, or resolving a difference between two managers as to how a problem with an employee might best be overcome).

Figure 5 Different types of negotiating situations

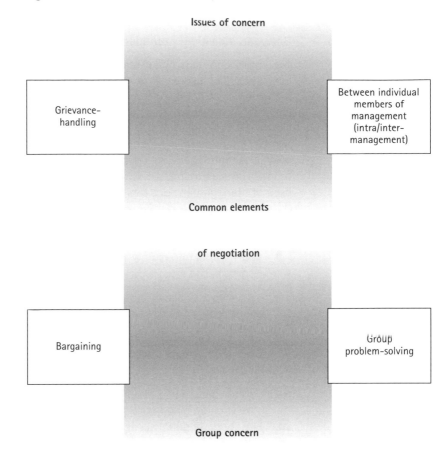

- grievance-handling to resolve a complaint by an employee that the behaviour of someone else at the workplace has breached his or her employment rights thereby causing an injustice, if not an intolerable situation – Grievances normally relate to individual employees, but if they are not handled with care they can develop to concern a group of employees.

- bargaining that results in a negotiated agreement to resolve issues of collective concern to employers and employees (for example, pay, hours of work, holidays and working practices) – However, bargaining can, and does, take place between management and individual employees (for example, in a non-union environment, particularly among middle management) resulting in a personal contract.

- group problem-solving that results in a negotiated agreement to resolve such issues as the conditions on which one party will co-operate with a second party with regard to action initiated by the second party.

Between individual managers

The most common negotiating situation in which employee relations managers/professionals are likely to find themselves is the one shown in the top right hand quadrant of Figure 5 – negotiation with their management colleagues. Each day managers find themselves negotiating with their colleagues either in the same management function or in another management function (for example, marketing, finance, sales, operations management). These managers may be of the same, higher or lower status than themselves. Negotiations between individual members of management are likely to be over such issues as:

- suggested courses of action (for example, how to deal with an employee's complaint against management behaviour)

- the introduction of new employment practices and procedures (for example, the introduction of an appropriate incentive scheme)

- securing the allocation of additional financial, staffing and equipment resources to support the people function

- gaining the commitment of managerial colleagues to a proposed course of action, particularly in the context of employee relations initiatives.

Negotiations between individual managers involve parties' protecting the same economic and political interests, so the style of negotiations in such situations is generally friendly and constructive, and certainly not adversarial.

Courses of action

Two or more managers may disagree on how a problem should/might be resolved. In such a situation each manager will seek purposefully to persuade the other of the merits of his or her proposed solution to the problem. If one is able to persuade the other that his or her proposed solution (or some compromise) is acceptable, then that is the agreement that will be implemented to solve the problem. However, if managers with different views on how a problem might be resolved cannot be persuaded to accept one or other approach, or they cannot agree a compromise solution between them, a senior manager will have to intervene and impose a resolution to the problem.

Gaining resources

Employee relations managers also frequently negotiate with senior managers to gain resources to enable them to implement new policies, procedures and practices they have devised on their own initiative or as requested by a more senior manager. In such circumstances, a junior manager seeks to persuade the senior manager to allocate the necessary resources. The outcome may be an agreement in which the junior manager obtains some resources – not perhaps what he or she would ideally have liked, but nevertheless sufficient to implement the new policies, procedures and practices. On the other hand, the senior manager may not be persuaded by the junior manager's arguments and may prefer instead to allocate resources to an alternative project that he or she considers to have a higher priority.

Gaining commitment

Managers in any management function and at any level of seniority cannot assume that their proposed actions, policies and arrangements will be accepted without question by their management colleagues. There is likely to be some opposition from those management colleagues who have different interests and priorities. Financial pressures may mean that one manager's progress is another's hold-up, and such interdepartmental rivalries can be a problem in organisations. So if unanimous management commitment to, and support for, proposed changes to policy and/or strategy are to be gained, some manager has to make a persuasive case that carries his or her colleagues along. An agreed management position to which all are committed (ie have bought into) is thus likely to emerge via the process of intra- or inter-management negotiation involving persuasion and often compromise.

Negotiation, then, is not – as is popularly thought – an activity confined to relationships between managers and employee representatives. It is a daily activity in which all managers, inside and outside the employee relations function, are involved. Negotiations take place day in and day out between managers of different and similar levels of executive authority and between the different managers from the different management functions. Nevertheless, some managers have difficulty viewing such circumstances as negotiating situations, preferring to regard them as a process of 'influencing others' and/or gaining the support/commitment of others.

When were you last involved in a negotiating situation where the other party was a management colleague? What was the issue? What arguments did you use to persuade your colleague that your view of handling the issue might be the right one? What counter-arguments did your manager colleague put forward? How were your differences of approach to solving the problem overcome?

Grievance-handling

What is a grievance?

A grievance is a complaint, real or ill-founded, by an employee that behaviour on the part of management (either by commission or by omission) has breached his or her employment rights. Such complaints, however, may be unjustified. If management believes that the employee's complaint is unfounded, perhaps because the employee has simply misunderstood the situation, then management must explain to the employee why it considers this to be the case. Not to do so carries the danger of adding another complaint to the original one, as well as sending a message to the employee that management is not taking the original complaint seriously.

Grievances are important to the individuals concerned. Each grievance has to be treated on its merit. One person's grievance cannot be 'traded off' against that of another individual – two separate grievances should not be linked.

Grievance issues

Complaints about management's behaviour tend to come from individual employees and can range over a wide number of issues, such as:

- a bonus payment has been calculated incorrectly

- a disciplinary penalty is too harsh

- promotion has been denied unreasonably

- access to a training opportunity has been refused

- a job is currently under-graded

- the employee has been sexually harassed by another employee or manager

- there are insufficient car-parking spaces in the company car park

- working conditions – eg heat, light, space – are unpleasant

- overtime opportunities are restricted to particular individuals rather than distributed equally across all employees in the department/section.

Although complaints about management behaviour usually come from individual employees, if they are not handled sensitively they can (and do) develop into collective employee complaints. The resolution of an employee grievance involves negotiation in that both management and the complaining employee seek to persuade each other that their own suggestion to resolve the grievance is the better one. However, such persuasion is rarely successful and a mutually acceptable solution will involve the parties' making concessions towards each other's positions.

Most grievances do not require the full procedure

Organisations virtually always have a set grievance procedure. Employee relations managers need to be familiar with this procedure. However, when an employee raises a grievance against management behaviour, the matter does not automatically trigger the full procedure. The vast majority of employee grievances are settled either informally or by a voluntarily negotiated agreed settlement *before* the procedure is triggered. Informal settlements can include an apology by the employer, or perhaps an admission of error by the employer who then rectifies the mistake that is the cause of the employee's complaint. Alternatively, the employer may explain to the employee why his or her grievance is ill-founded – an explanation that the employee then accepts.

What are the main issues of employee complaints in your organis-ation? Do these tend to get resolved informally, or do they require the full grievance procedure?

Bargaining

Bargaining is a situation where the parties involved have a 'shopping-list' of demands on each other. One party (usually the employees collectively) proposes a list of improvements to pay and other employment con-ditions (for example a shorter working week, longer holidays) and the other (normally the employer or an organisation of employers) responds with a set of counter-proposals covering changes in working practices and changes in the pattern of working hours, etc.

For example, in the 2001 annual pay negotiations between a trade union and a manufacturing company, the trade union presented the following shopping-list:

- an substantial increase on all basic rates of pay

- holiday pay to be improved to include all earnings in the 12 weeks prior to the holiday's being taken

- an improvement of shift premiums payable at weekends to double-time and payable for night-work to time-and-one-third

- overtime payments to be time-and-a-half for standard overtime and double-time plus time in lieu for customary holiday working

- drivers' overnight allowance to be increased to £20 per occasion.

The manufacturing company presented the following response:

- a wage increase of 1.5 per cent

- any additional costs arising from the 2001 national settlement to be recovered in full by efficiency and productivity improvements at plant level

- no changes to shift premiums

- no changes to overtime payments

- drivers' overnight allowance to be increased to £18 per occasion.

A bargaining situation involves issues of collective interest to the work-force, unlike an employee's grievance, which normally involves an issue of interest only to that individual. In a bargaining situation, a construc-tive compromise is achieved by 'trading' in the items that each party has flagged up to the other for negotiation. Identifying which items in their shopping-list the parties are prepared to trade is a key activity in preparing for the bargaining (see below). The aim of the parties is to use such 'trading' to advance, or protect, their own interests and thus create new 'prices' (new rules) at which labour services are bought and sold. Bargaining is thus about trading with the other party, and not about conceding anything specific to the other party. In the 2001 negotiations outlined above, the manufacturing company traded:

- a wage increase of 1.5 per cent

- an increase in the drivers' overnight allowance to £20 per occasion

- shift premiums for night-work to be increased to time-and-one-third.

In return the company received:

- the additional costs of the agreement being fully recovered by efficiency and productivity improvement at the workplace

- no changes to the basis of calculation of holiday pay

- no change to weekend working shift premiums

- no change to overtime premiums.

In most academic literature the words 'negotiation' and 'bargaining' are taken to be one and the same thing. This is incorrect. Bargaining is only one of a number of different negotiating situations in which a management might find itself. The tenor and style of negotiations in bargaining is likely to be more adversarial than in grievance-handling and group problem-solving situations in that by bargaining, the representatives of the buyers and sellers of labour services are seeking to protect and advance the interests of their constituents.

> Explain the difference in approach between bargaining and grievance-handling.

Group/joint problem-solving

This is a situation in which two or more parties negotiate over details whereby one party will co-operate with the other – most commonly in a situation where management is endeavouring to initiate some action to resolve a problem of concern to both parties. Let us consider an example.

The organisation is currently performing comfortably in terms of sales, profitability, etc, but recognises that in the near future product market competition will become more intense. Top management has started to consider suitable policy initiatives that might be introduced to minimise any adverse consequences in terms of sales and so forth when the greater product market competition becomes a reality.

As a first step the organisation has decided to invite a team of consultants to examine its work organisation and systems and to produce a feasibility study on what action/policies it might introduce and what their effect might be on improving its future product market competitiveness. The management has committed itself to implementing none of the report's recommendations until the workforce has been consulted and involved in thorough discussions on the report.

However, if the consultants are to gain a full picture for their report, they have to speak to and gain the co-operation of the workforce. The company believes that the best way to achieve this is for the consultants to go into the departments and to speak to the employees on an individual basis. But the consultants will have to inform the supervisor/team leader and the representative of the employees of what they intend to do in the department. Supervisors/team leaders have accordingly been told to release employees from their workstations so that they can speak to the consultants.

The workforce has an interest in seeing the organisation's efficiency improve because it will enhance their job security. They are therefore prepared to co-operate with the work of the consultants – but they have some concerns. First, they know that in other firms where this consultancy organisation has done work, redundancies have been declared shortly afterwards. Second, the employee representatives are worried that management wishes them to have no role when the consultants are speaking to their constituents. They would prefer to be present at any interviews the consultants carry out with individual employees in the various departments.

The workforce is not against the use of consultants as a matter of principle. Its representatives have decided to approach the management about its concerns. The ensuing negotiations between the parties are over:

- whether the firm of consultants preferred by management to produce the feasibility report will be used or whether a different firm of consultants could be brought in

- the procedure to be adopted by the consultants when in the departments – Will they have direct access to employees? Will employee representatives be present at interviews?

The example illustrates the manner in which a group problem-negotiating situation operates. Management is normally seeking the co-operation of its workforce to some proposed action to gain information which can then be used to solve a problem jointly, with the employees, to mutual gain. As a result, the management's negotiating style will not be adversarial. Management wants something from its employees, so it will start by demonstrating to them that there is an advantage in co-operating. For management to bang the table and to be insulting in the negotiations toward the employee representatives would be inappropriate to the context and unlikely to secure management's primary objective, which is to gain employee co-operation with the work of the consultants.

Has there recently been a joint problem-solving situation in your organisation? If there has, what was it about? What were the terms on which the employees co-operated? If there has been no joint problem-solving situation in your organisation, why do you think that has been the case?

Employee relations negotiations v commercial negotiations

Negotiating situations in employee relations are very different from commercial contract negotiations. Many managers outside the employee relations function find it difficult to understand why employee relations negotiations involve so much quasi-theatrical behaviour and take so long to conclude. So it is important for employee relations managers to understand just how employee relations negotiations are different from commercial contract negotiations. The main differences are summarised in the box below.

Main differences between employee relations and commercial negotiations

Unlike commercial negotiations, employee relations negotiations:

- involve an ongoing relationship

- are carried out by representatives

- do not result in legally enforceable contracts

- make more frequent use of adjournments

- always result in an agreement

Choice of negotiating partner

Commercial negotiations tend to be conducted on a more polite basis than those normally witnessed in grievance-handling or bargaining situations. In commercial negotiations, purchasers tend to buy from individuals or organisations they prefer and sellers can give preferential deals to those they like. In employee relations negotiations, the parties cannot deal only with those they prefer. Each party selects its own representatives, and management selects its best team to conduct the negotiations. In addition, the parties have to develop a professional relationship towards each other regardless of their feeling towards each other. Employee relations negotiations are always conducted by representatives of the parties who report back to constituents. Commercial contract negotiators are not accountable to constituents but usually to a line manager.

Face-to-face negotiations and adjournments

Many negotiations in the commercial field do not take place on a face-to-face basis. They may be undertaken by telephone (for example, telephone sales from call centres) or even by letter. Employee relations negotiations, however, always take place on a face-to-face basis. The use of adjournments is less common in commercial negotiations than in employee relations ones. In this case management (union) negotiators may adjourn several times in bargaining situations – but usually on fewer occasions in grievance-handling – to consider a union (management) proposal. Adjournments enable the parties to obtain and analyse more, new information, to reassess their objectives, aims, strategy and tactics, to re-group as a team where the negotiations are conducted via working parties, and, on occasions, to allow emotions to calm down.

The status of agreements

An important difference between employee relations and commercial negotiation is the legal status of the agreement that emerges. In the commercial contract world the contract outlining the conditions of the sale is legally binding and its contents can be enforced via the courts. The agreement that emerges from employee relations negotiations, as we saw in Chapter 1, is not legally binding. It is binding in honour only. Neither party can enforce its rights, as stipulated in the agreement, via the courts.

'No agreement'

In commercial negotiations, an outcome of 'no agreement' is quite acceptable – and quite common. Buyers and sellers may have every reason to conclude, after some negotiating, that a deal would not be in their interests and so amicably part and seek other suppliers or purchasers whose needs and terms are more acceptable. In employee relations negotiations, the aim – not just the possibility – is to reach an agreement, and the outcome is always a new or revised agreement, even if, on occasions, that agreement is unilaterally imposed by one party on the other.

The quality of future relationships

Grievance-handling, bargaining, joint problem-solving and intra-/inter-management negotiations all take place against an assumption that the parties mean to have an ongoing and permanent relationship. When the negotiations are over, the parties who have met on a basis of equality, have to meet again the next day and continue their employer–employee relationship in which the employees are in a subordinate role. Employee relations negotiators, unlike their commercial contractor counterparts, cannot simply walk away from the party with which they are currently dealing and make a more favourable agreement with another party. For a motorcar seller negotiating with a buyer, the relationship may well be confined to that one negotiation. Whether a sale is concluded or not the parties are unlikely to meet again in a buyer–seller relationship, so one party can insult the other with impunity. By the same token a cash buyer can use his or her bargaining power to obtain a discount on the price of the product or service he or she wishes to purchase.

The continuous relationship between employee relations negotiators at the workplace acts as a restraining influence on their behaviour during and after the negotiations. Each party must retain its dignity, preserve its professional self-respect and bear in mind the importance of preserving the quality of the future relationship. This means that management must avoid any implication that the outcome of the negotiations suggests the employee and/or the trade union has 'lost' and that management has 'won'. Both parties must be able to leave the negotiations (whatever the negotiating situation) without losing face. Once the negotiations have been concluded, regardless of the outcome, the parties have to return to a constructive working relationship as soon as possible. For management to use its 'victory' over its employees to humiliate them is not good practice. To behave in such a manner will result in lower employee morale, increased absenteeism and a poorer quality of product or service to the customer.

In employee relations negotiations, the negotiators have always to bear in mind the importance of preserving the quality of their future relationships. Whatever the outcome of the negotiations and whatever the atmosphere in which they are conducted, the two parties have to be able to co-operate and work together 24 hours a day, five or more days a week, indefinitely, at the end of the negotiations. However, if the employee representative with whom management has to deal is a national or regional one, rather than a workplace representative, and therefore not someone who works on the premises and with whom a day-to-day working relationship has to be maintained, the need to maintain amicable relationships is clearly less imperative because local management may not meet face-to-face with that particular employee representative again.

> List at least four ways in which employee relations negotiations are different from commercial contract negotiations.

Stages in the negotiation process

All negotiating situations involve the stages shown in the list below, although the length of time each stage will last and the degree of formality in each stage will vary. For example, in a negotiating situation between managers the 'agreement' on how to deal with a problem is unlikely to be written down except perhaps in the form of a letter and/or an internal memorandum to management colleagues. In all negotiating situations the preparation stage lasts the longest time. The amount of time the two parties spend actually bargaining, perhaps in a face-to-face situation across the table, is small relative to the total time spent by both sides in the whole negotiating process.

Stages in the negotiation process

- Preparation and analysis

- Presentation

- Searching for and identifying common ground

- Concluding the agreement

- Writing the agreement

The preparation stage

The selection of the negotiating team
The size of the management team will vary but there are advantages in its being small and of an uneven number. If the team is small, team discipline is easier to maintain. An odd number means that if the bargaining team has to take a vote to determine its position, there is always a majority view to prevail. The management bargaining team should represent all major interest groups in the business.

At least three functions have to be carried out by a negotiating team, who will work together under the guidance of its leader. The leader will be the main spokesperson and the principal negotiator, and will lead the negotiations. In addition, the leader will call for an adjournment if management considers one to be necessary, and will hold the chair during adjournments. It is the team leader who will enter corridor (private) discussions with the leader of the other side. The leader will also be responsible for finalising the agreement on behalf of the management. Leaders require a number of attributes. They have to have good interpersonal skills to build the team as a coherent whole, and they have to be acquainted with the employees' attitudes and, if appropriate, the policies and problems of any organisation which represents the employees. It is imperative that the leader shows leadership and is respected by the other members of the team. In addition, the leader must be firm, be capable of exercising good judgement, be patient, be a good listener and be skilful in communicating ideas and getting points across.

The negotiating team also requires a note-taker whose role in negotiations cannot be stressed enough. The note-taker's role includes:

- in adjournments, informing the negotiating team whether the negotiations are making progress or just going round in circles

- advising the negotiators whether the agreed strategy and tactics (see below) are being observed

- recording the proposals made by the other party

- indicating whether the negotiating team has – say, through lack of concentration – missed an offer/proposal from the other side (If this is happens, the negotiating team can return to it in the next or subsequent bargaining sessions.)

- ensuring that all issues are addressed; the note-taker summarises to the negotiating team what issues have been settled and what issues are still outstanding, and prevents issues that are on the negotiating agenda from being forgotten or overlooked

- supplying a complete and accurate record of what has been agreed, from which management drafts the agreement.

The team also requires a strategist whose role is to monitor the strategies of both sides and to identify and seek to confirm the anticipated basis of common ground and constructive compromise for both sides. The strategist also provides any additional information or details that may be required by the team. In addition, he or she monitors and assesses any proposals as and when they are made by the other party.

Some negotiating teams also find it useful to have a member whose sole purpose is to listen to what is being said and to make no spoken contribution in the bargaining sessions. Other teams may like also to have a person whose role is to watch the body and facial reactions of the members of the other side when they are receiving proposals from management or making proposals to management. These reactions can convey useful information and reveal the extent to which the other party is committed to its own proposals and prepared to listen to counter-proposals from the management side.

Regardless of the size of the management's negotiating team and of the division of labour between them, it is imperative – prior to both the first meeting with the other side and to meeting again after an adjournment – that each member of the management team be given the opportunity to contribute to the discussion and agree on the bargaining objectives, strategy and tactics (see below). Ideally, the negotiating team should determine these issues. This provides each team member with an insight into the overall plan and strategy and thereby generates commitment among the whole team to its objectives. So while the role of the team leader is most important during negotiations, the role of the whole team is very important in determining the policies and strategies.

Team discipline

Members of the management team should conduct themselves during the negotiations in line with the agreed position(s) established in the analysis stage (see below) so that the team in the actual negotiations is united and purposeful. It is important before meeting with the other side that the team agree that only one member should speak at a time in the bargaining sessions and that the team leader should not be interrupted unless it is absolutely necessary. However, all members of the team should be prepared to speak when called upon to do so by the team leader. If members of the team other than the leader are to make a spoken contribution during the bargaining sessions, then it should happen as part of a predetermined strategy, the leader having indicated to the other party that the new speaker is speaking at the leader's invitation.

It is also important before meeting with the other party that the team remind themselves of the importance of not disagreeing as a team in front of the other side, and that if team discipline begins to break down, the leader should seek an adjournment so that the necessary action to re-establish discipline can be taken (even to the extent, if necessary, of excluding a member of the team from participating any further in the face-to-face negotiating sessions). The maintenance of team discipline is easier if all members are fully acquainted with the negotiating objectives, and the necessary arguments and tradable items (see below) regarded as essential to achieving those objectives, and that if before meeting with the other side the team has agreed a non-verbal method of communication with each other (eg signals, passing notes, etc) during bargaining session.

The arguments from the management bargaining team have to be consistent, and despite any provocation or unprofessional behaviour on the part of the other side, should not deviate from the agreed format. If during negotiations the other side attempts to disrupt the discipline of the management team by trying to bring in another speaker from the management side against the planned sequence of contributors, the team leader must intervene immediately to make clear to the other side that all their remarks must be addressed to him or her as the team leader. If a member of the management bargaining team begins to talk out of turn, the leader must carefully restrain him or her, using appropriate language in the right tone of voice. It may, for example, only be necessary to tell the team member to keep quiet or to calm down for discipline to be restored – but if this does not work, an adjournment may be necessary during which discipline can be restored.

The members of the negotiating team must remain within their agreed roles and speak only when invited to do so unless a change of plan is agreed during adjournments in the negotiations. However, the team members should endeavour to help each other out of difficulty if the team comes under pressure. Getting rattled transmits to the other side a clear message that management may not be totally united in its commitment to its case, and that unexpected gains may be made by playing to these perceived differences.

What considerations should management take into account in selecting its team for bargaining with its employees' representatives? Justify your answer.

A management negotiating team goes through three further stages in preparing for negotiating. These are:

- analysis
- establishing the aims to be achieved in the forthcoming negotiating sessions
- planning the strategy and tactics to achieve these aims.

The analysis stage

The analysis stage of preparing for negotiating involves management's collecting and analysing relevant information to substantiate its claims and/or its proposals to be put to its employees' representatives. In preparing for negotiating, management is likely to have to analyse information derived from sources internal and external to the organisation. Internal sources are likely to provide information on such issues as:

- the labour productivity trends
- profitability
- labour turnover
- absenteeism statistics
- total sales
- investment
- pay changes
- orders pending
- the cashflow position.

External sources of information for negotiating purposes include employers' associations, the employee relations 'trade press' and UK Government departments. Government departments publish national data for the inflation rate and trends in earnings by occupation, industry, region, gender, etc. Much of this data may not be very useful, however, in local pay negotiations. For these negotiations, local pay and salary surveys that the organisation is likely to have arranged for itself are probably of more value.

Employers' associations are an important external source of information. They keep records about the types of agreements that exist in an industry and collect data on the size of pay-increase settlements that are being granted by member companies. Many employers' associations are also trade associations, and as such collect information on an industry basis over a number of subjects – eg total sales figures, the balance of foreign trade (export/import trends) and unit labour costs.

The analysis stage also involves the management negotiating team's checking on the relevance to the forthcoming negotiating situation of such existing arrangements as:

- collective or individual agreements
- custom and practice.

The employee relations manager should be familiar with the meaning and content of those policies that give effect to such rules and arrangements and to accepted custom and practice.

For those involved in annual pay negotiations there are a number of important sources of pay information. These are:

- Industrial Relations Services
- Incomes Data Services
- *Labour Market Trends*
- the *New Earnings Survey*.

Industrial Relations Services
The Industrial Relations Services (IRS) in its twice-monthly *Employment Review* provides information on employment trends and special features based on a survey of organisations, covering their employment policies and practices. It also contains a Pay and Benefits Bulletin which reviews trends in the general level of pay settlements and reports on pay deals concluded in private and public organisations as well as those involving a whole industry.

It also summarises the latest pay awards, showing the name and size of the group of workers involved, the effective date and length of the agreement, and brief details of the main changes. Its datafile contains information on price changes (the Retail Price Index), on changes in average earnings (Average Earnings Index) and on future forecasts of annual rates of change in prices and earnings. In addition, it contains a useful summary of the main statistics (inflation, average earnings, productivity/labour costs, hours worked, unemployment and employment) used by collective bargainers to pursuade the other party of the merits of their claims.

IRS also publish a monthly *Pay Intelligence* updating service. It features key statistics from its pay databank, including settlement levels for the public, private manual, private non-manual, manufacturing and services sectors, as well as for the economy as a whole. It also contains a summary of the IRS monthly pay analysis and settlement chart, and a 'state of play' table detailing news and deals in key negotiations, as well as the latest official inflation and earnings figures, together with the predictions of 10 leading forecasting organisations. The IRS pay databank is the only regularly published source of pay statistics independent of employers, trade unions and the UK Government. Each year it records the details of pay settlements for some 1,500 bargaining groups covering more than 9 million employees across all sectors of the economy.

Incomes Data Services

The Incomes Data Services (IDS) *Report*, published twice monthly, describes the changes to pay and conditions that are being agreed at company and industry level, and reports current developments in collective bargaining, quickly and simply. Pay settlements are given in detail and the latest statistics on wages, earnings and prices are reported and interpreted.

The IDS *Pay Directory* is published three times a year. It lists the wage rates, holidays, shift premiums, etc, of a wide range of occupations in a variety of companies, and records the wage rates that apply in selected industries and the public sector. It also publishes studies twice monthly which report on the results of research into single topics such as the pay of a particular group of workers, paid holiday entitlement, sick pay, pensions provisions, shift premium pay, redundancy and absenteeism. Its *Top Pay Review*, published monthly, monitors the changes to the pay and benefits of executives and professionals, and provides a comprehensive briefing on remuneration trends in companies and in the public sector.

Labour Market Trends

Labour Market Trends provides statistical information on the labour market, of which the most significant is on employment, unemployment, unfilled vacancies, and earnings. It also provides regular statistical information on inflation trends as the official outlet for the Index of Retail Prices, and supplies data on changes in unit wage costs for all employees for manufacturing, energy and water supply, production and construction industries, and for the economy as a whole.

The New Earnings Survey

The *New Earnings Survey* (NES) is the most comprehensive source of earnings information in Great Britain. It is a survey of the earnings of all those in employment in Great Britain, carried out in April of each year. The survey is based on a 1 per cent sample of employees who are members of PAYE income tax schemes and is designed to represent all categories of employees in businesses of all kinds and sizes. The sample each year comprises all those whose National Insurance numbers end with a specific pair of digits. The sample pair of digits has been used since 1975. Employers are then contacted to give details on the identified employees. The method covers about 90 per cent of the sample. The remaining 10 per cent is obtained directly from large employers. This same can include some employees not in a PAYE scheme. The coverage of full-time adult employees is virtually complete. The coverage of part-time employees is not comprehensive.

The NES provides an annual snapshot of earnings and hours worked analysed by industry, occupation, age-group, regions, county, and collective agreements. Its results are published in six parts:

- Part A is a streamlined analysis giving selected results for full-time employees in particular wage negotiation groups, industries, occupations, age-groups, regions and sub-regions.

- Part B provides analyses of earnings and hours for particular wage bargaining groups.

- Part C analyses hours and earnings for particular industries.

- Part D provides the same analysis for particular occupations.

- Part E provides the same analysis for regions and counties.

- Part F provides an analysis of the distribution of hours, joint distribution of earnings and hours, and an analysis of hours and earnings for part-time women employees.

The earnings data covers the level of earnings, the make-up of total earnings (basic pay, overtime pay, shift premiums, incentive payments, etc) and the distribution of total earnings (by decile, quartile and median).

Take a look at the *New Earnings Survey*. Write a report on how pay and conditions in your organisation compare with the national average. How would you account for any differences found?

Identifying tradable items

The most important activity, however, for the management team in preparing for negotiating is the identification of the key issues involved in the forthcoming negotiations, and the identification from among them of which of these issues management is prepared to trade on. It also involves anticipating which of the issues the employees' side is prepared to trade on, and which it is not. By identifying possible tradable items, the management bargaining team establishes the parameters within which it expects to be able to identify common ground with its employees and thereby the basis for a compromise agreement. In making these decisions about the possible tradable items management weighs up the significance of the issues at stake for the protection and advancement of its, and its employees', economic interests.

In negotiating, at any given time some of the issues are tradeable and others are not. Let us give an example. Management has just received a list of demands from its employees that include a 2.5 per cent increase in basic pay rates, the introduction of a productivity bonus, an increase in holidays, changes to paternity leave arrangements, and the removal of no-strike arrangements. After long consideration, management decides – because of market conditions – that any increase in basic pay rates and any removal of no-strike arrangements are not tradable items. However, it is prepared to trade the introduction of a productivity bonus if this can be made self-financing, an improvement in holiday entitlement, and changes to existing paternity benefits.

Having decided which items it is prepared to trade, the management negotiating team now starts to try to anticipate which issues it believes the employees (the union) will be willing to trade. In doing this, management must assesses the strength of feeling of the employees about each of the items on the negotiating agenda, including whether they feel sufficiently strongly that at the end of the day they would be willing to impose industrial sanctions against the organisation. Let us say, for example, that management anticipates that the employees and their representatives will feel most strongly about the introduction of a productivity bonus and gaining an increase in holiday entitlement (ie that these are their non-tradable items). So in this case management anticipates that its employees are willing to trade basic pay rate increases, the no-strike clause and paternity arrangements (ie that these are their tradeable items) to obtain improvements in holiday entitlement and the introduction of a productivity bonus. Management thus sees a basis for agreement around a productivity bonus, an increase in holiday and paternity leave changes in return for retention of a no-strike clause and no change in basic pay rates.

Establishing negotiating aims

The next phase of the preparation stage is the establishment by the management negotiating team of the objectives it wishes to achieve in the forthcoming negotiations. This phase also requires management to anticipate the negotiating aims and objectives of its employees and/or their representatives. It is a task that can be done more competently if the management knows and understands what motivates the representatives of the workforce with which it has to deal. Getting to know them does not mean agreeing with their position. However, it is only by knowing what makes them tick (for example, their attitudes, their reaction to pressures upon them, their personalities) that management can predict/anticipate with any reasonable degree of certainty:

- how the employees' representatives might react to management proposals
- the issues they are prepared to trade in bargaining

- the bargaining style they are likely to adopt

- the strategy and tactics they might develop.

By setting objectives, the negotiators know what they are trying to achieve. Negotiating is about compromise and flexibility, so it is normally unrealistic to set inflexible objectives because that usually gives only two options – win or lose. Negotiators have to arrive at some sort of prioritised approach. It is standard practice for negotiators to establish three positions for each item involved in the negotiations. These positions are:

- What would management ideally like to achieve?

- What does management realistically believe it can achieve?

- What is the least for which management will settle (the 'fall-back' or 'sticking' position)?

The fall-back position represents the lowest package for which management will settle. It is the minimum that can be accepted without failing to meet the negotiators' objectives. If this position cannot be achieved, management will prefer to enter into a dispute situation with its employees. It means that management is prepared to withstand industrial sanctions that the employees may take against them rather than settle for less than its fall-back position. Management, as part of preparing for negotiating, must therefore also draw up plans to minimise/offset any costs that may accrue to the organisation should a failure to agree result in industrial action by employees.

The aspiration grid

Having established its negotiating objectives, the next step for management is to anticipate the negotiating aims/objectives of the other party along the same lines – what is likely to be their ideal, realistic and fall-back position on each issue involved in the negotiating situation? Having considered which items it is prepared to trade, having anticipated the tradable items of the other party, having established its own bargaining objectives, and having anticipating those of the other party, management can now construct an 'aspiration grid' that sets out the parameters for the expected outcome of the negotiation. Such a grid shows the issues that management is prepared to trade as well as management's anticipation of the issues it expects its employees will be willing to trade. It gives the parameters within which the forthcoming bargaining might be expected to develop. It helps management to identify the information it requires from the other party, and the information it requires to convey to the other party (see the summary box overleaf).

An aspiration grid:

- sets parameters for the expected outcome of the negotiations

- shows the issues that management is prepared to trade on

- shows management's anticipation of the issues its employees or their representatives will trade on

- gives a picture of how the forthcoming negotiations are expected to develop

- helps management to identify the information it requires from the other party

- helps management to identify the information it must convey to the other party

An example of how the aspiration grid can be used is given in Table 27. An X indicates that a party is not prepared to trade that item. An O indicates that the party is prepared to trade that item. This grid is based on the example outlined previously. If both parties have an X against the same item in their fall-back column, it indicates that there will be no accommodation on that issue and the expectation must be that the negotiations will break down. There can be no basis for an agreement. In that eventuality management would have to give consideration to whether it is prepared to bear the costs that a failure to agree would involve. If it decides it is not, management will have hastily to reassess its position on the issue.

The grid shows that ideally management would like to trade no items with the employees. However, it knows this is unrealistic. The grid shows that management has therefore established a 'realistic' position of wishing to trade increases in holiday entitlement and changes to the paternity leave arrangements for no changes in pay and to the no-strike arrangements, and for there to be no productivity bonus introduced. The management's fall-back position is to introduce a productivity-based bonus scheme, to increase holiday entitlement and to change existing paternity leave arrangements in return for no increase in basic pay rates and the retention of the no-strike clause. The bottom line for the management negotiating team is to trade a productivity bonus, an increase in holiday entitlement and changes to paternity leave arrangements in return for no increase in pay and the retention of the no-strike clause.

The aspiration grid also shows what management expects to be the negotiating objectives of its employees' representatives. Management knows that the representatives would ideally like to trade no items. Management is of course aware, however, that the employee representatives will view that as unrealistic. The grid therefore shows that

Table 27 An aspiration grid

Items for negotiation	Management			Employees/Union		
	Ideal	Real	Fall-back	Fall-back	Real	Ideal
Basic pay increase of 2.5 per cent	X	X	X	O	O	X
Introduction of productivity bonus	X	X	O	X	X	X
Increase in holiday entitlement	X	O	O	X	X	X
Changes to paternity leave	X	O	O	O	O	X
Retention of no-strike clause	X	X	X	O	X	X

management anticipates the employees' realistic bargaining aim to be one of trading pay and changes in existing paternity leave arrangements in return for the introduction of a productivity-based bonus scheme, increased holiday entitlement and the removal of the no-strike clause. The grid further shows that the management negotiating team anticipates that the bottom line for the employees' representatives is likely to be to trade no increase in pay, no changes to the paternity leave arrangements and the retention of the no-strike clause in return for the introduction of a productivity-based bonus scheme and an increase in holiday entitlement.

The grid thus suggests that there is a basis for agreement between the parties. This is indicated in that the fall-back positions of the two parties do not have Xs against the same issue. Management is not prepared to trade a basic rate of pay increase and the removal of the no-strike clause. Management anticipates that the employees are prepared to trade these issues. The employees are expected by management not to be prepared to trade the introduction of a productivity-based bonus scheme and an increase in holiday entitlement. However, management has assessed that it can live with trading these issues. The management negotiating team now has a structure of how the bargaining can be expected to develop and evolve. In the face-to-face sessions with the representatives of its employees it will have to pass information to them on what issues management is prepared to trade and at the same time seek to gain information from the employees' side which confirms management's expectations of what the employees are prepared to trade.

The aspiration grid enables a negotiating party to structure its own position systematically and to record the expected outcomes of the other party's position. It sets out each side's objectives, known or anticipated, and their three positions. It indicates information the parties want to gain from, and give to, each other during the forthcoming negotiating sessions in order to confirm (or readjust) their expectations of the other party's position. If information received during the negotiating sessions suggests that expectations about the other party's intentions are inaccurate, the aspiration grid has to be reanalysed and amended.

The aspiration grid gives management a picture of how the bargaining sessions are likely to develop. In the actual bargaining sessions, management can test out whether its anticipation of the employees' bargaining objectives is correct or must be re-assessed by ensuring that the employees and their representatives receive clear information on management's bargaining objectives.

If management enters negotiations without having established objectives, the probability of reaching an unsatisfactory outcome or entering into a dispute situation is increased. It is essential that in establishing its 'realistic' and 'fall-back' bargaining objectives, management takes proper, and due, account of the relative balance of bargaining power between itself and its employees (see Chapters 1 and 2). The management's negotiating team must take all these factors into account. If the balance of bargaining power favours the employer, the aspiration grid will be different from one that relates to a situation in which the bargaining power lies with the employees and their representatives.

Planning strategy and tactics

The next phase of the preparation stage is when the negotiating team plans its strategy and tactics to deliver its negotiating objectives. This involves:

- deciding before meeting with the other party who is to speak, in what order, and on what issues

- anticipating the arguments and counter-arguments.

Anticipating the arguments and counter-arguments
An important part of planning the strategy and the tactics to achieve the bargaining objectives is to anticipate the arguments mostly likely to be used by the other party against your case and to consider how they might be countered. In this regard it is helpful if a member of the management negotiating team can play the 'devil's advocate' and probe management's case for its weak points, exploring how the employees' and/or their representatives' arguments against management's case may be exposed and answered. Plans can then be made to have responses immediately to hand.

Communicating with the team
During the negotiating sessions the team may find it necessary to communicate without the need to call for an adjournment (see below). Any agreed method of communication will have to be non-verbal. Research shows that the most common method used by negotiating teams is the passing of notes.

In conducting negotiations, the preparation stage is the longest and most important stage in the process. If management's analysis of the information it has gathered – whether by interview techniques or from statistical data – is incorrect, it will establish inappropriate bargaining objectives and develop an unrealistic strategy and tactics, with the result that the chances of its achieving its bargaining objectives will be significantly reduced. If it does achieve its objectives, despite inadequate preparation, it is likely to be because management holds the upper hand in the relative balance of bargaining power stakes or by good fortune. Good luck is not, however, a management skill. A 'seat-of-the-pants' approach to a bargaining situation is understandable – but any competent negotiator will tell you that there is no substitute for preparation. The golden rule to remember when preparing for negotiating is:

Failing to prepare
is
preparing to fail.

If management fails to prepare adequately, it is not a disaster. The situation can be rescued if management reassesses its negotiating analysis, objectives and strategy and tactics in the light of new information it gains that was not available at the preparation stage. Indeed, it is essential that management does reassess its bargaining objectives, and the analysis upon which they are based, every time it gains information it did not have or did not take into account, when getting ready for the next negotiating session. During any negotiating adjournments, management should frequently monitor and review its negotiating objectives (including a review of the aspiration grid) in the light of how the negotiations are developing and progressing.

Failing to prepare is preparing to fail. Explain the importance of this statement to employee relations managers involved in negotiation.

The first meeting

At the first meeting with the other side, if the negotiators are unknown to each other, it may be necessary to break the ice by the teams' introducing themselves to each other. On the other hand, if the negotiators are well known to each other some form of general greeting might help to start things off on the right foot.

Management begins the meeting
If management is making the initial presentation, the leader of the management delegation first gives a general summary of its case. After informing the employees, or their representatives, of the issues it is going to raise, management then substantiates the case it has already outlined by adducing supporting facts and figures, emphasising the rationale behind the proposals, and trying to suggest the strength of its feeling towards each of them. So the first part of the negotiating process involves both parties telling each other what they ideally want from each other.

Although it is perhaps not *common* practice, it is *good* practice for each party to put on the table all the issues they wish to be dealt with in the forthcoming negotiating sessions, and not just to present its views on selected issues. This avoids the possibility of a set of long negotiating sessions over many issues ending in apparent agreement only for one party then to say, 'Oh, by the way – we need to talk about X [a new issue] as well.' Some negotiators believe there are advantages in 'keeping something up your sleeve to hit them with later'. Bearing in mind that the purpose of negotiation is to come to an agreement, this is a dangerous tactic because:

- The hidden issue might be a non-negotiable issue for the other side or one on which it is prepared to trade only if the alternative is no agreement at all. If this is the case, there is a high probability that the negotiations will break down, losing with them the issues on which an accommodation has already been made.

- It can destroy the mutual trust between the leaders of the respective negotiating teams. Negotiators do not like to have negotiated in good faith and to have openly raised all the issues to secure an agreement only to find that the other party has behaved differently.

- If one party behaves consistently in bad faith, the other party will come to regard it as part of that party's negotiating tactic, and will take it into account in future negotiating sessions. Any new alleged surprise thereafter, hoping to evoke further improvements in the offer/claim made by the other side, is negated.

At best, a management may get away with the 'keep something up your sleeve' tactic once. The employee relations professional should be an open, and not a devious, negotiator who puts all the cards to be considered in the negotiations on the table from the outset.

Management receives proposal(s)

If management is receiving a proposal or proposals from its employees' representatives, it listens carefully to what they are saying and does not interrupt their presentation. When the employee side has completed its presentation, it is good management practice to avoid an unconsidered (ie knee-jerk) response. By the same token, it is unwise for management to reply with immediate counter-proposals unless they have been agreed beforehand. If management is receiving proposals for the first time, its response should be confined to asking questions to seek clarification of the proposals so that it can be confident that it genuinely understands what those proposals mean. Typical questions might be:

- What does the proposal actually mean? Could you please give us more details?

- What is the source of the statistic on wage rates/inflation rate, etc, that you have quoted?

- When you make reference to average earnings, what kind of average do you mean – mode, median, unweighted arithmetic?

It is essential that at the end of the presentation of the employees' proposals, management is 100 per cent certain as to what has been proposed and what it is that the employees' proposals actually mean. It is therefore good practice, before the employees' presentation session concludes, for management to summarise back in a neutral manner what it understands has been proposed on behalf of the employees. At the end of the employees' presentation, management should arrange to meet with the employees at a future date so that a full and measured response to the employees' proposal(s) can be given.

By the end of the presentation stage, both parties will have put to each other their ideal positions. There is unlikely, at this stage, to be much common ground between them. However, the issues to be resolved during the negotiating sessions are now known to both parties, who can forthwith begin the task of seeking confirmation of their anticipated common ground.

Identifying common ground

The emphasis and the tone of the negotiations now switches from concentrating on differences to identifying points of common ground that can form the basis of a possible agreement. The stage has now been reached at which both parties must seek to confirm the expected common ground from which an agreement can be built. Each team needs to obtain, in future bargaining sessions with the other party, information that will enable it to confirm whether its expectations as to the location of the common ground are correct.

Each subsequent bargaining session must be used constructively by both parties to gain this essential information. Management must supply information to the other party so that the employees can assess the correctness of their expectations as to management's position on the issues that are the subject of the negotiations. Negotiating sessions which do not provide the information needed by the two parties to confirm their anticipated areas of common ground are not a constructive use of time – although negotiating sessions do happen in which neither party gains relevant information. This generally occurs when either party tries to:

- score points off the other
- lay blame
- issue threats
- shout down the other side or be sarcastic
- interrupt
- talk too much
- attack personalities on the other side.

Management can seek to confirm its expectations as to where the common ground with the other side lies by using any of a number of techniques. The most important of these are:

- The 'if and then' technique, which involves using hypothetical statements such as 'If you are prepared to move closer to our position on issue y, then we are prepared to move closer to your position on x' – A positive response to this means that x and y have been identified as tradable items. The technique deliberately emphasises the requirement of the other side to move. It is a conditional offer.

- Open discussion within broad parameters: for example, management may indicate that an issue may be considered, but only in return for something else, say, a different set of employee representative arrangements – Management would then outline these arrangements so that they form the basis of discussion and negotiation.

- Questioning (interviewing) for clarification of the other side's position.

- Watching the body language of the other party (frowns, glances, nods, etc) as the members react to the proposals put forward.

- Listening carefully to exactly what is being said, including any conditions placed on any offers/proposals (see below).

- Every now and then summarising, using neutral language, the other party's position on an issue – This is particularly helpful if the issue concerned is complex. Such a summary might well begin with something like '... So what you are saying is that you understand our offer on issue x means that [at this point there is a complex example given of how the party believes what the other party has proposed will operate] and that we both have no problem with that.' Each separate negotiating meeting should begin with one or other party's summary of the stage the negotiations have reached. Such a summary usually outlines the areas upon which agreement has been reached and the issues upon which an agreement has still to be reached.

- Linking the issues that are crucial so that specific issues may together be precisely identified as ones the parties are prepared to trade on or not – Linking issues also ensures that the negotiations maintain a momentum.

- Seeking agreement in principle before discussing details – It is pointless discussing the details of (for example) how flexibility of employees between different tasks will operate if one party is totally opposed to employee flexibility.

Summary of techniques to test where the common ground lies

- the 'if and then' technique

- open discussion

- asking questions, seeking clarification

- watching the body language

- listening to what is said, and how

- periodic summarising

- linking issues

- looking for a general agreement before a detailed one

If the use of the techniques outlined above draws out new information, an adjournment can be called – if thought necessary – to consider the implications of that new information, including whether there is a need to reassess negotiating aims (ie amend the aspiration grid), to reopen analysis or to revise strategy and tactics.

Listening for disguised messages
In negotiating situations, listening skills enable a team to decode signals hidden within the spoken language. The meanings of the words are not always what they might seem when printed on the page. Let's look at some examples.

Statement as made	Likely meaning
At this stage we are not prepared to consider that.	That is a tradable item, but at this point we do not think it necessary to trade it.
We would find it extremely difficult to meet that demand.	Meeting that demand would not be entirely out of the question.
I am not empowered to negotiate on that point.	You will have to talk about that to my boss.
We can discuss that point.	That point is negotiable.
These are standard company terms.	These terms are negotiable up to a point.
It is not our policy to make bonus payments – and even if we did, they would not be as large as 10 per cent.	We'll let you have 2 per cent.
It is not our normal practice to . . .	We might . . . if you made it worth our while.

There is information significant enough to confirm tradable items in these statements. If either negotiating team neglects to listen for the true meaning hidden within such statements, it may miss out on learning what it needs to know.

The importance of momentum

Confirmation of what is the common ground gives the negotiating sessions a momentum. If they then become bogged down on a particular issue, the momentum can be sustained by switching to a new issue. This reinforces the importance of the negotiators' putting all the issues on the table from the outset. A thorny issue can be returned to later, and if it is then the only outstanding issue to an agreement's being secured, the parties are more than likely to readjust their attitude towards that issue to a more accommodating one. Both sides at that stage are faced with a stark choice. Either an accommodation is reached on the one outstanding issue or no agreement is made – and all the contributory agreements on issues that have been reached till then fall by the wayside. The party that has the stronger feelings on the remaining, but difficult, issue is thus faced with the very real possibility of 'throwing the baby out with the bathwater'.

Outline the various techniques by which a management negotiating team can search for the common ground and thereby the basis for an agreement with representatives of the workforce. Which of these techniques do you think is the most important – and why?

Adjournments

In bargaining the use of adjournments is useful in ensuring that the negotiating sessions are proceeding as planned. The number and frequency of adjournments depend upon the normal practice of negotiating sessions in the environment in which they being undertaken. Fowler (1996) points out that although adjournments may be suggested at any time, there are at least three constructive uses of the *ad hoc* (as distinct from scheduled) break:

- to give the parties an opportunity to withdraw and review progress among themselves or consider a proposal tabled by the other side

- to provide a break if the negotiations have reached an impasse or become bogged down in trivia or personal argument such that team discipline is in danger or has broken down

- to provide an opportunity for one or two members of each side to talk informally with each other away from the negotiating table in a manner that would not be appropriate in the formal negotiating sessions – This provides an opportunity for the leaders of the two teams to meet away from the negotiating table to discuss, without commitment, what it would take to unblock the impasse. The words 'without comment' are normally used in such situations to reassure the other members of the two teams that their leaders will not strike any formal deal without prior reference back.

Adjournments thus enable one or both parties to reconsider their position in private, and are very much part of negotiating situations. Their main purpose is to provide space in which to review and assess progress against the negotiating objectives and against the perceived objectives of the other party. They provide an opportunity to update the negotiating strategy in respect of how the negotiations are progressing. There are partial re-preparation sessions for a reconvened meeting. If the adjournment is taken to consider a specific proposal, it is important to remember that such adjournments create expectations of a response in the minds of the other party. Reading what is going on is vital, and keeping the mind focused on the negotiating objectives is essential. In such situations the warning by Cairns (1996) is salutary:

> *If the adjournment is to consider a new offer, don't take 10 minutes to reject it and 50 minutes discussing sport or the previous night's TV. Management may get the signal that if you took an hour to consider their offer they are close to an agreement.*

Adjournments should also be sought by management whenever it has any doubts about how the negotiating session is progressing or team discipline is about to break down (or has already broken down). The golden rule for management is:

If in doubt, get out.

Concluding the agreement

Entering this stage of the negotiating process is a matter of timing and judgement. The ability to recognise the best deal that in the circumstances could be reached and will be acceptable to the constituents represented is an important skill for the employee relations professional to acquire. In negotiating situations where increases in pay and other conditions are being offered in return for changes in working practices, the last item to be decided is what the amount of the increase in pay will be. There are a number of reasons for this.

First, the employer wants to know exactly what it is going to get in terms of increased work effort for the pay increase. It is only when an amount is on offer that the employer can make a considered judgement whether the 'price' for the changes in working practices gained is worth it. The same applies to the employees. It is only when they know what they have to do for it (ie the 'price' *they* have to pay) that they can make a considered decision on whether the proposed pay increase offers adequate compensation.

Second, if the pay issue is put on the table early in the negotiations, the negotiations themselves are likely to become deadlocked. The momentum to the negotiating session will come to a halt. Neither of the parties could move to accommodate the other's interests because it would not, at this early stage, be able to assess whether the overall 'price' was worthwhile.

Third, by negotiating over pay after all other issues have been agreed the negotiators are faced with a stark choice. If they cannot move to accommodate each other over pay, the whole agreement collapses. What has been agreed concerning the other items in the respective shopping-lists is withdrawn. The parties have to weigh up whether they want to 'throw the baby out with the bathwater'. Neither will want to see all its earlier hard work go to waste. Attitudes are thus more attuned to compromise than if there were more than one outstanding issue. Both sides also have to weigh up whether – if an agreement fails to materialise over the one outstanding issue of pay improvement – they are prepared to bear the costs that go with the other party's imposing industrial sanctions against them.

Factors to consider in concluding the agreement

There are a number of considerations that management should bear in mind when closing the negotiations. First, it must be satisfied all the issues have been discussed and agreed, and that both parties fully understand what they have accepted. If there is a misunderstanding over what has been agreed, the negotiating process must recommence. It is crucial that both sides have the same understanding of what they have agreed, or when the agreement is implemented, the parties will become embroiled in frequent disputes over how one party or the other is interpreting and/or applying the agreement.

Second, management has to convince the other party that its final offer *is* final. Management must be extremely careful not to allow any suggestion that what is effectively a bluff is its final position, or that what is genuinely its final position is no more than a bluff. A series of 'final offers' from management will destroy its credibility with the other party and undermine its ability to convince the workforce that the bottom line has been reached. Management gains little by telling its employees there can be no further improvement on its offer if the threat of industrial pressure from the employees – for example, by a ballot supporting industrial action – brings a further concession. In such circumstances management has demonstrated to the other side that it has not reached its fall-back position, and the employees will begin to expect even further improvement. When management tells the employees that its offer is final, *that must be the case*.

Third, management should avoid being rushed into concluding a final agreement, no matter how tempting an offer/proposal from the other side sounds. Management must make sure it has all the information it requires from the employees (or their representatives) and then seek an adjournment. This will enable the management negotiating team to examine the final offer and to identify any potential problems that may have gone unnoticed before.

Writing up the agreement

Once management has an oral agreement, it should run through a summary of the proceedings with the employees' representatives, noting precisely what has been agreed, and thereafter secure an agreement that what has been summarised is indeed what was agreed. It should then be written up in 'draft' form. The written agreement should state:

- who are the parties to the agreement

- the date it was concluded

- the date upon which it will become operative

- which groups/grades of employees are covered by the agreement

- the contents (clauses) of the agreement

- the duration of the agreement

- whether the agreement can be reopened before this end-date, and if so, in what circumstances

- how disputes over its interpretation and application will be settled (through the existing grievance/disputes procedure?)

- which other agreements, if any, it replaces.

The written agreement should contain the signatures of representatives of the parties covered by the agreement.

Explain why to write up the negotiating process is vital. Outline what techniques can be used for this purpose, and what the advantages are of each.

The agreement is usually drafted by management and then sent to the other party, which usually initials the clauses of which it accepts the wording. Only when both sides are happy with the wording is the agreement printed and formally signed.

There are some pitfalls management should avoid when writing up the agreement. First, it should check the wording very carefully. One word can make a big difference to the meaning of a clause in the agreement. (There is, for example, a vast difference in meaning between a statement that 'the management may provide' and the statement that 'the management will provide'.) No room for doubt should be left.

Second, management should retain full concentration in the latter stages of the negotiations. It is likely that by then the negotiating process will have been going on for some time. There is a danger that the management negotiating team will relax once it has an oral agreement, thinking perhaps that the hard work is over. However, management should bear in mind that all too quickly the details of what was said in negotiation may be forgotten. What has been agreed will be what is down in black and white on the signed agreement.

Third, the agreement must be straightforward and easy to understand. Unless it is fully understood by both parties and its wording and intent clear, its operation will cause endless disputes over its interpretation and application.

Fourth, it is important for the management's negotiating team to keep its own accurate record of what was agreed. It may turn out to be management's only protection against an attempt by the other party to interpolate into the agreement something that was not actually agreed during the negotiations. Fortunately, attempts to cheat when writing up an agreement are extremely rare among managements and employees' bargaining representatives. A party might get away with this type of behaviour once – but the cost could be high in terms of lost professionalism and of lost trust with the other party.

So throughout the stages of negotiation there is a gradual movement towards common points of agreement. At the end of the presentation stage there is little common ground between the parties, but at each subsequent meeting there should emerge – via the exchange of information – an increasing degree of common ground. Each meeting of the two parties should make progress towards a constructive compromise (see Figure 6).

Figure 6   The reconciliation of differences over time

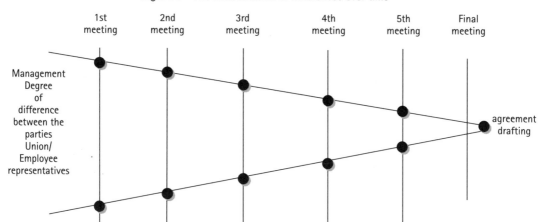

The outcome of negotiations

The best outcome of the bargaining process is one in which both parties make some gains – the so-called win/win situation. This is normally achieved by professional negotiators who concentrate on achieving well-prepared objectives, on maintaining long-term relationships with the other party, on emphasising a pragmatic approach, and on making an agreement that meets the needs of both parties. However, the relative balance of bargaining power between the two parties still heavily influences the outcome of the bargaining regardless of the professionalism the management bargaining team displays.

The opposite outcome is the lose/lose situation, which arises out of a lack of professionalism on the part of the negotiators. The result is that:

- neither party achieves its objectives

- no agreement is secured

- long-term relationships are soured

- the constituents of the negotiators no longer respect/trust them

- both parties become disillusioned with the negotiating process.

A third possible outcome is the so-called win/lose situation in which one party dominates the other and secures something from the other without giving anything in return. This outcome is often the result of unprofessional negotiating on the part of one or both parties. Such negotiations are characterised by an 'us and them' distinction between the parties. The bargaining teams' energies are directed towards victory ('I win – you lose'), a strong emphasis on immediate solutions regardless of their long-term consequences, personalised conflicts rather than the considered assessment of facts, information and arguments, and no consideration of the quality of future relations between the parties after the negotiations are over.

CONCLUSION

Negotiations can be defined as what happens when two or more parties come together to make an agreement by purposeful persuasion and by making constructive compromises.

- Four different negotiating situations can be identified – between managers, grievance-handling, bargaining, and group problem-solving.

- The most common negotiating situation in which employee relations professionals are likely to find themselves is negotiating with their managerial colleagues over various issues – for example, to determine the appropriate course of action to solve a problem.

- Grievance-handling is resolving an individual employee's complaint that the behaviour of management (or of another employee) has compromised his or her employment rights.

- Bargaining is where the parties involved reach an agreement by trading items in the list of demands they make of each other.

- Group problem-solving is a situation in which two or more parties negotiate the details whereby one party will co-operate with action proposed by the other that is of common interest to both parties.

- The main differences between employee relations negotiations and commercial negotiations lie in the choice of negotiating partner, face-to-face relationships, adjournments, the status of agreements reached, and the need to consider future relationships.

- There are five stages to the bargaining process – preparation and analysis, presentation, searching for the common ground, concluding the agreement, and writing up the agreement.

- The most important stage is preparation and analysis, and its importance can be summed up in the phrase 'Failing to prepare is preparing to fail'.

- An aspiration grid shows the issues the parties expect to trade with each other, and helps to identify the common ground likely to be the basis of reaching a compromise agreement.

- There are techniques available to management through which it can confirm its expectations of where the common ground lies.

- These include the 'if and then' technique, questioning, body-language watching, listening, and summarising.

- In writing up the agreement, clear wording is important if future disputes over the interpretation and operation of the agreement are to be avoided.

Further reading

CAIRNS L. (1996) *Negotiation Skills in the Workplace: A practical handbook*. London, Pluto Press.

FOWLER A. (1996) *Negotiating Skills and Strategies*. 2nd edition. London, Institute of Personnel and Development.

FOWLER A. (1998) *Negotiating, Persuading and Influencing*. London, Institute of Personnel and Development.

INCOMES DATA SERVICES, *Pay Directory*, published three times a year.

INCOMES DATA SERVICES, *Report*, published twice monthly.

INDUSTRIAL RELATIONS SERVICES, *Employment Trends*, published twice monthly.

INDUSTRIAL RELATIONS SERVICES, *Pay Intelligence*, published monthly.

KENNEDY G., BENSON J. *and* McMILLAN J. (1987) *Managing Negotiations*. 3rd edition. London, Hutchinson.

OFFICE FOR NATIONAL STATISTICS *Labour Market Trends*.

OFFICE FOR NATIONAL STATISTICS, *New Earnings Survey*, published annually and in six parts.

WALTON R. E. *and* McKERSIE R. B. (1991) *A Behavioural Theory of Labor Negotiations*. 2nd edition. New York, Ithaca.

WALTON R. E., CUTCHER-HERSHENFELD J. E. *and* McKERSIE R. B. (1994) *Strategic Negotiations*. Cambridge, Mass., Harvard Business School Press.

• Managing Employee Performance and Behaviour

Introduction

This chapter, and the one that follows, cover two related topics: discipline and grievance. Although they are to be dealt with separately, it is important to recognise that both are a two-way process and concern complaints, real or imagined, by one party against another. Both are covered by a specific Code of Practice, which is examined in detail later in the chapter. However, because of the way that the law has intervened in the disciplinary process – the unfair dismissal legislation – disciplinary issues have been afforded a much higher profile within organisations than grievance procedures, which are not as legally regulated.

What is discipline?

'Discipline' is an emotive word in the context of employment. The dictionary offers several definitions of the noun, ranging from 'punishment or chastisement' to 'systematic training in obedience'. There is no doubt that discipline at work can be one of the most difficult issues with which a manager has to deal. It brings to the forefront matters relating to an individual's performance, capability and conduct. In the context of employment, probably the most appropriate definition of it (as a verb) to adopt is

" *to improve or attempt to improve the behaviour, orderliness, etc., of by training, conditions or rules* ""

to improve or attempt to improve the behaviour, orderliness, etc., of by training, conditions or rules "

(Collins Concise Dictionary)

In this chapter we examine the practices and skills that are required of an employee relations professional if employee behaviour and performance is to be effectively managed. These depend on the principles of discipline-handling, the characteristics of a fair and effective disciplinary procedure, the legal aspects of discipline and dismissal, and the monitoring and evaluation of disciplinary procedures. A fair and effective disciplinary procedure is one that concentrates on improving or changing behaviour, and not one that relies on the principle of punishment.

Management problems with the discipline process

Many managers find it problematical to be responsible for employee behaviour and performance because they believe that the methodology available to them – the disciplinary process – is cumbersome and ineffective, or that the law on employment rights is heavily biased against them. This can often result in problems being ignored because they feel that effective action against individual employees either takes too long or is liable to mean an appearance before an employment tribunal at which the employee is more likely to be successful. Many managers share this basic misconception, and it is the responsibility of the employee relations professional to advise and guide their managerial colleagues through what, to many, is a minefield.

Good practice

It is important for managers, at all levels, to appreciate that the effectiveness of the business can be undermined if issues relating to conduct, capability and performance are not handled professionally and consistently, or, even worse, if such matters are ignored altogether. This chapter looks, *inter alia*, at the concept of 'good practice' in relation to performance and behaviour at work, at the steps that should be taken when managers are trying to alter existing behaviour or performance, and at how to ensure that all employees are treated fairly. 'Good practice' is a concept that many managers have difficulty with because it is a term that is difficult to define. In the context of discipline at work, it is about acting with just cause, using procedures correctly, acting consistently, following the rules of natural justice – it is all four of those things – and more. It is also about developing those good management habits which ensure that you do follow procedure, you do act consistently and you do take account of the rules of natural justice when taking disciplinary action. Good practice is therefore an important principle. Not only does it help to guarantee fairness and consistency, but it makes good business sense and can add value.

The origins of disciplinary procedures

Up to the beginning of the 1970s employers had almost unlimited power to discipline and dismiss individual employees, and in many instances they were not slow to exercise this power. Although it was possible for a dismissed employee to sue for 'wrongful dismissal' under the common law, it was rarely a practical option because of the time and heavy costs involved. The only time that the employers' power was likely to be restricted was where trade unions were present in the workplace and dismissal procedures were established through the collective bargaining process.

This changed with the Industrial Relations Act 1971. This Act gave individual employees the right, for the first time, to complain to an industrial tribunal that they had been unfairly dismissed. Industrial tribunals themselves had only been established in 1964 and so in 1971 were a relatively new feature of business life. They were renamed employment tribunals with effect from 1 August 1998 by the Employment Rights (Dispute Resolution) Act 1998, and this change has been carried through to all pre-existing enactments. As well as establishing the right not to be unfairly dismissed, the 1971 Act also introduced, in 1972, the Industrial Relations Code of Practice. This brought in the idea that there was a right and a wrong way to deal with issues of discipline. It was subsequently superseded by an ACAS Code of Practice on 'Disciplinary Practices and Procedures in Employment', which has itself now been superseded by a Code of Practice on 'Disciplinary and Grievance Procedures' (see below).

The 1971 Act was a turning-point in the relationship between employer and employee. The relative informality of the then industrial tribunals and the fact that access to them did not depend on lawyers or money meant that for many employees the threat of dismissal without good reason disappeared or diminished. This does not mean that employees cannot now be unfairly dismissed. They can. The law has never removed from management the ability to dismiss who it likes, when it likes and for whatever reason it likes. All that has happened since 1971 is that where employers are deemed to have acted unreasonably and unfairly in dismissing an employee, they can be forced to compensate that individual for the consequences of that action. Most employers have accepted this legal intervention without serious complaint, and seek to manage performance and behaviour issues in as fair a way as possible. Some clearly have not and do not, and take a cavalier attitude to individual employment rights. Others suffer from a misconception of what they can do and how the law impacts upon their actions.

The current legal position

Up until 1996 the law relating to discipline and dismissal was contained in the Employment Protection (Consolidation) Act 1978. In August of that year the Employment Rights Act 1996 came into force, consolidating provisions contained in the 1978 Act together with provisions of the Wages Act 1986, the Sunday Trading Act 1994 and the Trade Union Reform and Employment Rights Act (TURERA) 1993. The Employment Relations Act 1999 and the Employment Act 2002 have made further changes.

The starting-point for the disciplinary process is to be found in section 1 of the 1996 Act, which deals with an employee's right to a statement of employment particulars. Section 3 of the Act declares that any statement of particulars must also specify any disciplinary rules applicable to the employee or refer the employee to the provisions of a document specifying such rules that is reasonably accessible to the employee. The Employment Act 2002 has now inserted a further requirement that the statement must also include information about any procedures applicable to the taking of disciplinary decisions.

Section 3 of the 1996 Act goes on to assert that the statement of particulars must also specify who an employee can appeal to if he or she is dissatisfied with any disciplinary decision that is made.

Sections 94 to 134 of the Act deal specifically with unfair dismissal, and these set out:

- the legal definition of dismissal
- the specific reasons for which it is fair to dismiss an employee
- the position of shop workers who refuse to work on a Sunday
- the position of trade union officials
- the position of health and safety representatives
- the position of pension trustees.

Fair dismissals

There are three ways in which an individual can be legally dismissed. One: his or her employment is terminated with or without notice – this is the most common way and applies to circumstances in which somebody is summarily dismissed for gross misconduct or simply given notice of dismissal. Two: he or she is employed under a fixed-term contract and that contract comes to an end without being renewed. Three: he or she resigns (with or without notice) because of the employer's conduct – more usually known as 'constructive dismissal'. This book is not intended as a legal text – more detail on the meaning and applicability of these three definitions can be found in *Essentials of Employment*

Law by David Lewis and Malcom Sargeant (CIPD, 2002) or in the CIPD's Employment Law Service, which has been specifically designed to aid all practitioners in the legal aspects of their work.

Subsection 2 of the Employment Relations Act 1996 defines a number of reasons for which it can be fair to dismiss an employee. These are:

- insufficient capability or qualifications
- inappropriate conduct
- redundancy
- breach of statutory provision
- 'some other substantial reason'.

Dismissals relating to 'capability' (performance or absence) and 'conduct' (behaviour), together with 'some other substantial reason' (which is explained below), are probably the most common and have the most links with the disciplinary process. However, to be considered fair reasons for dismissal they have to pass the test of reasonableness set out in section 98 of the Employment Rights Act. This states in subsection 1 that:

In determining ... whether the dismissal of an employee is fair or unfair, it is for the employer to show (a) the reason for the dismissal, and (b) that it is either a reason falling within subsection 2 (see above) or that it is some other substantial reason.

Subsection 4 then goes on to say that:

the determination of the question whether the dismissal was fair or unfair, having regard to the reason shown by the employer, shall depend on whether, in the circumstances (including the size and administrative resources of the employer's undertaking), the employer acted reasonably or unreasonably in treating it as a sufficient reason for dismissing the employee; and that the question shall be determined in accordance with equity and the substantial merits of the case.

The requirement to act reasonably has been central to the operation of unfair dismissal legislation for some considerable time – one of the acid tests that employers defending a case at a tribunal can be judged on is the quality and fairness of their disciplinary procedures. This concept is supported by the legal validity given to the ACAS Code of Practice on 'Disciplinary and Grievance Procedures' and by the case of *Polkey v A E Dayton Services Ltd* [1987] IRLR 503. In the *Polkey* case the House of Lords effectively stated that failing to follow a proper procedure was unlikely to succeed as an effective defence unless the employer could prove that the outcome would have been no different irrespective of the procedure followed – a prospect that is, according to their lordships, fairly remote.

The Employment Act 2002 has now taken the principle of procedural fairness a step further. It contains a section on dismissal and disciplinary procedures which details how disciplinary matters are to be handled. These procedures are then referred to in a new section 98A of the Employment Rights Act 1996, which states that if the employer fails to follow or complete the procedure, an employee who is dismissed as a consequence will have been unfairly dismissed. This provision is further strengthened by a requirement that procedural arrangements must be complied with before cases are brought before employment tribunals, but there is also provision for a 'cooling-off period' in order to allow the parties to seek a compromise. These changes are important, and it is vital therefore that employee relations professionals make themselves familiar with the provisions of the 2002 Act.

Unfortunately, section 98A(2) then goes on to say that failure to follow a procedure is not unreasonable if employers can show that they would have decided to dismiss had a procedure been followed. For some, this makes an important change to the principle established in the *Polkey* case.

Although the Act sets out minimum qualifying periods of employment for the acquisition of employment rights, these limits can be, and have been, changed. For example, on 1 June 1999 the minimum period of continuous service with an employer to qualify for unfair dismissal was reduced from two years to one year. It is always disturbing when we hear – as we do – managers talk of having a free hand to take whatever actions they like during an individual's first months of employment. Making distinctions about how to deal with performance or behaviour issues based on an individual's length of service is to invite the possibility of inconsistency creeping into the process and to lay the organisation open to legal challenge. To avoid this possibility it is prudent for all managers and employee relations professionals to ignore an individual's length of service and treat all disciplinary issues in exactly the same way.

Disciplinary procedure

ACAS Codes of Practice

The ACAS Code of Practice on 'Disciplinary Practices and Procedures in Employment' is of great significance in the management and resolution of disciplinary issues. Although breach of the Code of Practice is, in itself, not unlawful, its provisions and impact are central to an understanding of the disciplinary process. The Code was issued under section 199 of the Trade Union and Labour Relations (Consolidation) Act 1992 and came into effect in September 2000. Its importance to the statutory process is made very clear in the preamble, which states that:

A failure on the part of any person to observe any provision of this Code of Practice does not of itself render that person liable to any proceedings. In any proceedings before an employment tribunal any Code of Practice used under sections 199 and 201 of the Trade Union and Labour Relations (Consolidation) Act 1992 is admissible in evidence, and any provision of the Code which appears to the tribunal to be relevant to any question arising in the proceedings is required to be taken into account in determining that question (Trade Union and Labour Relations (Consolidation) Act 1992, section 207). This Code has also to be taken into account by the arbitrators appointed by ACAS to determine cases brought under the ACAS Arbitration Scheme (see Section 212A of the Trade Union and Labour Relations (Consolidation) Act 1992).

Given such a very clear statement of the Code's status and taking into account the statutory underpinning of procedures by the Employment Act 2002, it is a foolish organisation that does not take seriously the need to invest time in ensuring that its own disciplinary procedures and practice are appropriate.

Because of the importance that ACAS places on drawing up disciplinary procedures and company rules, it has produced a handbook *Discipline and Grievances at Work* which provides advice on dealing with disciplinary matters. The handbook, which is based on the Code of Practice, examines:

- the need for rules and disciplinary procedures
- handling a disciplinary matter
- holding a disciplinary hearing
- deciding and implementing disciplinary or other action
- the appeals process.

An organisation's disciplinary procedure

If you examine your own organisation's disciplinary code against the ACAS template, you are likely to identify – if not a mirror image – remarkable similarities. The organisation's actual procedure should comprise:

- an oral warning
  - a subsequent written warning if the required improvement is not forthcoming
    - a final written warning if conduct or performance is still unsatisfactory
      - finally, dismissal.

There are a number of important points to note about this staged procedure. Firstly, it is important that a record be kept of every disciplinary warning issued, even an oral warning. Secondly, it is important to advise individuals how long a warning will be 'live'. 'Live' in this context indicates the length of time that a particular disciplinary sanction will 'stay on the record'. Warnings can be taken into account if further disciplinary issues arise, but warnings that have expired cannot. Many organisations will have different time-scales for different levels of warning – for example, an oral warning might be 'live' for only six months whereas a written warning might be 'live' for 12 months. Finally, it is important that employees are advised of what will happen next if the desired changes to performance or behaviour are not made. One important point to note at this stage is the rights that individual employees now have under Data Protection legislation. Under the provisions of this legislation, employees have the right to see anything that the employer holds in their personnel file – and this would include any notes made as part of the disciplinary process.

The purpose and scope of a disciplinary procedure should be very clear. It should allow all employees to understand what is expected of them in respect of conduct, attendance and job performance, and should set out the rules by which such matters will be governed. The aim is to ensure consistent and fair treatment for all.

To what extent does your organisation's disciplinary procedure meet the criterion of clarity? Does it set out the time that individual warnings will be 'live', and is it capable of ensuring consistent and fair treatment for all employees? You may consider it worth reviewing your procedure against these benchmarks.

Principles underlying the disciplinary procedure

When we look at handling discipline later in the chapter, you will note that the only way to ensure consistency is by taking a 'good practice' approach and recognising that a disciplinary procedure is more than just a series of stages. There are a number of principles underlying the procedure which are extremely important and help to ensure good personnel management practice. As with the mechanics of the procedure itself, ACAS offers guidance on good disciplinary procedures which, ACAS says, should:

- be in writing
- specify to whom they apply
- be non-discriminatory
- provide for matters to be dealt with without undue delay
- provide for proceedings, witness statements and records to be kept confidential

- indicate the disciplinary actions that may be taken

- specify the levels of management which have the authority to take the various forms of disciplinary action

- provide for workers to be informed of the complaints against them and, where possible, to see all relevant evidence before any hearing

- provide workers with an opportunity to state their case before decisions are reached

- provide workers with the right to be accompanied

- ensure that except for gross misconduct, no worker is dismissed for a first breach of discipline

- ensure that disciplinary action is not taken until the case has been carefully investigated

- ensure that workers are given an explanation for any penalty imposed

- provide a right of appeal – normally to a more senior manager – and specify the procedure to be followed.

The right to be accompanied by a shop steward or other trade union official used only to apply to workplaces where there was a recognised union. However, the Employment Relations Act 1999 has now provided all workers with the statutory right to be accompanied at disciplinary and grievance hearings. The right applies where the worker is required or invited by his or her employer to attend certain disciplinary or grievance hearings and when he or she has formally made a reasonable request to be so accompanied. In Chapter 3 we examined the concept of 'worker' and how certain employment rights had now been extended to cover them. This right is one of them, and the statutory right to be accompanied in such circumstances applies to all workers, not just employees working under a contract of employment.

It is important to emphasise that the right to be accompanied applies to every individual, not just union members, and it is of no consequence whether the organisation recognises unions or not.

Whether a worker has a statutory right to be accompanied at a disciplinary hearing depends on the nature of the hearing. When a problem first surfaces, employers often choose initially to deal with it by means of an informal interview or counselling session. So long as the informal interview or counselling session does not result in a formal warning or some other similar action, it is often more appropriate to try to resolve matters between just worker and manager. Equally, employers should not allow an investigation into the facts surrounding a disciplinary case to extend into a disciplinary hearing. If it becomes clear during the course of the informal or investigative interview that formal disciplinary action may be needed, the interview should be terminated and a formal hearing convened at which the worker should be afforded the statutory right to be accompanied.

The statutory right to be accompanied applies specifically to hearings which could result in any of these circumstances:

- the administration of a formal warning to a worker by his or her employer (ie a warning, whether about conduct or capability, that will be placed on the worker's record)

- the taking of some other action in respect of a worker by his or her employer (eg suspension without pay, demotion, or dismissal)

- the confirmation of a warning issued, or some further action taken.

After 'live' warnings expire

Although it is to be hoped that any disciplinary problems within an organisation can be resolved at the earliest opportunity, and without recourse to all levels of the procedure, the world of work is not so simple. Many managers complain that having given an individual an oral warning – or, in some cases, having got all the way through to final written warning stage – the problem to which the disciplinary action related resurfaces once the warning ceases to be 'live'. It is then assumed, mistakenly, that the whole process must begin again.

That is not so. Three points should be considered here. Firstly, for what length of time do warnings stay 'live'? If it is for too short a time, you run the risk of achieving only short-term changes in behaviour – yet on the other hand you do not want it to be too long. A sanction that remains on an employee's record for an excessive period of time relative to the original breach of discipline can certainly act as a demotivating influence. Secondly, has the warning been too narrow? Very often it makes more sense to issue a warning in such a way that an employee is left in no doubt that 'any further breaches of the company rules will result in further disciplinary action'. Thirdly, as the ACAS principles set out above indicate, the procedure may be implemented *at any stage*. If you have an employee against whom you constantly have to invoke the disciplinary procedure, or if the offence is serious but does not amount to gross misconduct, then it may be appropriate to begin with a written rather than an oral warning. In extreme cases, a final written warning could be appropriate.

Gross misconduct

Before leaving procedural requirements it is necessary to examine what the concept of gross misconduct means. You will have noted that according to the ACAS principles above it is permissible to dismiss an individual without notice if he or she has committed an act of gross misconduct. 'Gross misconduct' can be notoriously difficult to define and often difficult to prove – but ACAS very helpfully provides a list of actions that would normally fall into this category. They are:

- theft

- fraud

- deliberate falsification of records

- fighting

- assault on another person

- deliberate damage to company property

- serious incapability through alcohol or under the influence of illegal drugs

- serious negligence

- injury or damage

- acts of serious insubordination.

Quite an extensive list, it is notable also for its lack of clarity. For example, what is an act of serious insubordination? Would it cover a refusal to carry out instructions received from a supervisor? What is serious negligence, or serious incapability through alcohol?

The potential difficulties caused by this lack of clarity mean that whatever procedure you establish, it reflects the organisation's structure and culture – the norms and beliefs within which an organisation functions. This is where the writing of clear company rules is so important. Not only do they help to distinguish between ordinary and gross misconduct, but they provide employees with clear guidelines on what is acceptable in the workplace, in terms of both behaviour and performance.

> How sure are you that your organisation's disciplinary procedure is working as it should? What criteria would you use to assess whether it is or is not?

Rules in employment

Rules should be written for the benefit of both employer and employee. Their purpose should be to define and make clear exactly what standards of behaviour are expected in the workplace. Typically, rules cover the following areas:

- time-keeping

- absence

- health and safety

- misconduct

- use of company facilities

- confidentiality

- discrimination.

There are some (including ACAS) who would argue that rules about poor performance should also be included – but there are some practical difficulties about writing rules in respect of poor performance. Individuals need to know what is expected of them in respect of performance, yet the best way to do that is through a clearly written job description that sets out their prime tasks and responsibilities and tells them how their performance will be measured. Obviously, if rules relating to behaviour are broken and, as a consequence, performance is impaired – as might happen, for example, if an employee gets drunk every lunchtime – then it is easy to see a link between poor performance and rule-breaking such that the disciplinary procedure should be used to correct the problem.

But if someone is simply not competent to carry out the tasks for which he or she has been employed, it is hard to see what sort of rule has been broken – notwithstanding the fact that the disciplinary procedure may be used as a means of correcting the problem. This, though, is a minor point. The important point is to ensure that the following principles are followed whatever rules are established:

- they are clear

- they cannot be misinterpreted

- they are capable of distinguishing between ordinary misconduct and gross misconduct.

The importance of clear rules

Failure to be clear and failing to make a proper distinction between types of misconduct have caused many organisations to suffer losses at employment tribunals. It is no good having a very clear procedure, laying down the type and number of warnings that an individual should receive, if the rules being applied are imprecise or do not reflect the attitudes and requirements of the particular business. As Edwards (1994) said:

How people expect to behave depends as much on day-to-day understanding as on formal rules. Workplaces may have identical rule-books, but in one it may be accepted practice to leave early near holidays; in another, on Fridays; in a third, when a relatively lenient supervisor is in charge; and so on.

There is also a need to ensure that rules reflect current industrial practice, as is illustrated by the following case. The applicant, who was a union representative, had been dismissed for gross misconduct for gaining unauthorised access to his employer's computer system. He had gained access to a part of the system that would normally be inaccessible to him by using another employee's password. In his defence it was argued that 'he had only been playing around' with the system and that there had been no intent to obtain information to which he was not entitled. Furthermore, although he might have been doing something wrong, it was not 'gross misconduct' and could have been covered by a disciplinary warning. In upholding the dismissal for gross misconduct the Employment Appeal Tribunal (EAT) stated:

> the industrial members are clear in their view that in this modern industrial world if an employee deliberately uses an unauthorised password in order to enter or to attempt to enter a computer known to contain information to which he is not entitled, then that of itself is gross misconduct which prima facie will attract summary dismissal, although there may be some exceptional circumstances in which such a response might be held unreasonable.

Denco v Joinson (1991) IRLR 63

In essence the EAT were making the same point that had been made some years earlier in *C A Parsons & Co Ltd v McLaughlin* (1978) IRLR 65 – that some things should be so obvious it ought not to be necessary to have a rule forbidding them. However, for the avoidance of doubt, the EAT went on to say in the *Denco* case that:

> It is desirable, however, that management should make it abundantly clear to the workforce that interfering with computers will carry severe penalties. Rules concerning access to and use of computers should be reduced to writing and left near the computers for reference.

Although the comments of the Employment Appeal Tribunal, about certain things being obvious, may seem perfectly reasonable, it should be remembered that employers have an absolute duty to demonstrate that they have acted reasonably when they dismiss somebody. In *Denco*, even the EAT acknowledged that there might be circumstances in which an employer's particular response might be 'unreasonable' – and this in respect of something supposedly obvious. The message is very clear. If something is not allowed – say so, and spell out the consequences of breaching the rule. Because technology – or the ownership of the business – can change, what may have been acceptable once may later be frowned on. The prudent employee relations professional will ensure that the organisation's rules are the subject of regular monitoring to guarantee that they properly reflect the organisation's current values and requirements.

To be clear about the behavioural standards expected in any workplace, and the sanctions to be applied for non-compliance, is particularly important in distinguishing between gross and ordinary misconduct. Frequently, organisations commit the error of making vague statements in their company rules to the effect that 'certain actions *may* be treated as gross misconduct', or that 'a failure to do something *could* leave an individual liable to disciplinary action'. For example, many rules on theft that we have seen simply state that 'Theft may be considered to be gross misconduct.'

This sort of wording can only leave room for doubt and confusion. If an employee stole a large sum of money from the company, there is little doubt that he or she would be charged with gross misconduct and, if the allegation was proved, dismissed without notice. What, though, would happen if the alleged theft were of items of company stationery or spare parts for machinery? Would every manager treat the matter as one of gross misconduct and dismiss, or would the value of the items taken be a consideration? Employee relations professionals must be aware of these potential contradictions when helping to frame rules that govern the employment relationship. If it is normal practice to turn a blind eye to the misappropriation of items like stationery, then this can cause problems when someone is accused of a more serious theft. We have already high-lighted how important it is that discipline is applied fairly and consistently. Is this happening if different managers are given the opportunity to apply different standards to the same actions? Allowing different managers to take a different view about the seriousness of certain acts of theft brings inconsistency into the process. This could prove very costly at an employment tribunal. One way to avoid this problem is to stick to positive statements – for example, that theft *will* be treated as gross misconduct.

A better rule on theft might be:

Theft
Stealing from the company, its suppliers or fellow-employees is unacceptable, whatever the value or amount involved, and will be treated as gross misconduct.

Using this style of wording should help to ensure that every employee in the organisation knows the consequences of any dishonest action on his or her part. Getting managers to apply the sanction consistently is another problem – one we will deal with later in the chapter.

How often are the rules in your organisation reviewed, and when were they last updated? Do you know whether different standards apply to the enforcing of the rules?

Theft, whatever standards different organisations might apply, is usually associated in the public mind with gross misconduct, notwithstanding the problems of definition that we have just looked at. The distinction between gross misconduct and other serious infractions of the rules can often be harder to identify. The first thing to acknowledge is that no clear distinction exists, but that it is possible to apply common sense to the issue. For example, it is easy to understand that a serious assault on another person ought to be treated as gross misconduct, whereas poor timekeeping should not. Although a consistent failure to observe timekeeping standards might ultimately lead to dismissal, the two offences clearly initially indicate different outcomes – immediate dismissal in the first case and normally a verbal warning in the second. Perhaps one way in which a distinction might be drawn, therefore, is by reference to the expected outcome of the disciplinary process and to the relationship of trust that has to exist between employer and employee.

It is implicit in every contract of employment that for an employment relationship to be maintained there has to be mutual trust and confidence between employer and employee. When issues of discipline arise, that relationship is damaged. One of the purposes of disciplinary action is to bring about a change in behaviour – and if the offence is one of poor timekeeping, there is usually no question of a total breakdown of trust so that the expected outcome of disciplinary action is of improved timekeeping and a rebuilding of the relationship. If the cause of the disciplinary action was a serious assault on another employee, perhaps a manager, a disciplinary sanction might bring about a change in behaviour or ensure that the offence is not repeated, but there is a high probability that the relationship of mutual trust and confidence might be damaged beyond repair, and it might be impossible for the employment relationship to be maintained.

Handling disciplinary issues

The way in which managers and employee relations professionals approach disciplinary issues is subtly different, depending on the nature of the problem. Most organisations have some form of disciplinary procedure, and probably some company rules, but the use and application of the procedure may vary from company to company and from manager to manager. In some organisations disciplinary action is very rarely taken, either because standards are clear and accepted by employees or because standards are vague and applied haphazardly. In others, standards are maintained by an over-reliance on mechanical procedures which usually act as a demotivating influence on the workforce.

The purpose of any disciplinary procedures should be to promote:

orderly employment relations as well as fairness and consistency in the treatment of individuals. They enable organisations to influence the conduct of workers and deal with problems of poor performance and attendance thereby assisting organisations to operate effectively.

(ACAS Code)

The principles of fairness and consistency are at the heart of 'good practice', and the aim of all managers should be to handle disciplinary issues in as fair and equitable a way as is possible. They should do this because it represents 'good practice' in terms of management skill, not just because of the influence of the law. If managers are concerned only with legal compliance, they will not be as effective as those who are driven by the need to maintain 'good practice'. The law on unfair dismissal is now so ingrained into the fabric of the workplace that only by keeping to such standards does it cease to be an issue. Good managers have nothing to fear from the laws relating to individual employment rights. That is not to say that the law should be ignored, but neither should it be feared. In an ideal world managers would act in such a way that they avoided accusations of unfair treatment. But this is not an ideal world and even the best managers can find themselves defending their actions before an employment tribunal – which is why it is important for the concept of 'good practice' to become part of an organisation's ethos.

Not only does this allow employers to demonstrate consistent and fair treatment for all, but it ensures that they meet their absolute duty to act reasonably, which is set out in section 98(4)(a) of the Employment Rights Act 1996. Furthermore, such an approach not only makes good business sense, it fits the concept of 'natural justice' that is so important in handling disciplinary issues.

The 1996 Act identifies reasons for fairly dismissing an employee as poor conduct, insufficient capability and 'some other substantial reason', and all of these severally require the implementation of a disciplinary process in order for any action taken to be reasonable. However, before resorting to the disciplinary procedure, a good manager will consider whether some other route might be more appropriate. Maintaining good standards of discipline within an organisation is not just about applying the rules or operating the procedure. It is about the ability to achieve standards of performance and behaviour without using the 'big stick'. One way this might be done – and one that avoids anyone becoming embroiled in the disciplinary process – is counselling, which might provide the required change in behaviour without making the individual concerned feel that he or she was some kind of dissident.

Counselling

Counselling is more than simply offering help and advice. It is helping, in a non-threatening way, an individual to come to terms with a particular problem. The problem may be about performance, about timekeeping, about drug or alcohol abuse, or about another employee (for example, an accusation of sexual harassment). Counselling an employee, whatever the nature of the problem, needs careful preparation. With a drug or alcohol problem most managers lack the necessary skills to carry out such a sensitive task, but even if they conclude that specialist help is required, they can still help to bring the problem out into the open. In other cases, provided the problem is approached in a systematic way, this type of intervention may avoid disciplinary action.

One example of where counselling might be an appropriate first step would be in respect of an allegation of sexual harassment or bullying. Provided the complainant has not suffered any physical assault, and, most importantly, that the complainant is happy for the matter to be handled in an informal way, then counselling can be very helpful – not only to the alleged harasser but also to the victim. Without wishing to minimise or condone what can be a very serious problem in some workplaces, it can often be the case that the alleged harasser or bully does not realise that his or her behaviour or actions are causing offence or fear. Sitting down with an individual and explaining that some of his or her words or actions are causing distress to another employee can often be very effective. However, it is important not to leave it there but to monitor the situation thereafter, to ensure that the behavioural change is permanent and that the complainant is satisfied with the action taken and the eventual outcome. If not, you may find yourself dealing with a formal grievance or even a claim for 'constructive dismissal'.

> Does your organisation's disciplinary code say anything about equal opportunities or discrimination? Is there, for example, a clear rule that says sexual harassment or racial discrimination will not be tolerated? Do you have a Code of Practice that gives guidance on how to manage these sorts of problems?

Similarly, if the problem concerns poor performance, 'good practice' would be to discuss the problem with the employee concerned rather than go straight into the disciplinary procedure. The first step would be to speak to the employee, in private, explaining what aspects of performance were falling short of the desired standard and, most importantly, what actions were required by the employee to put matters right. The golden rule to remember is to set clear standards. If the employee does not know what is expected of him or her, how can he or she deliver the performance that is required? Another step in this process might be to consider whether some additional training might be an option. All of this might be best dealt with under a formal appraisal scheme, if one exists within the organisation.

The formal approach

However, if after following the counselling route there are still complaints of harassment, or the quality of work being carried out still falls below standard, then it may be necessary to begin disciplinary proceedings. Again it is important to remember the principle of 'good practice'. The operation of the disciplinary procedure can often lead to managerial disenchantment because of the claim that 'it takes too long'. This is where the employee relations professional has a clear duty to advise and guide management colleagues. Since starting down the disciplinary path can, ultimately, lead to a dismissal, it is important to remember the requirement that in taking a decision to dismiss somebody you should act reasonably and in accordance with natural justice.

It is easy to understand the frustration a line manager might feel if the disciplinary process takes a long time, but it is the employer who is in control of the process and can determine the timing. The question of fairness relates not to how long the process takes but to the quality of the procedures followed. For example, say you had an experienced employee who was responsible for carrying out a very important task within the organisation and which had serious cost implications if it were not carried out efficiently. If the task was not being performed satisfactorily, the amount of time you could allow the employee to improve his performance would be limited. Alternatively, if the employee was inexperienced and performing a task that was less cost-sensitive and important, the time allowed for improvement should be longer.

It is also necessary to consider how long a substandard performance has been allowed to continue unchallenged, because it may be the case that a previous manager was prepared to accept a lower standard of performance.

What is important in both of these scenarios is that the employee is made aware of the standard that is required and understands the importance of achieving that standard in whatever time-scale is agreed. Under the ACAS Code it is acceptable to miss out stages in the disciplinary procedure, and this may be the more obvious solution if the consequences of the poor performance are so serious.

Using the disciplinary procedure

Whatever the nature of the problem, once the decision has been taken to invoke the formal disciplinary procedure it is important to ensure that its application cannot be challenged. The following guidelines, which are broken down into two stages, help to ensure a consistent and fair approach.

Preparing for the disciplinary hearing

Now that the Employment Act 2002 sets out minimum procedural standards for the conduct of dismissal and disciplinary meetings, the preparatory process becomes particularly important. There are various steps that must be taken in preparing to conduct a disciplinary interview, and a number of points to consider, some of which are statutory requirements:

1   Prepare carefully and ensure that the person conducting the disciplinary hearing has all the facts. This seems straightforward, but it is not always possible to obtain all the facts. Frequently, the evidence of alleged misconduct is no more than circumstantial, particularly in cases involving theft. However, the guiding principle is to ensure that a thorough investigation takes place, and that whatever facts are available are presented – including, where appropriate, written witness statements. Sometimes people will ask to remain anonymous when providing information during a disciplinary investigation, and such a request has to be treated with a great deal of care. If possible, seek some form of corroborative evidence and try to check whether the anonymous informant's motives are genuine.

2   Ensure that the employee under a cloud knows what the nature of the complaint is. This again seems straightforward, but is often the point at which things begin to go wrong. For example, it would not be sufficient to tell an employee that he or she is to attend a disciplinary hearing in respect of their poor performance. He or she must be provided with sufficient detail in order to be able to prepare an adequate defence.

3   Ensure that the employee knows the procedure to be followed. Simply because an individual was provided with a copy of the organisation's disciplinary code when commencing employment does not imply that he or she is totally familiar with the procedure to be followed. It is always wise to provide such individuals with a new copy of the disciplinary procedure – not least because there may have been amendments since they received their original version.

4   Advise the employee of his or her right to be accompanied (see above). Where individuals work in a unionised environment, this tends to be automatic, so that an invitation to attend the meeting is sent directly to the appropriate union official. However, in non-unionised environments, people are not always sure who would be an appropriate person to accompany them or whether they want to be accompanied at all. As a matter of good practice it is wise to encourage people to be accompanied, but if they refuse, that refusal has to be respected. Following such a refusal the fact that the employee wishes to attend a disciplinary interview alone should be recorded.

5 Enquire if there are any mitigating circumstances. What is or is not a mitigating circumstance is dictated by each case. It is not for the employer to identify matters of mitigation, but it is important to ask the employee facing a disciplinary sanction whether there are any particular circumstances that might account for his or her actions. Whether an individual manager accepts what may seem to be no more than excuses is a question of fact determined by individual circumstances. For example, an employee with a bad timekeeping record might be excused if he or she was having to care for a sick relative before attending work, whereas another employee might put forward a less acceptable excuse, such as a broken alarm clock.

6 Are you being consistent? This is where the employee relations professional can provide invaluable assistance for the line manager. Most line managers deal very rarely with disciplinary issues and may not be aware of previous actions or approaches that have been taken in respect of disciplinary issues. The employee relations professional can provide the advice and information that ensures a consistent approach.

7 Consider explanations. This is not the same as mitigating circumstances or excuses. This is the opportunity that you must give an employee to explain his or her acts or omissions. For example, if the hearing was about poor performance, the employee might want to point out factors that have inhibited performance but which might not be immediately apparent to the line manager conducting the hearing. There may be issues around the quality of training received or the quality of instructions given.

8 Allow the employee time to prepare a case. The question here is of how much time. It is important that issues of discipline are dealt with speedily once an employee has been advised of the complaint against him or her, but it is important for the employee not to feel unfairly pressured in putting together any defence he or she may have.

9 Arrange a suitable time and place for the interview. This would seem to be obvious, but as with so many things in employee relations, what may seem obvious to the specialist is not always apparent to the busy line manager. There is a tendency for managers to arrange meetings within their own offices where the potential for being interrupted is more pronounced or privacy less easily guaranteed. It is also important to remember that the employee might request an alternative date to the one suggested, particularly if his or her chosen companion or trade union official cannot attend.

10 Ensure that personnel records etc are available. This means not just basic information about the individual but also records

relating to any previous disciplinary warnings, attendance, performance appraisals, etc.

11 Where possible, the manager too should be accompanied. It is very unwise for a manager to conduct a disciplinary interview alone because of the possible need at some future time to have corroboration of what was said. It also helps to rebut any allegations of bullying or intimidation that may be made by a disgruntled employee.

12 Try to ensure the attendance of witnesses. This should not be a problem if the people concerned are in your company's employ, but might prove difficult if they are outsiders.

The importance of careful preparation cannot be stressed too strongly, for it is at this stage that things often go wrong. Where tribunals often express concern, for example, is in relation to the preliminary stages of the disciplinary process. Employers are often criticised for failing to give sufficient information to the employee about the nature of the complaint against him or her. We have certainly found examples of employers who have deliberately withheld information to prevent employees from constructing plausible explanations for their conduct or actions.

The disciplinary interview

Good preparation helps the second part of the process – conducting the actual disciplinary interview. There are seven points to remember at this stage:

1 Introduce those present – not just on the grounds of courtesy but because an employee facing a possible sanction is entitled to know who is going to be involved in any decision. In a small workplace this may be unnecessary, but it can be important in larger establishments.

2 Explain the purpose of the interview and how it will be conducted. This builds on the need to ensure that the employee fully understands the nature of the complaint against him or her and the procedure to be followed. As with any hearing, however informal, what it is for, what the possible outcomes are, and the method by which it is to be conducted are important prerequisites for demonstrating that natural justice may be seen to be done.

3 Set out precisely the nature of the complaint and outline the case by briefly going through the evidence. This may seem like overkill, but it is important to ensure that there are no misunderstandings. It is important also to ensure that that the employee and his or her representative, if there is one, are given copies of any witness statements and afforded a proper opportunity to read them.

4 Give the employee the right to reply. Put simply: no right of reply – no evident natural justice.

5   Allow time for general questioning, cross-examination of wit-nesses, etc. If this does not happen, it might later be difficult to persuade a tribunal that the test of reasonableness had been achieved.

6   No matter how carefully you prepare, or how well you are con-ducting a disciplinary hearing, things may not always proceed smoothly. People may get upset or angry and the whole process become very emotional. In such circumstances it might be advis-able to adjourn and reconvene at a later date. If this happens, it is important to make it clear to the employee that the issue cannot be avoided and a further hearing will be held.

7   Sum up afterwards. There is a need to be clear about what con-clusions have been reached and what decisions are still to be made, and for this reason it is better to adjourn so that these decisions may be properly considered and thought through.

Careful preparation and a well-conducted interview are not guarantees that individuals will not complain of unfairness, but they are essential if the test of reasonableness is to be satisfied.

Misconduct during employment

There are two distinct types of misconduct: persistent rule-breaking and gross misconduct. In most instances, dealing with the persistent rule-breaker is relatively straightforward, provided that the organisation's disciplinary code is applied in a sensible and equitable manner. Assuming that it has been possible to go through some form of coun-selling with the employee, but that the required change in behaviour has not materialised, then it is likely that the only alternative is to begin the disciplinary process. The likely first step is a verbal or written warning followed, if necessary, by the subsequent stages in the procedure, lead-ing ultimately to dismissal.

Although the dismissal of an employee is never an easy task for a man-ager, it can – if the steps outlined above are followed – be a relatively straightforward process. Furthermore, individuals who are dismissed for persistent infringements of the rules, about which they have had a series of warnings and an opportunity to appeal, rarely go to employ-ment tribunals. It is difficult for an individual to claim that the employer acted unreasonably when he or she has been given a number of oppor-tunities to modify his or her actions. The only complaint that an individ-ual might have in such circumstances is that the procedure itself was unfair or had been applied contrary to the rules of natural justice. This might happen if, for instance, some people were disciplined for breaches of the rules and others were not.

> Imagine that your organisation had dismissed somebody for bad time-keeping and unauthorised absences, and the employee had challenged this in an employment tribunal. What evidence would you need to present in support of your organisation's action?

Gross misconduct

Gross misconduct, on the other hand, presents totally different problems for the manager. We earlier examined some of the issues surrounding the concept of gross misconduct, and the need to be absolutely clear what breaches of the rules *will* mean as opposed to what they *might* mean. For the manager who is called upon to deal with a case of alleged gross misconduct it is vitally important that all procedural steps are strictly adhered to because mistakes can be costly. Managers are often under extreme pressure to resolve matters quickly, not just because it is much fairer to the accused individual that the matter be got out of the way speedily but because other colleagues may have already prejudged the outcome. Pressure cannot always be avoided, but it is necessary that in such circumstances the requirements to prepare properly and conduct a fair hearing are not forgotten.

Some cases of gross misconduct are very clear-cut – the employee concerned either admits the offence or there are sufficient witnesses to confirm that the alleged offence was indeed committed by the employee in question. In such cases the first decision for the employer is to decide whether to treat the matter as gross misconduct – for which the penalty is summary dismissal without notice, or with pay in lieu of notice – or to take a more lenient line It is a decision that is made easier if the company rules are clear and unambiguous about what constitutes gross misconduct. But in our experience many cases of gross misconduct are not clear-cut, and managers are very unsure about how to deal with them. Some of the cases in which we have been asked to assist include suspected theft of goods or money, suspicion of tampering with time-recording devices, suspected false expense claims, or seeking the payment of sick pay while fit for work. One reason managers can be unsure about dealing with such offences is that some of them could lead to criminal charges being laid against the employee or employees concerned.

One way to approach this very sensitive issue is to ensure that 'the Burchell test' is applied. This test relates to a case that was decided in 1978 involving an incident of alleged theft (*British Home Stores v Burchell* 1978 IRLR 379). The specific facts of the case are not particularly important, but the case itself is significant because of the test of reasonableness that flowed from it. The Burchell test states that where an employee is suspected of a dismissable offence and then dismissed, an employer must show that:

- the dismissal was genuinely for that offence and the offence was not used as a pretext

- the belief that the employee committed the offence was based on reasonable grounds – that is, on the evidence produced, the employer was entitled to say that it was more probable that the employee did, in fact, commit the offence than that he or she did not

- the belief was based on a reasonable investigation in the circumstances – that the employer's investigation took place before the employee was dismissed and included an opportunity for the employee to offer an explanation.

Implications of the Burchell test

Let us look at the test in a little more detail and try to relate it to events as they might take place in the working environment. Take the example of an expenses claim that seems fraudulent. The first part of Burchell says that the dismissal must be genuine and not use the alleged offence as a pretext – as a convenient means of dismissing an employee whose face no longer fits, or who has a history of misconduct over which no previous action has been taken. The second and third parts of Burchell relate to the employer's belief in the employee's guilt and to the standard of the investigation carried out. As Lewis and Sargeant (2000, p262) state:

> *The question to be determined is not whether, by an objective standard, the employer's belief that the employee was guilty of the misconduct was well-founded, but whether the employer believed that the employee was guilty and was entitled so to believe having regard to the investigation conducted.*

Using the Burchell test in the case of a suspected fraudulent expenses claim, the employer would have to be very diligent in assembling the evidence. What guidelines were laid down for the benefit of those allowed to claim expenses? What expenses had been accepted in the past? Were the same standards applied consistently to all staff? Had any other employee made a similar claim in the past without challenge? Assembling such an array of evidence is only likely to happen if there is a thorough investigation. But this is only the first part of the process – the employee is also entitled to offer an explanation. What do you do if the explanation is linked to the lack of guidelines about what is and what is not claimable?

Although the findings in the *Parsons* case (see above) – that some things are so obvious that they do not need a rule – are relevant, the seniority of the employee concerned might also be relevant. A 'reasonable' belief that a senior employee, who regularly claimed expenses, was acting dishonestly might be easier to demonstrate than a situation in which a junior employee was claiming expenses for the first time. We acknowledged above the uncertainties that are sometimes encountered when the possibility of criminal proceedings is on the agenda. The question is, can we dismiss somebody if we have asked the police to investigate with a view to prosecution? The short answer is Yes – provided that the Burchell test guidelines are followed. Quite properly, the burden of proof placed on an employer in such circumstances is totally different from the burden of proof imposed by the criminal justice system. In a criminal trial the prosecution must prove 'beyond all reasonable doubt' that an offence was committed. This is entirely reasonable when an individual's liberty is at risk, and it is why, under the Burchell test, somebody can be dismissed 'fairly' for dishonesty who may then be found 'not guilty' in a criminal trial.

Insufficient capability

This is the second of the fair reasons for dismissing an employee, and we need to consider it under two subheadings – firstly, insufficient capability that is linked to an employee's simple inability to do the job properly (lack of competence), and secondly, insufficient capability that relates to an individual's being unable to do the job because of poor health.

Advising a line manager whose team includes a member delivering a less than adequate performance is something that the employee relations specialist does frequently. Very often the initial step in this advisory role is to persuade the line manager not to take precipitate action. It is not unusual for the personnel professional to be told by a manager that a particular employee is 'useless', and that he or she 'needs help to get rid of them'. Convincing a line manager in these circumstances not to launch into a formal disciplinary process without considering what other options are open is very important. Earlier, we looked at the question of counselling and noted that in the event of an ultimate dismissal, an employment tribunal would want to satisfy itself that the employee knew what standards were expected of him or her, and that he or she had been given an opportunity to achieve them – and that this had happened before any formal disciplinary procedures had begun. Another option might be the provision of alternative work for the employee concerned if he or she has demonstrated incapability for the tasks currently allocated.

Whatever option is taken, the employee is entitled, on the grounds of fairness, to be told exactly what is required of him or her, what new standards are being set, and the time-scale in which he or she is expected to achieve them. During the period of time the individual is given to reach the desired standards, a good manager ensures that he or she is kept informed of progress – this again is the operation of the principle of 'good practice' or good management habits.

One important point to remember in looking at capability is the obligation placed on employers by the Disability Discrimination Act 1995, the principal purpose of which is to protect disabled people from discrimination in the field of employment. The issue is dealt with below.

Similarly, insuffcent capability through poor health frequently results in long spells of absence from work. This issue too is dealt with in the section below.

Managing absence

Absence can be one of the most emotive issues that any manager has to face and has always to be handled with sensitivity. There is limitless scope for disputes to arise in this difficult area, and it is important that the employee relations professional is aware of all the circumstances in which absences can occur, and where these involve legal rights – time off work for domestic emergencies is one example – understands the breadth of such rights.

Absence from work can occur for a number of reasons. Some absences – like holidays or paternity leave – are normally arranged in advance and cause minimum disruption to the employing organisation. The absences that really cause disruption within an organisation are those that are unplanned, because the employee concerned is sick, has simply failed to turn up for work, or has been overtaken by a domestic emergency. Only for the second reason would it be normal to treat it as a breach of the rules on unauthorised absence and deal with it as a case of misconduct.

One reason for unauthorised absence might be that an employee has failed to return from an authorised absence – say, a holiday – at the due time. An individual's returning late from holiday has become a much more widespread problem in recent years due to the increase in overseas travel: for most people who return to work late in such circumstances the fault lies with delayed air flights or other travel problems. On the part of some employers the effect of a late return from holiday may be minimal, and they may treat it as no more than an irritation – but for others, particularly at a time of the year when large numbers of people are on holiday, the disruption caused can be serious. Notwithstanding the fact that the cause of the problem (a late flight) was outside the employee's control, the employer might take the view that steps which could have been taken to minimise the disruption – for example, a telephone call – were not. Whether disciplinary action follows in such circumstances will clearly rest on the facts of each individual case, but in any event if action is taken it should follow the guidance given above for preparing and conducting a disciplinary interview, particularly in respect of mitigating circumstances and presenting an explanation.

However, in most establishments the most widespread cause of absence from work is sickness, or alleged sickness – and although it would be wholly unreasonable to treat a case of genuine sickness as a disciplinary matter, incapacity for work on the grounds of poor health *can* be a fair reason for dismissing an employee. For this reason in particular, the way in which an employer deals with health-related absences is very important.

Sickness absence

Dealing with sickness absence can be a minefield for any manager, but for the employee relations specialist expected to give clear and timely advice it is even more so. Estimates of the annual cost to the UK economy of sickness absence currently hover around the £10 billion mark – so absence really does require to be managed effectively. Unauthorised absence is usually a disciplinary matter, but most absences do not fall into this category. They are recorded as sickness. Without wishing to suggest that any employee deliberately seeks to be untruthful, notifying the employer of 'sickness' remains the most common reason for absence from work. It has also to be said that although the overwhelming majority of employees have minimal periods of sickness absence, most organisations include staff whose sickness record is poor. Such people may well consistently notch up as many as 25–30 sick days per annum through bouts of 'flu', 'migraine' and 'stomach upsets'.

The second CIPD annual survey into employee absence, published in 2001, exposes high levels of 'hidden absence' among employees, and reveals that up to a third of all absences are considered by employers to be less than genuine. That on average every single employee now takes three days off per annum causes the survey to put the annual cost of sickness absence at £487 per employee. Not surprisingly, 94 per cent of the survey respondents described sickness absence as 'a very significant business burden'.

In order to manage such a problem effectively, the starting-point has to be adequate record-keeping. ACAS advises that 'Records showing lateness and the duration of and reason for all spells of absence should be kept to help monitor absence levels.' Such records enable a manager to substantiate whether a problem of persistent absence is real or imagined. All too often the employee relations specialist who is asked for advice is expected to work with insufficient data. Managing absence is not just about applying rules or following procedure: it is about addressing problems of persistent absence quickly and acting consistently. This sends out a clear and unambiguous message to all employees that absence is regarded as a serious matter.

But how do you act rigorously and at the same time retain fairness and consistency? The most effective way is through the 'return-to-work' interview. This has been shown to be the most effective method of controlling sickness absence. The employer demonstrates that absence matters – that the company has noticed the employee's absence, and that it cares.

In their booklet *Discipline and Grievance at Work*, ACAS sets out guidelines for handling frequent and persistent short-term absences which support the principle of the return-to-work interview and help to ensure a consistency of approach. Factors that must be taken into account are:

- Absences should be investigated promptly and the employee asked to give an explanation.

- Where there is no medical advice to support frequent self-certified absences, the employee should be asked to consult a doctor to establish whether medical treatment is necessary and whether the underlying reason for absence is work-related.

- If after investigation it appears that there were no good reasons for the absences, the matter should be dealt with under the disciplinary procedure.

- Where absences arise from temporary domestic problems, the employer in deciding appropriate action should consider whether an improvement in attendance is likely. It is also important to consider whether any of the absences should, or could have been, covered by the Maternity and Parental Leave (Time off for dependants in an emergency) Regulations 1999. These regulations are discussed in more detail below.

- In all cases the employee should be told what improvement is expected and warned of the likely consequences if it does not occur.

- If there is no improvement, the employee's age, length of service, performance, the likelihood of a change in attendance, the availability of suitable alternative work, and the effect of past and future absences on the business should all be taken into account on deciding appropriate action.

Persistent absence

Frequent short-term absences can be very difficult to manage and may become the cause of serious conflict between employees. Where one individual within a work group is constantly absent, it is usually his or her colleagues who suffer because they have to take on additional duties or alter their hours at short notice. It is they, not the management, who are inconvenienced – and they are entitled to expect that their employer will do something to manage the problem. So if doubt still remains about the nature of the illness, injury or disability that is causing the employee's absence, the employee should be asked if he or she is prepared to be examined by an independent doctor to be appointed by the company. Normally, unless there is some form of contractual provision which allows for this, an employee cannot be compelled to comply.

However, with the growth of occupational sick pay schemes, many organisations have overcome this problem by building compulsion into their scheme rules. And indeed, advising an employee that such an examination will be required if attendance does not improve is often sufficient to resolve the problem.

Complications can arise, however, when the injury or illness responsible for the persistent short-term absences is genuine. It would never be reasonable to discipline an individual in such circumstances – but it *can* be fair to dismiss him or her. Where such a situation does arise, it is absolutely imperative that a careful process of assessment and examination is carried out. This would include obtaining a comprehensive medical report setting out full details of the individual's capacity to work and consideration of other options – part-time work, reduced hours, alternative work, etc.

All of the above makes good sense and is consistent with the principle of managing absence with a 'good practice' ethos. Employee relations professionals must, however, consider what other methods they can use for managing absence. They might include the introduction of flexitime and annual hours schemes so that employees could manage domestic commitments without resorting to 'taking a day off sick'. In short, employers might do well to consider how they can become more family-friendly.

Long-term absence

The section above dealt with the persistent short-term absentee and noted that although some absences might not be genuine, many were. A similar problem arises in respect of employees whose absence is long-term. It is reasonable to presume that the majority of long-term absences are also genuine and would certainly be covered by some form of medical certification. Nevertheless, they still have to be managed – and again, ACAS provides guidance. In its view, it is important that:

- The employee should be contacted periodically so that he or she maintains regular contact with the employer.

- The employee should be advised if employment is at risk.

- The employee should be asked if he or she will consent to his or her own doctor's being contacted. The employee's right to refuse consent, to see any report that is made, and to request amendments to it, must be clearly spelled out.

- The employee's doctor should be asked if the employee will be able to return to work and the nature of the work he or she will be capable of carrying out.

- On the basis of the report received, the employer should consider whether alternative work is available.

- Employers are not expected to create special jobs, nor are they expected to be medical experts. They should simply take action on the basis of the medical evidence.

- As with other absences, the possibility of an independent medical examination should be considered.

- Where an employee refuses to co-operate in providing medical evidence, he or she should be told, in writing, that a decision will have to be taken on the basis of what information is available, and that the decision may be to dismiss.

- Where the employee's job can no longer be kept open and no suitable alternative is available, the employee should be informed of the likelihood of dismissal.

This last point can be very emotive. When dealing with an employee who has long service, who boasts an exemplary work record and who is genuinely suffering from or incapacitated by a serious illness, telling him or her that he or she is likely to lose the job can be very difficult – not only because the employer is genuinely concerned about the impact on the employee of such a decision, but because the employer may be concerned also about the possibility of legal action for unfair dismissal being taken against the company.

In cases where illness or injury is obvious and the medical prognosis reasonably clear, following the ACAS guidelines will help to ensure that the decisions that are made will stand up to external scrutiny. But what happens when the injury or illness is not so obvious? 'Bad backs' and stress are two examples that spring to mind. Because the words 'stress' and 'backache' are used so loosely – even by doctors on medical certificates – an employer must deal with these cases both carefully and critically. The way forward may only emerge over time. Often both employer and employee will have to wait for many weeks, if not months, for further medical investigations to be carried out before the appropriate form of action can be decided. For personnel professionals this can be a difficult time; they are often under pressure from line manager colleagues to support a premature decision to dismiss so that a replacement can be recruited. Effective employee relations professionals who have developed their influencing skills should, however, be able to persuade colleagues that acting precipitately is not in the best interests of the organisation.

Disabilities and absence

It is possible that individuals who have contracted a serious illness, have suffered a serious injury or are suffering from 'stress' will be deemed to be labouring under a disability. So what happens if the reason for absence is held to be a disability as defined by the Disability Discrimination Act (DDA)?

In the context of managing absence, section 4(2)(d) of the Act states that 'It is unlawful for an employer to discriminate against a disabled person by dismissing them or subjecting them to any other detriment.' Because the Act applies equally to existing employees as well as to new recruits, employers should be careful when initiating action in respect of employees with a permanent health problem to pay due regard to the legislation. Section 6(1) of the Act states that an employer has a duty to make 'reasonable adjustments' if any employee is disadvantaged by either the physical features of the workplace or by the arrangements for the work itself. The Code of Practice which accompanies the Act lists a number of 'reasonable adjustments' that an employer might have to consider. These include:

- making adjustments to premises
- allocating some of the disabled person's duties to another person
- transferring the person to fill an existing vacancy
- altering the person's working hours
- assigning the person to a different place of work
- allowing the person to be absent during working hours as necessary for rehabilitation, assessment or treatment
- giving the person training, or arranging for training to be given
- acquiring or modifying equipment to suit the person
- modifying instructions or reference manuals to apply to a person so disabled
- modifying procedures for testing or assessment
- providing a reader or interpreter as and when necessary
- providing supervision.

Clearly, employers will not have to make 'reasonable adjustments' in respect of all 'sick' employees – only those who fit the Act's definition of disability. A disabled person is a person with 'a physical or mental impairment which has a substantial and long-term adverse effect on [the] ability to carry out normal day-to-day activities' (section 1). This chapter is about discipline, not disability, but employee relations specialists must be aware that the disability legislation imposes challenges that must be taken into account when managing absence. Most importantly, it must be remembered that dismissal of a disabled employee because of the disability is automatically unfair, and on that basis is almost certainly impossible to defend.

Absence and domestic emergencies

The Employment Relations Act 1999 amended the Employment Rights Act 1996 to provide employees with a right to take a reasonable amount of time off work to deal with unexpected or sudden emergencies – for example:

- if a dependant falls ill or has been injured or assaulted

- when a dependant is having a baby (this does not include taking time off after the birth of a child)

- to make longer-term care arrangements for a dependant who is ill or injured

- to deal with the death of a dependant

- to deal with a disruption in care arrangements for a dependant

- to deal with an incident involving a young son or daughter during school hours.

The details of the right to time off are contained in the Maternity and Parental Leave (Time off for dependants in an emergency) Regulations 1999, which set out the circumstances in which employees can use the provisions and describes how they can, if necessary, enforce their rights. Essentially, the emergency for which an employee is claiming time off must involve a dependant of theirs. A dependant is the husband, wife, child or parent of the employee, although the definition also includes someone who resides in the same household as the employee – for example, a partner or an elderly relative. It does not include tenants or boarders.

Neither the number of times an employee can be absent from work nor the length of the time off that can be taken is specified in the regulations, but in most cases one or two days should be sufficient to deal with the problem. The fact that such time off is unpaid is, in most circumstances, enough to limit the length of the absence anyway.

However, any right is open to abuse either by unscrupulous employers or by employees acting in bad faith. Where an employee believes that he or she has suffered a detriment, or in extreme cases, been dismissed in seeking to take time off, he or she has the right to take the matter to an employment tribunal. An employer who believes that the right is being abused should deal with the situation according to the organisation's normal disciplinary procedures.

In the context of employee relations, this right might be said to offer an opportunity to an employer. In Chapter 2 we noted that it was important for the employee relations professional to see the law as more than an object of compliance – that some rights could be seen as a minimum standard which could be built on by a progressive employer, and that the proactive employee relations professional could provide the evidence to support such development. We also said, more recently above, that in order to reduce some absences employers might do well to consider more family-friendly policies. The right to time off for domestic emergencies could be the springboard for the creation of such a policy.

Some other substantial reason

The final grounds on which a dismissal is fair, as set out in the 1996 Employment Rights Act, is 'some other substantial reason'. This concept was introduced into the legislation 'so as to give tribunals the discretion to accept as a fair reason for dismissal something that would not conveniently fit into any of the other categories' (Lewis and Sargeant, 2000). Dismissals for 'some other substantial reason' have, as Lewis and Sargeant point out, been upheld in respect of employees who have been sentenced to a term of imprisonment, employees who cannot get on with each other, or employees who have problems with one of the organisation's customers. Interestingly, the cases which Lewis and Sargeant quote all relate to the 1970s and 1980s, which might indicate that businesses are now less reliant on this rather vague concept. It is certainly the case that the more professional employee relations specialists, recognising that such issues and conflicts do arise, have amended their disciplinary procedures accordingly and many organisations now have a rule relating to general conduct which may be worded in something like the following way:

> Any conduct detrimental to the interests of the company, its relations with the public, its customers and suppliers, damaging to its public image or offensive to other employees in the company, constitutes a disciplinary offence.

It is easy to see how such a rule could be used to deal with any of the examples cited by Lewis and Sargeant. In the context of managing discipline, however, what is needed is a much more systematic route. To someone who is not a lawyer 'some other substantial reason' can be a rather vague concept – being able to proceed against an individual for a breach of a specific rule is much clearer to everybody involved.

Appeals

Every disciplinary procedure must contain an appeals process – otherwise, it is almost impossible to demonstrate that the organisation has acted reasonably within the law. In common with every other aspect of the disciplinary process, it is important to ensure fairness and consistency within an appeals procedure which should provide for appeals to be dealt with as quickly as possible. An employee should be able to appeal at every stage of the disciplinary process, and common sense dictates that any appeal should be heard by someone who is senior to the person imposing the disciplinary sanction. This will not always be possible, particularly in smaller organisations, but if the person who hears the appeal is the same as the person who imposed the original sanction, then ACAS advise that the person should hear the appeal and act as impartially as possible. In essence, an appeal in these circumstances is going to be no more than a review of the original decision, but perhaps in a calmer and more objective manner.

As with the original disciplinary hearing, an appeal falls into two parts: action prior to the appeal, and the actual hearing itself. Before any appeal hearing the employee should be told what the arrangements are and what his or her rights under the procedure are. At the same time it is important that the employer obtains, and reads, any relevant documentation. It is equally essential that at the appeal hearing the appellant should be told its purpose, how it will be conducted and what decisions the person or persons hearing the appeal may make. Any new evidence must be considered and all relevant issues properly examined. Although appeals are not to be regarded as an opportunity to seek a more sympathetic assessment of the issue in question, it is true that appeals are not routinely dismissed. Overturning a bad or unjust decision is just as important as confirming a fair decision. It is an effective way of signalling to employees that all disciplinary issues are dealt with consistently and objectively.

Many organisations fall into the trap of using their grievance procedure in place of a proper appeals process. This is to be avoided wherever possible. The grievance procedure should be reserved for resolving problems that arise out of employment, and is covered in the next chapter. Finally, not only should appeals be dealt with in a timely fashion but the disciplinary procedure beforehand should specify time-limits within which appeals should be lodged.

CONCLUSION

In this chapter we have explained why managing employee performance and behaviour is such a key area. We have looked at the origins of disciplinary procedures and how they have developed over time. We have also provided an outline of the current legal position – although it is important to remember that this is not a legal text and that because the law is constantly evolving an employee relations professional should check legal facts each time a performance or behaviour problem arises.

Poor management of performance and behaviour can create employee relations problems, and for that reason we make no apology for the emphasis we place on the importance of good practice and the need to act professionally. We have tried to reflect the realities of managing these issues within an organisational context because discussions that we have had with managers from a whole range of organisations show that these are the issues that can cause major employee relations problems, often because breaches of the rules are treated with differing degrees of seriousness (even to the extent sometimes of being utterly ignored) by different managers.

There is also an overwhelming business case for the effective management of employee performance and behaviour. More and more organisations are recognising the value that can be added by involving employees in the business and gaining their commitment to organisational objectives. Assuming that this is a trend that most organisations would wish to see continue, an employee relations climate that recognises the rights and responsibilities of both parties to the employment relationship is absolutely vital.

KEY POINTS

- A fair and effective disciplinary procedure is one that concentrates on improving or changing behaviour and not one that relies on the principle of punishment.

- There must always be a just cause for disciplinary action, whether it is misconduct, inability to perform the job in a satisfactory manner, or some other reason.

- Good practice is an important principle because it helps to ensure fairness and consistency.

- The statement of particulars of employment must specify any disciplinary rules applicable to the employee and must also include information about any procedures applicable to the taking of disciplinary decisions.

- There is a need for clear and unambiguous rules within the workplace, and both procedures and rules should be regularly monitored.

- It is important to discuss performance and behavioural problems with the employee (counselling) before using the disciplinary procedures.

- Disciplinary interviews should be thoroughly prepared for and then conducted in a professional manner.

- Employees are entitled to know the cause of complaints against them, entitled to representation, entitled to challenge evidence, and entitled to a right of appeal.

- Managing absence should be a priority for any organisation, and appropriate polices should be established for the purpose.

Further reading

ADVISORY, CONCILIATION AND ARBITRATION SERVICE (2001a) *Discipline and Grievances at Work: The ACAS advisory handbook.* London, ACAS.

ADVISORY, CONCILIATION AND ARBITRATION SERVICE (2001b) *Disciplinary and Grievance Procedures: The ACAS Code of Practice.* London, ACAS.

CHARTERED INSTITUTE OF PERSONNEL AND DEVELOPMENT Employment Law Service.

CHARTERED INSTITUTE OF PERSONNEL AND DEVELOPMENT (2001) *Employee Absence: A survey of management policy and practice.* London, CIPD. June.

EDWARDS P. (1994) 'Discipline and the creation of order', in K. Sisson (ed.), *Personnel Management: A comprehensive guide to theory and practice in Britain.* Oxford, Blackwell.

Employment Rights Act 1996.

Employment Rights (Dispute Resolution) Act 1998.

Employment Relations Act 1999.

Employment Act 2002.

LEWIS D. *and* SARGEANT M. (2000) *Essentials of Employment Law.* 6th edn. London, Chartered Institute of Personnel and Development.

LEWIS D. *and* SARGEANT M. (2002) *Essentials of Employment Law.* 7th edn. London, Chartered Institute of Personnel and Development.

Introduction

A grievance is a complaint by an employee that something in the management's behaviour has breached his or her employment rights – and that he or she is unhappy about it. It may be real or it may be the result of a misconception or a misunderstanding. In either case, settling it quickly and effectively is important. To individuals concerned, their grievance is important. In addition, employee grievances cannot be ignored by the organisation because an individual grievance that is mishandled can escalate to a serious collective dispute. The purpose of managing grievances is to rectify matters that have been and are going wrong, by:

● investigating the situation

● identifying what has caused the employee complaint

● taking the appropriate action to resolve the complaint to the mutual satisfaction of the employee and the management.

A grievance must be resolved at the earliest possible stage. A key aspect of fairness at work is the opportunity for the individual employee to complain about, and receive redress for, unfair treatment. In this chapter we examine the fundamentals of managing employee grievances as an important element in the work of the employee relations professional. The 1998 Workplace Employee Relations Survey reported that in 95 per cent of the workplaces it surveyed the responsibilities of employee relations managers included managing employee grievances.

Managing grievances is, however, primarily a line manager's responsibility. In this line managers require help, advice, support and expertise from the employee relations professional. Such assistance includes devising effective grievance procedures and training line managers to operate these procedures in a fair, reasonable and consistent manner. The employee relations professional is also responsible for monitoring and reviewing the effectiveness of the operation of grievance procedures, especially in terms of outcomes.

The business case for resolving grievances

Employee grievances may arise even in the best-run organisations on a wide variety of issues, including discrimination, harassment and bullying. If grievances are not dealt with or handled quickly, they are likely to fester and harm the employment relationship. A grievance may be felt by a group as well as an individual, and in that case if left unresolved, may develop into a major collective dispute involving a trade union. However, whether individual or collective, all employee grievances have the potential to damage the quality of an organisation's employee relations and thereby its competitive position. The golden rule to bear in managing employee grievances is that they are important to those who express them and must be treated seriously by management.

Employee grievances are an outward expression of worker dissatisfaction which, if not resolved, can result in unsatisfactory work behaviour which has adverse consequences for the organisation's competitive position. Unresolved dissatisfaction gives rise to:

- employee frustration
- deteriorating interpersonal relationships
- low morale
- poor performance, seen in lower productivity and a poorer quality of output or service
- disciplinary problems, including poor performance by employees
- the resignation and loss of good staff (increased labour turnover)
- increased employee absenteeism
- the withdrawal of employee goodwill
- a resistance to change – if employees feel they have been treated badly, they are likely to be resistant to proposed changes.

In addition, unresolved grievances can cause employees who that feel their employment rights have not been respected to resign from their employment and to claim a fundamental breach of contract amounting to 'constructive dismissal'.

If an organisation has the reputation of having a high level of employee dissatisfaction, it will represent a disincentive for individuals or organisations to purchase goods and/or services from it, fearing that the goods and/or services are likely to be of poor quality. A reputation for employee dissatisfaction also gives an organisation a 'bad employer' image in the labour market. Such an image accentuates an organisation's problems in recruiting and retaining the appropriate quantity and quality of labour services necessary to achieve its corporate objectives.

Organisations in which there are employee feelings of unfair treatment will have relatively higher cost structures than competitor organisations that have absolutely and relatively lower levels of employee dissatisfaction. The former organisation has a competitive disadvantage relative to the latter, which will be expressed in worse sales, revenue and profitability.

If grievances are not addressed, they can adversely affect an organisation and the quality of life of its employees. It is therefore essential to the continued prosperity and wellbeing of the company and its employees that employee complaints about management behaviour are addressed as quickly as possible and as near to their source as can be. There is a clear business case for the effective and professional management of employee grievances.

It is important that employees know to whom they can take a grievance, and that new employees are informed of the grievance procedure, which should be readily accessible – it might well, for example, be set out in the company handbook – and written in simple straightforward language. The 1998 Workplace Employee Relations Survey reported that the most common way in which employees are informed of the existence and content of the organisation's grievance procedure is to read it in their letter of appointment (47 per cent of workplaces surveyed), the staff handbook (55 per cent of workplaces) or on a notice board (10 per cent of workplaces). Training for team leaders, supervisors and other line managers in dealing with employee grievances effectively is a business priority. A survey of grievance-handling published in 2001 by Industrial Relations Services revealed that 72 per cent of 102 organisations surveyed provided training for managers who might be expected to deal with a grievance.

What is a grievance?

A grievance usually arises because an aggrieved individual regards some management decision (or act of indecision) as 'unfair'. However, not all employee complaints are justified. The management action complained of may in fact be legitimate behaviour within the terms and spirit of a collective agreement between the employees and the management, within a company rule contained in the company's staff handbook, or within the necessities of the business. In managing employee grievances, management acquires and develops an ability to distinguish real from unfounded grievances, and then – if appropriate – to explain clearly to the employee why his or her complaint merits no action by management.

However, all grievances, whether real or unfounded, are important to the individual concerned and have to be treated on their merits. If management receives a complaint which appears somewhat frivolous, it is not good practice to reject it without at least an investigation into how it has arisen. If such an enquiry reveals the employee's complaint to be ill-founded, then why this is the case must be explained to the individual. By acting after investigation in a fair, reasonable and consistent manner, management demonstrates to its employees that both unfounded and genuine complaints are treated seriously and in a businesslike and effective way.

Non-trading of grievances

In negotiating the settlement of grievances, management treats each on its merits, thereby demonstrating to each complainant that management accepts the complaint as a serious issue for that individual. An employee's grievance has to be dealt with independently of that of any another employee. In managing employee grievances, management proceeds on the basis of one at a time. It negotiates an agreement to settle the individual's grievance of a particular issue and then moves on to negotiate an agreement to settle another employee's grievance over a different issue.

The effective negotiation of grievances, unlike bargaining, excludes a trade-off between employee complaints about employer behaviour. Management does not offer to settle one person's grievance in exchange for getting another employee to agree to drop his or her grievance. In grievance-handling neither management nor employee representatives take part in such trading. Yet the employee relations professional should not fall into the trap of being forced to deal simultaneously with a whole list of different grievances over different issues from a number of different employees.

The most common employee grievances

Complaints from individual employees can centre on many aspects of management behaviour. An employee may complain that the employer has acted in breach of a collective agreement (ie management is not applying it as the parties intended); that tools and/or machinery have not been properly maintained; that the canteen facilities are poor and inadequate; that the workplace is too dark, too cold (or hot) and/or unhealthy; and that the disciplinary penalty imposed upon them is too harsh. Other areas of individual employee complaint against management may include that they have been passed over for promotion; that they have been denied access to a training and development opportunity; that their holiday allocation does not meet their family circumstances; that there has been a late payment of a bonus; that a new working practice has been introduced without prior consultation; or that their job is graded at an inappropriate level.

In 2001 Industrial Relations Services published the results of its survey into the handling of individual grievances (see IRS No.726, April 2001). It had sent a questionnaire to 102 organisations employing all together more than 600,000 employees. The organisations surveyed varied in size from 72,000 employees to 25 people: 102 usable returns were received. Of the 102 organisations surveyed, 100 had formal written policies to deal with individual employee grievances. This compares with the 1998 Workplace Employee Relations Survey, which reported that 91 per cent of the workplaces it surveyed had a formal procedure in place for dealing with individual grievances raised by non-managerial employees. Over half of the organisations in the IRS survey had first introduced a grievance policy more than 10 years previously.

The most common subjects of employee grievances as revealed in the Industrial Relations Services' 2001 survey are shown in Table 28. Pay and grading was ranked as the most common source of grievance, followed by terms and conditions and then working practices. Disciplinary matters was the fourth most common source of employee grievances despite several organisations' specifically excluding this issue from their grievance policies.

Of the 1,000 people interviewed in 1998 for the (then) IPD study of the psychological contract, 17 per cent reported that they had been treated unfairly in the last 12 months on the grounds of age, race, gender, disability, experience, qualifications or on other grounds. The highest

Table 28 The subjects of the most common employee grievances (IRS survey, 2001)

Issue	Number of organisations
Pay and grading	40
Terms and conditions	38
Working practices	32
Discipline	29
Work allocation	22
Bullying	20
Discrimination	15
Health and safety	7
Sexual harassment	4
Management style	4
Personality clash	3

proportion of complaints was among employees employed in the health sector and among young workers. The main stated reasons for unfair treatment were:

- personality clashes   (19 per cent)
- lack of experience   (11 per cent)
- gender   (10 per cent)
- age   (8 per cent)
- lack of qualifications   (6 per cent)
- race   (4 per cent).

Increasingly, then, many employee complaints are falling into what can broadly be described as 'equality' issues. Women employees are increasingly complaining to management that their jobs are inappropriately graded and paid. An increasing number of employee complaints are based on claims of injustice in that the behaviour complained of is motivated by a dislike of the employee on the grounds of their gender, race, creed, colour or disability. Sexual harassment also constitutes an employee grievance. Such complaints can be difficult in that in some cases the behaviour complained of is by an individual who is also the person supposed to manage the complaint.

Employee grievances can be collective, in that a group of employees may have a common complaint relating to their employment or an individual may have a grievance which has collective implications. All the employees in an office, for example, may complain that the temperature is too high or too low, or employees collectively in one workroom may complain that their level of pay or bonuses seem unfair compared with those of other groups of employees in other sections of the organisation. Research indicates that the main causes of grievances raised by a group of employees are:

- the interpretation and application of an existing agreement
- pay and bonus arrangements
- organisational change
- new working practices
- grading issues.

The IRS Survey mentioned above revealed that 49 organisations (out of 102) had a formal written procedure for dealing with collective disputes. Most of the organisations with distinct policies for individual and collective grievance were in the public sector. In some organisations, however, the collective grievance procedure is known as a disputes procedure. Interestingly, in the IRS Survey (2001), of the 46 organisations without any collective procedure, half of them recognised trade unions for collective bargaining purposes. So unionised workplaces are only marginally more likely than non-unionised establishments to have a collective grievance policy.

What are the main sources of employee grievances in your organisation? How would you explain this pattern?

The take-up of grievances

Employees who are unable to resolve a grievance informally are obliged to follow their organisation's formal grievance procedure (see below). The aim of such a procedure is to encourage employees who believe they have been treated unfairly to raise the matter without fear of reprisal, to have it discussed and resolved as fairly and as quickly as possible, in order to prevent a usually minor disagreement developing into a more serious disputes and to help build an organisational climate based on openness and trust. Management needs a knowledge and understanding of how to operate these procedures and – as we have already seen – most organisations provide training for team leaders and other frontline managers in managing employee grievances effectively. All organisations require appropriate mechanisms to ensure that employee dissatisfaction is identified quickly and is dealt with, to mutual satisfaction, if possible *before* the individual's complaint is put into the formal grievance procedure. Activating the grievance procedure is costly in terms of management time.

Most employees' complaints against management behaviour do not reach the formal grievance procedure. Of the workplaces with formal grievance procedures surveyed in the Workplace Employee Relations Survey (1998), only 30 per cent reported that those procedures had been activated in the previous 12 months. In the smallest workplaces, the corresponding figure was 20 per cent, and in large workplaces 79 per cent.

There are many reasons why employee complaints may not go into formal procedure. First, something may happen to render it unnecessary. As Torrington and Hall (1998) point out, an employee's dissatisfaction can disappear after a good night's sleep and/or after a cup of tea with a colleague.

Second, the employee may just want to make a point, to relieve his or her frustration. The grievance may be resolved at once if an appropriate manager listens to the employee. 'A shoulder to cry on' may thus provide sufficient satisfaction for the employee to withdraw his or her gesture of disapproval at management's behaviour.

Third, in times of high unemployment individuals may be reluctant to raise a grievance formally with the company because of a fear that management may hold it against them and react by denying them promotion, access to training and development programmes or merit award payments. Fourth, employees may see little point in raising a grievance because they believe the procedure is not a particularly effective mechanism for resolving problems. Fifth, some individuals may be unwilling to express their dissatisfaction with management for fear of offending their immediate superior who may regard the complaint as a criticism of their competency. And finally, it may be that employees have nothing to complain about. The IPD Survey of Surveys into Worker Dissatisfaction and Insecurity (1999) found that the majority of British employees are satisfied with their jobs, do not feel insecure, and have a high level of commitment to their employers.

The IPD publication *Fairness at Work and the Psychological Contract* (1998) interviewed 1,000 people of whom only 10 per cent said they had made a formal complaint about the way they had been treated in their organisation. Indeed, only 28 per cent said they had ever made a complaint against their organisation. Either they did not regard their unfair treatment as really serious or they had no faith in or knowledge of any complaints procedure.

Of the 10 per cent who had laid a complaint, 21 per cent reported that the procedure in their organisation was fair in dealing with their complaint, whereas 28 per cent claimed it was reasonably fair, 18 per cent said it was not fair and 27 per cent considered it very unfair. This is a very uneven distribution but suggests that many of those who formally complained were unhappy with the operation of the grievance procedures. While this high level of dissatisfaction is perhaps an inevitable consequence of the failure to uphold some complaints, it is, at the same time, disturbingly high. The results may also help to explain why many of those who felt they had been unfairly treated did not follow up their grievance.

That individual grievances may not be put formally into the grievance procedure does not mean that the quality (the overall climate) of employee relations in the organisation is in good shape. However, employee dissatisfaction identified at an early stage can generally be settled quickly through informal discussions. Behaving in this way reduces considerably the probability that the employees' level of dissatisfaction will reach a point at which they are prepared to make a formal complaint against management's behaviour.

A situation in which complaints are being repressed because employees feel that senior management will not act against a team leader/supervisor whose style of management is the cause of the grievance cannot be allowed to continue. Senior management might, for example, counsel the team leader/frontline manager as to why his or her management style has to change or provide formal training after which his or her style should change for the better. If such action fails to produce a more constructive management style, management must either redeploy the team leader/frontline manager elsewhere or consider dispensing with his or her services. If employee complaints are shown, following thorough investigation, to be the result of a personality clash between the team leader/frontline manager and an individual employee, the grievance may be best resolved by redeploying the individual to another area of employment.

Has the grievance procedure in your organisation been activated in the last 12 months? If it has, what were the issues and who were the workers involved? If it hasn't, why do you think that is the case?

The grievance procedure

The grievance procedure provides the means whereby individual employees process their complaint against management behaviour. Procedures for dealing with grievances are to be found in organisations which operate without trade unions as well as in those that operate with them. In organisations without trade unions, the procedure's first element must be to inform the individual of the action required to raise the grievance and the steps management will take to give it consideration.

A grievance procedure benefits employees because with one in operation they know where they stand and they know what to expect. The purpose of the procedure is to:

- ensure the fair and consistent treatment of employees
- reduce the risk of 'unpredictable' action
- clarify how grievances will be dealt with
- maintain a good employee relations environment
- help the employer to avoid disputes or costly legal action.

Underlying principles

In managing employee complaints, management is guided by a number of principles – fairness, consistency, representation, and promptness. Fairness is ensured in that the procedure prevents management from dismissing employee grievances out of hand on the grounds that they are trivial, too time-consuming and/or too costly, guarantees that there is a full investigation by an unbiased individual to establish the facts of the case, provides the employee with adequate time to prepare his or her case and to question management witnesses, allows for the case to be heard by individuals not directly involved in the complaint, and provides for the right of appeal to a higher level of management and, in some cases, to an independent external body. A grievance procedure with a clearly demarcated number of stages and standards of behaviour at each stage ensures consistency of treatment and reduces the influence of subjectivity.

In raising a complaint, the procedure provides an individual with the right to be represented by a person comparatively independent of the employer, other than that such a representative is usually internal to the organisation (for example, an employee representative, a shop steward, a work colleague) rather than external (for example, a full-time trade union official, a solicitor). However, the Employment Relations Act 1999 gives individual employees the statutory right to be accompanied by a representative of their choice (who may be a full-time trade union official regardless of whether the employer recognises a trade union and regardless of whether the individual is a member). The promptness principle may be achieved if the procedure has a small number of stages, each of which has a time-limit for its completion. This enables the grievance to be resolved as quickly and as simply as possible.

The grievance procedure ensures the right of employees to complain if they feel aggrieved and, if they exercise this right, to be treated in a fair and reasonable manner in accordance with procedural rules which conform to the principles of natural justice. The individual employee is treated with dignity and respect. A grievance procedure thus provides 'order and stability' in the workplace by establishing standards of behaviour, and due processes to resolve employee grievances in a peaceful and constructive manner.

The form of a procedure

The form of grievance procedures varies immensely. In a small non-union establishment, the procedure is likely to be written into an employee's contract of employment, where the following language would be typical:

> If you have a grievance relating to your employment, you should raise it with your immediate supervisor.

In larger organisations a grievance procedure is likely to be constituted by a clause in a collective agreement. However, in large non-union organisations the grievance procedure is likely to be reproduced in the company handbook, where a typical wording might be:

> If you have any grievance relating to your employment, you should raise it with your immediate supervisor. If the matter is not settled at this level, you may pursue it through the grievance procedure agreed between the company and the trade union representatives. Further details of such procedural agreements are maintained separately in writing and may be consulted on request to management.

A typical procedure

A typical grievance procedure follows a standard format which:

- opens with a policy statement that might very well look something like this:

  The organisation encourages open and honest communication at all levels. It recognises, however, that from time to time employees may wish to seek redress for grievances relating to their employment. Although this procedure for handling grievances is in written form, it is not intended to replace any initial informal approach to try to resolve such an issue. Managers and staff are therefore encouraged to make every effort to resolve problems amicably before resorting to the formal procedure. Matters should be dealt with on a day-to-day basis as they occur, and be settled as near to the point of origin as possible and as quickly as is reasonably practicable. It is, however, recognised that a formal procedure may be necessary to resolve true grievances quickly, to allow employees to pursue concerns relating to their working conditions without fear or recrimination, to prevent conflict, and to maintain positive employee relations.

- may then contain further general principles and perhaps a definition of what constitutes a grievance

- consists of a number of stages – At each stage the aim is to identify action that will stop the problem recurring or continuing. The number of stages in a procedure usually ranges from two to five: three is the most common

- defines time-limits for the completion of each stage designed to ensure a speedy resolution of the grievance

- provides the disgruntled employee with the right to representation by an individual (comparatively) independent of the employer.

In most large organisations (and particularly if unionised) procedures for managing employee complaints relating to health and safety provision, job grading (the job evaluation scheme), sexual harassment and discrimination, and 'whistle-blowing' are distinct from the general grievance/disputes procedure. Grievances about job grading, sexual harassment, etc are thus normally dealt with by means of a purpose-built procedure. The degree of its differentiation from the general grievance procedure depends on the volume of business and on the speed, efficacy and acceptability required by the parties. These specific procedures are discussed in greater detail later in the chapter.

Stages

There are a number of stages in a typical grievance procedure. Common factors to all the stages are:

- the spelling out of the details of who, at that stage, is to hear the case (eg the departmental manager, the managing director) and the individuals to be present (eg the personnel manager, the line manger and the employee concerned), including who can represent the employee (eg a colleague, friend or shop steward)

- an explanation of any appeal mechanisms available to employees at that stage

- a definition of the time-limit within which the stage must be completed

- information about what will happen next if the grievance is not resolved or remains unsettled at that stage.

The aim of grievance procedures is to reach a resolution of the employee's complaint as quickly as possible but without undue haste. As we have seen, a grievance procedure usually specifies how, and to whom, employees can raise a grievance, and spells out the stages through which the complaint may be processed. To ensure a speedy settlement, time-limits are specified by which each stage of the procedure must be completed (see above). The first stage is invariably one in which any employee who feels that he or she has a complaint against management should, in the first instance, raise it with his or her immediate manager. If that manager is unable to resolve the matter, the parties move on to the second stage of the procedure, which usually means that the employee finds a representative who then represents him or her in taking up the complaint at the appropriate level of management. If the complaint still remains unresolved, the third stage is entered in which the employee and the representative take their case to higher levels of management (for example, the departmental manager).

If there is no resolution to the grievance at this stage, the complaint is normally next considered by the employee's representative and the general manager. In unionised establishments at this fourth stage the local union branch secretary usually becomes involved. If a resolution still eludes the parties, the formal procedure may be exhausted – which may effectively mean that all that can be done on the matter without going to a tribunal or to court has been done. However, some procedures (especially those designed to deal with collective grievances) contain a fifth stage which involves external parties such as an independent arbitrator or conciliator, a representative of an employers' association and a district/regional trade union official. The IRS 2001 Survey of grievances and their handling found that just 11 organisations out of the 102 surveyed provided for employees to appeal to an independent third party, such as the Advisory, Conciliation and Arbitration Service (ACAS), should they be dissatisfied with the final stage of the in-house process.

In managing grievances, management's objective is to settle the complaint as near as possible to the point of its source. If employee complaints are allowed to progress to a higher level than necessary, this principle is undermined. A professional employee relations manager ensures that managerial colleagues, particularly line managers, understand the limits of their authority when acting within the constraints of the grievance procedure. The problem-solving objective of the procedure is achieved and the significance of the different procedural stages maintained when grievances are settled as near as possible to the point of origin.

Although defined stages through which a grievance can be processed are essential, there is no ideal number of stages. The number is a function of many factors, including the size of the organisation. However, the principles of natural justice would point to a minimum of two stages, in that two stages ensure at least one level of appeal after the immediate decision. Nor should the procedure contain too many stages because that just prolongs the process and is in conflict with the principle of resolving grievances as quickly as possible and as close as can be to their origin.

> Do you have a grievance procedure in your organisation? If not, why not? If you do, how many stages does it have? Why does it have that number?

Time-limits

An employee with a complaint wants his or her grievance settled as soon as possible, and is likely to regard it as the highest priority for the manager to whom the complaint is made. That manager, on the other hand, needs time to gather the facts, consult with other managers and consider what action to take, all of which has to be fitted around all the other tasks for which that manager is responsible. The idea behind a time-limit is that it provides a manager with an opportunity to consider the problem seriously while at the same time also committing him or her to providing an answer within a fixed period of time. This relaxes the pressures on the employee, or his or her representative, who now knows that if a satisfactory answer has not been provided at the end of the time-limit, the grievance goes forward to the next stage in the procedure.

The usual practice is to allow longer time-limits for the completion for each successive stage. Internal stages' time-limits can vary from a low of 24 hours to a maximum of five days, but such limits are longer for external stages. Time-limits alone do not ensure the expeditious handling of grievances, but they are useful in establishing standards of reasonable behaviour by the parties. When the external stages of a grievance procedure are triggered, time-limits for their completion again provide reassurance for the employee that inordinately lengthy delays in dealing with their complaint should not be possible. Most of the doubts and criticisms against time-limits (for example, loss of flexibility, undermining mutual trust, the issue is not dealt with properly at the lower levels) are overcome if there is a proviso in the procedure to permit, by mutual agreement, the extension of the time-limits by which each stage of the process must be completed. The guiding principle is that the employee's complaint progresses *quickly* to the level needed to find a solution to the problem, and that managers do not 'sit on' grievances.

Employee representation

Fair and reasonable behaviour by an employer in managing employee grievances requires the employee, as in disciplinary cases, to have the opportunity of representation by an individual who advocates the case on his or her behalf. Representation assists the individual employee who lacks confidence and experience to deal with his or her line manager or senior manager, especially managerial luminaries operating at the executive level (for example, the managing director). The representative – who, as we have seen is likely to be internal to the organisation – is nonetheless independent of the interests of the employer and is not present merely to witness what management says to the individual.

The Workplace Employee Relations Survey (1998) showed that only 4 per cent of the workplaces surveyed did not allow employees to be accompanied by a third party in grievance hearings. In workplaces where the employer allows the employee to be independently accompanied, 41 per cent allowed them to choose whoever they wished to accompany them. The remaining half specified a variety of options including a trade union official (45 per cent), a full-time official (27 per cent) and another work colleague (87 per cent). In workplaces where union members were present but there was no recognition, nearly half (46 per cent) of managers said that workers might be accompanied by anyone of their choosing. Of those chosen to be representatives, with the option left open to employees, full-time union officials were mentioned by 20 per cent of managers.

The Employment Relations Act 1999 gives workers a statutory right to be accompanied by a fellow worker or trade union official when they are required or invited by their employer to attend certain grievance hearings and when they make a reasonable request to be so accompanied. The chosen companion has a statutory right to address the hearing, but no statutory right to answer questions on the worker's behalf. Workers are free to choose an official from any trade union to accompany them at a grievance hearing regardless of whether the union is recognised or not. However, the ACAS Code of Practice (see below) on Discipline and Grievances at Work recommends that where a trade union is recognised in a workplace, it is good practice for an official from that union to accompany the worker at a hearing.

Representation at what stage?

In many procedures, representation starts at the second stage after the individual has raised his or her complaint with the immediate manager. Representation then only becomes necessary if the employee is dissatisfied with the response from the immediate manager and wishes to take the matter to a higher level of management. The assumption behind this is that a grievance is not a grievance if the individual employee's immediate manager resolves the problem.

However, there are employee relations managers who believe that an employee should have representation from the very start of his or her complaint. In these circumstances the employee's first step is to take the grievance to a workplace representative (where there is one) rather than to his or her immediate superior, persuade the representative that he or she has a genuine grievance, and ask for representation in processing the complaint. The employee's representative then has an important responsibility to act as a useful 'filter' and sift genuine grievances from the unfounded.

The equality of representatives

In the internal stages of the procedure, the individual employee's representative is also an employee of the organisation. Such a representative wears two hats – one as an employee and the other as an employee representative. His or her relationship with management, in status terms, is very different depending upon which hat he or she is wearing. As employees they are in a subordinate position to management who give them instructions, empower them, verify the quality of their work, monitor their timekeeping and initiate disciplinary action against them. Employees' workplace representatives are contracted to supply work to the employer.

However, when they wear the employee representative hat they interact with management as partners of equal status. This equality is expressed in the grievance procedure which sets out the 'players' to be involved in each stage of processing the grievance. When management and the employee's representative meet at different stages, they do so on the basis of equality. So if, for example, the third stage of the procedure states that the employee's representative and the chief executive/managing director will meet to try to resolve the grievance, and the meeting is held in the managing director's office, they meet there as employee relations players of equal status. The managing director thus treats the employee's representative as such and ensures that he or she has the proper facilities (seating, appropriate space for documents, etc) to represent his or her 'client' in a professional manner.

The procedure also protects the employee's representative from a frontline manager's/team leader's refusal to allow him or her time away from work duties to represent the 'client's' interests. The procedure is management's acceptance that in certain circumstances the individual employee's role as an employee relations player takes preference over his or her role as an employee. If, in managing grievances, management and employee representatives are equal partners, they have a joint responsibility for settling grievances.

This equality relationship in grievance-handling is difficult for some line managers to accept. Many find it difficult – if not impossible – to recognise employee representatives other than as employees of the company and therefore subject to their own control and direction. Such managers feel that their authority is undermined if more senior managers treat employees, when wearing their representative's hat, as equal. They find it difficult to understand why their senior managers show so much consideration and grant such facilities towards individuals who they perceive as merely employees of the organisation.

> When managing grievances, is the employee's representative – in relation to the manager who is representing management's interests – in a superior, inferior or equal-status position? Justify your answer.

Operating the procedure

The role of the employee relations professional

Grievance procedures are an integral part of the whole way in which an organisation is managed. They directly affect line management at all levels. Line managers have always had the main responsibility for operating the procedure, assisted and advised by the employee relations professional. Yet for the employee relations professional it is important not to take on board line managers' problems or take responsibility for them. It is becoming standard practice in modern organisations for team leaders/frontline managers to manage people *in partnership with* human resource managers (Kelly and Gennard, 1997). The role of the employee relations professional in managing grievance is therefore to:

- identify and meet line management training and development needs with regard to managing grievances

- ensure that line managers have a clear understanding of the way in which grievance procedures are intended to operate

- devise a grievance procedure which conforms with 'good practice' and spells out not only what has to happen at each stage but why

- promote awareness of 'good practice' in managing grievances among line managers

- make sure that employees are aware of their rights under the procedure

- promote a constructive grievance policy at board level.

The employee relations professional also has an important role to play in monitoring and reviewing the operation of the grievance procedure and in recommending revisions to its design or operation. This involves reviewing the outcomes of the grievances taken through the procedure and noting whether these outcomes were ones that management wanted or not, and if not, why not. (For example, was an unexpectedly adverse outcome the result of inadequate investigation of the complaint?) This review and monitoring function also requires the employee relations professional to analyse the subject matter of individual employee grievances and to check that the procedure has been applied in all cases fairly and consistently (ie that management has behaved reasonably in processing employee grievances). The IRS Survey (2001) of the handling of employee grievances showed that of the 102 organisations surveyed only 25 monitored the outcome of resolving employee grievances. This compared with 40 per cent of organisations in its 1997 survey.

The role of the line manager

The first line manager remains a key player in the operation of the grievance procedure. An employee who files a grievance may be regarded by a first line manager as reflecting badly on his or her managerial competence. If grievance procedures are to operate effectively, senior management must reassure first line managers that it does not automatically see any such problem. On the contrary, line managers should be encouraged to hear grievances. It is important that they are aware of employee dissatisfaction as early as possible. It is usually easier to resolve grievances informally in a satisfactory manner for the individual and management if they are handled as quickly and as close to the source of the complaint as may be.

First line managers have the least executive authority, however, which limits their ability to make decisions without reference to more senior managers. If a frontline manager/team leader has continuously to refer a grievance up to a superior, employees will soon realise that the best way to have their problems resolved is to short-circuit the first line manager and go directly to the superior manager. When this happens, the legitimate authority of the frontline manager is undermined and the whole credibility of the procedure is threatened – although in reality all that is happening is that the number of procedural stages is being reduced. The worst impact is that it removes the grievance from its source of origin, slows down the process by requiring a U-turn to go back through the correct stages, and causes confusion and bad feeling. To avoid all this, the employee relations professional must ensure three things:

- that everyone knows, within the procedure, the limits of their own and others' authority

- that the procedures are adhered to consistently by line managers

- that first line managers have the authority to settle grievances.

In situations where union workplace representatives believe line managers are unable to take a decision at the appropriate level, good practice requires management to insist that the protocol of the procedure is followed. By doing this, management demonstrates that it will apply the procedure consistently and that its operation is understood by those managers who have a part to play in its operation. It is important that first line managers have authority to deal with as many types of grievance as possible. The frontline manager/team leader must be able to say 'Yes' as well as 'No'.

It is equally important that first line management continues to be involved in the settling of grievances even when grievances technically pass out of their hands. Managers should do this either by being at subsequent meetings or at the very least by asking to be informed of the outcome of the further grievance process. It is bad management practice if a first line manager hears of the outcome of an employee's complaint from the employee or from his or her representative.

Grievance records

When a grievance passes to a higher stage in the procedure, documentation of what happened at the previous stage is necessary for the benefit of those managers who are not familiar with the complaint, with the individual employee or with his or her supporting arguments and evidence. In practice, the extent to which records of grievances are kept varies widely. In some organisations the completion of grievance records is a required activity for line management. In others only the personnel/HRM department keeps records. In yet others no documentation of any kind is kept except when an employee complaint progresses to the external stage of the procedure. The ACAS Code of Practice on Disciplinary and Grievance Procedures advises that records should be kept detailing the nature of each grievance raised, the employer response, any action taken and the reasons for it. The Data Protection Act, however, means that management may also have to release to the employee notes they have taken at grievance hearings/meetings.

Grievance records serve several useful purposes for management. If there is a failure to agree at any stage, a written record clarifies the complaint, and the arguments in favour of it presented by the employee. This is also helpful to those managers involved in the next stage of the procedure. If the record is agreed by both parties – commonly completed by the manager concerned and countersigned by the employee and/or the representative – it is even more valuable. Grievance record forms assist the personnel/HRM function to keep in touch with the progress of unresolved grievances.

Grievance records are also useful because the resolution of the grievance may provide a significant interpretation or perhaps an important precedent. Records are particularly useful for analysing trends in the use of the grievance procedure. Analysis of the record will show where, and why, delays in the procedure occurred more than once. When a resolution to the individual's grievance has been reached, a written and agreed statement helps to ensure that there are no misunderstandings over what has been agreed. In the absence of an agreed statement, the parties may find they remember different versions of what they thought they actually agreed. A written statement is also useful for communicating the outcome of the employee's complaint.

However, systems which require line management to keep records of grievances are not easy to keep going unless management keeps a watchful eye on matters. Some frontline managers who handle grievances often complain that having to keep grievance records is an extra, irksome administrative chore. Without a watchful eye from more senior management, grievance records systems at the first-line level may not operate effectively.

> Does your organisation keep grievance records? If not, why not? If it does, what information does the record keep, and why?

Grievances and the law

Under the Employment Rights Act 1996 the basic statutory requirement that applies to an employee grievance is that the employer has to specify, by description or otherwise, a person to whom the employee can apply if he or she is dissatisfied with a disciplinary decision or has a grievance. This information is to be given to the individual employee in the statement of particulars of terms of employment. A formal grievance procedure is not legally required, but almost every organisation finds it useful to adopt one. When they do, the statement of particulars specifies any further steps available to the employee beyond the first point of contact. This, as we have seen, is often in a separate document setting out the organisation's full grievance procedure.

Goold v McConnell (1995)

However, employers who do not have a formal grievance procedure can fall foul of the law. In *W A Goold (Pearmack) Ltd v McConnell* (1995) an industrial tribunal held that the employer's failure to supply a grievance procedure to its employees amounted to a breach of the employment contract, which entitled the employees to resign and therefore claim constructive dismissal. The two employees concerned were also held to be unfairly dismissed. The facts of the case were simple. Mr McConnell and Mr Richmond were jewellery salesmen paid a basic salary and commission. In 1992 their employer changed sales methods and, as a result, commission suffered. The employees wished to complain about this issue but there was no established grievance procedure and the employer had not issued them with a written statement of main terms and conditions of employment.

In July 1992 a new managing director joined the firm and the employees tried to complain to him. He told them he was unable to deal with their complaint immediately. The two employees then decided to seek an interview with the chairman but were prevented by his secretary. The employees resigned and claimed constructive dismissal. The Employment Appeals Tribunal (EAT) agreed with the industrial tribunal's view that it was an implied term in any employment contract that employers should reasonably and promptly give employees an opportunity to obtain redress of any grievance.

Reed and Another v Stedman (1999)

In this case the EAT gave employment tribunals general guidance on how they should approach complaints to sexual harassment at work. Ms Stedman was employed by Bull Information Systems Ltd from 1 June 1995, initially as a temporary secretary and then in a permanent position to Mr Reed, the marketing manager. She found working with him intolerable and resigned on 28 June 1996.

He had behaved in an unwelcome sexual manner towards her and her health had begun to deteriorate, which she had put down to his behaviour. Although she had complained to him only once about that, she had complained about it to her mother and to colleagues at work. Members of the company's personnel department were aware of those complaints and of her deteriorating health. Ms Stedman thus had a grievance which company personnel had failed to investigate. In finding that Ms Stedman had been constructively dismissed by the company and sexually harassed by Mr Reed, the EAT ruled that the company had breached the contract of employment by failing to investigate the cause of Ms Stedman's ill health and complaints she had made to colleagues. This case demonstrates the importance of management's investigating every employee grievance. Indeed, it is incumbent on a company to do so because not to do so may justify a legal ruling that such behaviour breaches trust and confidence.

Metcalf Ltd v Maddocks (1985)

The benefits of having procedures for handling employee grievances – even though the law does not require them – are also clear from the case of Chris Metcalf Ltd v Maddocks (1985). The crux of the matter was that an employee had refused to carry out a particular instruction and had been dismissed. In this case the company had no formal grievance procedure for its 90 employees and had failed to issue statements of particulars to its employees. In the tribunal hearing the argument was that these omissions by management had caused a breakdown in communications between management and the employee, to the point where the employee's reasons for refusing to carry out the instruction had no means of being expressed or heard properly. The industrial tribunal ruled that a grievance procedure would have enabled employees to articulate their worries and anxieties and thus have prevented the problem occurring. An appeal by the firm against the decision failed.

The Employment Relations Act 1999

As we have already noted, the Employment Relations Act 1999 requires employers to permit workers to be accompanied at specified disciplinary and grievance meetings. This clause came into effect on 4 September 2000, and applies to any grievance hearing that concerns the performance of a duty by an employer in relation to a worker. The accompanying person may be a fellow-worker, a full-time official or lay trade union official. This right applies equally to workers in unionised and non-unionised environments. The chosen companion may address the hearing, ask questions and confer privately with the worker but has no legal right to answer questions on behalf of the worker.

The ACAS Code of Practice

The ACAS Code of Practice on Disciplinary and Grievance Procedures came into operation on 4 September 2000. Although a failure to follow the Code does not render an employer liable to any proceedings, the Code is admissible in evidence and may be taken into account by employment tribunals. The Code aims to help employers, workers and their representatives by giving practical guidance on how to deal with grievance issues in employment. It also provides guidance on the statutory right to be accompanied at a grievance hearing, on the suitability of such companions and on the reasonableness of requests by workers to be accompanied. It advises that although workers are free to choose any one fellow-worker or trade union official, workers should bear in mind that it would not be appropriate to insist on being accompanied by a colleague whose presence would prejudice the hearing or who might have a conflict of interest. It also advises that it would not be sensible for a worker to request accompaniment by a colleague from a geographically remote location when somebody qualified was available on site.

> How has your organisation responded to the right of employees to be accompanied in grievance hearings? If it has not responded, why is that the case? If it has reacted, why did it react in the way it has?

Organisations are fairly tightly constrained by the law with regard to disciplinary matters (see Chapter 10). An employee grievance, on the other hand, is bound by much less case and statute law. Some argue that it is the strength of the legal framework for discipline, as distinct from the legal framework for grievance, that is the central reason why discipline rates a higher priority in organisations than grievance-handling.

The day-to-day management of grievances

Much of an employee relations professional's time may be taken up with individual employees' problems or complaints. However, most employee grievances are dealt with satisfactorily before they reach the formal grievance procedure. For example, take the case of an employee who claims that she has received an incorrect amount of pay.

There are a number of possibilities:

- On checking, management accepts that the amount of pay due has been miscalculated and rectifies the matter immediately. In that case, the grievance has quickly and permanently been resolved at the individual level to everyone's satisfaction.

or

- The payment is correct although the employee believes she has been underpaid. There is no real grievance here, but either of two things might happen:

  - the situation is discussed and explained adequately, and the matter is resolved

  - the employer fails to explain the details to the satisfaction of the employee who still believes she has been treated unfairly even though she has not. Now there is a danger that a collective dispute might develop, taking a simple problem to an inappropriate level.

or

- The details of the complaint are accepted by the employer who nevertheless fails to take corrective action quickly. Such tardiness causes another grievance to arise, which takes the place of the original. The employee was relying on a correct payment to meet commitments but now cannot do so because the company is 'holding on' to her money.

The first contingency is obviously the most preferable one, in that it puts right a genuine error promptly and efficiently. The second and third possibilities carry the risk of generating feelings of mistrust and suspicion.

However, not all grievances are of as simple a nature and resolvable so quickly. Management must deal with all grievances in a competent and systematic manner, and the full procedure to facilitate that involves a number of stages:

- hearing the grievance

- preparing to meet with the employee and/or his or her representative

- meeting with the employee and/or his or her representative

- confirming common ground between the employee and the management

- resolving the grievance

- reporting the outcome.

The grievance interview

The purpose of the grievance interview is to enable an individual to state his or her complaint and for management to discover, and remove, the cause of the employee's dissatisfaction. From the interview, management obtains the facts of the situation, analyses the problem and, if appropriate, decides on the action to take to resolve the grievance.

Good management practice in preparation for a grievance interview is to check the employee's employment record with the organisation. Although circumstances and time pressures may make this impossible, it is worth bearing in mind that an employee with a grievance against management may possibly adopt an aggressive attitude. If this turns out to be the case, management should endeavour to calm the individual down – perhaps by referring positively to the employee's record of service to date. When dealing with an individual who has become unreasonable in their anger, management must guard against responding in a similar way or being provoked into such a reaction. It can happen all too easily when faced with an aggressive employee critical of management's behaviour.

Gathering information about an employee's grievance is extremely important. If incorrect, or insufficient, information is collected, any analysis is likely to be wrong and an incorrect decision may well be made. Competent interviewing, watching and listening skills are crucial in this regard.

At the end of the interview, the manager should have a good understanding of the employee's grievance and how he or she would like to see it resolved. If the employee's grievance is, for example, that he or she has been denied access to a training opportunity, the employee should be told first *why* he or she was denied the opportunity but should then be given the opportunity to explain to management how he or she would ideally like the situation to be resolved – perhaps by being sent on the next available appropriate training opportunity. The 'why' question is always the most difficult, since an individual always presents a favourable view of the case, possibly withholding information that weakens it. However, remember the golden rule – the manager must get all the facts, including those that might make the individual's case against management less clear-cut.

The management has got to have all the facts. It is seeking to make a decision on whether the employee's grievance is genuine and well-founded, and if so, on what action to take. If the grievance interview fails to bring out vital information the manager may conclude, wrongly, with adverse consequences, that the employee does not have a genuine complaint. On the basis of the information gained from the grievance interview the manager makes an assessment of the situation. He or she decides upon an appropriate course of action and explains to the individual employee, to his or her representative and to managerial colleagues why he or she has decided upon that action.

Unfounded grievances

At the end of the interview, management may conclude that the grievance is unfounded because:

- the real problem is a clash of personality between the individual employee and his or her immediate manager

- the employee has misunderstood something crucial (for example, a works rule).

Alternatively, the employee may drop the grievance because he or she is happy that management has listened sympathetically, or because he or she feels that to take it further will only make matters worse.

Grievances can be genuine or unfounded – and distinguishing between them is an important responsibility for both employer and employee representatives. They have a common interest to avoid wasting time, resources, effort and emotion in putting inappropriate issues through formal procedures. However, all grievances are important and must be treated on their merits. If management receives a complaint which it judges to be ill-founded, it is not good practice to dismiss it in an arbitrary manner. Management should:

- find out why and how it has arisen

- explain clearly and openly why it is a complaint that merits no action.

This not only sets the record straight but also allows everyone to see that even an imagined rather than a real complaint is being handled seriously. For instance, some organisations have agreed employment conditions which include the option of changing the location at which individuals work. Local authorities, for example, with offices in towns across their areas sometimes need to move their officers around to cover short- or long-term pressures, and this is set out in employment contracts and/or collective agreements. An employee who was required to move location but was reluctant to do so would not have a legitimate grievance. However, if he or she did raise the complaint, it would have to be discussed and resolved at the earliest possible stage. This would both clarify the facts of the situation and avoid treating the individual in a way that might lead to long-term resentment and thus damage long-term relationships.

In this case, the grievance is imagined rather than real. Management's action (ie relocation) is within agreed procedures. Because nobody is acting contrary to the accepted way of behaving – even though the employee does not like the action taking place – there is no real grievance to be managed. Nonetheless, the employee has to be heard and the issue dealt with, if only to clarify the facts. It is important that the issue is handled in a way which precludes the individual's feeling ignored or snubbed.

Genuine grievances

On the other hand, the manager may conclude – after interviewing the employee laying the complaint – that further information is required about the grievance before management's attitude to the issue can be established. (For example: what does the agreement say? What is company policy on the issue? Are there any witnesses or other people with relevant information who should also be interviewed?) In such circumstances management will make arrangements with the employee and his or her representative for a further meeting. Alternatively, following the grievance interview management may decide that the employee's grievance is genuine, be prepared to seek a resolution to the matter, but require time to prepare a considered response. In this situation, management will also try to make arrangements on when and where next to meet with the employee and/or his or her representative to resolve the issue.

> Explain the importance of interviewing skills if the employee relations professional is to be competent in managing employee grievances.

Preparing to meet with the employee and his or her representative

There are three main stages to preparing to meet with the individual employee and his or her representative in order to negotiate a settlement to the individual's grievance. These are:

- analysis

- establishing how to achieve the aim of resolving the grievance while at the same time protecting management's interests

- planning the strategy and tactics to achieve the established aim.

Analysis

The analysis stage involves management in collecting and analysing relevant information to substantiate its proposals for resolving the individual employee's grievance. It also includes developing the argument to be put to the employee and his or her representative to support management's case. In managing grievances most of the necessary information is obtained by interviewing management colleagues and employees who have something relevant to say about the issue at stake (for example, they witnessed the incident about which the employee is complaining).

The analysis stage also involves management in checking whether the subject of the grievance has been complained of previously by employees, and if so, what the outcome was. Such an outcome might represent a precedent for dealing with the current employee's grievance. Other important management activities in the analysis stage include asking those who should know whether:

- there are any relevant company rules

- custom and practice are relevant to the employee's complaint

- any collective or personal contracts are relevant.

The most important activity for management in the preparation stage of handling grievances is the identification of the exact details of the employee's complaint. Some of these details are more important to the complainant's argument than others, and some of them are more significant to the management's view of the matter than others. Any agreement on a resolution may be reached by the parties' 'trading off' the importance of these details surrounding the issue, but retaining certain principles. In making a decision about which 'details' to trade, management assesses their significance to the complainant and tries to anticipate which 'details' it believes the employee will be prepared to trade in return.

Let's assume that management has encountered a young male employee swearing in the presence of a frontline manager and suspended him for three working days without pay. The lad considers the penalty too harsh and with his representative approaches management to register this fact. In analysing the situation, management identifies three issues – suspension, the length of the suspension, and no pay for the period of suspension. From a management perspective, given the offence, for the employee to escape any disciplinary penalty would be unacceptable. However, before finally making this decision, management assesses how strongly the individual's work colleagues feel about the harshness of the disciplinary penalty. Would they, for example, be prepared to impose industrial sanctions against the company? If they would, how successful might such action be? So, if it persists with retaining the initial penalty, management has to weigh up whether the grievance might not escalate into a collective dispute involving with it all the associated costs. If management concludes that the employees would not take the issue to a collective dispute, it can be confident in its view that the initial penalty should be upheld. But if the conclusion is the opposite, then management is likely to take the view that although the principle of the imposition of a disciplinary penalty cannot be compromised, the severity of the penalty might be reduced.

If management comes to this conclusion, it then turns to consider the length of the suspension and lost pay. Again, the management is unlikely to see the payment of wages during a period of suspension as a matter upon which a compromise can be made. If management assesses that to maintain this stance will not provoke a collective dispute, the non-payment of wages during a period of suspension will become non-negotiable. However, if management's assessment is that the employees feel strongly about non-payment, it will announce that it is prepared to negotiate on the issue.

On the basis of the above analysis, management will hope for a resolution based on some compromise on the length of the suspension in return for the retention of lost pay and some disciplinary penalty. Management has decided which details it is prepared to trade in the light of assessing its bargaining power relative to the group of workers concerned, should the individual complaint of too harsh a disciplinary penalty develop into a collective dispute. Management has anticipated that the employee will accept the principle of suspension but will trade the details surrounding the length of the suspension and the lost pay.

Establishing aims

Having completed its analysis, management then establishes objectives for the forthcoming meeting with the individual employee and his representative (we are still using the example above). Management establishes three aims:

- how it would ideally like the grievance to be resolved
- how it thinks the grievance can realistically be resolved
- what the least is for which management will settle (the fall-back position).

Management establishes these three positions for each of the issues involved in the employee's grievance. Having established its own aims/objectives, management turns its attention to anticipating the aims/objectives of the employee making the complaint: what is the individual employee ideally, realistically and minimally expecting to achieve as a resolution to his grievance?

Management can now construct an aspiration grid (see Chapter 9) setting the parameters for the expected outcome from the forthcoming grievance-handling meetings. A possible aspiration grid for management is shown in Table 29. It shows that management would ideally like to trade no details surrounding the grievance with the employee. However, management knows this is unrealistic and has established, on the basis of its analysis of the situation, a realistic position of some compromise around a retention of the suspension and no pay in return for a reduction in the period of the suspension from three days to two days. Its fall-back position is to retain the suspension and lost pay for a further reduction in the length of the suspension (to one day).

The grid shows that management anticipates that the employee expects management to be unwilling to compromise on suspension and the lost pay accompanying it. It also demonstrates that management anticipates that the employee will accept a reduction in the length of suspension

Table 29 An aspiration grid on the matter of three days' suspension without pay

Possible resolution to grievance	Management			Employee		
	Ideal	Real	Fall-back	Fall-back	Real	Ideal
3 days' suspension – pay restored	X	X	X	O	O	X
2 days' suspension – pay restored	X	X	X	O	O	X
1 day's suspension – pay restored	X	X	X	O	X	X
2 days' suspension – no pay	X	X	O	O	O	X
1 day's suspension – no pay	X	O	O	O	O	X

O = prepared to trade
X = not prepared to trade

and, if a mutually acceptable solution is to be achieved, that it will centre on this issue. It also indicates that no problems are anticipated over the loss-of-pay issue because although management is not prepared to make compromises on this aspect of the grievance, management thinks the employee is.

The aspiration grid shows that there is a basis for a resolution to the employee's complaint that management has imposed too harsh a disciplinary penalty. In the fall-back position, although management is not prepared to compromise on the principle of the suspension, it is on its duration. However, it is not prepared to compromise on the 'no pay during suspension' issue. The employee is prepared to make compromises on the length of suspension and to accept 'no pay during the period of suspension'. Through the use of appropriate techniques (see Chapter 9) during subsequent meetings management will test whether the expected employee (and his representative's) objectives are as anticipated. Management, at the same time, will seek to pass on to the employee by appropriate coded language and techniques its attitude towards the issues of the length of the suspension and no pay during the period of suspension. Should new information come to light in their subsequent meetings, the management team will have to review, and amend, its aspiration grid.

Planning strategy and tactics
Having established its negotiating aims, management now moves to planning its strategy and tactics to realise those objectives. There are a number of issues for management to consider:

- who will speak for management, and in what order

- communication methods within the management team (for example, the passing of notes)

- management's arguments, and how these can in turn be countered

- an anticipation of arguments to be made by the employee in support of his case, and how these might be countered.

The anticipation of the likely arguments to be used by the other side in support of its case and how management might counter them is particularly important. Insights into these sets of counter-arguments can be gained by a member of the management 'playing the devil's advocate' to probe management's case for weaknesses. In the light of this exercise, management can strengthen its case.

The preparation stage is the most important stage in managing employee grievances. The golden rule in preparing is:

> *Failing to prepare*
> *is*
> *preparing to fail.*

However, if management prepares inadequately, the situation can be rescued if necessary by management's reassessing its analysis, aims and strategy in the light of new information which it failed, for whatever reason, to obtain while preparing its original case.

Meeting with the employee and his or her representative

In presenting its case to the individual employee and/or his representative, management outlines the matters it intends to raise and then:

- presents a broad picture of its proposals for resolving the grievance

- gives the details of its proposals backed by supporting evidence

- summarises its proposals to resolve the grievance.

The employee will have stated his case at the grievance interview.

The parties now move on to seek confirmation of their expected common ground for the basis of a resolution to the employee grievance. There are a number of techniques management can use for this purpose – the 'if and then' technique, questioning for clarification, watching, listening, etc (see Chapter 9). However, information to confirm the expected basis for an agreement will not arise if the meetings with the employee are unconstructive – if, for example, the parties merely blame each other for the grievance, if they keep interrupting each other, if one side attacks personalities on the other side, and so on. In most grievance-handling situations adjournments are called more often to confirm facts or to speak to a witness who can confirm the facts than because of the provision of significantly new information which requires the parties to reconsider their strategy and tactics and their objectives.

Summary of the working of a grievance procedure

Employee makes complaint.

Manager carries out grievance interview.

Possible outcomes of grievance interview:

- Grievance is unfounded – management behaviour complained of is legitimate.

- Employee decides to drop grievance.

- Management decides the grievance is genuine – management can deal with the problem immediately (miscalculated pay is corrected, holiday allocation changed, whatever).

- Management needs to consider its response.

Preparation for meeting with employee and his or her representative:

- Analysis
  - what are the issues?
  - on what will management be prepared to compromise?
  - on what will employee and his or her representative be prepared to compromise?

- Aims
  - ideal, realistic, fall-back

- Strategy and tactics.

Resolution of grievance:

- Common ground

- Write up resolution.

Resolving a grievance

If a manager is unable to find a resolution to the grievance, the matter can be referred to the next stage in the procedure at which a higher-level manager will prepare, present and try to find a mutually acceptable solution. When a grievance remains unresolved, the manager in passing the matter on to the next stage must check that the complaint is taken up at that level, and not just lost sight of.

However, when a resolution to a grievance is found, but before finally accepting that the resolution has been agreed, management must:

- be convinced that the employee understands what has been agreed

- 'play back' to the employee what management understands the resolution of the grievance actually means, to prevent any misunderstanding arising.

If this process reveals that the employee has indeed misunderstood what has been agreed and the misunderstanding cannot be cleared up in further discussion, the negotiations will have to restart.

Once management has an oral agreement for the resolution of the employee's grievance, it should be written up. In many grievances this will take the form of an internal memo/letter to another manager and to the employee recording what has been agreed. For example, if the complaint was one of denial of access to a training opportunity, and it is upheld via the grievance-handling process, then a manager will write to the personnel or other appropriate department, reporting that it has been agreed that the individual concerned should attend the next available appropriate training course. On the other hand, it can – depending on the issue – take the form of an agreement signed by the manager concerned, the individual employee and his or her representative. The outcome is then reported to the appropriate interested parties. Clarity is important, and the manner in which what has been agreed is recorded should leave no room for doubt.

> Outline the skills required of managers in successfully handling grievances. Which do you consider to be the most important, and why?

Specific issues/specific procedures

The grievance procedure deals with a broad range of complaints and problems. However, some areas of organisational life have their own specific list of potentially thorny issues. These include:

- job grading and evaluation
- complaints by one employee about the behaviour of another
- sexual harassment
- discrimination in promotion and advancement.

So while some employee complaints remain as general grievances, others are best dealt with by specific procedures designed to deal with the type of difficulties specific to certain issues.

> Does your organisation have special issues/grievance procedures? What issues do they cover? Why do these specific procedures exist?

Job grading/evaluation appeals procedures

These procedures are far more common in the public sector than in the private sector. Job evaluation helps determine the appropriate level of a job as measured against criteria such as decision-making, working conditions (for example, exposure to hazards, working in the open air as against in an office, etc), contacts with and outside the organisation, the degree of supervision received, the complexity of the work (for example, gathering and inputting data as opposed to gathering and then manipulating data to produce a report with recommendations) within the organisation's structure. The appropriate level in the structure influences the pay level and seniority associated with the job.

A grievance that centres on such an issue arises mostly when an individual claims that his or her job has changed relative to when it was last evaluated because it now carries greater responsibility for

- people (in terms of supervising and training them)

- financial resources (an increased budget, greater financial control)

- physical resources (modern high-tech expensive equipment)

and therefore warrants a higher grading and level of remuneration.

On the other hand, management may argue that the job has not changed in responsibility and what has changed is an increase in the volume of tasks, at the same level of responsibility. It therefore makes sense in resolving such a dispute to have a procedure tailored to cover the specific circumstances of job grading, including access to specialist and expert individuals.

In a typical job evaluation appeals procedure, the first stage normally requires the individual employee to discuss the basis of his or her appeal with the immediate line manager/team leader. The second stage normally requires the individual to complete a Formal Appeal Form, which then goes before a meeting of a Job Evaluation Appeals Panel. The complainant, accompanied by his or her representative, presents a case to the Appeals Panel, as does the employer. The Appeals Panel will decide either to upgrade the job or to reject the appeal. The decision is usually communicated to the individual through his or her line manager. If the appeal is upheld, the decision will be implemented from the date of the Panel's decision.

If the job-holder is dissatisfied with the decision of the Appeals Panel, he or she may request that the case goes to a third stage and be heard by an Independent Appeals Body. At this stage the job-holder (assisted by his or her representative) will present the basis of the appeal. A member of the Appeals Panel will present justification for their decision, and the Independent Appeals Body – which is usually chaired by an independent chairperson acceptable to both parties – will make a decision that is final and binding. In some organisations with job-evaluated grad-ing structures, this means that individual grievances over job gradings are at the end of the day decided by arbitration.

A job evaluation procedure is relatively clear-cut and straightforward. It has the advantage over the standard grievance procedure of building in access to experts at each appeal stage and providing more specialist panels to hear the appeals.

Dignity at work

Harassment, based on gender or race, and bullying at work have received increasing attention in recent years as organisations and worker-representative bodies have become more concerned about the dignity of individuals in the workplace. Many organisations have policies and procedures which link the complaints procedure on harassment with the existing grievance procedure rather than establishing separate arrangements for such complaints. Others have treated it as a specific issue. Both approaches work.

In organisations where a harassment policy exists, it is normal for a dual system to operate. The initial action is usually confined to the specifics of the complaint within the procedure laid down for managing sexual harassment. If the problem cannot be resolved within the limits of the policy and is proved to be an issue that merits disciplinary proceedings, then the disciplinary procedure is triggered.

When an employee complains that he or she has suffered sexual harassment from another employee, whether a manager or not, he or she has a grievance. He or she is, in fact, making a complaint to man-agement. In dealing with an allegation of sexual harassment, the man-ager first conducts a thorough investigation to establish whether there is a *prima facie* case of sexual harassment for the accused employee to answer. If the manager decides, on the basis of the investigation, that there is a case to answer, disciplinary proceedings are likely to be insti-gated against the accused employee. However, this is conditional on the 'victim's' agreeing to allow the issue to be taken to this stage. If the victim refuses to proceed any further with the matter, that is the end of it. If the disciplinary proceedings are started against the accused indi-vidual and the charge of sexual harassment is upheld, an appropriate penalty will be imposed, up to and including, often as a last resort, dis-missal of the accused. If, on the other hand, the manager decides that the sexual harassment allegation has no foundation, the manager must explain fully to the 'victim' and his or her representative why this is the case.

So if a manager is sitting in his or her office and a woman employee comes in claiming she has been sexually harassed, and she has wit-nesses and wants action taken against the individual concerned, it is clear what the manager must do:

- investigate the claim thoroughly

- decide whether there is a case to answer

- if there is a case to answer and it cannot be settled amicably and the 'victim' insists on pressing the complaint, the disciplinary procedure is triggered

- if there is no case to answer, it must be explained carefully and sensitively to the 'victim'.

Different organisations define differently their acceptable standards of behaviour, particularly with respect to gross misconduct. In some organisations sexual harassment is regarded as gross misconduct, carrying a penalty of instant dismissal if proven. That this is the case will be spelled out to employees in the organisation's policy statement on sexual harassment and/or dignity at work. It is not the case in all organisations, however, for in some lesser penalties can be, and are, imposed on the harasser.

There are therefore good reasons for dealing with sexual harassment complaints outside of the general grievance procedure. First, there is a reasonable chance that the person who is the subject of the complaint is the line manager of the employee making the complaint. This makes it difficult to resolve the grievance as near to the point of its origin as possible. Second, there is a link between grievance, discipline and harassment. The role of the employee relations professional in sexual harassment complaints is to act as a catalyst for line managers to manage the issue by providing them with general expertise and support, including access to training programmes to handle dignity at work issues.

> Explain briefly the process you would adopt when dealing with a case of alleged sexual harassment or bullying by one employee against another.

Other areas

Other complex areas of employee complaint which justify having separate grievance procedures include discrimination in promotion, bullying, and alleged unequal treatment in terms of pay, overtime, travel, etc. Each case is unique and requires thorough investigation before deciding whether the grievance is real or imagined, whether the offence is proven and whether informal or formal action through procedures is appropriate. All cases of grievance have to be handled with equal care. Procedures offer a way for management to behave in a fair, reasonable and consistent manner in managing grievances.

CONCLUSION

- A grievance is a complaint by an employee that management behaviour has breached his or her employment rights, causing a detriment and considerable resentment.

- If grievances are not dealt with quickly or handled with care, they are likely to fester and harm the employment relationship by causing, *inter alia*, low employee morale, poor performance, high labour turnover, increased absenteeism and resistance to change.

- In managing employee grievances, management acquires and develops an ability to distinguish genuine from unfounded grievances, and in the latter case to explain clearly to the employee why his or her complaint merits no action by management.

- The most common focus of employee grievances is pay and conditions followed by working practices.

- Most employee complaints against management behaviour do not reach the formal grievance procedure, and there are many reasons for this – for example, individuals may be unwilling to raise their grievance for fear management may hold it against them.

- The grievance procedure provides the means whereby individual employees process their complaints against management behaviour, informs the individual of the action he or she must take to raise a grievance, and the steps management should take in giving it consideration.

- In managing employee grievances, management is guided by the principles of fairness, consistency and promptness, while the employee should always have right to be represented/accompanied by an individual independent of the employer.

- A typical grievance procedure opens with a policy statement, contains a number of stages, defines time-limits by which each must be completed, and explains what happens next if the grievance is not resolved.

- The role of employee relations professional in managing grievances is to:

  - meet line management training development needs

- devise a procedure which conforms with good practice

- promote awareness of good practice among line managers

- make sure that employees are aware of their rights under the procedure

- monitor the effectiveness of grievance procedures and identify appropriate criteria for it.

● Employers are not specifically required by law to have grievance procedures, but there are a number of strong legal arguments to support the case for formal grievance procedures within all employing organisations.

● The managing of formal employee grievances involves a number of steps – the grievance interview, preparing to meet the employee (analysis, establishing aims, planning strategy and tactics), meeting with the employee and/or his or her representative, confirming the basis for a successful resolution of the agreement, resolving the grievance, and writing up the outcome.

● The grievance procedure deals with a broad range of employee complaints but some issues are best dealt with by specific procedures designed to deal with specific difficulties that can arise (such as job grading, sexual harassment and bullying).

Further reading

ADVISORY, CONCILIATION AND ARBITRATION SERVICE (1997) *Guide for Small Firms: Dealing with grievances*. London, ACAS.

ADVISORY, CONCILIATION AND ARBITRATION SERVICE (2000) *Code of Practice on Discipline and Grievance Procedures*. London, ACAS.

ADVISORY, CONCILIATION AND ARBITRATION SERVICE (2001) *Discipline and Grievance at Work*, Advisory Handbook. London, ACAS.

ADVISORY, CONCILIATION AND ARBITRATION SERVICE (2002) *Bullying and Harassment: A guide for employers*. London, ACAS.

CULLY M., WOODLANDS S., O'REILLY A. *and* DIX G. (1999) *Britain at Work as Depicted by the 1998 Workplace Employee Relations Survey*. London and New York, Routledge.

FOWLER A. (1996) *Negotiating Skills and Strategy*. 2nd edition. London, Institute of Personnel and Development.

INDUSTRIAL RELATIONS SERVICES (2001) 'Airing a grievance: how to handle employee complaints', *Employment Trends*, No.726, April.

INSTITUTE OF PERSONNEL AND DEVELOPMENT (1998) *Fairness at Work and the Psychological Contract*. London, IPD.

INSTITUTE OF PERSONNEL AND DEVELOPMENT (1999) *How Dissatisfied are British Workers? A Survey of Surveys*. London, IPD.

JACKSON T. (2000) *Handling Grievances*. London, Chartered Institute of Personnel and Development.

KELLY J. *and* GENNARD J. (1997) 'The unimportance of labels: the diffusion of the personnel/HRM function', *Industrial Relations Journal*, Vol. 28, No. 1

RENWICK D. *and* GENNARD J. (2001) 'Grievance and discipline: a new set of concerns', in T. Redman and A. Wilkinson (eds) *Contemporary Human Resource Management*. London, Pearson Education Ltd.

ROLLINSON D., BROADFIELD A. *and* EDWARDS E. (1996) 'Supervisor and management styles in handling discipline and grievance: Part 2 – Approaches to handling discipline and grievance', *Personnel Review*, Vol. 25, No.4.

TORRINGTON D. *and* HALL L. (1998) *Personnel Management*. Hemel Hempstead, Prentice Hall.

12 • Managing Redundancies

CHAPTER OBJECTIVES

When you have completed this chapter you will be able to:

- understand the connection between redundancy and the management of change

- produce a redundancy policy and associated procedures

- explain the legal framework in respect of redundancy, in particular the requirements on consultation

- understand the need to have clear policies for managing the 'survivors' of a redundancy exercise.

Introduction

Over the past quarter of a century British business has been exposed to ever-increasing competition in its own and world markets. In the 1960s, 1970s and early 1980s this tended to impact more heavily on manufacturing industry, which therefore experienced the greatest job losses. However, in the last 15 years this increase in competition has spread to the public and service sectors.

Notwithstanding the significant improvements in competitiveness of many UK businesses in the last decade, Britain has not always been successful in competing in overseas markets, nor in defending home markets. In the 1970s and 1980s this supposed weakness of the British economy was variously blamed on trade union resistance to change, poor and badly trained management, too much or too little UK Government spending, and a whole range of other economic and social factors. Since the mid-1990s, however, the view of Britain's economy has changed and is perceived, relative to its competitors', as reasonably strong and stable. Yet despite this, we still see many organisations having to reduce their labour force. As always, a number of factors are held to be at fault – an exchange rate that is too high, non-membership of the euro, a financial system geared to shareholder reward rather than to capital investment, and so forth. That capital investment has been neglected is borne out by a survey of 600 chief executives worldwide, carried out anonymously by PricewaterhouseCoopers. This survey showed that although UK bosses pretend to focus on the long term and ignore daily fluctuations in their company's share price, what they actually do is the reverse:

The increase in redundancy

Every few years, the fluctuating nature of our economic life-cycle means that we become used to hearing the words 'downturn', 'slowdown' and 'downsize'. A combination of problems in the global market and the knock-on effects of 11 September have, once again, raised the spectre of large-scale redundancies. As Jane Pickard has reported (*People Management*, 22 November 2001), the 'dot.com slump, the general economic downturn in the USA ... and the collapse of the airline industry have pushed the British economy into a state of caution, where companies are looking to pare back costs'. This combination of events meant, said Pickard, 'that jobs in sectors as diverse as publishing and consultancy, finance and hospitality, not to mention the massive cuts made by companies in the thick of the crisis, such as British Airways and Rolls-Royce' were under threat. These cyclical economic fluctuations are likely always to be with us in some form or other, so it is no surprise that a survey carried out by career consultants Penna Sanders & Sidney (reported in *People Management*, 5 April 2001) found that 70 per cent of their respondents said that either they or someone they were close to had been made redundant.

As always, whenever there are major job losses it will have a cascade effect downwards on to smaller businesses which are somewhere in the supply chain, or which are affected by changes in consumer spending. This means that the employee relations professional must always be alive to the potential for redundancy – which is the reason we are devoting a whole chapter to redundancy issues.

The legal regulation of redundancy

Prior to 1965 employees had no statutory protection in respect of redundancy. The right of organisations to hire and fire at will was seen as one of those inalienable 'management rights' that were necessary if organisations were to compete successfully in a commercial world. However, by the beginning of the 1960s there was a widespread belief that economic growth was being held back because of a lack of labour mobility. The Redundancy Payments Act 1965 was part of the answer to this problem and enjoyed the support of both major political parties as well as both sides of industry – a classic example of the post-war consensus that we mentioned in Chapter 2! The Act stipulated for the first time that a worker with a minimum period of service was entitled to compensation for the loss of his or her job through redundancy. Compensation was decided on the basis of age and length of service, and was subject to both a maximum and a minimum amount. The basic law in relation to redundancy compensation has not changed much in the intervening years, but there have been significant developments in respect of consultation, selection and transfers of undertakings.

The definition of redundancy

In order to properly understand the way in which the law seeks to offer protection to those facing the loss of their employment there are a number of factors which must be considered. The first of these concerns the definition of redundancy, which is set out in section 139 of the Employment Rights Act 1996. Principally, there are two ways in which a redundancy can occur, and these are set out in section 139(1) as follows:

(a) The fact that [the] employer has ceased or intends to cease –
   i) to carry on the business for the purposes of which the employee was employed by him, or
   ii) to carry on that business in the place where the employee was so employed, or

(b) The fact that the requirements of that business –
   i) for employees to carry out work of a particular kind, or
   ii) for employees to carry out work of a particular kind in the place where the employee was employed by the employer, have ceased or diminished or are expected to cease or diminish.

To put that in everyday language: redundancy occurs when the employer closes down completely, moves premises, requires fewer people for particular jobs or requires no people for particular jobs. Redundancy can also occur when an individual has been laid off or kept on short-time for a period that is defined in sections 147 to 152 of the 1996 Act. Assuming that the reason an individual's employment comes to an end is within one of the statutory definitions, or that he or she has been laid off or kept on short-time, and assuming that he or she has been employed there for at least a minimum period of qualifying employment, then he or she is entitled to a statutory redundancy payment.

Redundancy 'can mean different things to different people. Even as a specific legal concept it has been the subject of differences and errors of interpretation' (Fowler, 1993). For that reason it is an area in which the employee relations professional must develop particular skills.

The need for a redundancy policy and procedures

For personnel professionals, job security policies and the avoidance of redundancy are an increasingly important part of the employee relations framework. In Chapter 6, in examining the management of change we said that organisations have a continuing need to evolve, to constantly search for their distinctive capabilities. This in turn means undergoing a continuing process of change and leads to the inevitable weakening of employees' confidence in their employer's ability to maintain job security. Where redundancy is unavoidable, 'good practice' dictates that organisations have in place policies and procedures that enable them to deal with a difficult situation with sensitivity and equity. The employee relations specialist has a key role to play in this process in informing managerial colleagues of the scope and extent of any policies, and in advising them how to manage the redundancy process.

Policies and procedures are important not only because the law dictates certain minimum requirements but also because, like most activities connected with employee relations, there is a good business case for doing so. An important element in the management of redundancy situations is the need to provide effective counselling and support for the redundant employee – support in terms of job-seeking, outplacement, etc. Of equal importance is the need to ensure that those who are to remain in employment, and may be fearful for their future, are not ignored. Ignoring the 'survivors' is likely to produce a demotivated workforce that is prone to conflict with management.

Redundancy and the management of change

In the context of redundancy we should look at what it is that causes firms to have to change and ask whether job losses have to be the inevitable result. In many cases, organisations have had no option but to declare redundancies – for example, an urgent need to cut costs or a failure to win an important contract. These are just two examples of where immediate action has to be taken. But redundancies might sometimes have been avoided if organisations had invested more time in human resource planning, training or skills development.

The PricewaterhouseCoopers survey referred to above concluded that in many cases job cuts represented no more than the easy option. The lack of foresight shown by many business leaders is pointed out by Duncan Brown of Towers Perrin (*People Management*, 22 November 2001) in his report on the 'boardroom rejection of a number of HR initiatives to do with recruiting and retaining top talent, including, ironically, one concerned with leadership development'. They were rejected, Brown noted, 'not on principle but for expediency'. In his view the 'traditional UK corporate response to a downturn – pay freezes and ... redundancies –' can often prove disastrous.

In a complex business world we have to recognise that business change will continue to lead to reduced workforces because organisations are under continuous pressure to

- improve their effectiveness

- increase profitability

- reduce costs

- yet remain innovative.

But businesses can be changed without wholesale job losses. Changes in markets have created a need for organisations to be much more responsive to their customers' requirements. In manufacturing, for example, consumers demand higher and higher quality standards combined with greater value for money. But better long-term planning might indicate that costs, other than people ones, could be reduced – costs of items such as wasted information technology and bloated administration, and costs of uncontrolled purchasing.

> Has your organisation had cause to declare any redundancies in the past two years? If so, could those redundancies have been avoided?

In Chapter 6 we looked in detail at the need for organisations to develop clear business strategies that would, in turn, help to identify what their people strategies ought to be and how they should manage change. For many the answer has been to downsize the organisation or to introduce flexible working practices. These responses, according to Sparrow and Marchington (1998):

> *raise questions about the most appropriate organisational form ... Under the burden of economic and competitive pressure, a range of organisational strategies is aimed at competing not just on cost but on quality and speed of response.*

Evidence suggests that had alternatives to redundancy been at the top of everybody's agenda, some of the large numbers of jobs that have disappeared over the past three decades might have been saved. For many senior managers the need to deliver very large productivity increases and cost savings made redundancy the only option (P. Lewis, 1993). Although this lack of choice has to be acknowledged, there are two reasons why employers ought to be considering the alternatives to redundancy. One is that every organisation must endeavour to maintain some form of competitive advantage. Two, it is a reasonable presumption to say that competitive advantage is unlikely to be achieved and maintained without a committed and motivated workforce.

Decisions over redundancy – because they are often made to address an immediate and short-term problem – can create an entirely wrong effect, the opposite of the one intended. They can engender a mood of disillusionment and cynicism that, if allowed to fester, can destroy any of the short-term financial gains of a redundancy exercise, together with any hope of gaining employee commitment to the future. Sparrow and Marchington (1998) make the point that in relation to downsizing and de-layering:

immediate financial and performance measurements made today cannot assess the implications of correct or incorrect decision-making, because such decisions now tend to operate and be proved effective over a longer time-span.

Employee commitment

If employee commitment is to be obtained, together with high levels of motivation, then employees have to feel secure in their employment, not afraid for their future. In 1983, when UK unemployment was at over 3 million, Ron Todd – then General Secretary of the Transport Workers' Union (TGWU) – commented that there were 3 million people on the dole, and another 23 million who were scared to death (Blyton and Turnbull, 1994). There is little evidence to suggest that the fear factor has gone away. In a 1996 report the IPD stated that 'insecurity has damaged people's commitment', a state of affairs that if not remedied 'has the potential to damage competitive performance'. The Penna Sanders & Sidney survey is further evidence that redundancy remains a spectre that can affect individuals' perceptions of their job security. Although we can acknowledge that all businesses have to worry about competition, about retaining their competitive edge, about growth and even about survival, these worries might be eased if they know they have a committed and loyal workforce. The challenge is how to overcome the 'fear factor' and to achieve the necessary commitment that is so important.

There is no magic formula for achieving commitment, but a 1995 survey by the IPD and Templeton College, Oxford, identifies some important elements that can help management towards getting close to this objective. One of these is trust, on which, says the survey, the 'psychological contract' that the employer has with employees must rest. The employees will have trust if they are confident that the employer will continue to search for new customers and new markets, thus making it possible for their talents to be employed. Clearly, as the survey points out, 'trust is vulnerable to the incidence of redundancy in an organisation', and serious questions 'are now being raised about some of the cost-reduction, redundancy and downsizing policies' that have been prevalent in recent years. This, said the survey, had caused some employers to declare that they would offer continual employment except in the most unprecedented circumstances. Where businesses find it impossible to underwrite job security, they should commit to consulting on those strategic issues that can affect security of employment.

Whether or not there have been redundancies in your own organisation, what do think is the current position in respect of employee
security? Do you and your colleagues feel secure, or is there some
concern about the future?

Much depends on the interaction between managers and the workforce
that can correspond to a means of fostering the levels of commitment
and loyalty being sought. Such imperatives constitute the major reason
for the concerted push by human resource specialists to integrate
people management issues into strategic management. As Pettigrew
and Whipp (1991) argue, one of the central contributors to competitive
performance is the way in which people within a firm are managed. In
employee relations terms, this means creating a partnership between
workers and their managers that is collaborative, not adversarial. There
are quite a few examples of cases in which employers and employees
have been prepared to negotiate and make agreements over job security, although they have tended to be in unionised environments.

Are you aware of any other arrangements of this kind? Is it something your organisation has considered?

Policies and procedures

No matter what sort of strategic vision an organisation employs, there
will sometimes be no alternatives to reducing the numbers employed.
The possibility that this will occur is much higher now than it was 20
years ago. Good employee relations practice dictates a need for clear
policies and procedures which allow redundancy situations to be dealt
with in a professional and equitable manner. Not only are there legal
regulations to be taken into account, but the 'psychological contract'
has to be maintained.

Policy

A statement of policy on redundancy might, in some ways, be better
classified as an organisation's statement of intent in respect of its commitment to maintaining employment. For example, a policy statement on
redundancy might be set out as follows:

> The company intends to develop and expand its business activi-
> ties in order to maintain its competitive advantage within our
> existing marketplace. It is also our intention to seek new prod-
> ucts and markets, provided they have a strategic fit with the rest
> of the business. To achieve these objectives we need the active

co-operation and commitment of the whole workforce. In return our aim is to provide a stable work environment and a high level of job security. However, we must also do our best to ensure the economic viability of the business in the competitive world in which we now have to operate. In such a world, changes in markets, technology or the corporate environment may cause us to consider the need for reductions in staffing levels. In order to mitigate the impact of any reductions in staff the following procedure will be adopted.

Such a policy statement does not make any commitment to no compulsory redundancies, but it is an important first step in recognising people as an important asset. Evidence is already beginning to suggest that the downsizing, re-engineering culture of the late 1980s/early 1990s can have a detrimental effect on businesses that are seeking to grow. A study by International Survey Research cites responses from a number of senior HR managers which revealed that downsizing went too far and the overall effect was negative (*People Management*, November 1996). We have already quoted the Sparrow and Marchington view that decision-making must be evaluated over a longer time-scale. Many organisations are now beginning to recognise that they have lost valuable experience and skills which are proving difficult to replace.

Mumford and Hendricks, in charting the rapid rise and fall of the business re-engineering concept (*People Management*, May 1996), argued that it failed as a technique because many of its followers did not understand people and change management techniques. They pointed to evidence that re-engineering always took longer than expected, involved more resources than were available, and presented unforeseen problems. Developing a redundancy policy, or statement of intent, as described above should be driven by an organisation's overall business strategy and can be an important first step in building that important management/workforce partnership. But even in the most strategically aware organisations, not everything is predictable and there may be situations in which job losses cannot be avoided. This is where the procedure mentioned in our example of a policy statement comes into play.

> Does your organisation have a redundancy policy? If so, what does it say about job security?

Procedure

The first thing to say about a redundancy procedure, as with any other procedure, is that it must fit the business. That is, it must be written and designed to cater for the individuality of one specific organisation. Draft procedures can be obtained from professional bodies like the CIPD or from commercial organisations like Croner's, but they should always be treated as guidelines or templates and be amended to meet individual organisations' requirements.

As a basic minimum, there are a number of things that a redundancy procedure should cover, starting with alternative courses of action. Where the possibility of a reduction in employee numbers arises, management should begin a process of consultation. Several legal rules relate to the necessity for consultation, which must take place with either trade unions, elected workplace representatives or individuals. The purpose of this consultation is to establish whether any potential job losses can be achieved by means other than compulsory redundancies. Some of the factors that would normally be considered at this juncture would be:

- a ban on recruitment (unless unavoidable)
- the retraining of staff
- a redeployment of staff
- restrictions on the use of subcontracted labour and temporary and casual staff
- a reduction in the amount of overtime working.

Depending on the nature of the business, other considerations might include temporary layoffs, short-time working or even job sharing.

Early retirement

If there are any employees who are already over normal retirement age it may be necessary to insist on their immediate retirement – and at the same time it may be appropriate to ask for volunteers for early retirement. This is only an option if the business has its own regulated pension scheme and even then requires careful consideration. As an absolute minimum the pension scheme must allow for the payment of pensions early on the grounds of redundancy. Most schemes certainly allow for some form of early retirement, but there is usually a penalty in the form of a reduced pension. So for any individual to seriously consider such an option, early retirement has to be associated with some form of financial inducement. In effect, the potential retiree is credited with more years of pensionable service than he or she has actually worked. The question of how many extra years to credit will depend on how near to normal retirement age a particular employee is, and the ability of the employer to make the necessary payments into the fund. It is possible that the employer might have to make a substantial payment into the pension fund – more than a redundancy payment, in many cases – to ensure that there is no detriment to the early-retired employee. Alternatively, the employer may have to provide a one-off lump sum that will take the employee up to an agreed date for receiving the pension.

It is important that these financial considerations are taken into account by employee relations professionals when they are asked, as they often are, to cost the available options for reducing the workforce. A further point to remember in considering early retirement is the position of pension trustees. Following the Maxwell pensions scandal, trustees now have much more responsibility for the management of individual schemes. Whether to allow early retirement on redundancy grounds or to enhance the value of an individuals pension is not a management decision. It is a trustee decision. For the employee relations professional all of this means that whether early retirement as an alternative to compulsory redundancy represents a viable option has to be carefully costed and researched.

If management, after giving very careful consideration to the alternatives listed above, nonetheless concludes that the need for redundancies still remains, the next step in the procedure is to give employees, or their representatives, written details of its proposals. These would include details of the criteria management proposes to use for selecting individuals for redundancy.

Voluntary redundancy

Management may indicate at this stage that it is prepared to accept volunteers, but that voluntary redundancy must be subject to the company's need to retain a balanced workforce, with the appropriate mix of skills and knowledge. As P. Lewis (1993) and others have noted, the concept of voluntary redundancy has become the most widely acceptable method of dealing with redundancy, and there are obviously a number of advantages in adopting the voluntary approach. Firstly, it can help to avoid some of the demotivating effects that redundancy inevitably has on an organisation.

Secondly, it can be cost-effective. Although persuading people to go – rather than obliging them to leave – may well require higher individual payments (possibly in pension costs), the financial benefits of a redundancy exercise can begin to impact much earlier if a costly and time-consuming consultation exercise can be avoided. It may be possible to reduce the workforce by a higher number than was originally envisaged if a voluntary approach is adopted, as British Telecom found with their 'Release 92' scheme, which was considerably over-subscribed. Accepting more people in this way obviously has unbudgeted cost implications, and it is important, before paying extra costs in this way, that a comprehensive human resource planning exercise is carried out in order to assess future labour requirements.

Another factor that must be considered before making any announcements about voluntary redundancy is an assessment of who might volunteer. It is the authors' experience that individuals who have volunteered and then been turned down display a serious lack of commitment to any reorganisation precipitated by the redundancy situation. Avoiding this requires a careful evaluation of which individuals would be allowed to go, if they volunteered – and again it is the authors' experience that too many managers make assumptions about individuals within their teams. This is where the employee relations professional, in the role of objective adviser, can make a valuable contribution.

Compulsory redundancy

If the voluntary option is not feasible, because the wrong people are volunteering or because insufficient numbers are coming forward, the next step has to be compulsory redundancy. At this point in the procedure there should be an acknowledgement that the organisation will, as far in advance of any proposed termination date as possible, notify all employees that compulsory redundancies are proposed and that a provisional selection has been made. This part of the procedure fulfils a statutory requirement. The easiest and most non-contentious method of selection is 'last in, first out' (LIFO), but the Employment Appeal Tribunal has now challenged even this. In the case of *Blatchfords v Berger and Others* (2001) the EAT observed that 'it could not be said with certainty either that selection on the basis of LIFO would always be reasonable or that no reasonable employer today would adopt LIFO as the sole criterion'. Even if LIFO is deemed to be a reasonable selection process, it can, nevertheless, have significant downside effects. To use LIFO can, for many organisations, mean losing their youngest employees or those with the most up-to-date skills. For this reason many organisations have adopted a selection system that is based on a number of criteria such as attendance records, range of work experience, disciplinary records, etc. Such criteria – which have to be as objective as possible, and be based on a system of points scores – tend to be looked on very favourably by tribunals. It would be important to stress that any selection was provisional and subject to change following consultation with the employees affected.

Creating a points score

Once management has determined what criteria should be used, it is suggested that each employee should be scored by an appropriate number of points for each criterion (usually on a scale of 10). For the managers asked to score their workers there should be clear guidance on the number of points each individual may receive for each aspect of work, and some thought should be given also to weighting each criterion by a factor in order to take into account the importance of that factor to the employer.

For example, the manager might be asked to decide which particular attribute or criterion is the most important and then to multiply the score for that criterion by a factor of, say, 5. The criterion that has the lowest importance might be multiplied by a factor of, perhaps, 1.

It is important that great care is taken in setting scoring guidelines. When all the scores have been calculated, those employees with the lowest scores are the ones who should be selected for redundancy – yet it is often the case that companies produce scores in this way but still feel unhappy about the results. In other words, they feel unhappy about dismissing certain employees even though those employees have scored badly. In such cases the employers should consider very carefully *why* they would be unhappy about selecting those employees. There may be an objective reason for retaining them and, had the selection criteria been drafted to take that reason into account, those employees would have scored more highly. An employee may be engaged in a particular project (eg to introduce information technology into the workplace), and as such the employer may be loath to choose that employee for redundancy. For this reason, the selection criteria should include whether or not someone is engaged on a particular project, and that particular criterion should be assigned an appropriate weighting factor. Alternatively, employees who have some unique or special skill that is essential for the employer to retain could be taken out of the pool for selection altogether. The important point is that such considerations must be made when deciding on the type of system to be used. It is our experience that tampering with the results when they do not deliver the desired outcomes is more likely to lead to a legal challenge from those who are selected. Graham Judge, in an interview for *People Management*, November 2001, made it clear that:

The key to devising a selection process that is seen to be fair and can withstand scrutiny by trade unions and employment tribunals is to be clear about the skills and experience the company will need in the future. This is only possible if business objectives are clear to all employees.

In summary, therefore, an employer should make a note of those objective criteria which it considers appropriate, decide upon a scoring system, and then decide upon the weighting factor for each criterion. A specimen matrix and score-sheet is set out in Table 30 opposite.

> Do you think that in your organisation line managers have sufficient information about the skills of the workforce and the future skill requirements of the business?

Assistance to redundant employees

Once the selection of individuals has been confirmed, it is important – particularly if the procedure is to be consistent with the policy – that some sincere gesture is made in respect of alternative employment. Of course, alternative employment is not always possible, nor is it always desired by those to be made redundant. Nevertheless, it is incumbent on the employer to make every effort to look for alternatives, and where they exist, to consider redundant employees for suitable vacancies. But whenever the organisation, or the number of jobs to be reduced, is very small, options in respect of alternatives are rare.

Yet the procedure must set out the basis on which employees will be interviewed for any vacancies, and the terms and conditions on which

Table 30   Specimen matrix and score-sheet

Name:		Age:	
Date of birth:		Years of service:	
Department:		Job role:	

	Employee assessment		
Criterion	**Score out of 10**	**Weighting (max. × 5)**	**Total**
Skills		χ	
Attendance		χ	
Flexibility		χ	
Etc		χ	
		χ	
		χ	
		χ	
GRAND TOTAL			
Assessed by:		Checked by:	

Source: CIPD Employment Law Service

such alternative jobs will be offered. Terms and conditions may be the standard terms for the job in question. They may be the terms enjoyed by the individual previously concerned, or there may be some form of transitional terms. These are all issues that the employee relations specialist has to consider. Naturally, the procedure must say something about trial periods.

It would be normal practice for a redundancy procedure to set out what steps the organisation proposes to take in assisting a redundant employee who cannot be found alternative employment within the business. Such steps should include provisions for paid time off to attend interviews, to seek retraining opportunities or to attend counselling sessions. This latter point will be dealt with in more detail later in the chapter.

Compensation for redundancy
Finally, the procedure might set out the basis on which employees will be compensated for the loss of their employment. There is a statutory entitlement to a minimum amount of redundancy pay, set out in section 162 (2) of the 1996 Act as follows:

- one and a half weeks' pay for each year of employment in which the employee was not below the age of 41

- one week's pay for each year of employment that the employee was between the ages of 22 and 40

- half a week's pay for each year of employment under the age of 22.

No more than 20 years' service can be taken into account in calculating an individual's redundancy payment, and there is also a maximum weekly amount that an individual can receive irrespective of how much he or she earns. This maximum amount is now reviewed *and uprated* by the UK Government on an annual basis. However, some organisations are prepared to make enhanced payments in order to ease the trauma that redundancy can cause or in order to encourage volunteers to come forward. They may also pay for more than 20 years' service if they so wish, but it is important to remember that any enhancements, to either amounts or length of service, are entirely at the employers' discretion, unless there is a specific contractual arrangement. Employee relations professionals who are charged with drawing up a procedure should be aware of the pitfalls of setting out too much detail on compensation. It is important to ensure that the organisation retains some flexibility on the issue of enhanced payments. Whatever motives lie behind paying more than the statutory amount, no organisation can predict the future or the circumstances in which redundancies may occur. It is important therefore to ensure that any payments set out in a procedure document are not to be regarded as contractual.

Entitlement to compensation

In the context of redundancy payments, the definitions of redundancy can be of particular importance. Before 1990 an employer had certain rights to reclaim part of any redundancy payment made to an individual employee, and although this rebate applied only to the statutory part of a redundancy payment, it was an important factor for an employer to take into consideration when thinking about making an enhanced payment. With the ending of the rebate, employers now have to meet the total cost of all redundancy payments, and as a consequence have become much more concerned with ensuring that any loss, or diminution of work, does actually justify a payment.

Business reorganisation
There are three sets of circumstances which, an employer might argue, create no entitlement to a redundancy payment. In the context of so much change management an employer might say that the events which led to an individual's leaving employment had nothing to do with redundancy but was simply the consequences of a legitimate and lawful business reorganisation which was unacceptable to the employee concerned. The likely scenario is that employees in such circumstances would resign and claim that they had been 'constructively dismissed'. It is quite probable that the employee will argue that the 'work of a particular kind' that he or she had been carrying out had 'ceased or diminished', and that he or she is entitled to at least the statutory rights. This would then have to be resolved by a tribunal, which Lewis and Sargeant (2000) describe as one of such tribunals' more difficult tasks. In the case of *Lesney Products v Nolan* (1977) IRLR 77, Mr Nolan and some of his colleagues argued that the change from a long day shift with

overtime to a double day shift was a diminution in the employer's requirements for work of a particular kind, and that they should have received a redundancy payment. The Court of Appeal held that such a change was a legitimate reorganisation, based on efficiency, and that therefore no payment was due.

The employee's workplace

The second set of circumstances in which an employer might refuse to make a redundancy payment concerns the words 'in the place where the employee was so employed'. This raises the whole question of mobility clauses in the contract of employment, and how much the employer can rely on them. For example, if the contract requires that an employee work anywhere he or she is sent, a refusal to do so could lead to a dismissal for misconduct, but not for redundancy. For the employer to rely on the terms of a mobility clause to rebut a claim for a redundancy payment there must be an express clause in the contract that allows an employer to ask an employee to work at a different location or locations. Even then it is by no means certain that the employer will win the argument.

In 1995 the Court of Appeal held that a clause contained in a contract of employment requiring an employee to work in such parts of the UK as her employers might dictate constituted unlawful sex discrimination within the Sex Discrimination Act 1975. The case in question, *Meade-Hill and Another v British Council*, revolved around the British Council's decision to require Ms Meade-Hill to accept the incorporation of a mobility clause into her contract as a consequence of a promotion. Although this particular case – which was decided in Ms Meade-Hill's favour – was more concerned with sex discrimination than with redundancy payments, it is important because of statements made by the Court of Appeal in respect of mobility clauses generally. The Court commented that even if this particular mobility clause could not be justified in its present form, the objectionable aspects would disappear if it were modified in a relatively minor respect. In the Court's view there was no great cause for celebration by employees as a result of this particular decision.

For most employee relations professionals the question of mobility is more likely to arise when the whole, or part, of a business is moving, either to a new geographical location some distance from the present workplace or to new premises broadly within the existing geographical location. In order that an organisation may retain a degree of flexibility in terms of its location it is important to be clear about an employee's 'place of work'. For this reason it is essential, when drawing up the employee's statement of terms and particulars of employment as required by the Employment Rights Act 1996, to identify whether 'the employee is required or permitted to work at various places' [s1(4)(h)].

The case of *Blatchfords v Berger and Others* referred to above is a classic example of how important it is not only to issue a statement of terms but to be clear about where an individual can be expected to work. In the *Blatchfords* case the Employment Appeal Tribunal examined whether a mobility clause could be implied into the employees' contracts of employment. There were seven applicants to the employment tribunal, six of them secretaries and one a cashier. They were all employed by the respondent (a firm of solicitors) at the same office in Holborn, and did not have written contracts of employment or section 1 statements. Blatchfords had two other offices in the Greater London area, one at South Harrow, the other at Croxley Green. Largely due to the loss of an important client, the firm decided to amalgamate the Holborn and South Harrow offices and to close the Holborn office on 27 November 1998. The six secretaries were offered the opportunity of relocating to the South Harrow office. Two initially said they were prepared to do so, but then changed their minds. In the end, all six refused. However, Blatchfords required them all to relocate and argued that there was an implied term in their contract requiring them to do so. None of the seven applicants took up employment at South Harrow: all left the company's employment. They claimed unfair dismissal, but the tribunal found that the employer's requirement for them to relocate to South Harrow was, on the facts, a fundamental breach of their contracts – ie they were constructively dismissed. The employer's appeal to the EAT was also unsuccessful.

> What does your organisation's standard contract say about mobility? Are there any circumstances in which the current wording could bring the company into conflict with an employee?

Alternative employment

The third set of circumstances that might lead to refusal to make a redundancy payment is when an employee refuses an offer of 'suitable alternative employment'. If the employee is offered a new contract of employment, to begin immediately, or within four weeks of the termination of the old contract, and the offer is unreasonably refused, there is no entitlement to a redundancy payment. However, the burden of proving that an offer is suitable lies with the employer. If the employee were to express the view that the proposed new job was inferior to the old one, it would be for the employer to demonstrate that it was not. How an employer can do this has been the subject of many industrial tribunal cases. In *Hindes v Supersine Ltd* (1979) IRLR 343 it was argued that whether the proposed employment was 'substantially equivalent' to the former job was as objective an assessment as any. In *Cambridge and District Co-op v Ruse* (1993) IRLR 156, the Employment Appeal Tribunal held that 'it is possible for an employee reasonably to refuse an objectively suitable offer of alternative employment on the ground of his personal perception of the job offered'. In this case Mr Ruse had refused an alternative job because he considered it represented a demotion and a loss of status.

It is very difficult to give absolute advice on such matters as alternative employment. The sensible employee relations specialist will deal with each case individually and on its merits. It may be that what is suitable for one employee may be totally unsuitable for another. One alternative is the provision within section 138(3) of the legislation that allows for a 'trial period'. This gives the redundant employee an opportunity to try a new job for a period of four weeks, or such longer (specified) period as may be agreed to allow for retraining. If, having opted for a trial period, the employee decides at the end of it that the job is not suitable, then a redundancy payment is still payable.

The law and consultation

Since the mid-1970s all member states of the European Union have been required to enact legislation which obliges employers to consult with workers' representatives about redundancy. This was generally assumed to mean consultation with recognised trade unions and was first implemented into the legal framework by sections 99 to 107 of the Employment Protection Act 1975. The relevant provisions are now contained in sections 188 to 198 of the Trade Union and Labour Relations (Consolidation) Act 1992.

During 1992 the European Commission claimed that there were imperfections within the UK legislation because:

- there was no provision for consulting with employees in the absence of a recognised trade union

- the scope of the UK legislation was more limited than was envisaged by the original European Directive (75/129/EEC)

- there was no requirement that an employer considering collective redundancies had to consult workers' representatives with a view to reaching agreement in relation to the matters specified in the Directive.

The Commission's complaints were considered to be well-founded, and amendments effected by the Trade Union Reform and Employment Rights Act 1993 made it a requirement that consultations about proposed redundancies must include discussion and consultation about ways of avoiding dismissals altogether. This change to the legislation was also considered to be insufficient, and in 1994 the European Court of Justice ruled that the UK could not limit the right to be consulted to representatives of recognised trade unions. As a response to this, additional regulations – the Collective Redundancies and Transfer of Undertakings (Protection of Employment) (Amendment) Regulations 1995 – were introduced and took effect from March 1996.

Further changes, in the shape of the European Directive on Information and Consultation of Workers at National Level (which we examined in

Chapter 3), are currently due to take place. The main purpose of legislation arising from the Directive will be to:

- recognise at an EU level the fundamental rights of employees to be informed and consulted on any decisions likely to affect them significantly

- develop arrangements for anticipating and forestalling the social consequences that may arise from changes in the life, organisation and running of a company

- strengthen the link between information and consultation on strategic and economic issues, and consultation on how to address the social consequences arising therefrom.

Irrespective of what may or may not be on the horizon, what does this plethora of Directives, legislation and regulation mean in practical terms for the employee relations specialist? What is an employer required to do if there is a possibility that employees will be made redundant? The question should be considered from two angles – collective redundancies and individual redundancies.

Collective redundancies

The Trade Union and Labour Relations (Consolidation) Act 1992 together with the 1995 Regulations oblige any employer who wishes to make 20 or more redundancies to consult with 'appropriate representatives'. These appropriate representatives should be union representatives where there is a recognised union in the workplace, but where that is not the case there is provision for employees to elect representatives. Where employees do decide that they want some form of collective representation in such circumstances the intention is that:

- employers will have to make suitable arrangements for the election of employee representatives which ensure that an election is carried out sufficiently early to allow for information to be given and consultation to take place in good time

- the number of representatives to be elected and the terms for which they are to be elected will be matters for the employer to determine, so long as the number of employee representatives is sufficient to represent all employees properly and the period of office is long enough to complete the consultation

- the candidates for election must be members of the affected workforce at the date of election

- no one who is a member of the workforce may be unreasonably excluded from standing for election

- everyone who is a member of the affected workforce at the date of election must be entitled to vote, and each person may cast as many votes as there are representatives to be elected

- the election should be conducted in such a way that those voting do so in secret and that the votes given at the election are fairly and accurately counted

- in the event of any dispute as to the validity of the election, any of the affected employees may complain to a tribunal, and it will be for the employer to show that the election conditions were complied with.

The timetable for consultation

Section 188(2) of TULR(C)A 1992 requires consultation about proposed redundancies to begin at the earliest opportunity, but in cases involving 20 or more people minimum time-periods are a necessity. If the employer is proposing to dismiss over 100 employees, the consultation process must begin at least 90 days before the first dismissal takes effect. If the proposal is to dismiss less than 100 but 20 or more, the consultation process must begin no later than 30 days before the first dismissal. Some commentators have expressed doubt about how the phrase 'proposing redundancies' should be interpreted, particularly as the Collective Redundancies Directive uses the phrase 'contemplating redundancies'. There is a degree of agreement that the Directive requires consultation at an earlier stage than TULR(C)A, but there is very little case law which helps to clarify the problem, and the safest course for any employer is to start the consultation as soon as possible.

Information required by employee representatives

The timetable described above can only start to run once employees or their representatives have been provided with certain information:

- the reasons for the employer's proposals

- the numbers and descriptions of the employees to be dismissed

- the method of selection the employer proposes for dismissal

- the method of carrying out the dismissals the employer proposes, having due regard to any procedural agreement that might be in existence

- the period of time over which the programme of redundancies is to be carried out

- the method the employer intends to use in calculating redundancy payments, unless the statutory formula is being applied.

Should an employer fail to provide any or all of the information required, or if the information that is provided is insufficient, the consultation period will be deemed not to have started. In such circumstances the employer faces the risk of a penalty being imposed (see below) for failing to consult at the earliest opportunity. It is difficult to give precise guidance on what, and how much, detail must be provided, but vague and open-ended statements will not be acceptable. The employee relations specialist will just have to acknowledge that every case must be decided on its merits and be thoroughly researched.

It is no good relying on 'what happened last time'. That may not be good enough. In *MSF v GEC Ferranti (Defence Systems) Ltd* (1994) IRLR 113 the Employment Appeal Tribunal held that:

> *Whether a union has been provided with information which is adequate to permit meaningful consultation to commence is a question of facts and circumstances. There is no rule that full and specific information under each of the heads [of the legislation] must be provided before the consultation period can begin.*

The Tribunal went on to confirm an earlier judgement, which held that a failure to give information on one of the heads may be a serious default, but that there is nothing to say that it must be treated as a serious default.

Consultation must be genuine

For consultation to be deemed genuine it has to be undertaken with 'a view to reaching agreement' with employees' representatives. Three things have to happen. An examination has to take place on possible ways to avoid dismissals. If there is no possible way, any means of reducing the numbers to be dismissed should be investigated. Finally, ways should be found to mitigate the consequences of the dismissals for those that are dismissed. How tribunals will measure whether these obligations have been fulfilled is open to question. It would be strange if the legislation, as amended, meant that the employer and the representatives have to reach an agreement. What is more likely is that employers must approach the discussions with an open mind and where possible take account of any proposals put to them by the representatives. This in itself can cause problems, insofar as the distinction between consultation and negotiation is concerned. Very often union representatives will see employer proposals as a matter for negotiation, and this can sometimes be a cause of conflict, particularly where an employer perceives that the organisation has little room for manoeuvre.

Penalties for failing to consult

If there has been a failure to follow the proper consultation process, an application can be made to an employment tribunal for a declaration to that effect and for a 'protective award' to be paid. This requires the employer to go on paying the employee remuneration for a protected period. The legislation relating to protective awards are quite complex, but the important elements include:

- the affected employee receives payment at the rate of one week's gross pay for each week of the 'protected' period

- unlike some compensatory awards there are no statutory limits on a week's pay

- subject to certain maximums, the length of a protected period is at the employment tribunal's discretion; the test is what is just and equitable having regard to the seriousness of the employer's default

- the maximum periods are 90 days when 90 days should have been the consultation period and 30 days when 30 days should have been the consultation period; in any other case the maximum is 28 days.

As P. Lewis points out (1993) the financial implications of protective awards can be quite significant because there are often substantial numbers of employees involved – and yet, according to a report commissioned by law firm Nabarro Nathanson, around one in five companies was unsure about the requirements of the legislation (*People Management*, 25 December 1996).

Employers with well-established redundancy procedures are unlikely to come into conflict with the law over a failure to consult. Notwithstanding this, the prudent employee relations specialist will keep his or her organisation's procedure under review in the light of any relevant tribunal decisions. The real problems arise for those organisations that do not have a procedure or who try to put together a procedure in a hasty and unprepared manner when redundancies are imminent. Such organisations may find that the price they pay for a lack of preparedness is extremely high. Tribunals have shown an increasing tendency to take a very narrow view of any special pleading by employers that there was no time to consult, and the guidelines set out by the Employment Appeal Tribunal in 1982 are still of very great relevance.

CASE STUDY

The EAT has stressed (*Williams v Compair Maxam* {1982} ICR 156, EAT) that:

- the employer should consult the union as the best means by which the management result can be achieved fairly and with as little hardship to employees as possible

- the employer should try to agree with the union the criteria to be applied in selecting the employees to be made redundant

- when a selection has been made, the employer should consider with the union whether the selection has been made in accordance with these criteria.

To be acceptable, non-consultation would have to be the result of some event that was quite out of the ordinary – but it would be very unwise to be confident that circumstances you believe to 'be out of the ordinary' would be accepted as such by a tribunal.

Individual redundancies: consultation

Consultation with trade unions and now with the wider constituency of 'employee representatives' has tended to attract most of the attention in studies of redundancy, and there is certainly a good deal of case law on the subject. But the necessity for individual consultation must not be overlooked. Many managers have fallen into the trap of assuming that when only one or two individuals are to be made redundant there is no obligation to consult or that consultation can be cursory. This is an incor-

CASE STUDY

Nicky H has been made redundant three times in her working life, but the first occasion was the worst.

She worked for a publishing company as head of the central marketing team, which acted as an internal agency. The first inkling that anything was wrong came from a colleague who heard via an e-mail that the team was to be disbanded in a reorganisation.

Nicky immediately tried to see her boss, but was told he was tied up in meetings all day. When they did meet, he was accompanied by a woman she had never seen before.

'He told me I was out of a job,' she says. 'Then he said: "But that's not the point. The point is that you are completely incompetent. The team can't stand you, you have no management skills, and I don't know why we hired you – you can't even photocopy anything."

'I was then told I would be escorted straight to the HR department and would not be allowed to speak to my team. When I got to HR, the manager said she had no idea what was going on and offered me a box of tissues.'

The incident came a few weeks after Nicky's three-month review, at which, she says, no criticisms were made of her competence. 'I have never felt like such a piece of trash in my life,' she says. 'I had bad dreams about that day for a year afterwards, and it killed my confidence. To be treated like that in front of a complete stranger was absolutely horrendous.'

She did manage to get a message to her team, however. They met her in the pub later and were sympathetic. But she could do nothing more, having been at the company for less than six months.

Shortly afterwards, she took a low-level job at a friend's firm to help rebuild her confidence – until that company suffered cashflow problems and had to shed some staff. She then joined a major management consultancy, but again found herself a victim of cutbacks.

This latest redundancy was a complete contrast to Nicky's earlier experience: she got three months' salary, outplacement support and backing from the company, which allowed her to send e-mails to contacts, kept in touch and invited her back for social events.

With the help of the consultancy, she has now decided to start her own business giving style advice to executives. She could also offer a few tips on redundancy.

rect assumption. Although there is no statutory framework for individual consultation as there is when collective redundancies are on the agenda, tribunals can still intervene. The Employment Rights Act 1996 identifies redundancy as a fair reason for dismissal (section 98 (2) (c)), provided that the employer has acted 'reasonably'. This requirement opens the door for an employee to claim unfair dismissal on the grounds that the employer, by failing to consult, has not acted reasonably.

Although not giving rise to an employment tribunal claim, an article in *People Management* (22 November 2001) provides a classic case study on 'How Not to Shed Staff'.

Most claims for unfair dismissal in respect of redundancy are in either of two areas: unfair selection and lack of consultation. If the scenario reported above had concerned an employee with the required length of service to register a claim for unfair dismissal, it is inconceivable that the employer's actions would have been judged anything other than unreasonable. But, as we stated in Chapter 10, 'good practice' demands that a firm operate reasonably and with just cause on every occasion, not just when it thinks an employee can make a claim against it. Too often we hear managers say 'He has only been here a few months! Do I really have to go through all the procedure?'

Many employers have argued that because the redundancy situation has affected only one or two individuals, consultation would not have made any difference. This defence has been virtually closed to employers since the decision of the House of Lords in *Polkey v A E Dayton Services Ltd* (1987) IRLR 503 – although unwise and unprofessional employers still try to use it. In *Polkey* the House of Lords did not say that consultation was an absolute requirement, but that the onus is on the employer to demonstrate that consultation would have been 'utterly useless'. In the majority of cases it would be difficult to demonstrate the uselessness of something that had not been tried. What impact the changes introduced by the Employment Act 2002 will have on the *Polkey* principle (as mentioned in Chapter 10) remains to be seen.

By far the best option for employers is to recognise that good employee relations would be best served by adopting a systematic approach to consultation, whether the proposed redundancies are going to affect five people or 50 people. This means that you should always allow enough time for a proper consultation exercise even when it is only one or two people that are to be made redundant. You should give very careful consideration to the possibilities of alternative employment – even lower-paid alternative employment. You must allow people time to:

- consider their options
- challenge the need for redundancy
- propose their own alternatives.

The employer does not have to go along with any alternatives proposed, but the organisation must be able to demonstrate that it gave them careful and objective consideration. It is sometimes too easy to be dismissive about suggestions made by a potentially redundant employee, but the way in which an organisation approaches the question of alternative employment will very often determine a tribunal's view of its reasonableness. Good practice dictates that you should always allow for the possibility of error in the judgements that you make. We have seen too many managers make the arrogant assumption that they must be right.

It is important not to assume someone is dead wood unless you can be sure that they have no potential to develop new skills. I have known people take on a second lease of life because of the challenge posed by a redundancy.

(*Judge,* People Management, *22 November 2001*)

Are you confident, having read the sections on consultation, that you fully understand the legal requirements? Do you now think you should advise any of your colleagues of their obligations?

Transfers of undertakings

When the ownership of a business transfers, there is always the possibility that redundancies will be one of the results. Under the Acquired Rights Directive of the European Union (Directive 77/187/EEC) member states are required to ensure, in broad terms, that all employees who are covered by employment protection legislation receive additional protection in respect of job security if the identity of their employer changes. This does not mean that an employer who acquires a new business is obliged to retain all the inherited employees irrespective of the commercial realities, but equally the new employer cannot just dispense with those employees without just cause. Should employers find that, on the transfer of a business, there are sound commercial reasons for reducing the headcount, then subject to the normal rules on consultation and the operation of a fair selection procedure, the law will not stand in their way. What the law does insist on, however, is that the transferred employees' rights are retained. This means that if they have had the requisite period of service with their old employer to qualify for a redundancy payment, the new employer cannot avoid making a redundancy payment to them. In the context of consultation, all the issues of representation and the right to information that we have noted above in respect of collective redundancies apply equally to transfers of undertakings.

Post-redundancy

The massive rise in unemployment in recent years has meant that more attention is now paid to the needs of redundant employees. In this section we look at the growth in both counselling and outplacement services, and in addition at the position of those employees who remain in employment. The latter may well suffer from the so-called 'survivor syndrome'.

Counselling

In this section we have decided to examine counselling and outplacement separately, notwithstanding that they overlap in many ways. Here, we are talking about counselling in the sense of helping employees to come to terms with the fact that they have lost their jobs. Counselling in respect of personal skills, job search and financial planning is dealt with under 'outplacement'.

Although redundancy has become part of everyday life, the loss of one's job usually comes as a tremendous personal blow. Even when 'the writing is on the wall' and the prospect of job losses in the organisation is inevitable, individuals still hope that they will be unaffected.

There can be a similarly blinkered tendency for employers to want a redundancy exercise to be forgotten as quickly as possible afterwards, and this can manifest itself in a very uncaring attitude. The employee relations specialist should be reminding managerial colleagues that they have a continuing responsibility for their redundant employees and, as the CIPD Guide on Redundancy says, be taking steps to provide displaced employees with a counselling service. Redundant employees can feel anger, resentment and even guilt – emotions which, if not carefully managed, can inhibit the employees from moving forward to the next phase of their careers – and this is where effective counselling becomes crucial. However, it is important to proceed cautiously, and earlier in this book, in another reference to counselling, we stressed the need for proper training. As Fowler (1993) said:

> *Handling the first stage of redundancy counselling requires considerable skill, and should not be attempted by anyone who does not, as a minimum, understand the general principles of all forms of counselling.*

Not every redundant employee will agree to or want counselling, yet it is important to understand its key purpose all the same. If you talk to redundant employees, as we have done, you are struck by the violent mood swings that can occur during the initial post-redundancy phase. Depending on the personality of the individual concerned, his or her mood can swing from pessimism about the future to unfounded optimism, from anger at the former employer to a feeling that they have been given an opportunity to do something different. The objective of counselling is to bring all these emotions out into the open and to help individuals to make decisions about their future. It is not a panacea, it will not stop people being angry or feeling betrayed, but it might help them to view their future constructively.

For the employee relations specialist there is a further dimension to the provision of counselling. Not only is there a moral imperative but there are sound business reasons. Unless the organisation is closing down completely, there will be other employees left who you will want to rebuild the organisation around. Richard Baker, Director of Human Resources at Hoechst Roussel, made a very valid point when he said (*People Management*, 2 January 1996): 'People . . . never forget the way they are treated when they are made redundant, and neither do the friends and colleagues who remain behind.'

Outplacement

Outplacement is a process in which individuals who have been made redundant by their employer are given support and counselling to assist them in achieving the next stage of their career. There are a large number of organisations that offer outplacement services, but the range and quality of their services varies greatly and the employee relations specialist must carefully research prospective suppliers if the decision to use outplacement is taken.

Broadly, outplacement consultancies offer services on a group or individual basis which fall into the following general categories:

- CV preparation
- researching the job market
- communication techniques
- interview presentation
- managing the job search.

Each organisation operates differently, but in the best organisations the process generally starts at a personal counselling session with a trained counsellor. Once this has been carried out, the next step is the preparation of a CV. This involves identifying key skills and past achievements so that the job-hunter can 'self-market' from a position of strength. Step 3 is to make decisions about job search methods (cold contact, advertisement, recruitment consultants, etc) and contact development – for example, networking. Step 4 is to ensure that the key communication skills of letter-writing, telephone fluency and interview presentation are of a sufficiently high standard to enhance the job search. Where skills ought to be improved, the better consultancies provide the necessary training at no extra cost. The final step is to manage the actual job search, setting personal targets, keeping records of letters and phone calls, maintaining notes of interviews and carrying out a regular job search evaluation.

Running alongside these basic services there should be a range of support services, such as secretarial help, free telephone and office space, and financial planning advice. What individuals get will depend on the particular package that the former employer purchases on their behalf.

Of course, not every employer can afford the cost of outplacement, particularly if large numbers of employees are affected by the redundancies. In such circumstances, organisations have to consider what they can do to help from within their own resources, or by using a mixture of internal and external resources. A classic example of a company that took its responsibilities seriously is evidenced by the following case study.

CASE STUDY

When aero engine company Rolls-Royce had to axe 4,800 jobs worldwide in the wake of the 11 September 2001 attacks on targets in the USA, it was well placed to deal with the crisis.

Here in Britain, the company had set up six resource centres in early 2000 to handle an anticipated downturn in the market.

The centres, one at each of the company's main UK sites, provide a three-day career-transition training programme leading to an Investors in People-recognised award and continuing, open-ended support and advice.

The centres take CIPD good practice as a model, and each is staffed with a manager, a counsellor, several other dedicated Rolls-Royce personnel and a flexible team from the company's two external outplacement providers, Capita Grosvenor and Winchester Consulting. The providers give access to national jobs databases with online search facilities.

Since the centres opened, hundreds of employees affected by cutbacks have used them for careers guidance, advice on writing CVs, training, and so on. Eighty-five per cent have found new employment, typically after a few weeks.

'One of the challenges was the reputation that resource centres have in other organisations,' says John McKell, Rolls-Royce head of employment policy. 'They are renowned for providing minimal provision to lower-paid workers in pokey surroundings, while managers get executive packages. But at Rolls-Royce, the service is gold-plated for everyone.'

The company has involved employees and unions from the start. In response to a proposal from union officers it set up a resourcing committee by means of which employee and union representatives could review redundancy support. Several improvements, such as better communications, have resulted.

Does your organisation have any sort of policy on counselling and outplacement? If not, who would make the decisions about what level of support to offer?

'Survivor syndrome'

When people are forced to leave employment because of redundancy, those who are left behind can be affected just as much as those who have left. Anecdotal evidence we have gathered from the finance sector and local UK Government indicate that disenchantment, pessimism and stress are the likely result of even a small-scale redundancy exercise. Survivor syndrome, as it is called, can be minimised if, as we pointed out above, those who are to be made redundant are treated fairly and equitably, and if the decision is made to invest in an effective post-redundancy programme. This usually means a time commitment from senior managers and a good communications process.

The disenchantment, pessimism and stress referred to above are the result of two factors. The first corresponds to the fact that remaining employees are often asked to 'pick up' the work of their former colleagues, either directly or indirectly, as the consequence of the reorganisation. In one local authority individuals had to reapply for their own jobs three times in three years following a series of redundancies and reorganisations. The second factor concerns communications. The anecdotal evidence that we have suggests that in many organisations the remaining employees are not always communicated with effectively, so allowing an opportunity for rumour and disenchantment. Getting the message across about why redundancies were necessary and what happens next is vitally important – and yet most people we have spoken to identify poor communications as one of the principal causes of their dissatisfaction.

Blakstad and Cooper (1995) identify three sets of stimuli which can interfere with communications, one of which is internal stress. Internal stress can be caused by a number of variables, but one of the causes identified is 'group concerns'. The aftermath of a redundancy exercise is a classic example of 'group concerns', and yet many managers do not take this into account when communicating with the survivors. For the professional manager who wishes to minimise the effect of survivor syndrome, communications and communications methodology must be carefully worked out. 'While it is usually impossible to understand the individual concerns of each member of the [group], structuring the communication around an awareness of group tensions can be used to strengthen retention of messages' (Blakstad and Cooper, 1995).

CONCLUSION

Redundancy is one of the most emotive issues that any manager can be called upon to deal with. Calling individuals one by one into your office and informing them that they no longer have a job is never easy. For the employee relations specialist who is at the beginning of his or her career, managing a redundancy exercise can be just as traumatic as for the redundant employee.

No matter how experienced you become, managing redundancy is never straightforward, but in this chapter we have attempted to set the process into some sort of organised framework. Most redundancies occur because organisations need to change, and although we have recognised this, we nevertheless feel it is important that employee relations specialists recognise there should be alternatives when reducing an organisation's headcount. In particular, we stressed that in an era of constant change businesses must retain their competitive advantage. This is unlikely to happen if their employees are constantly looking over their shoulders, fearing for their jobs. One of the challenges that all managers, whether or not they are personnel practitioners, face in the twenty-first century is how to reconcile the need for organisational change with the individual's need for contentment and security at work.

KEY POINTS

- The definition of when redundancy occurs is important because it determines an individual's legal right to compensation, consultation, etc.

- Redundancy should always be a last resort – but it is a last resort for which it is important to have effective policies and procedures.

- Selection in redundancy situations must be objective and capable of withstanding external scrutiny.

- If employers do not wish to pay out large sums in compensation, they must ensure that they fulfil their statutory obligations. Evidence from numerous tribunal cases demonstrates that the most expensive failure is that of not consulting with the employees.

- People do not forget how a redundancy exercise was handled, and the professional personnel practitioner will take care to ensure that any redundancy exercise considers the needs of all individuals, as well as those of the organisation.

- Because the 'survivors' of a redundancy episode are just as likely to be affected by its consequences as those who are actually made redundant, it is important that they understand why redundancy was necessary.

Further reading

BLAKSTAD M. *and* COOPER A. (1995) *The Communicating Organisation*. London, Institute of Personnel and Development.

BLYTON P. *and* TURNBULL P. (1994) *The Dynamics of Employee Relations*. London, Macmillan.

BROWN D. (2001) 'Lopsided view', *People Management*, Vol. 7, No.23, November. pp36–37.

FOWLER A. *Redundancy*. (1993) London, Institute of Personnel and Development.

HENDRICKS R. *and* MUMFORD E. (1996) 'Business process re-engineering RIP', *People Management*, Vol. 2, No.9, May. pp22–29.

JUDGE G. (2001) 'The judge who has to sit in judgement', *People Management*, Vol. 7, No.23, November. p32.

KAY J. (1993) *Foundations of Corporate Success*. Oxford, OUP.

LEWIS D. *and* SARGEANT M. (2000) *Essentials of Employment Law*. 6th edn London, Chartered Institute of Personnel and Development.

LEWIS D. *and* SARGEANT M. (2002) *Essentials of Employment Law*. 7th edn London, Chartered Institute of Personnel and Development.

LEWIS P. *The Successful Management of Redundancy*. (1993) Oxford, Blackwell.

PETTIGREW A. *and* WHIPP R. (1991) *Managing Change for Competitive Success*. Oxford, Blackwell.

PICKARD J. 'When push comes to shove', *People Management*, Vol. 7, No.23, November. pp30–35.

SPARROW P. (1998) 'New organisational forms, processes, jobs and psychological contracts', in P. Sparrow and M. Marchington, *Human Resource Management: The new agenda.* London, Pitman Publishing/Financial Times.

SPARROW P. *and* MARCHINGTON M. (1998) *Human Resource Management: The new agenda.* London, Pitman Publishing/Financial Times.

SUMMERFIELD J. (1996) 'Lean firms cannot afford to be mean', *People Management*, Vol. 2, No.2, January. pp30–32.

CHAPTER

13 • Managing Health and Safety

CHAPTER OBJECTIVES

When you have finished this chapter you will understand:

● the nature of the institutions that formulate and introduce health and safety laws and regulations

● the legal framework under which organisations have to operate in the fields of health and safety

● the health and safety duties imposed on employers and employees

● the role of trade unions in ensuring, promoting and monitoring health and safety

● the importance of risk assessment.

Introduction

Employee relations is concerned with gaining people's commitment to the achievement by an organisation of a series of business goals and objectives. Such goals and objectives can be achieved only if the individuals who work in the organisation believe that they themselves are valued by their employer – and yet in many organisations, employees can gain the impression that they do not really matter, that they are expendable. Organisations like this may have a good reward system, may have effective systems of communication, may have well-trained line managers and effective policies to deal with a range of people issues, but in one key area they are found wanting. That key area is health and safety. The CIPD Professional Standards state that:

> *The underlying aim of health and safety is to promote the wellbeing of employees and others affected by the operation of any business, service or organisation. When a workplace is safe and people see that their wellbeing is respected, it is likely to improve morale and support other human resource policies. Work itself can have positive or negative long-term effects on employee health: it is an increasingly important aspect of health and safety to ensure that risks to physical or mental health are identified and controlled.*

If, on the other hand, people consider that their health, safety or welfare at work is of little or no consequence to their manager, or worse, to the organisation as a whole, their commitment to the business will diminish. And yet, as the CIPD Standards go on to say,

> *Those organisations successfully managing health and safety recognise that health and safety policies align with their other human resource management policies.*

Too often, when the words 'health and safety' are mentioned, management teams raise a collective groan of despair.

Why is this? It is widely acknowledged that injuries and disease from workplace activity constitute a moral, legal and economic problem. The cost of accidents and disease to the country as a whole is extremely difficult to calculate, especially when a substantial proportion of accidents are of a minor nature and go unreported. Yet it has been estimated that every year more than 2 million people suffer ill health caused by work, and that more than 30 million working days are lost through injury or ill health. This has immense consequences for productivity within an individual organisation, but also for UK Ltd.

Nevertheless, it is not all bad news. Despite a clear distaste for health and safety legislation and the lack of popularity for the enforcement mechanisms, there is little doubt that Britain has come a long way in protecting the health and safety of the workforce. In 1884 Her Majesty's Factories Inspector reported that 403 people had been killed while at work in the country's factories during the previous year. By the start of the present decade the Health and Safety Commission (HSC) annual statistics showed 'only' 31 deaths in the manufacturing sector. In mining, Her Majesty's Inspector of Mines reported 998 miners killed in 1884; in 2000 this had been reduced to 6. However, as Figure 7 demonstrates, we must not be complacent. The year 2000/2001 saw an unwelcome upturn in the fatal injury rate, representing the deaths of 295 workers (both employed and self-employed) – an increase of 75 more work-related deaths across Britain than during the previous year. Nor should we be concerned just about fatal injuries. In the financial year 1999/2000, the Health and Safety Executive (HSE) estimated that there were 343,000 reportable injuries to employees. Not only do these figures represent serious distress to those involved, and to their families, but they are a drain on national resources. Current estimates put the cost of reported injuries at around £18 billion a year. Then there is the cost to an individual business if employees are injured or disabled at work. Even if there is no occupational sick-pay scheme in place, statutory sick pay is due, there is a cost in lost productivity, the cost of management time in carrying out an accident investigation, and finally, the possibility that an individual can claim damages through legal action. For more information on a range of health and safety statistics readers are encouraged to visit the HSE website, www.hse.gov.uk. Such is the concern at the ever-mounting cost of lack of awareness that the Health and Safety Commission has called:

Figure 7   The annual fatal injury rates for UK employees (per 100,000), 1971–2001

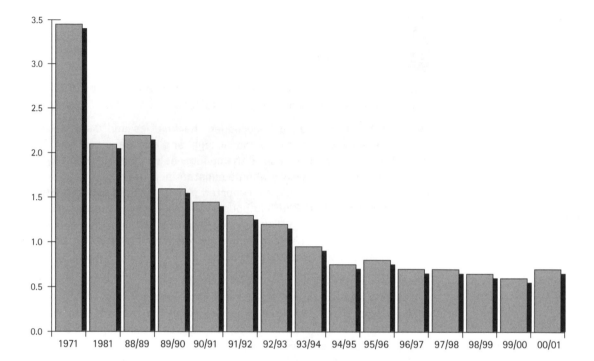

 for a compulsory duty on all organisations to investigate all reportable incidents, cases of ill health or even 'near misses' that could have resulted in injuries. The Commission believes that the proposals can save the UK £1.8 billion a year, including £600 million for business, if employers turn their attention to those incidents not currently investigated. 　

(C. Taylor, People Management)

Try to get hold of statistics that tell you how much accidents at work and sickness cost your organisation each year.

Because of the clear link between health and safety and employee commitment and productivity, it is important that personnel professionals play their part in creating a positive health and safety culture in the workplace. As a further extract from the CIPD Professional Standards emphasises:

Health and safety is an all-embracing multi-disciplinary topic and requires a knowledge of a wide range of subjects such as law, risk/safety management, occupational health and hygiene, ergonomics and human factors.

How seriously is health and safety taken in your organisation? Is the individual with operational responsibility a senior manager?

The Health and Safety at Work etc Act 1974

The statistics quoted above on deaths at work mean that it would be churlish to pretend that there have not been real increases in the standard of health and safety management. The major breakthrough came at the beginning of the 1970s. The report of the Committee on Safety and Health at Work (the Robens Report) was published in 1972 and was directly responsible for the introduction of the present system of safety management. This came into being in 1974, when the Health and Safety at Work etc Act (the HSW Act) set up new institutions and provided for the progressive revision and replacement of all health and safety law as it was then.

Health and safety institutions

The Act created a number of institutions of which the two most important are the Health and Safety Commission (HSC) and the Health and Safety Executive (HSE).

The Health and Safety Commission is a body of up to ten people appointed by the Secretary of State (currently, the Secretary of State for Transport, Local Government and the Regions) after consultation with organisations representing employers, employees, local authorities and others, as appropriate. A recent innovation is that one of the present members of the Commission has been appointed to represent the public interest, which, given issues like rail safety, can be seen as a highly progressive step. HSC's primary function is to make arrangements to secure the health, safety and welfare of people at work, and the public, in the way undertakings are conducted, including proposing new laws and standards, conducting research, providing information and advice, and being responsible for the control of explosives and other dangerous substances. It has a specific duty to maintain the Employment Medical Advisory Service, which provides advice on occupational health matters. It also has a general duty to help and encourage people concerned with all these matters.

The Health and Safety Executive is a body of three people appointed by the Commission with the consent of the Secretary of State. The Executive advises and assists the Commission in its functions. It has some specific statutory responsibilities of its own, notably for the enforcement of health and safety law. The Executive employs approximately 4,000 people including policy advisers, technologists, scientific and medical experts, and a larger body of inspectors (who are their best-known personnel). They are collectively known as the HSE.

Local authorities also have statutory responsibilities for the enforcement of health and safety law. These apply mainly in the distribution, retail, office, leisure and catering sectors. HSE liaises closely with local authorities on enforcement matters through the Health and Safety Executive/Local Authorities Enforcement Liaison Committee (HELA). An enforcement liaison officer network in HSE regional offices across Britain also provides advice and support for local authorities.

Ministerial responsibilities

Health and safety is regulated in the same way across the whole of Great Britain. A number of different Secretaries of State are responsible to Parliament at Westminster for the activities of the HSC and the HSE in different areas. The Secretary of State for Transport, Local Government and the Regions answers to Parliament on the HSC and the HSE's staffing and resourcing, on matters affecting the protection of workers and on all other activities of the Commission and Executive, except when these come within the specific area of responsibility of another Secretary of State. For example, the Secretary of State for Trade and Industry answers on nuclear safety and health, and the safety aspects of barriers to trade, whereas the Secretary of State for the Environment and Rural Affairs is responsible for certain aspects of pesticide safety. In most of these matters the Commission and Executive act by virtue of their powers and duties under the Health and Safety at Work etc Act and its associated legislation, or European legislation. In a few they act under agreements as the agent of the Secretary of State concerned.

Secretaries of State have the power to direct the Commission in particular matters, and they themselves may introduce health and safety law, provided that they consult the Commission. In practice, the Commission has put forward almost all health and safety proposals since the 1974 Act to Ministers. In exercising their responsibilities for negotiating and implementing European health and safety law, Ministers have always looked to the Commission for help and advice.

Advisory committees

The HSE provides the Commission with policy, technological and professional advice. Other expert advice comes from HSC's network of advisory committees. Some deal with particular hazard areas such as hazardous substances, and some with particular industries like construction or the railways. Each includes a balance of employer and employee representatives and, where appropriate, technological and professional experts. Each is serviced by the HSE. Their main function is to recommend standards and guidance and, in some cases, to comment on policy issues confronting the HSC or to recommend an approach to a particular new problem.

The Commission and Executive have links with other bodies, notably with the universities, engineering institutions and the National Radiological

Protection Board, which has a national function in relation to ionising and other radiations. They also maintain close contact with professional and scientific societies – for example, the Royal Society, the British Occupational Hygiene Society, the Institute of Occupational Hygienists and the Royal Society of Chemistry – which make a major input into the development of the scientific and technical base of occupational health and safety in the UK.

One example of the research that is carried out in respect of health and safety issues, and that is very relevant to organisations with a mobile workforce such as sales representatives or delivery drivers, may be seen in the work of the Work-Related Road Safety Task Group. This group has been set up by the Commission to consider occupational road risk. It is estimated that around 800 employees die every year when driving for work purposes. This equates to a quarter of all fatal road traffic accidents.

Fatigue is a major problem (as evidenced by the Selby rail crash), and if employees are travelling long distances and then attending high-pressure meetings, they are unlikely to be getting sufficient rest. Failure by employers to address the risks of excessive driving can lead to the courts' imposing heavy penalties. In one case at the Old Bailey, the directors of a haulage company were found to have been grossly negligent after one of their drivers fell asleep at the wheel and killed two people. The court held that the directors should have realised that the driver – who spent 60 hours a week behind the wheel – had failed to take proper breaks and was in a 'dangerously exhausted state'.

Figure 8 Health and safety in Great Britain – the main institutions

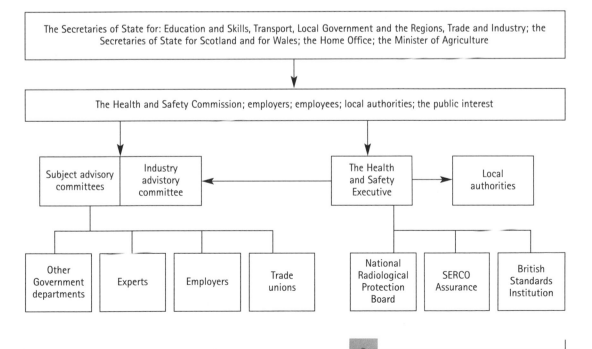

> If your organisation employs individuals who drive as part of their work (sales representatives, van drivers, etc), what checks are made on their driving hours, and are they encouraged to take breaks?

Duties imposed by the Act

The Health and Safety at Work etc Act applies to all work situations. The starting-point and main principle of the Health and Safety at Work etc Act is that it is those who create risk from work activity who are responsible for the protection of workers and the public from any consequences to their health or safety. The Act places specific responsibilities on employers, the self-employed, employees, designers, manufacturers, importers and suppliers. Associated legislation places additional duties on owners, licensees, managers and people in charge of premises. The main provisions of the Act express general duties – for example, upon employers to maintain a safe workplace, upon anyone who undertakes work activity to protect the public – and require that goods are designed so as to be safe and without risks to health. Employees are required to co-operate with their employers in taking care.

The general duties of employers

The Act imposes a duty on all employers to ensure, so far as is reasonably practicable, the health, safety and welfare at work of their employees. In particular this duty includes:

- providing and maintaining plant and systems of work that are safe and without risks to health

- making arrangements to ensure safety and the absence of risks to health in connection with the use, handling, storage and transport of articles and substances

- providing information, instruction, training and supervision to ensure the health and safety at work of all employees

- maintaining a workplace that is safe and without risks to health

- providing and maintaining safe means of access to, and egress from, the workplace

providing adequate welfare facilities

- for employers who employ five people or more, preparing, and keeping up to date, a written statement of their policy showing how management intends to provide a safe working environment, and also giving details of the organisational arrangements for carrying this out

- ensuring that non-employees (eg contractors, the general public, work-experience staff, temporary staff, visitors) are not exposed to any risks resulting from workplace activities

- providing employees free of charge with anything necessary, or required by law, in the interests of health and safety at work (eg personal protective equipment).

The general duties of employees

The Act also acknowledges the importance of employees' involvement in health and safety at work. Employees are required:

- to take reasonable care for the health and safety of themselves and others who may be affected by their acts or omissions

- to co-operate with employers and any other persons so far as is necessary to enable them to carry out statutory provisions

- not to intentionally or recklessly interfere with or misuse anything provided in the interests of health, safety and welfare.

For managers or designated leaders, not only does the Act impose duties on them as ordinary employees but it also imposes extra duties on them. These other duties are in relation to their obligation to supervise the work of others – tho Act states that:

- Where a person by his/her act or default causes another person to commit an offence, then he/she, as well as that other person, may be charged with the offence, or,

- Where an offence committed by a body corporate is shown to have been committed due to the consent, connivance or neglect of a director or senior manager, then he/she, as well as the body corporate, shall be guilty of an offence.

Safety policy

One of the strict duties imposed on employers under the Health and Safety at Work Act is that they are obliged to have a safety policy that must be communicated to all employees. This does not mean that every single employee must be given a copy but that the policy must be prominently displayed where it can easily be seen. Some organisations manage this process by including a copy of the policy in the employee handbook; others have a specific 'health and safety' notice-board. There is no format laid down for a health and safety policy, but the HSE does provide guidelines (again available from its website) on what form a policy statement should take. An intrinsic part of the health and safety policy is the organisational arrangements that have been put in place for the actual management of safety issues. Such organisational arrangements will specify who in the organisation has what responsibilities for particular issues. This is a key document, because whereas the policy can be seen as a sort of 'apple pie and motherhood' statement, the organisational document clearly spells out who should do what. The following example of a policy statement and the organisational arrangements that flow from it demonstrates this point.

Health and Safety at Work Act 1974 – General policy statement

It is Company policy to promote the highest standard of health and safety at all levels of business. The policy is to do all that is reasonable to prevent personal injury and damage to property and to protect everyone (including our clients) from foreseeable hazards. In particular this Company has responsibility:

- to provide and maintain a safe and healthy working environment for employees, taking account of any statutory requirements

- to provide and maintain safe plant, equipment and systems of work, taking account of any statutory requirements

- to provide information, training and instruction to enable employees to perform their work safely and efficiently

- to make available all necessary and relevant safety devices, protective clothing and equipment and to supervise their correct use

- to maintain a constant and continuing interest in health and safety matters applicable to the Company's activities, in particular by consulting and involving employees and/or their representatives wherever possible

- to make reports and keep records taking account of statutory requirements.

Employees have a duty to co-operate in the operation of this policy:

- by working safely and efficiently, having regard for others

- by meeting statutory obligations

- by promptly reporting incidents involving other employees, clients or plant, equipment, or working practices that have resulted or may result in injury or damage

- by observing company procedures and rules in a manner appropriate to securing a safe and healthy workplace

- by assisting in the investigation of accidents with the object of introducing measures to prevent a recurrence.

Signed

Managing Director

Organisational arrangements

The Managing Director will be responsible for ensuring that Group policy is carried out.

A Competent Person will advise the Managing Director on safety matters and formulate the Company's health and safety policy. He/she will draw up or assist in drawing up risk assessments and safe working practices and carry out safety audits.

A Safety Officer is to be nominated, in writing, by operational managers and managers for each [department or location]. The Safety Officer bears direct responsibility for health and safety and environmental matters. The Safety Officer's duties include checking that regulations and Company safety policies are being complied with, and promoting the safe conduct of the work. The Safety Officer may be the [departmental or site manager].

The operations manager and managers will be responsible for maintaining high health and safety standards in their areas of control, including appropriate consultation with staff and contact with local authorities. They will review accident reports and progress action, where appropriate. They will be responsible for ensuring that all employees in their departments or sections are instructed in the policy of health and safety, and that the arrangements are being applied effectively. They will be responsible for the maintenance of equipment and processes on which personal safety depends, and for the safe introduction of new materials, machinery and processes.

Safety representatives are to be [elected or appointed] for each [department or location] and will sit on the Safety Committee, while carrying no additional responsibility. They will communicate safety concerns to their management and the committee, and will keep a watchful eye on safety matters [in their department/at their site].

Individual employees will be responsible for complying with the Company's health and safety policy by observing the Company rules on such matters and taking reasonable care for the health and safety of themselves, other employees and our clients.

The Grievance Procedure will be the means by which employees register a grievance to supervision on a matter of health or safety. The procedure provides for rapid consideration of any problem.

Arrangements: all employees are expected to study the detailed health and safety arrangements under the heading 'Organisation and Administration' applicable to their working location, or to the location being visited, which is available from their line manager.

> If it is your company's practice to issue the health and safety policy to all employees, are you sure that they understand it? If that is not the company's practice, should you be thinking of other ways of getting the message of the organisation's safety intentions across?

Some of the legal duties imposed by or under the Act are very specific. For example, a mine must always have two exits, and laboratories that offer particular services must be approved by the HSE. The duty to assess risks and take appropriate action is fundamental and absolute. Beyond that, many duties are expressed as goals or targets which are to be met 'so far as is reasonably practicable' or through exercising 'adequate control'. The phrase 'so far as is reasonably practicable' is key within the Health and Safety at Work Act. For example, employers must weigh up the costs of providing a safe system of work against the risk to health and safety if such a system was not provided, Only if the costs are grossly disproportionate to the risks can the safety precaution be considered unreasonable. Most everyday health and safety issues, however, do have 'reasonably practicable' solutions. The cost of keeping walkways and fire exits clear, for example, is not disproportionately high compared with the risk to safety.

The thinking behind this comes from a legal case, *Edwards v NCB* (1949), in which the judge stated: 'A computation must be made in which the quantum of risk is placed on one scale, and the sacrifice involved in the measure for averting the risk is placed on the other.' When deciding 'cost versus risk' (in which 'risk' is effectively shorthand for the size of the risk and the sacrifice needed to reduce the risk), two factors must also be looked at. Firstly, just how likely is it that injury will in fact be caused (the greater the probability that an accident will occur, the greater the duty to guard against it)? Secondly, what severity of injury is it that is being risked?

Within the legislation are various words that qualify an organisation's legal duties:

- *absolute* – compulsory: you have to do this (there is no choice)

- *practicable* – feasible, possible to carry out without genuine detriment even if difficult

- *'reasonably practicable'* – a formula that corresponds to requiring a decision on 'cost versus risk'.

These qualifications imply some degree of latitude or judgement as to how far it is reasonable to go. To do something 'so far as is reasonably practicable' is, as we note above, something of a balancing act, but it can also mean, for example, to ascertain and apply up-to-date good practice wherever it is established, since clearly it is always reasonably practicable to do that. Where good practice is not specified or obvious, it is reasonable to weigh the *seriousness* of the risk against the difficulty and cost of reducing or removing it. In such cases, risk-reducing measures must legally be pursued up to the point where the taking of any further steps would be grossly disproportionate to any residual risk. These rules are regardless of company size or economic circumstances.

In a very few cases the requirement of a regulation may be to do what is practicable or technically feasible. This means that whatever is specified must be done regardless of the expense.

Regulations, codes of practice and guidance

The Health and Safety at Work Act provided that legislation passed before 1974 would be 'progressively replaced by a system of regulations and approved codes of practice'. At the time the Act came into force there were some 30 statutes and 500 sets of regulations. In carrying out the reform of the law, the general principle has been that regulations, like the Act itself, should, so far as possible, express general duties, principles and goals, and that subordinate detail should be set out in approved codes and guidance. In 1994 there was a 'Review of Regulation', but it would be fair to say that the process of reform continues. Further change may result from the European legislative process, which sometimes imposes more detailed and specific requirements than would be envisaged under the Act, or alternatively, change may be driven by public pressure to provide safer workplaces.

The appropriate Government Minister makes regulations, normally on the basis of proposals submitted by the Commission after the consultation process mentioned above has been exhausted. Such proposals have to be laid before Parliament and, unless objection is made, they then automatically become law 21 days after being submitted for parliamentary scrutiny.

Approved codes of practice (ACOPs) are approved by the HSC with the consent of the appropriate Secretary of State; they do not require agreement from Parliament. Approved codes on health and safety have a special authority in law, as codes do in disciplinary and other matters. Failure to comply with the provisions may be taken by a court in criminal proceedings as evidence of a failure to comply with the requirements of the Act or of regulations to which the ACOP relates, unless it can be shown that those requirements were complied with in some equally effective way. Approved codes (which can be updated fairly easily) thus provide flexibility to cope with invention and technological change without a lowering of standards.

Other guidance is issued by the Commission or its advisory committees, or by the HSE, in effect as a notification of the standards its inspectors will expect. Following HSC/E guidance is not compulsory and employers are free to take other action. In addition, the HSE issues a large volume of guidance adapted to the needs of local authority inspection. Each year the HSC and HSE publish over 350 documents giving information, advice and guidance about different sectors or processes – at any one time there are approximately 1,200 priced titles and 800 free titles in print, many of the latter also available on the HSE websites.

Other legislation

Some legislation existing prior to the 1974 Act remains in force, including legislation covering mines, railways and nuclear safety, some parts of the Factories Act 1961 and the Offices, Shops and Railway Premises Act 1963.

Under the Nuclear Installations Act 1965, the Executive is the licensing authority for nuclear installations. The HSE supervises mining qualifications under the Management and Administration of Safety and Health at Mines Regulations 1993. The Railway Inspectorate approves new railway works and changes to existing works, by means of regulations made under the Transport and Works Act 1992.

European legislation

In recent years, most legislation on health and safety has been introduced to implement European Directives – mainly directly promoting minimum standards for the health and safety of workers but also via measures designed to complete and maintain the single market or protect the environment. There is now a developed body of EU health and safety law. A key element is the Framework Directive (implemented in 1993 by the Management Regulations) which established broadly based obligations on employers to evaluate, avoid and reduce workplace risks, etc. EU Directives on health and safety are based on a set of common principles and themes, which are likely to follow the same format in the future:

- the avoidance of risks
- the evaluation of risks that cannot be avoided
- the need to combat and deal with risk at source
- the replacement of the dangerous by the non-dangerous or the less dangerous
- the need to give collective protective measures priority over individual protective measures.

In 1992 six major pieces of European legislation – known in the UK as 'the six-pack' – came into being. The practical impact of this new legislation was not simply to add more requirements but rather to make explicit what was already implicit in the Health and Safety at Work Act.

'The six-pack' consists of:

- the Management of Health and Safety at Work Regulations 1992 (amended)

- the Workplace (Health, Safety and Welfare) Regulations 1992

- the Provision and Use of Work Equipment Regulations 1992 (PUWER) (updated 1998 – PUWER 98)

- the Manual Handling Operations Regulations 1992

- the Personal Protective Equipment at Work Regulations 1992 (PPE)

- the Health and Safety (Display Screen Equipment) Regulations 1992 (DSE).

Do all your organisation's managers fully understand the responsibilities these regulations impose? What training do they receive, if any?

The development of European occupational health and safety legislation is underpinned by the concept of social dialogue (explained in more detail in Chapter 4), by which consultations are required with representatives of the employers, workers and governments across the member states. Britain plays a strong role in this process: the HSE provides experts for the various groups that are working on proposed legislation, and exchanges experience with equivalent regulators across Europe. This means that the UK is usually in a good position both to influence the formation of the legislation and, subsequently, to convert the resulting Directives into national legislation through its own policy process.

The policy process

In developing policy, the HSE follows the principles of good regulation, as adopted by the UK Government, under the following headings:

- *Transparent* – Legislation must be clear and easy to understand, with aims written in clear and simple language, and people and businesses given an opportunity to comment and time to comply before introduction.

- *Accountable* – The HSE/HSC answers to Ministers, Parliament and the public for any legislation it proposes, with appeals procedures for enforcement actions.

- *Targeted* – Legislation is focused on the problems and reduces adverse side-effects to a minimum, where possible being goal-based and regularly reviewed for effectiveness.

- *Consistent* – New legislation is consistent with existing regulations in health and safety and other subjects, and compatible with international law and standards.

• *Proportionate* – The effect which regulations have on people and businesses provides a balance between risk and cost, and alternatives to state regulation are fully considered.

In order to follow these principles it is incumbent on policy staff to take responsibility for considering a wide range of options during the development of any legislative initiative, whether these originate from the identification of an issue peculiar to Great Britain or from a European or international initiative. The starting-point is the collection of evidence to justify the intervention. Evidence can come from various sources, such as experience with the enforcement of existing legislation, scientific data, or, if necessary, specially commissioned research. Alternative solutions, including non-legislative ones, are considered, their impacts assessed (see below), and associated existing legislation considered for contradictions or compatibility. The HSE has to take particular care in order to ensure that its proposals do not discriminate unfairly against any person or group.

Once the alternative solutions have been developed, this analysis is made available to a wide range of interest groups and the public for their views. Such consultations frequently take place in two stages – the issue of a Discussion Document, in which the problem is described and views are sought on appropriate action, and then of a Consultation Document, in which the details of the options are presented and views sought on practicability. The results of this policy development process and the consultations are then presented to the HSC for it to advise Ministers on the appropriateness of the regulations – if that is the option selected. If all agree that regulation is necessary, associated guidance is produced and issued well in advance of the implementation date of the regulations. This process is designed to obtain broad public support, avoid unintentional consequences, produce a solution that is enforceable, and balance the risks, costs and benefits.

A current topic of concern to many individuals is the liability of company directors for fatal accidents that are caused by a less than rigorous safety regime, and whether such individuals should be prosecuted for 'corporate manslaughter'. This is a key issue for the Government and the Commission as they try to bring home to the leaders of British industry their responsibility for leadership on risk management issues. It fits in well with wider initiatives, like moves towards greater social and environmental responsibility in business. As part of this process the Commission issued guidance on 'Directors' responsibilities for health and safety', which set out what they thought directors ought to do to make sure that occupational risks are properly managed in their organisations. And 'organisations', in this context, includes both companies and public sector employers. In 2002 the HSC, for the first time, spelled out how companies can be prosecuted for breach of health and safety law. A 'new enforcement policy' states under what circumstances prosecution should take place and what factors must be considered in decisions to investigate incidents. The HSC Chairman stated (*People Management*, February 2002) that the

changes emphasise the central role of the director in health and safety. The [new] policy warns inspectors to ensure that they consider the role of the management chain, and of individual directors and managers, in any possible offences. It also describes how to take action against them if evidence shows it is justified.

As with many other topics of current interest, details and guidance can be found on the HSE website.

Regulatory Impact Assessments

All proposals for legislation, and published guidance that has the force of law, have to be supported by a Regulatory Impact Assessment (RIA) if they have an impact on businesses, charities or the voluntary sector This assessment:

- identifies the problems and the specific objectives of the proposals

- assesses the risks

- compares the benefits and costs of a range of options, including a 'do nothing' case, and non-regulatory solutions

- summarises who or what sectors bear these costs and benefits, and identifies any issues of equity or fairness

- outlines the impact on small firms and any measures to help them comply

- sets out the arrangements for securing compliance, with details of sanctions for non-compliance

- identifies how the policy will be monitored and evaluated, such that results feed back into the process of policy development.

The impact assessment develops throughout the policy process: a draft accompanies the consultation document and feedback is used to refine the analysis. The final results are presented to Ministers, who sign a statement that having read the RIA, they are satisfied that ' . . . The benefits justify the costs.'

Evaluation and review

Plans for evaluation of the impact of the legislation are required before the legislation is introduced. These use the data gathered earlier in the process (to justify the intervention) to contribute to a definition of a baseline and to allow the impact of the regulations to be quantified. The success of the legislation will be judged against how well it meets its objectives. Legislation, once introduced, is normally evaluated against a pre-announced timetable. The aim is to repeat this process at intervals to identify whether the legislation should be modified or repealed. This avoids having a growing raft of archaic legislation – which could potentially be a problem given Britain's long, unbroken, legislative history.

In 1994 the Health and Safety Commission completed a comprehensive review of its regulation, following a request by Employment Department Ministers to remove any unnecessary burdens on business, as part of the Government's wider deregulation initiative. The review set a series of challenging and far-sighted recommendations which looked fundamentally at the law in place, how it was understood and interpreted, and how it was enforced. The recommendations were fully implemented by 1998 and have involved a series of actions and initiatives to improve the way the health and safety system is regulated.

Enforcement

For most personnel professionals, and their line manager colleagues, their principal contact with health and safety institutions is through the process of inspection. The objective of inspection is to stimulate compliance with health and safety legislation and to ensure that a good standard of protection is maintained. Inspectors have, and make use of, important statutory powers. They can enter any premises where work is carried out, without giving notice. They can talk to employees and safety representatives, take photographs and samples, and impound dangerous equipment and substances. If the levels of health and safety standards being achieved do not satisfy them, they have several means of obtaining improvements:

- advice or warnings

- improvement or prohibition notices (the former requires a contravention of the Act to be remedied in a specific time, and the latter requires an activity to be stopped immediately, or after a specific time, unless remedial action is taken)

- prosecution in the criminal law courts

- in the case of a death resulting from a work activity, the possibility that manslaughter might be involved is always considered – manslaughter investigations are the responsibility of the police

- informal investigation of particular accidents or incidents, so as to learn lessons or prepare legal action.

Inspectors decide what enforcement action is appropriate in accordance with the Commission's published enforcement policy statement. Commission policy requires that enforcement action should be proportionate to the risk created, targeted on the most serious risks (or where hazards are least well controlled), consistent, and transparent. This policy is currently being revised and has been subject to a major consultation exercise in its own right.

The HSE was the first central government enforcing body to sign up to the Enforcement Concordat, which provides a blueprint for fair, practical and consistent enforcement of regulations and was a joint initiative by the Cabinet Office and Local Government Authority. As part of its commitment to this initiative, the HSC requires local authorities to follow its enforcement policy.

Prosecution

If an enforcement officer does decide to prosecute – because an organisation or an individual is contravening legislation, failing to comply with an improvement or prohibition notice, or committing any other specified offence, such as obstructing an enforcement officer or making false statements – he or she must take into account all the circumstances of the case, including its seriousness, the employer's record and the effectiveness of health and safety arrangements.

In most cases, prosecutions are heard in magistrates' courts (lower courts) where, on a guilty verdict, fines of up to £20,000 per breach for sections 2–6 of the Health and Safety at Work Act 1974 can be levied. For all other breaches of health and safety regulations, the fine in a lower court is limited to £5,000. A lower court can alternatively impose community service orders or imprison individuals for up to six months. Offences heard in the lower courts are known as 'summary offences'.

All of these options are regularly exercised by the lower courts, and each year some 2,500 charges are laid against employers by the HSE and local authority inspectors (the Crown Office, or Procurator Fiscal Service in Scotland). The fines can be substantial because most incidents involve more than a single breach of legislation, so a form of 'totting up' takes place. These fines can be levied against the organisation and/or individuals within it. In a serious case, an individual or an organisation may be indicted to Crown court, where the penalties are more severe – potentially an unlimited fine or up to two years' imprisonment.

The HSE has a firm belief that, where there are problems in persuading businesses to take a proactive approach to health and safety, the organisation's stakeholders – eg customers, insurers, investors – can create *pressure* for improvements. This pressure is amplified by the HSE's policy of maintaining a database of convictions and naming, on its website, those convicted.

Risk assessment

The most proactive basis for managing health and safety at work is through the process of health and safety risk assessments – and it is a clear legal requirement that every organisation must carry out such assessments: there is no choice.

But for risk assessment to have any meaningful benefit to an organis- ation and its employees it has to be more than a ritual exercise to satisfy a legal requirement. In the introduction to this chapter we noted that gaining people's commitment to business objectives could be undermined if health and safety was not taken seriously. Where this happens, employer/employee relations are inevitably damaged because people perceive that they are undervalued as individuals. In the context of employee relations, risk assessment therefore becomes a vital tool in the process of gaining that commitment. Looked at from this perspec- tive, risk assessment becomes less of a chore and more a means of enhancing other employee involvement and participation initiatives. Success, however, depends on the extent that the organisation involves those who actually carry out the tasks in the risk assessment pro- gramme. Sensible managers take every opportunity to involve as many people as possible in the programme because they understand that risk assessment is a proactive activity that will help their organisation to avoid needless injuries to its people and incurring losses. Three factors underpin the requirement to carry out risk assessments:

- *moral reasons* – Not many people would wish to see others become ill, get injured or die through work activities they are responsible for. It is extremely upsetting for all concerned when a serious accident takes place. It is difficult to have to explain to the relatives/partners of the injured person what has actually happened. It is even more difficult to attend the funeral of someone who has been killed by the activities of your organisation. How do you face the bereaved family? What can you say?

- *legal reasons* – There is no doubt that the law is being tightened up with more and more specific regulations. The most recently introduced legislation includes a specific requirement to carry out risk assessments, and it is impossible to fully comply with the Health and Safety at Work Act without doing so.

- *economic reasons* – Enormous financial implications arise from the mismanagement of health and safety at work. HSE studies have shown that in accident situations, uninsured costs heavily outweigh insured costs. The possible uninsured losses to be incurred from accidents at work which must be taken into account include such things as:
  - the loss of key workers
  - the loss of service to clients

- damage to the company's image – for instance, when an organisation from the caring sector, such as a Health Service Trust, is featured in the media following work-related injuries or illness to staff or patients
- damage to supplier relationship – if you are a total-quality organisation and you suffer accidents which are featured in the media, what is implied about your management control systems, and how would this be interpreted by your major customers?

Legislation requiring risk assessment

Although the personnel professional may not be directly responsible for the carrying out of risk assessments, the outcome of such assessments, or the failure to have them carried out, may impact on his or her work. This is because individual employees are likely to raise grievances, either formally or informally, about unaddressed health and safety issues. The resolution of such grievances then becomes part of the HR function. For this reason it is vitally important that HR professionals fully understand the legal framework of risk assessment and the methodologies involved.

The Management of Health and Safety at Work Regulations 1992 specify the overall requirement to risk-assess every work activity and environment. Other more specific Regulations requiring risk assessments include:

- the Manual Handling Operations Regulations 1992

- the Personal Protective Equipment at Work Regulations 1992 (PPE)

- the Health and Safety (Display Screen Equipment) Regulations 1992 (DSE)

- the Noise at Work Regulations 1989

- the Control of Substances Hazardous to Health Regulations 1999 (COSHH 99)

- the Control of Asbestos at Work (Amendment) Regulations 1998

- the Control of Lead at Work Regulations 1998

- the Fire Precautions (Workplace) Regulations 1997.

In general, risk assessment is only common sense – we would never cross a busy street without looking to see if it was safe to do so (an everyday example of risk assessment).

The Management of Health and Safety at Work Regulations stipulate the following general duty:

The carrying out of suitable and sufficient risk assessment of all risks to the health and safety of employees and non-employees [in fact anyone] arising from the work activities, and the identification of the necessary preventive and protective measures to prevent injury.

A risk assessment that is suitable and sufficient is defined in the approved Code of Practice as follows:

- It should identify the significant risk arising out of work.

- It should enable the employer or self-employed person to identify and prioritise the measures that must be taken to comply with the relevant statutory provisions.

- It should be appropriate to the nature of the work and such that it remains valid for a reasonable period of time.

The duty to assess risks under these Regulations is general, and applies to all eventualities that may arise at and from work. If a more specific Regulation – ie COSHH, DSE, PPE or Manual Handling, etc – applies to an activity or situation, it will not be necessary to repeat the existing risk assessment carried out for those Regulations, provided that:

- the assessment is still valid

- the assessment is 'suitable and sufficient'.

The various specific Regulations do not define how risk assessments should be carried out – they only give guidance as to what the out-come of risk assessment should be, and this allows the personnel pro-fessional the flexibility of selecting a method that suits his or her organisation's particular needs. Similarly, there is no one method that suits all organisations, and it is recommended that a method broadly fitting the needs of the organisation is taken and adapted to fit the specific situation.

In order to understand fully the process of risk assessment it is advis-able to become familiar with the following definitions:

- A *hazard* is something with the potential to 'cause harm'.

- *Risk* is the chance or likelihood that that potential to do harm will be realised.

- *Risk assessment* is a process of identifying the hazards in any work situation and making a competent judgement of the likelihood that that hazard will actually constitute a risk of harm. It involves rating the severity of that risk and identifying measures to ensure that the risk is eliminated or, if that is not possible, adequately controlled so as to prevent harm.

- *Preventive* and *protective measures* are those measures that have to be taken as a result of carrying out a risk assessment.

Some are dependent on the specific legislation involved, but HSE guidance is as follows:
- if possible, avoid the risk altogether
- combat risks at source
- wherever possible, adapt the work to the individual (not vice versa)
- take advantage of 'technological and technical progress'
- risk-prevention measures must form part of a coherent policy and approach
- give priority to those measures that protect the whole workplace and those who work there or visit it
- workers must understand what they have to do.

Anti-risk measures should form part of an approach that builds an active health and safety culture in the organisation. The combating of risk at source is an important point to grasp – all too often we treat the symptom rather than the root cause. If we regularly find water on the floor, yes, it is important to clean it up to prevent people slipping on it – but it is vital that we repair the real cause of the risk, the faulty tap (or question why the tap was there in the first place!).

Risk assessment methodologies

Methods of risk assessment vary from organisation to organisation and it is important to evaluate the method most suited to your organis-ation's needs.

The five-step approach
This well-thought out and very easy-to-use system published by the HSE (HSE Leaflet IND(G) 163L) consists of one sheet that gives useful advice to guide the user through each of the five steps, and a second sheet with headings and prompts for each step, with a column under each heading to record personal findings.

The five-steps are:

1   Look for hazards.

2   Decide who might be harmed, and how.

3   Evaluate the risks arising from the hazards and decide whether existing precautions are adequate or whether more should be done.

4   Record your findings.

5   Review your assessment from time to time and revise it if necessary.

This system should be suitable for most organisations. Some people have commented that it is not sophisticated enough, but experience demonstrates that simple, effective systems usually deliver the required result because they are more likely to receive management buy-in.

Team-based risk assessment

This is another easy-to-use form-based system but it ensures that the risk assessment process is a team activity. The system, developed by The Industrial Society (now called The Work Foundation), is based on the logic that drives such initiatives as quality circles and product improvement groups. It harnesses people's creative powers and gets them involved not just with designing safer working practices but also with more productive and economic outcomes.

The process of team-based risk assessment has as its objective the involvement of the people close to the action. In this respect it is similar to product improvement groups. The team studies the method(s) being used to carry out an activity or the features of a work area by breaking the activity down into component parts (easily digestible chunks) and asking a series of questions about each stage. Firstly, are any hazards present? If so, do those hazards represent a risk, and if so, do we rate the risk as low, medium or high? Thirdly, are we using the most appropriate method, equipment, material for what we are trying to achieve, and if we are, what controlling action/s is/are necessary? Fourthly, how are the controls to be implemented, and when? Fifthly, who is involved? And finally, what monitoring is to be carried out, how often, and who is involved?

The team should be encouraged to estimate the cost of any changes required and the likely benefits of proposed changes.

Computer-based risk assessment systems

There are numerous examples of computer-based risk assessment systems. The important points to be considered when selecting such an option are:

- Will it fulfil the organisation's needs, and is it flexible enough for the organisation to use in its risk assessment programme without having to utilise other more traditional methods as well?

- How difficult is it to operate – bearing in mind that you wish to involve those close to the action – and how long will it take to train them in its use?

A factor common to all systems is the need for some means of rating the risks assessed so as to allocate priorities for action (and available budget). A number of systems feature the simple concept of applying the description 'low', 'medium' or 'high' to the assessed risk and concentrating on the 'highs' first, and so on. This will be perfectly adequate for most organisations that in general are fairly low-risk environments.

However, some organisations – because of the nature of their processes, etc – have a number of inherent risks of varying severity which must be classified and managed accordingly. Also, many managers are more comfortable with numerical rating systems. These are many and varied but have a common theme of:

- applying numbers to gradations of the severity of hazard potential, and to the gradations of the severity and likelihood of realisation of risk

- rating those numerical factors in a given circumstance

- multiplying these factors together to give a rating.

Points to bear in mind when designing or choosing such a system include not having too large a scale of gradation for hazard and risk. This will only confuse those attempting to use the system and lead to inconsistent results. Some people have an aversion to numbers, and this could get in the way of successful risk assessment.

Experienced safety professionals would point out that many people who have carried out risk assessments have experienced some difficulty with rating risks. This difficulty centres on the assessors' tendency to focus on the potential severity of harm to be suffered from a hazard rather than assessing the likelihood of the risk's being realised, and thus marking everything as high-risk. Instead, separate judgements should be made of the level of severity of harm (injury or illness) and the likelihood that the risk will be realised.

> What system of risk assessment is used in your organisation? How often is it reviewed?

The process

Firstly, it is important to observe what is actually going on in the workplace. This means 'walking the job', observing, talking, and listening to people. For instance, what is the 'normal' work activity – does it comply with the operating manual or has there been some 'drift'? What happens in pressurised/abnormal situations?

Secondly, look for any hazards, anything with the potential to cause harm to people. It is a search that provides an opportunity for employee involvement. Get the people working in that environment to help with this. Those closest to the action are in the best position to know what really goes on and can help rate the severity of the hazard. As with any aspect of personnel, good records are vital – in this case, your findings.

Thirdly, do these hazards represent any risk? Are the hazards adequately controlled, or should more be done to prevent the 'potential to cause harm' being realised? What is the severity of the risk? How many people could be affected? Who are they? Don't forget risks to visitors, contractors, customers, etc. Again, it is vital that those who work in the area or use the equipment/methods are fully involved. Consider what might present a risk to any particularly vulnerable person such as new or expectant mothers, new employees, young persons.

Fourthly, design safe systems of work. Design protective and preventive measures to eliminate or adequately control any risks. Using the 'team' approach to do this is again vital. People will support what they have had a hand in creating. People are also ingenious, and this is an excellent opportunity to tap the talent that undoubtedly exists. The result is often not only a safer method of working but also an improvement in service, efficiency and effectiveness.

Having done all of this, three further things must happen. Whatever safe system of work has been identified has to be implemented, and once implemented, it has to be monitored. Managers must be encouraged to talk and listen to people, and to look for evidence that the safe system is being used.

One methodology employed by many organisations is to use an initial process of self-assessment – of the type that the following example in respect of display screen equipment demonstrates:

Title: Display screen equipment – self-assessment	Date:

Name: .... Date: ....

Main use of workstation? ....

How much time on average do your spend using a display screen each week?

(Please delete as appropriate)

Less than 5 hours	5–10 hours	10–20 hours	20+ hours

Do you touch type? Yes/No

Equipment present at workstation

Screen ☐ **Keyboard** ☐ **Mouse** ☐ **Other input device** ☐ **Printer** ☐

Chair ☐ **Lamp** ☐ **Phone** ☐ **Document holder** ☐ **Footrest** ☐

Desk ☐ **Other items** ☐

Display screen	Yes	No	Assessor
Are the display characters easy to read and of adequate size?			
Are the screen characters stable and free from flickering?			
Are there controls for brightness and contrast?			

	Yes	No	Assessor
Can the screen be tilted and swivelled easily?			
Can the height of the screen be adjusted?			
Is the screen free from uncomfortable glare and reflections?			
Is the screen regularly and adequately cleaned?			

Keyboard

	Yes	No	Assessor
Is the keyboard separate from the screen?			
Is the keyboard tiltable?			
Is there enough space in front for the user to rest hands and wrists?			

Assessor

	Yes	No	Assessor
Is there a keyboard pad?			
Is the keyboard non-reflective?			
Is the layout of the keys easy to use?			
Are the keyboard symbols easy to read?			
Does the keyboard remain still on the work surface when in use?			

Work surface or desk

	Yes	No	Assessor
Does the surface have low reflection?			
Are you able to rearrange the layout of equipment?			
Is the document-holder stable and adjustable?			
Is work positioned to lessen head/eye movement?			
Are all electrical cables/equipment in good condition?			
When in a sitting position are your legs clear of the underside of your desk?			

Work chair

	Yes	No	Assessor
Is the chair stable?			

	Yes	No	Assessor

Does it allow ease of movement and a comfortable position?

Can the seat be adjusted in height while sitting?

Is the seat-back adjustable both for height and tilt?

Can you place your feet flat on the floor?

If the answer to the above is no, do you have a footrest?

Does the armrest help to achieve a comfortable position?

Environment

Does the layout of your immediate work area allow you to do your job properly?

Are you able to gain access to the equipment you need in order to perform your job properly without excessive reaching, stretching or twisting?

Is your workstation free from glare caused by internal lighting?

Do windows have adjustable blinds/coverings?

Is the work area free from excessive noise?

Other items

Has health and safety training been provided in the aspects of using a workstation?

Do you feel that you have received adequate training in the IT skills required to do your job?

Have you received and understood the DSE information sheet offered to you?

Do you know who to contact within the company if you wish to discuss any aspect of DSE?

	Yes	No	Assessor

Are you aware of the accident/incident reporting procedure as documented in the H&S handbook?

Do you suffer from any recurring discomfort which you believe is caused by the use of display screen equipment?

Assessor use only.

Notes and advice given to the user:

Model assessment and proposed action report:

Workstation fig. 1	Workstation fig. 2

Other comments:

Proposed action: **Date for completion**

User's signature: **Date:**

Assessor's signature: **Date:**

Has your organisation recently introduced any new equipment, changed working processes, or recruited new staff? If the answer to any of these is yes, have new risk assessments been carried out?

Consultation with employees

In its booklet *Consulting Employees on Health and Safety – A guide to the law*, the Health and Safety Executive makes the point that 'consulting employees on health and safety matters can be very important in creating and maintaining a safe and healthy working environment'. Notwithstanding the fact that, by law, employers *must* consult all of their employees on health and safety matters, the above sentiments support the theme that we have been pursuing in this chapter – that by involving employees an employer can motivate them into having a greater awareness of health and safety issues. The upside of such motivation is likely to be a more efficient business as accidents and work-related illnesses decline.

By law, employers must consult all their employees on the following health and safety matters:

- any change that may substantially affect their health and safety at work – for example, in procedures, equipment or ways of working
- the employer's arrangements for getting 'competent persons' to help him or her satisfy health and safety laws
- the information that employees must be given on the likely risks and dangers arising from their work, on measures to reduce or get rid of these risks, and on what they should do if they have to deal with a risk or danger
- the planning of health and safety training
- the health and safety consequences of introducing new technology.

In the context of consultation, one of the most important initiatives contained in the Robens Report (1972, mentioned at the beginning of this chapter) was a significant role for trade unions in the management of health and safety. Section 2(4) of the Health and Safety at Work Act 1974 provides for the appointment of safety representatives when there is a recognised trade union in the workplace. 'Recognised' in this context means having formal recognition for the purposes of collective bargaining, although it does not necessarily mean statutory recognition as set out in the Employee Relations Act 1999. Where a union is voluntarily recognised, that is sufficient to trigger its rights to a formal role in health and safety management.

Where safety representatives are appointed by a trade union, their activities are governed by the Safety Representatives and Safety Committees Regulations 1977 (SRSC Regulations), and employers cannot refuse to recognise them. Once appointed, they are entitled to be consulted over the making and maintenance of health and safety arrangements. Any employees not in groups covered by trade union safety representatives must be consulted by their employers under the Health and Safety (Consultation with Employees) Regulations 1996 (HSCER). The employer can choose to consult them directly or through elected representatives. If the employer consults employees directly, he or she can choose whichever method suits everyone best. If the employer decides to consult the employees through an elected representative, the employees then have to elect one or more people to represent them. Figure 9 demonstrates how the system works.

Figure 9   Health and safety consultation with employees

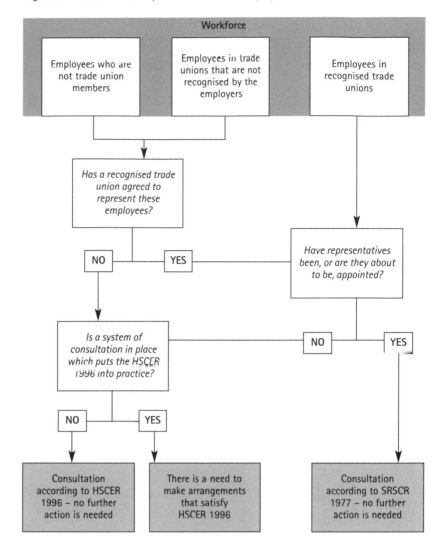

Basically, the difference between the roles of trade union safety representatives and elected representatives of employee safety (representatives elected by groups of employees not covered by trade union safety representatives) is as follows.

Under the SRSC Regulation the roles of trade union safety representatives are:

● to investigate possible dangers at work, the causes of accidents there, and general complaints by employees on health and safety and welfare issues, and to take these matters up with the employer

- to carry out inspections of the workplace, particularly following accidents, diseases or other traumatic events

- to represent employees in discussions with health and safety inspectors and to receive information from those inspectors

- to go to meetings of safety committees.

The employer must set up a safety committee if two or more trade union safety representatives ask for one.

The separate HSCER 1996 give elected representatives of employee safety the following roles:

- to take up with the employers any concerns about possible risks and dangerous events in the workplace that may affect the employees they represent

- to take up with the employers any general matters affecting the health and safety of the employees they represent

- to represent the employees who elected them in consultations with health and safety inspectors.

Union safety representatives may be elected or appointed, and the SRSC Regulations stipulate that if an employer has received written notification from a recognised independent trade union of the names of the people appointed as union safety representatives, such persons have the functions set out in Regulation 4 of the SRSC Regulations. Although it is always preferable to have representatives who have an interest in safety management, so far as is reasonably practicable union safety representatives will either have been employed by their employer throughout the preceding two years or have had at least two years' experience in similar employment. Employees cease to be union safety representatives for the purpose of these Regulations when:

- the trade union which appointed them notifies the employer in writing that their appointment has been terminated

- they cease to be employed at the workplace

- they resign.

There is nothing in the legislation which stipulates the number of union safety representatives who can be appointed, but guidance notes published with the SRSC Regulations suggest appropriate criteria for assessment of the numbers. It is important to note that none of these functions imposes a duty on 'safety representatives', although they will be liable for the actions they take as ordinary employees.

In view of the range of activities that representatives have to cover, it is in everybody's interests that they are well trained, and employers who consult the representatives of employees on issues of safety have a duty to ensure that those representatives are provided with such training in respect of their functions as is reasonable in all the circumstances. The employer must also meet any reasonable costs associated with such training, including travel and subsistence costs.

Inspection

Regulation 5 of the SRSC Regulations entitles safety representatives to inspect the workplace at least every three months, but they must give reasonable notice in writing of their intention to do so. Of course, inspections may take place more frequently if the employer agrees. Additional inspections may be made if there has been a substantial change in the conditions of work or new information has been published by the HSC or HSE relevant to the hazards of the workplace. Inspections may also be conducted where, for example, there has been a notifiable accident or dangerous occurrence. The employer must provide reasonable facilities and assistance for the purpose of carrying out an inspection, including facilities for independent investigation by the union representatives and private discussion with the employees. However, there is nothing to prevent the employers or their representatives from being present during an inspection.

It is also important to recognise that a trade union safety representative or a representative of employee safety is entitled to time off, with normal or average pay, during working hours to perform his or her functions and to undergo such training as may be reasonable in the circumstances.

Safety committees

One of the most effective methods of creating a culture of health and safety is to establish an effective safety committee. One that is genuinely effective should be comprised of a group of individuals (managers and employees) who have a real interest in safety matters and who meet together on a regular basis to seek ways of improving the health, safety and welfare of the workforce. All too often safety committees are no more than talking-shops – there because somebody thinks they ought to be. There is, however, a statutory underpinning of this process. Where at least two union safety representatives submit a written request, employers must establish a safety committee, but before doing so they must consult the union safety representatives who made the request and the representatives of recognised trade unions. Such a committee must be formed within three months of the request being made, and a notice must be posted stating the composition of the committee and the workplaces covered. Under section 2(7) HASAWA 1974 the function of safety committees is to keep under review the measures taken to ensure the health and safety at work of employees.

> Does your organisation have a safety committee? If it does, does it play a proactive role in health and safety issues? If there is no safety committee, how does your organisation communicate health and safety matters to the workforce?

Detriment

It should be noted that the Code of Practice advises employers, recognised unions and union safety representatives to make full and proper use of existing industrial relations machinery to reach the degree of agreement necessary to achieve the purpose of the SRSC Regulations and to resolve any differences. However, where an employee suffers a detriment as a result of health and safety activities, a complaint may be brought under section 100 of the Employment Rights Act 1996 (if the individual was dismissed) or section 44 of the Act. Section 100 states that health-and-safety-related dismissals are to be regarded as automatically unfair. In such cases the compensation available for the aggrieved employee is not, as it is in ordinary dismissals, capped. This means that tribunals are free to decide the size of any award. The remedies available for infringement of section 44 mirror those available from detriment on trade union grounds, but in essence it means that any individual who believes that he or she has suffered a detriment could resign and claim unfair dismissal. In *Goodwin v Cabletel* (quoted in Lewis and Sargeant, 2000) a construction manager who had responsibility for health and safety matters on site was unhappy with one subcontractor and took an aggressive approach to dealing with the matter. The manager's employer, however, wished to be more conciliatory and imposed a detriment by demoting him. The manager resigned and claimed constructive dismissal. The EAT subsequently confirmed that protection extended to the way duties were carried out.

Current and future issues

In June 2000, the HSC and the then Department for Environment, Transport and the Regions issued a strategy statement called *Revitalising Health and Safety*. This was designed to:

- inject new impetus into the health and safety agenda

- identify new approaches to further reduce rates of accidents and ill health caused by work, especially approaches relevant to small firms

- ensure that the UK's approach to health and safety regulation remains relevant for the changing world of work over the next 25 years

- gain maximum benefit from links between occupational health and safety and other Government programmes.

The strategy statement followed a consultation which had been launched in 1999 and sought the views of all those with a stake in health and safety management. The action plan presented in the statement incorporated many ideas suggested in the consultation and included measures to:

- motivate employers, through a detailed menu of the benefits of good health and safety, through a new challenge issued to industry on annual reporting, and through changes to the enforcement regime

- engage small firms more effectively, in conjunction with the Small Business Service, through a programme of tailored sector-specific guidance and support schemes

- put the Government's own house in order through the removal of Crown immunity

- promote coverage of occupational health in local health improvement programmes and take action on rehabilitation

- secure greater coverage of risk concepts in education, both through the nationa1 curriculum and specifically for safety-critical professionals.

It also set some challenging targets for the country to achieve by 2010 which, if achieved, would:

- reduce the number of working days lost per 100,000 workers from work-related injury and ill health by 30 per cent

- reduce the incident rate of fatal and major injury accidents by 10 per cent

- reduce the incidence of cases of work-related ill health by 20 per cent.

The aim is to achieve half of the improvements under each target by 2004.

Work on the action plan is proceeding and will dictate a good deal of the activity of the HSE over the next few years. In the circumstances it is reasonable to assume that some of this activity will cascade down to individual organisations during the next decade. The first step in the implementation of the action plan has been a revision of the HSC's/HSE's Strategic Plan which has used statistics to target those sectors and topics that are the cause of the majority of work-related accidents and ill health. This has identified eight priority programmes that target five generic hazards and three sectors:

- falls from a height
- accidents relating to workplace transport
- musculo-skeletal disorders
- stress
- lips and trips

- construction

- agriculture

- health services

In each of these priority programmes the objective is to improve compliance with the law, promote continuous improvement, and develop the necessary knowledge, skills and support systems. Even if you are not employed in one of the specific sectors cited above, the five generic issues under the spotlight should be of concern to you and your organisation. The blend of activities programmed for individual organisations will depend on the organisations' particular circumstances and how they relate to each sector or hazard.

Stress at work

We have already mentioned the issue of excessive driving, but figures from the HSE suggest that 60 per cent of the 67 million working days lost each year are stress-related. Time off through stress is clearly on the increase and can be extremely costly for any business. Richard Lister of the solicitors Lewis Silkin says that 'Employers must take steps to alleviate stress in the workplace to avoid personal injury claims' (*People Management*, February 2002):

On 5 February 2002, the Court of Appeal (CA) overturned three judgments – and upheld one – against employers over claims for stress-related psychological illness. The judgments were made by county courts, as opposed to tribunals, and the ruling is an attempt by the CA to establish a consistent framework across the legal system for dealing with stress-related personal injury claims.

The CA confirmed that the basis for a claim was whether the harm an employee suffered was reasonably foreseeable. This depends on what the employer knew or ought reasonably to have known. The judges said that employers are entitled to assume that employees can withstand the normal pressures of the job unless [the employers] know of a specific work problem or that a particular employee is vulnerable. They said that the duty of care test was the same whatever the employment – this means that reputedly stressful jobs do not qualify for special treatment. On the other hand, the nature and extent of the work, and signs from the employee of impending harm to health, were both relevant.

The CA gave clear advice on what was 'reasonable' to expect of an employer in fulfilling its duty of care. The indications of harm to health arising from stress at work had to be plain enough for any reasonable employer to realise it should act. In deciding what was reasonable, the judges said a court could take account of the size and scope of the employer's operation, its resources and the demands it faced.

They also said an employer can only be expected to take steps likely to do good (courts will probably need expert evidence on treating stress-related illness). If the only reasonable and effective step would have been to dismiss or demote the employee, an employer will not be in breach of its duty of care if it allows a willing employee to continue to work. In all cases courts had to identify the steps an employer should have taken, before finding it in breach of duty.

There is a risk, says Lister,

that the guidelines specified by the court could lull employers into a false sense of security, and ... therefore employers should not be complacent and assume this new ruling provides a green light for ignoring workplace stress. There are other legal avenues that stressed employees can pursue apart from an action for personal injury [and] employers should remain vigilant. Staff may suffer significant stress as a result of work and organisations should provide support. Perhaps the most significant part of the ruling is the suggestion that employers who offer confidential advice, counselling and treatment are unlikely to be found guilty of negligence. Prudent employers will put these in place if they have not already done so.

Board responsibility

There are a number of issues that are being developed as part of the *Revitalising Health and Safety* Action Plan, and one aspect of this work is encouraging large organisations to adopt consistent ways to deal with health and safety issues in their published reports. Scrutiny by shareholders – and by the wider public – of how organisations perform on health and safety will help provide a benchmark, and the Chair of the HSC and Ministers have written to 350 of the top businesses in the country encouraging them to adopt the HSC's guidance on reporting. Once again, the guidance is available on the HSE website.

There is no doubt that effective leadership from directors and senior managers is essential if organisations are to deliver the improved health and safety performance envisaged by the *Revitalising Health and Safety* strategy. As with most aspects of organisational behaviour, leadership from the top is vital if employee commitment is to be obtained.

CONCLUSION

This chapter has tried to do a number of things. We have explained the approach which the HSC and HSE take in the development and enforcement of health and safety law, and we have noted that the system for enforcement is designed to achieve a high degree of accountability, with extensive use made of alternatives to regulation such as self-help guidance materials, the promotion of good practice, awareness campaigns and advice. Where enforcement is deemed necessary there is a range of enforcement tools to allow the action to be proportional. The extensive negotiations which precede the introduction of European legislation, with its tripartite consultation, and the subsequent national system for developing legislation, including extensive consultation across industry and government, is intended to achieve consistency with existing legislation. The mature, yet still highly relevant, primary legislation in the form of the Health and Safety at Work Act 1974, with its goal-setting basis and powers to introduce supporting secondary legislation, allows the system of health and safety legislation to be targeted on those sectors or hazards which produce greatest risk.

We have stressed that it is important for safety to be taken seriously, and that if managers ignore safety policies and procedures, the wrong message is sent out. What does it say about the organisation if, when employees break safety rules, they are not appropriately disciplined because management turn a blind eye in the name of expediency?

Overall, as the CIPD Standards state:

> By playing a central role in preventing accidents and illness at work and limiting the risk of adverse effects on other stakeholders, the personnel professional adds real value. Accidents and illness affect not only those directly involved. They impact on productivity, morale, the organisation's image and the bottom line, as downtime and the costs of insurance, investigation and possible legal penalties have to be met.

Safety is not, if it ever was, an option – it is a high priority for all.

KEY POINTS

- Systems in place are designed to achieve a high degree of *transparency* on the need for legislation, through the inclusive nature of the composition of the Health and Safety Commission, the extensive use of consultation prior to introduction, and the production of accessible and definitive guidance.

- At the organisational level it should be understood that managing and creating a health and safety culture in the workplace can be considered under three main areas – *principles of accident prevention*, *strategies*, and *techniques*.

- Good management has to come from above. Employees should be able to see that their health, safety and welfare is part of the strategy of the organisation and is being taken seriously – that there is a balance between quality and production.

- Irrespective of whether the organisation does or does not recognise one or more unions, employees must be consulted in order to feel part of the decision-making process and to know that they are being listened to (effective communication).

- Any safety policy should be well communicated if it is to be understood.

- As a personnel professional you should be aware that commitment is the result of leadership. You can help develop this process by convincing line manager colleagues that they will help to further a safety culture by the way they act.

- You should be able to explain how important it is for everybody to have a clear understanding of their accountability and responsibility for health and safety and of measures for their implementation, and how important it is to identify the hazards within the workplace.

Further reading

HEALTH and SAFETY EXECUTIVE (1998) *The Health and Safety System in Great Britain*. HSE Books.

HEALTH and SAFETY EXECUTIVE (1999) *Reducing Risks, Protecting People*. HSE Discussion Document.

HEALTH and SAFETY EXECUTIVE (2000/2001) *Health and Safety Statistics*. HSE Books.

LEWIS D. and SARGEANT M. (2000) *Essentials of Employment Law*. 6th edn. London, Chartered Institute of Personnel and Development.

LEWIS D. and SARGEANT M. (2002) *Essentials of Employment Law*. 7th edn. London, Chartered Institute of Personnel and Development.

LISTER R. (2002) 'The benefit of foresight', *People Management*, Vol. 8, No.4. pp20–21.

STRANKS J. (2001) *A Managers Guide to: Health and Safety at Work*. London, Kogan Page.

TAYLOR C. (2001) 'HSC demands tougher regulation of accidents', *People Management*, June.

CHAPTER OBJECTIVES

The purpose of this final chapter is to review the reader's knowledge and understanding of the major issues dealt with in the book. The chapter should prove useful for those students preparing for the CIPD Professional Development Scheme (PDS) Standards Generalist Module, Employee Relations, in that it provides questions similar to those likely to be found on the nationally set examination paper. At the same time, however, it should prove beneficial also to readers who are studying for internally set examinations, since it provides a framework for revision, and to those who are interested in posing questions about employee relations in their own organisation.

The chapter contains a section outlining the philosophy underpinning the PDS Standards in Employee Relations, followed by two sections which adopt the format of the CIPD national examination paper in employee relations, and a third section which provides advice on how to tackle the paper.

Introduction

The philosophy

The underpinning philosophy of the PDS Standards in Employee Relations is:

- The drivers for both its content and approach are the 'thinking performer' vision and the CIPD 'business partner' paradigm.

- The aim is not principally to train personnel/HR professionals to perform their current roles for their existing employers more efficiently, but rather to prepare them for a multi-faceted future within the profession.

- To be an effective professional in the employee relations field requires continuous improvement, self-evaluation and a business-focused mentality. In other words, compliance (both legal and ethical), though important, is not enough. The former IPD's discussion document *People Make the Difference* pointed out clearly that an adherence to procedure and systems does not make the difference between organisational success and failure in the marketplace. Compliance does not give competitive advantage – although non-compliance can lead to competitive disadvantage.

- It is expected that candidates who enter the examination will become, where appropriate, advocates for their proposals and implementation plans, and will be capable of selling their ideas to a target audience.

The examination paper

The paper is divided into two sections. Section A is a mini-case-study which is designed to test a significant range of the operational indicators and knowledge indicators of the employee relations standards. It is also linked closely to several elements of the Indicative Content of the Standards. In the case study, candidates are expected to identify the problems it poses for management, to produce and justify solutions to the identified problem(s), and to explain how they would gain the commitment of their managerial colleagues and, if appropriate, the workforce, to their proposals and to discuss the research/financial, staffing and physical implications of their proposals.

Section B contains ten questions, and candidates must answer seven of these. These ten questions cover employee relations institutions, processes, outcomes, skills, and the external environment surrounding management's employee relations activities. These ten questions are designed to test the candidate's knowledge and understanding across the whole range of the CIPD Professional Development Scheme's Employee Relations Standards.

The examination paper also contains important statements on its front page. The most important of these are:

- The duration of the examination is two hours plus ten minutes' reading time.

- Equal marks are allocated to each section of the paper.

- If a question includes reference to 'your organisation', this may be interpreted as covering any organisation with which you are familiar.

- You are likely to fail the examination if (a) you fail to answer the seven questions in Section B and/or (b) you achieve less than 40 per cent of the available marks in either section.

Section A: Specimen case studies

Case study 1

Threats from the external environment
Edward Johns is a public sector organisation located in southeast England. It employs 400 people. Two hundred and fifty are manual employees, of whom half are male and the other half female. There are 100 administrative, clerical and technical and lower-level professional

staff. The remaining 50 employees are at senior, middle and supervisory levels of management. They are all highly qualified professionally. They find managing distasteful – but someone has to do it. The majority of employees work full-time, although there are some part-timers among the clerical staff.

The delivery of the HRM function is highly structured. There is a relatively large HRM department with a number of personnel assistants, officers and managers. The attitude of the HRM department is reactive and very procedural. Its ethos relies on compliance with agreements, rules, regulations, legislation, etc. The thought of being proactive is not even raised. Things work well but nobody ever takes any initiatives.

The working hours for the manual workers are 37 hours per week but 35 hours per week for all other employees. Paid holidays for manual employees are five weeks but six weeks for other employees. There are pay differentials between, and within, the main occupational categories at Edward Johns. There is a company pension scheme. The company maintains regular communications and information-giving sessions with its employees. It has the usual procedures to be found in any organisation – grievance, discipline, promotion, job grading and redundancy – and these work satisfactorily. Indeed, relationships with employees have been good and employees regard employment at Edward Johns as relatively secure. This has been helped in that the pace of change in the organisation has been slow and evolutionary. It has certainly not been revolutionary.

However, Edward Johns has just appointed a new managing director whose background and work experience has been in the private sector. This appointment has been made because important changes in the external environment are anticipated:

- The Government has announced that it will be encouraging the public sector to appoint to management positions at all levels of the organisation individuals with experience of having worked in the private sector.

- The introduction of measures reflecting the 'social dimension' of the European Union is likely to be accelerated.

- Technology is changing as computers, lasers and telecommunications continue to develop.

- The Government has let it be known that it will remove Edward Johns' sole public supplier position and will allow private sector companies to begin to compete with it.

The stable predictable environment in which Edward Johns has long operated is undoubtedly coming to an end.

The task

Produce a report addressed to the new managing director outlining:

- the employee relations policies the organisation might introduce to deal with the expected changes in the external environment, and

  - possible changes in the way the employee relations management functions are delivered.

Your report should also include an action plan.

You should devote 75 per cent of your time to outlining the policies required and the possible changes involved, and 25 per cent to drawing up the action plan.

Case study 2

Lack of strategic direction

Geoff Hayward plc is engaged in the leisure industry. It has a total workforce of 300, of which 100 are based in the company's head office undertaking a range of financial, administrative and property management tasks. A further 200 are distributed evenly across the company's 18 leisure outlets located in the southern part of the UK.

There is a site manager at each outlet plus a multiskilled workforce carrying out a range of duties for the company's customers. The 18 outlets each operate on a 7-days-a-week 24-hour basis so staff have to be flexible and capable of working with the minimum of supervision. Staff and managers from the 18 outlets meet informally together on a regular basis. There are some *ad hoc* working parties which discuss a range of issues including health and safety, customer service and training. Staff regularly transfer from one outlet to another when vacancies occur.

Geoff Hayward plc has not, until now, had a specialist personnel manager. Each outlet manager is encouraged to solve its own people management problems using, where necessary, external advice from the leisure industry employers' association. This policy has not proved successful, and the company has faced a number of legal challenges to some of its decisions. These issues related to working time, dismissals on the grounds of ill health, and claims for payment of wages.

Geoff Hayward plc has no proper salary structure and there has been considerable dissatisfaction with the salaries paid at each outlet. In some cases, outlets operating in the same labour market conditions are paying widely different salaries to staff who undertake the same work. This has led to a serious decline in staff morale, a rise in labour turnover and a fall in profitability as customers withdraw their demand for services because of poor customer service.

There are no trade unions recognised at any of the 18 outlets, but some staff are beginning to exercise their right to trade union representation at grievance and disciplinary hearings.

An exhaustive review by a firm of consultants reported that Geoff Hayward plc lacked strategic direction. They recommended the appointment of a new managing director whose brief is to address the current profitability and people problems and to prepare the company for expansion into the European Union. The consultant's report also recommended the appointment of a specialist in personnel management.

The task
The managing director has asked you, as the newly appointed personnel manager, to produce a report, as a matter of urgency, that will provide her with the following:

- Recommendations
    - to improve staff retention
    - to improve staff morale
    - on the appropriate form of 'employee voice' to be adopted.

- An assessment of the personnel issues that must be considered if the company is to start to operate in one or two member states of the European Union.

You are advised to spend 70 per cent of your time on the recommendations, and 30 per cent of your time on the assessment.

Section B: Examination questions

1   A line manager comes into your office and asks you to give him *two* reasons why the European Social Dialogue process of the European Union should be supported by employers. Briefly outline your answer to the line manager.

2   Your chief executive telephones you in your office stating that she is to speak next week at a CIPD seminar on 'good practice' in employee relations, but she is not at all sure what the term 'good practice' means. Outline the definition you would give to the chief executive, giving your reasons.

3   You are stopped by your immediate manager who asks you to explain the importance of interviewing skills in managing employee discipline. What would you tell him?

4   You have just read a letter in a quality newspaper arguing that now strikes hardly ever seem to happen in the UK, the days of conflict between employers and employees have gone. Your colleagues tell you they have also read the letter and agree with it. But you don't agree with the argument in the letter. Why not?

5   A line manager stops you in the corridor and asks you to outline at

least two key principles that should underpin a grievance procedure. Outline your reply.

6   You have been asked to address a CIPD branch on the reasons
    why the state makes payments to individuals who have lost their
    jobs. Outline what you would you say in your talk, and give full
    reasons.

7   Your marketing director telephones and asks if you could explain
    the difference between commercial and employee relations nego-
    tiations. Outline your reply to her.

8   Your reporting manager believes that too many employees are
    performing below expected standards with respect to the quality
    of their work. You are asked to review the operation of the disci-
    plinary procedure. Outline the criteria you would use to decide
    whether the disciplinary procedure is operating satisfactorily from
    a management perspective.

9   During a conversation around the lunch table one of your col-
    leagues remarks that he was at a lecture the night before given by
    an academic who kept describing trade unions as 'job-conscious,
    not class-conscious'. This claim has puzzled your colleague who
    asks what it means. Explain it briefly for him.

10 You receive a request from a senior manager asking if you can
    explain why trade union bargaining power has declined over the
    last two decades. She is asking because she has to give a talk on
    this subject tomorrow. Given a brief, but informative, reply to this
    request.

11 A line manager has had an argument with an employee over a
    complaint that he pressurised the employee into working more
    weekend shifts than other workers in the department. The line
    manager wants guidance from you specifically on:
    ● whether the employee has a genuine grievance
    ● what the key points to be borne in mind are when handling an
      employee grievance
    ● how this situation should be handled.

12 Framework agreements have been negotiated at a European level
    with regard to workers on fixed-term contracts, part-time workers
    and parental leave. Briefly explain:
    ● who the parties are that negotiate such agreements
    ● how long the parties can take to reach such an agreement
    ● how such agreements are enforced throughout the member
      states of the EU.

13 Your line manager approaches you and informs you that she wants
    to introduce a major employee relations initiative. She also tells
    you that because it is a controversial proposal she wants to write

a report on it designed to gain the commitment to the initiative of their managerial colleagues. She further points out that she has little experience of report-writing and asks your advice. Explain to your line manager what the most important ground rules to be borne in mind are when producing employee relations reports to gain the commitment of one's managerial colleagues to a proposed employee relations initiative. Give full reasons.

14 A work colleague approaches you in your office just before the end of the working day explaining that some managers have said they are confused about the key differences between conciliation, mediation and arbitration. Your colleague asks if you can help them. Explain to them the difference between conciliation and arbitration.

15 Explain to a line manager the key differences in the roles and functions of the Central Arbitration Committee (CAC) and the Advisory, Conciliation and Arbitration Service (ACAS).

16 Your line manager tells you that the chief executive officer (CEO) of the organisation has decided that if the organisation is to have a competitive edge it will need to gain the commitment of its employees to the success of the organisation. Your line manager also tells you that he is to report back to the CEO on the employee relations mechanisms the organisation might introduce to achieve this. Outline to your line manager *two* employee relations mechanisms your organisation might introduce to gain the commitment of its employees to its future success.

17 The Government believes that unions and employers should work in partnership in the workplace to achieve common goals such as fairness and competitiveness. One of your work colleagues asks you to explain:
  ● the principles that underpin successful and strong workplace partnership agreements
  ● what employers gain from such agreements.

What would you tell your colleague?

18 You hear that your organisation has dismissed an employee for bad timekeeping and unauthorised absence, and that she has made a claim of unfair dismissal to an employment tribunal. Your line manager seeks your advice on the type of evidence your organisation should prepare in order to justify its actions to the tribunal. What advice would you give your line manager, and why?

19 Your organisation has decided that a reduction in the size of its workforce is unavoidable. Its senior managers have never dealt with such a situation previously. They have heard that consultation with the workforce must take place but are unsure of the details. Your line manager asks you to explain to them the key information

that employers should provide so that they can prove afterwards that effective and meaningful consultation over the proposed redundancies have taken place. First, outline how you would explain to your line manager that it's not as simple as that, and second, outline what you would therefore tell the senior managers.

20 Your organisation has decided to promote good health by raising awareness through health surveillance and training. You have been asked to produce a report, devising and implementing such a programme. Outline what you would say in your report, giving full reasons.

Examination guidelines

The purpose of this final section is to provide students with some guidance on how to tackle examination questions on the Employee Relations (Generalist Module) paper. A number of broad comments are appropriate, in that students tend to make mistakes on every part of the paper, but these are supplemented with our reservations relating to specific sections of the paper. In assessing the performance of the candidates, the examiners take into account:

- the knowledge and understanding the candidate demonstrates of the issues raised by the question

- the ability the candidate demonstrates to apply, describe and analyse appropriate management techniques

- evidence of the application of the core management skills required to solve everyday employee relations problems

- the extent to which the candidate's answers reflect a practical, managerial and businesslike approach.

The 'bottom line' test for the examiners is that the CIPD Qualification (Graduate CIPD) is an indication to employers that the holder of such a qualification can be reasonably expected to be aware and informed of the prevailing trends, topics, skills and techniques in employee relations and in human resource management in general, and to display the level of proficiency in terms of operational skills that might be expected of a graduate member of CIPD.

Five other general points can be made:

- To pass the case study question, candidates are expected to:
  - demonstrate that they understand the problem(s) the case study poses for management
  - provide specific proposals to overcome these problems. The solutions must include some details. General statements like 'We would introduce measures to gain employee commitment to the objectives of the organisation' are unacceptably vague

    – provide a rationale for their proposals. Candidates must therefore explain what problems their proposals will overcome.

However, to gain a mark in the merit or distinction grade category, candidates must go on to:

    – explain how they would gain the commitment of their managerial colleagues and the workforce to their proposals – in short, how they would deal with any implementation problems arising from their proposals

    – discuss the physical, human and financial resources implications of their proposals

    – provide an action plan.

● Many candidates fail to answer all parts of a multi-part question.

● Many candidates fail to address the question that has been set, preferring to tell the examiners all they know about the subject matter of the question. Although this can be very interesting, it demonstrates that the candidate has not read the question set and then answered that set question. Similarly, it is common for candidates to write an essay rather than a report or draft grievance-/discipline-handling programme when that is requested. One of the skills the examiners seek to assess in the paper is the ability of candidates to write in a clear, concise and convincing manner. You are advised to produce a shorter answer that is well planned and that reveals knowledge and understanding of the subject matter of the question rather than a long, unstructured answer which produces the relevant points by accident rather than by design. The golden rule to apply is:

> Read the question (RQ)
> then
> Answer the question (AQ).

● Many candidates seem to lose sight of the overall objectives when answering a question and provide an unbalanced answer which devotes too much time to one part of the question, to the detriment of others. Clear planning before starting to write an answer can obviously reduce the chances that such a problem will arise. All too frequently candidates seem to believe that making references to well-known academics demonstrates knowledge and understanding of the principal issues surrounding the subject matter of the question. This is all very well if the references are relevant and appropriate – and do not appear to be bolted on to a somewhat peripheral answer.

● Many candidates fail to locate their answers in the wider commercial and environmental context, showing little appreciation of national or European Union-wide trends or longer-term developments in the economy as a whole, in the legal framework surrounding management employee relations strategies and policies, or in employee relations in particular. There is often a temptation to assume that current fads and fashions represent a superior solution to organisational problems, and little recognition that they may be superficial and trite. When discussing current 'new' management practices candidates must demonstrate that they are capable of analysing and evaluating whether the success (or alleged success) of the introduction of such practices in one organisation is relevant to and capable of being successfully replicated in another organisation. Candidates all too often fail to recognise the force of existing cultural norms and traditions when putting forward recommendations, somehow assuming that all options are feasible. It is important to demonstrate an awareness of the constraints (financial, resistance from one's managerial colleagues, etc) as well as the opportunities when answering questions. One of the things which the Professional Development Scheme aims to develop in candidates is the ability to persuade line managers of the usefulness of employee relations strategy, policies and practices in solving specific problems and adding value to the organisation.

Taking a more positive stance, there are certain guidelines which students might like to bear in mind when preparing for the examination, some of which build upon what has been said in the previous paragraphs. These are:

1   Make sure that the whole indicative content is understood – otherwise, you may have difficulty in providing answers to the seven of the 10 questions in Section B of the paper. In addition, when addressing the case study in Section A, students must be able to demonstrate a holistic appreciation of employee relations.

2   Provide examples, as appropriate, to support a particular answer and arguments. These may be drawn from any organisation, not only the one for which the candidate currently works, and it is useful if contemporary examples are provided because they show that the candidate is up-to-date and is reading the professional journals.

3   Write concisely and clearly, providing signposts to an answer. There is nothing worse for an examiner than having to reread an answer several times in order to try to identify precisely what the candidate is trying to say. A clear introduction stating explicitly what will be contained in the answer helps considerably in this respect, as does the use of paragraphs, sections and numbering. The precise technique used matters less than the overall impact, and candidates should therefore use the approach with which they feel most comfortable.

4   Ensure that the examination is paced so that an attempt can be made at all questions. It is worthwhile repeating that

approximately one hour should be allocated to each section in the examination paper. This means that in Section B, each question should be answered in about eight minutes.

These guidelines should not be seen as an attempt to impose unrealistic professional standards on CIPD students. Rather, they reflect the fact that central to all aspects of managerial work are these very same skills: addressing the question posed, choosing from alternatives to formulate a realistic answer, justifying recommendations, and writing in a clear and well-structured manner that is above all persuasive and convincing.

There are a number of more specific comments relating to each of the sections.

When addressing the case study, candidates must ensure that they understand the case as a whole and are able to identify the key points within it. In suggesting solutions to the problems posed in the case study, candidates should demonstrate:

- that they can integrate the different aspects of employee relations

- that they can discuss policy options, including the pros and cons of each, and decide which on balance they would select, and explain why

- whether 'new' management practices (fads) are relevant, and explain how this is so — but more importantly, that they can explain how the adoption of these practices would help solve the organisation's problems and how they could be successfully introduced

- how the employee relations solution would contribute to the achievement of the organisation's objectives

- that they understand commercial realities. Candidates frequently argue that they would reduce an organisation's headcount by early retirement schemes – but without telling the examiners whether the organisation's pension fund scheme could finance such a policy or without recognising that early retirement is a matter for the fund's trustees and not the chief executive. Candidates have in the past also often demonstrated that they do not realise that the implementation of technological change takes time as well as money in that the technology has to be ordered, delivered and installed, and technical problems ironed out.

Section B comprises a number of questions which require short paragraph-length answers. These can be drawn from all parts of the indicative content and require candidates to present fairly basic core information in order to demonstrate their knowledge and understanding of the topics under consideration. The answers in this section must be concise, but can usefully be supplemented with examples to illustrate the candidate's overall comprehension of the issue. It is important that all seven questions required in this section are answered.

• Index